Heinemann

SOCIOLOGY A2

for AQA

Warren Kidd   David Abbott   Gerry Czerniawski

www.heinemann.co.uk

✓ Free online support
✓ Useful weblinks
✓ 24 hour online ordering

01865 888058

Heinemann

Inspiring generations

Heinemann Educational Publishers
Halley Court, Jordan Hill, Oxford OX2 8EJ
Part of Harcourt Education

Heinemann is the registered trademark of
Harcourt Education Limited

© Warren Kidd, David Abbott and Gerry Czerniawski, 2004

First published 2004

09 08 07 06 05 04
10 9 8 7 6 5 4 3 2 1

British Library Cataloguing in Publication Data is available
from the British Library on request.

ISBN 0 435 46709 3

Typeset by 𝒯 Tek-Art

Printed in the UK by Bath Press

Cover illustration by Matt Buckley

Picture research by Thelma Gilbert

Acknowledgements
Every effort has been made to contact copyright holders of material reproduced in this book. Any omissions will be
rectified in subsequent printings if notice is given to the publishers.

T=top; c=centre; b=bottom; l=left; r=right

Page 14 , Hulton Archive; page 16, Rex Features; page 24, Rex Features; page 26, Photofusion/ Steve Morgan; page
30, Corbis/Hulton; page 32, Panos Pictures; page 34, Alexander Milgram; page 40, Rex Features; page 43, Topham
Picturepoint; page 46, Bentham Collection, University College London; page 48, Hulton Archive; page 56 ASDA; page
58, PA Photos; page 62, Rex Features; page 64, Rex Features; page 66, Photofusion/Mark Campbell; page 68, Rex
Features; page 76, Rex Features; page 82, Rx Features; page 86, Robert Harding; page 88, Popperfoto; page 90,
Topham Picturepoint; page 92, Mary Evans Picture Library; page 97, Photofusion; page 101, Rex Features; page 102,
Press Association; page 105, Collections/Eric Lewis; page 107, Corbis; page 110, Popperfoto; page 112, Topham
Picturepoint; page 113, Popperfoto; page 116, Camera Press; page 132, Science Photo Library; page 136, AKG; page
142, David Tothill; page 146, Rex Features; page 148, Topham Picturepoint; page 153, Photofusion/Steve Eason; page
154, Science Photo Library; page 158, Hulton Archive; page 161, Topham Picturepoint; page 166, Zygmunt Bauman;
page 187, Sally & Richard Greenhill; page 198t, Rex Features; page 198b, Topham Picturepoint; page 200, The
Wellcome Trust; page 208, Corbis; page 211, Rex Features; page 212, Rex Features; page 222, Rex Features; page
224, John Frost Newspaper Services; page 226, Rex Features; page 228, Photofusion/Paul Doyle; page 230, Carlton
TV; page 232, Rex Features; page 248, Rex Features; page 250, Rex Features; page 254, Rex Features; page 258, Erik
Olin Wright; page 260, Rex Features; page 262, Rex Features; page 268, Sally & Richard Greenhill; page 273, Rex
Features; page 276, PA Photos; page 278, Charles Murray; page 285, Gosta Esping-Anderson; page 295, Topham
Picturepoint; page 302, Topham Picturepoint; page 324, Rex Features.

Tel: 01865 888058 www.heinemann.co.uk

Contents

Book

CD

Introduction

What is sociology like at A2 level?
What are the main differences between the AS
and the A2 level?
What is the specification like for AQA sociology?

Power and politics

Power and politics case studies
Power and politics webquest
Power and politics revision cards
Power and politics multiple-choice questions
Power and politics: test your evaluation skills
Power and politics key word quiz

Contents

Contents

Theory, methods and methodology

Theory, methods and methodology case studies
Theory, methods and methodology webquest
Theory, methods and methodology revision cards
Theory, methods and methodology multiple-choice questions
Theory, methods and methodology: test your evaluation skills
Theory, methods and methodology key word quiz

Contents

How to be synoptic

What tricks are there to demonstrate synopticity?
How can we make power and politics synoptic?
How can we make religion synoptic?
How can we make theory, methods and methodology synoptic?
How can we make crime and deviance synoptic?
How can we make stratification and differentiation synoptic?

Crime and deviance

Crime and deviance case studies
Crime and deviance webquest
Crime and deviance revision cards
Crime and deviance multiple-choice questions
Crime and deviance: test your evaluation skills
Crime and deviance key word quiz

Contents

Contents

Exam and revision tips

Margin boxes:
Key ideas
Key definitions
Key facts
What, when and why?
Who is this person?
Synoptic links
Methods links
Classic study
Coursework suggestions
Top exam hints
Revision tips
Pushing your grades up higher:
Power and politics
Religion
Theory, methods and methodology
Crime and deviance
Stratification and differentiation

Webography

Foreword

This book has been written as the follow-up to *Heinemann Sociology AS for AQA* (2003). It is intended to be used in the second year of an A Level course, ideally as a follow-up to the AS course book, but it can also be accessed if the AS book was not used for the previous year.

Sociology A2 for AQA is designed to take off from the point where the AS course, and book, halted. What does it mean to be a student of A2 sociology and how does the A2 course extend, develop from and differ to the previous AS one? What are the challenges of the A2 year? What are the differences in terms of knowledge, both in breadth and depth?

This book seeks to strip A2 sociology down to its essentials; to show students how all the ingredients of sociology work together. We aim to get students thinking about the relationships between theory, key words and studies, and how the ideas from their previous AS year relate to the topics studied in the A2 year. The book also seeks to unite subject content with skills development and examination advice and technique. We have written the book with the examination in mind, yet at the same time tried to show how sociology as a discipline works, and how evaluation skills can be developed by thinking in a sociological fashion.

We hope you like this book, and we wish you every success with your examinations.

Warren Kidd
David Abbott
Gerry Czerniawski
2004

Foreword

Author biographies

Warren Kidd is the Senior Tutor for the Social Sciences at Newham Sixth Form College ('New Vic') in East London, where he teaches sociology. Warren is an accomplished textbook author for the AS and A level market and has previously been a vice president of the Association for the Teaching of the Social Sciences (ATSS). He is an experienced provider of teacher INSET and contributor to student sociology conferences. He is the series editor for both this book and *Heinemann Sociology AS for AQA* and has written the introduction, synoptic skills, coursework skills and examination skills chapters of this book.

David Abbott teaches at Hills Road Sixth Form College in Cambridge. He has written several textbooks and articles for AS/A2 level sociology. David has written the theory, methods and methodology, crime and deviance, and stratification and differentiation chapters of this book.

Gerry Czerniawski is a former member of the executive of the ATSS and teaches sociology on AS and A2 courses in London. He is an associate lecturer in social sciences for the Open University and tutors in sociology at the London School of Economics and Political Science (LSE) on the Saturday School programme for A level students. As well as producing resources for the ATSS, Gerry has provided INSET courses in sociology and is also a teacher trainer on the City and Guilds teacher-training course. Gerry has written the power and politics, and religion chapters of this book.

Dedication

Warren dedicates this book to his family, his friends, his loved ones, and his students. He would like to thank Jane, for making it all so much easier, and the students at Newham Sixth Form College, who provided the inspiration for so many of the ideas behind this book.

David dedicates this book to Rosie, Christopher, and Olivia.

Gerry would like to dedicate this book to Vivian Archer and the Newham Book Shop.

Chapter 1

Introduction: making the transition from AS to A2

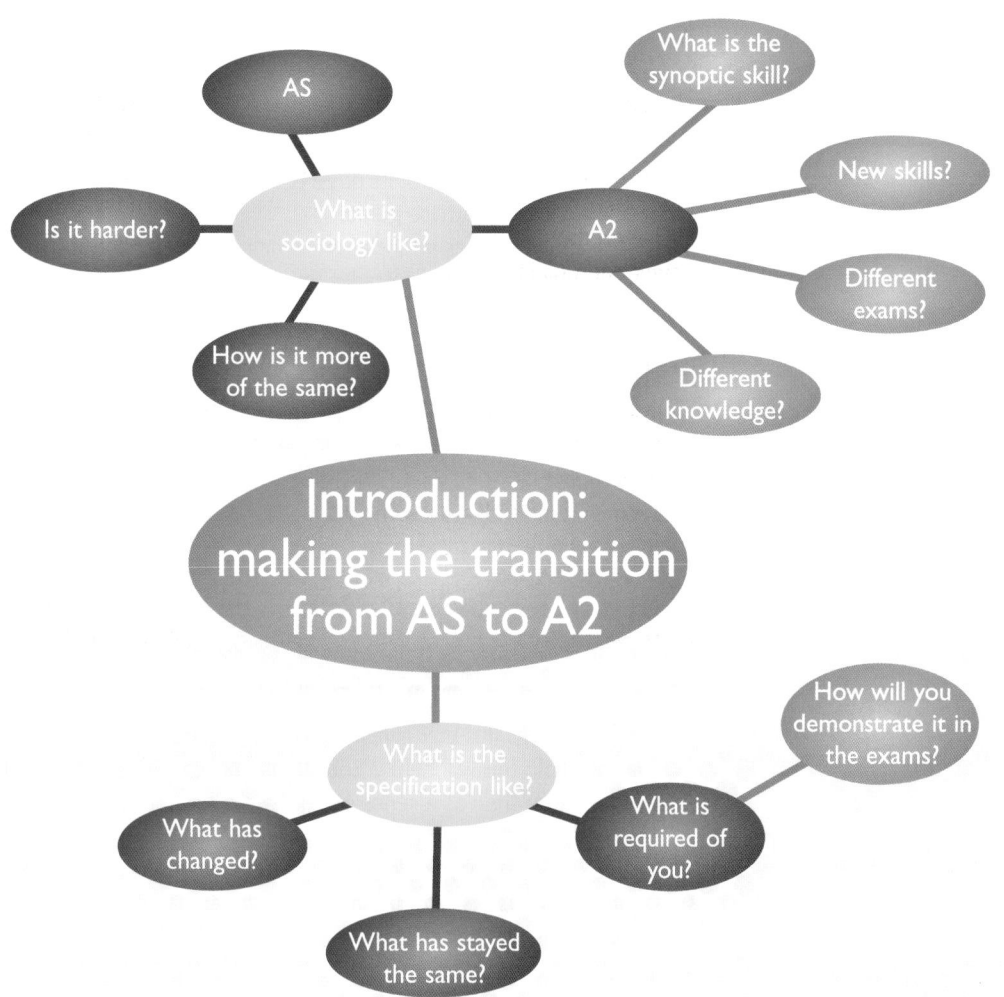

How to use this book

This book aims to help you to be successful on your sociology course. Exam success is not simply a case of knowing the subject content, it is also a case of being able to apply what you know in the way the exam and the examiner requires. You will find this book helpful in the following ways:

- It contains a lot of knowledge, but also provides you with support for the exam.
- It focuses on what the exam board specification says about the course you are following.
- It shows you what sociology is all about and what the tricks and shortcuts are to learning the subject.
- It breaks sociology down into manageable sections, focusing on the idea that there are four essential or key ingredients that you have to use in order to 'do' sociology well.
- It provides both classic and up-to-date sociological studies and theories.

What features does this book have?

This book provides the following features:

- Coloured pages which indicate the exam advice in each chapter. You will also notice that the contents page is colour-coded in the same way to give you a quick exam advice guide.
- Each section contains information to help you think about the exam, and also to try and push your grades up as high as possible.
- Margin boxes that give you tips and advice.
- Each chapter begins with a look back at the AS course, showing how synoptic links can be made. Plus, at the end of every chapter, you will find information on Module 6 and the Unit 6 Synoptic exam and links between each topic. In this sense, we have tried to be synoptic both forwards and backwards.
- Each chapter ends with some frequently asked questions that you may need to know the answers to.

What do the boxes in the margin do?

In the margin of every section, you will come across a variety of different boxes. They each do a slightly different thing, and they are there to help you.

- Top exam hint: this box gives you some very quick exam tips (AO1/2).
- Synoptic link: this will help you to think about your sociology course as a whole, rather than as a series of separate topics or options (AO1).
- Methods link: this box integrates methods into every topic (AO1) – this is a very important synoptic skill, and is central to thinking like a sociologist.
- Coursework suggestion: handy hints or an actual proposed idea for linking topics to coursework at A2 level are provided (AO1/2).
- Key definition: this box contains a key term and its definition (AO1).

- Key idea: this box contains an important sociological idea explained (AO1).
- Key fact: this provides a relevant statistic, to give your exam answers that bit more depth (AO2).
- Classic study: these boxes focus upon a really important or well-known piece of research to help you support your arguments in the exam (AO2).
- What, when and why?: this box will help you to locate the ideas and people you are reading about within the historical period they come from. This is useful for evaluation purposes (AO2).
- People box: when studying sociology, you will find that you come across many different sociologists who all have different ideas. This will help you to understand a bit more about the people behind the ideas you are learning (AO1).

How is the book divided up?

This A2 book is divided into distinct areas:
- **Introduction** – The introduction focuses on the requirements of the specification and gives an introduction to Sociology at A2 level
- **Section 1 Topic areas** – This section looks at the unit 4 exam topics, plus the Theory and methods topic for unit 5W, if you are taking this exam rather than doing the coursework.
- **Section 2 The synoptic unit** – This section covers Crime and deviance and Stratification and differentiation, the two topics for unit 6 (you will be studying one of the two choices). There is also a complete chapter giving advice on the important skill of synopticity.
- **Section 3 Skills for success** – This section looks at important skills such as essay writing and evaluation skills. There is also a separate chapter on the optional unit 5C coursework, providing ideas, advice, hints and tips.

The CD-ROM

The CD-ROM that accompanies this book gives you the opportunity to print off the margin boxes in specific combinations to suit your own needs. These will be invaluable for revision and for coursework so make good use of this facility throughout your course.

Along with exam and revision tips, the CD-ROM also contains new case studies for your revision, web activities, handy revision cards and key word exercises, multiple-choice assessment tests, evaluation skills exercises and a bibliography of useful websites. A CD-ROM symbol will appear throughout the book and will direct you to the relevant sections of the CD.

What is sociology like at A2 level?

Auguste Comte 1798–1857. Comte was lucky. He invented sociology, so he did not have to learn about many new ideas or harder theories as they did not exist. For you, however, this A2 year will be both easier and harder. There are many new ideas to learn, but also plenty of opportunities to use ideas from last year again.

Welcome to sociology

First, welcome to A2 sociology. The aim of this book is to try to help you to be as successful as possible by giving all you need to know in manageable-sized pieces. The aim is not to provide a great long list of ideas to learn, but rather to show you how sociology works as a way of thinking about society, and to show you how the sociology examinations work. This book continues where the AS book left off; showing you what you need to know, explaining what it means, and trying to show you how to develop the necessary skills you will need in order to pass the final examinations successfully.

Sociology at A2 level is both the same and different to sociology at AS level. It is both easier and harder.

How is sociology at A2 easier?

- Sociology has not changed much. We have not re-interpreted any of the theories you learned at AS level. Nothing in the world of sociology has changed so much that you will not recognise it when you see it again in these pages.
- This means, sociology is actually easier this year. You do not need to worry about what you are getting yourself into as you already know. There are still the four important ingredients of sociology to focus on: theory, key words, named examples and evaluation.
- You can use much of what you learned in your AS year again this year. In fact, this will actually save you time, as you do not need to learn again what you learned last year. There are theories from last year that you now know, and so you will not need to spend time re-learning them, just take a little time to remind yourself of them. This is also true for the language that sociologists use. Most of the key words from last year will also be used this year. You will be familiar with what sociologists say and how they say it, but this time around it will not seem as strange and unfamiliar as it might have at the start of last year.
- There is also possibly more time this year. You will certainly find yourself going at a quicker pace once you start the course, as your teachers can proceed faster because of your existing knowledge base of sociology. They do not have to progress slowly to make sure you understand the basics because you already have them. The A2 exams are also a little bit later in the year than the AS exams are. Again, this means a few more lessons; a little bit more time.

How is sociology at A2 harder?

At the same time as it gets easier, it also gets a bit harder – a typically confusing sociological statement!

- There will be some new theories that you will have to learn; theories that you will not have been taught at AS level.
- You might need to go into more depth for some of the theories you learned last year. There might be more case studies to know, or slightly different interpretations to learn. However, the important thing to remember is that you always have the basics from last year's work.
- Arguably, the A2 examination is harder than the AS one. Obviously, this depends on the individual, but the A2 examination does ask you to be much more evaluative than the AS exam.
- The A2 examination also requires you to write essays, which is very different from the 20-mark questions at the end of the AS exam. The exam also requires you to demonstrate the important skill of 'synopticity' – the ability to show links to all the units you have studied in the final Unit 6 exam.
- Finally, coursework in A2 sociology is much more demanding than at AS, especially in terms of the time it might take to complete it. However, again, it is not really much harder – it just takes longer to do. All you have to do is start it early, and follow the advice of your teachers and the guidance in Chapter 8 of this book.

What is sociology at A2 level like?

As you can see, nothing much has changed except the nature of the examinations and the skills you are required to demonstrate. Sociology is still sociology. The ideas remain the same, but at A2 you are expected to do more with them. It is not sufficient just to learn the ideas, you need to show that you can manipulate them, and that you really understand how sociology works inside and out. This is also the aim of this book.

Key points to remember

- Sociology as a subject has not changed between AS and A2 levels.
- A2 sociology is harder since there is more to learn and harder skills to master.
- A2 sociology is also easier since you are starting A2 with a whole year's worth of sociology behind you.

✓ Top Exam Hint

Remember in the AS book we encouraged you to make revision cards of all the studies that you needed to know in the AS year. This year, early on in the course, go through these cards and sort out those that might link to the topics you are doing at A2. Consult your teacher if you are unsure. Now you have the cards, use them. Use them in class and in essay answers – try to establish connections between this year and last year.

✳ Key Idea

Being synoptic means being able to show links and connections between things. This is a major skill in the second year of your sociology course – as it is for all A2 subjects.

● Synoptic Link

Go through your AS folder early on in the course – consider how what you did in the AS year might relate to what you will be doing this year. Take pages from your notes and insert them at the beginning of this year's class, ready for the skill of synopticity.

What are the main differences between the AS and the A2 level?

What does this mean?

Think back to the start of your AS year. One of the big concerns you might have had then was understanding what AS level was. Also, in the case of sociology and perhaps some other subjects that do not often get taught at GCSE level in schools, you might have wondered what the new subject would be about.

This year you will not have these concerns. You know already what to expect from sociology. You may have already sat AS examinations and you have already begun to learn the basics of the subject. You now need to concern yourself with how the A2 level might differ from the AS.

What are the differences of knowledge?

- The AS course is like an introduction to the ideas of sociology. The A2 course takes these same ideas, but asks you to apply them to different topics and, while doing so, to develop new skills.
- The AS theories will still be used at A2, although some new theories might be added. Most theories are still either 'macro' or 'micro', or they are either 'consensus' or 'conflict' in their approach to viewing society. You might find that the number increases, but you will also find that many new theories seem very similar to the old ones you already know.
- You will still need to know all the key concepts you learned last year. The way you speak and write sociology has not changed, but for the essay questions in the exam you will really need to be able to manipulate these technical and conceptual terms. They are a priority in order for your essay answers to have depth.

What are the differences of examination?

- The AS exam relied upon more short answer questions than the A2 exam will do. Equally the AS exam was more concerned with how you responded to the items and sources provided, whereas the A2 exam is much more about what you bring to the exam – your knowledge of key terms, theories, studies and your skills to evaluate and manipulate them.
- The AS exam did not require you to write long, extended pieces of writing. This year, however, the 40-mark essay answer really needs to be thought of in terms of approximately three to four sides of A4 writing. This is a much more detailed piece of work, which tests your written skills and ability to provide a detailed argument.

Start this year with confidence – you already have a whole year of sociology behind you.

✓ Top Exam Hints

- In the AS book we encouraged you to keep a vocabulary book – dust it down and get it out for this year's course too. Since you will have lots of words in it already, it means you start this year much better off than you did last year. Just make sure that you refer to it and use the words in your exam answers for depth.

- Look at Chapter 9 in this book for detailed advice on how to write good-quality essays.

What are the differences of skill?

- The greatest difference is in the weighting of the skill of evaluation. For the A2 course it is much more important than in the AS year.
- You will also be required to demonstrate your ability to think and to manipulate information synoptically. In other words, your ability to be able to draw on other areas of sociology in order to make connections. Sociology always used to ask students to think like this, but now your skill in this is actually tested on the Unit 6 exam paper. You will either be doing crime and deviance or the topic of stratification and differentiation for this unit.

Key points to remember

- There will be more theories to learn this year, but they will not necessarily be any harder.
- The exam will require much more detailed pieces of writing from you.
- You will need to demonstrate both synoptic and evaluation skills in the exam at A2 level.

✓ **Top Exam Hints**

Look at Chapter 5 in this book to seek advice on how to master the skill of synopticity.

What is the specification like for AQA sociology?

What does this mean?

As with all qualifications, the examination body, in this case AQA, lays out what it wants students and teachers to do unit by unit, year by year.

- The AS exam is made up of three units.
- The A2 exam is made up of a further three units, making a total of six units in all – this is what is known as a 'six unit award'.
- For sociology at AS you would have taken either two exams and produced a piece of coursework, or you would have taken three exams.

The A2 sociology course follows the same pattern.

- The Unit 4 exam is one hour and 30 minutes long, and you study either power and politics, religion, or world sociology. As last year, the exam has some shorter questions and some longer questions, along with a piece of data – a source item. Unlike last year, there is only one source item and the questions are worth 8 marks and 12 marks followed by a 40-mark essay question. You get a choice of essay questions at the end and you must select one question.
- Unit 5 is about theory and method; you will either do a piece of coursework for this unit or sit an examination. If you do the exam, it is the same format as the Unit 4 exam, as described above. If you do the coursework option, unlike last year, you are required to actually design, carry out and evaluate your own research based on the tasks in the specification. See Chapter 8 of this book for guidance on how to do this.
- Finally, Unit 6 is what we refer to as the synoptic paper; in other words, even though this paper has a theme or a 'topic' you will also be expected to illustrate how the topic might link to all the other topics you have studied both this year and last. The topic of this unit will be either crime and deviance or stratification and differentiation. Whichever topic you do, the question paper is similar to that for Units 4 and 5, but with some significant differences. You still answer 8-, 12- and 40-mark questions, but you do not get a choice for the 40-mark essay – you have to do the one you are presented with. Also, each of the three questions do something quite particular: one question will link the topic to the previous topics you have studied; one will link it to methods; and the other question will link the topic to theory. This is why the paper is the 'synoptic' paper.

What has changed from the AS year?

Unlike AS, A2 exams are longer in terms of time, and they are scheduled on different days. You might remember that, in the AS course, Units 1 and 2 were 'back-to-back'; they happen one after the other. In the A2 year, the exams are on separate days, with the Unit 6 paper usually being the last exam.

✓ **Top Exam Hint**

Do not forget what you already know about sociological theory. You might like to keep a list in the front of your folder of all the key words associated with each of the theories you know so far. This might help you when you come to write essays as you can use the words to create depth and detail.

● **Synoptic Link**

Synopticity will be tested formally in Unit 6, but good students are always synoptic – even in the other units. Always try to make connections; try to see sociology as a whole world view rather than simply as a series of unrelated topics. Since everything in society is connected somehow, so too is everything in sociology.

The exam papers have fewer questions, but the style of the paper is the same. There is a source item, a few short-answer questions and a longer question. The longer question requires the demonstration of more skills.

The 8-mark question asks you to identify two aspects of something. The 12-mark question requires a more detailed explanation of an issue or idea. The 40-mark question is an essay, and should take up the majority of the time allowed for the whole exam, probably about 55 minutes to one hour of the total time, which is one hour and 30 minutes. This means that your answers need to be more detailed, and certainly more evaluative than in the AS exam.

The synoptic paper (either crime and deviance or stratification and differentiation depending which one you are doing) is worth 20 per cent of the whole A2 exam. It is the highest weighted part of the whole two-year course.

What will the A2 year be like?

The exam board says that the units can be taken in any order, although they recommend that the synoptic unit (Unit 6) is taken at the end as it is a summary for the whole course. Technically speaking, you could do the units in whatever order your teachers choose, but most teachers will probably teach them in order.

You might start the year with a re-cap of AS work, and you might also look at the Unit 5 coursework option, if you are taking this. Most schools and colleges will probably try and get you started on this quite early on as it is a sizable piece of work, although it is worth remembering that is it worth only 15 per cent of the total A2 level marks. Having said this, if you can get a high grade for coursework it might take some pressure off you for the final two examinations.

Key points to remember

- The skill of evaluation is more important this year than in the AS exam.
- Unit 5 might be either an exam on theory and methods or a piece of coursework.
- Unit 6 is the 'synoptic' unit.

✓ **Top Exam Hint**

Do not forget that, for the Unit 6 paper, the three set questions do different things. One question will test links to methods, one will test links to theory and the other will test links to other topics. Usually the questions on the paper tell you which is which in italics after the actual question. This is a feature of the Unit 6 paper only.

Frequently asked questions

Q. How much harder does sociology get at A2?

A. This depends upon who you are and what you may or may not be good at already. For some people, it is the thought of having to write full essays, for others it is having to be much more evaluative than before. The ideas do not really get any more difficult, but there are more of them, and you will need to remember a lot more, especially since Unit 6 is synoptic and requires you to make connections and links with other ideas and topics.

Q. What is the most challenging thing about A2 sociology?

A. Most students think that the ideas will be harder at A2 than at AS, but it is more the case that the skills get more challenging. In fact, sociology is sociology – the ideas in A2 are the same as the ideas and theories in AS. What is challenging is what you are now required to do with them.

Q. What skills do I now need to develop?

A. The most important skill for A2 sociology is that of evaluation. You really need to be able to do things with the ideas you are given, rather than just repeat them. You need to be able to say what is good or bad about an idea or a theory; to say if you think a theory does or does not have any real evidence to support or disprove it. You will most notice the need for this skill in essay answers, and in coursework (if you do it). You can develop this skill by following the advice in Chapter 9 on exam skills.

Part 1 TOPIC AREAS – UNITS 4 & 5W

Chapter 2

Power and politics

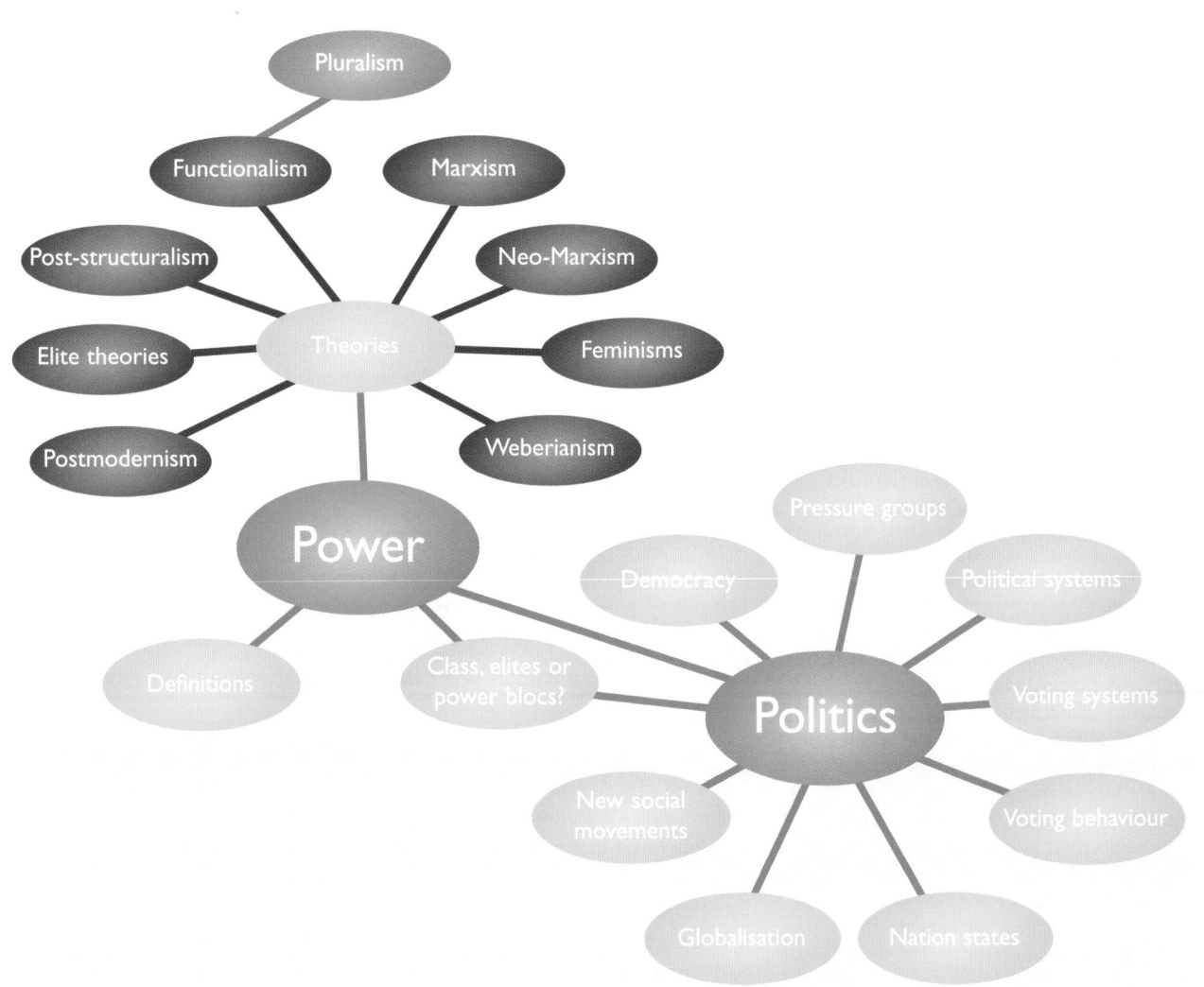

2.1 | # Key issues in power and politics

Do public demonstrations like this anti-war march in London in 2003 confirm an interest or dissatisfaction with politics?

✳ Key Idea

When reading this chapter, try to make a distinction between 'old' and 'new' sociologies of politics. Theories of the **old sociology of politics** tended to focus on issues to do with power as a form of domination of one group by another; the role that the community played in making decisions in society; the way that power operates at both macro/structural levels or micro/individual levels; the role of elites and their use of power in their own interests and the importance of class as a primary explanation for relationships of power and politics.

The **new sociology of politics** tends to focus on 'micro' levels of power struggle such as language or interpersonal interaction; political struggle surrounding lifestyles that include those to do with sexuality, ethnicity or the environment; cultural politics i.e. the ability of small groups to define or control certain areas of life for example within areas of medicine or religion; a focus on the role the media plays in controlling or persuading different groups; and the impact of uncertainty and diversity and our belief in political, religious or scientific 'claims to truth'.

Why are sociologists interested in power and politics?

Political issues continue to explode onto the pages of tabloid and broadsheet newspapers on a daily basis. Stories about 9-11, the stoning of women in Nigeria, gang warfare on the streets of Hackney in East London, and the accusations levelled at rap music fans that their music encourages a 'violent society' are all issues that help sociologists in their attempt to understand the relationship between power, politics, the individual and society.

At the start of this chapter, we can say that by 'power' sociologists mean **possessing the ability to do things that affect other people's lives**, in some cases even when they do not want their lives to be affected. While this can sometimes rely on the threat or use of force, 'legitimate' power (some sociologists refer to this as 'authority') relies on the acceptance of people to whom the power is directed.

By 'politics' sociologists do not just refer to the workings of government and those in official positions of power, such as government ministers. Sociologists also use the term to refer to **the exercise, struggle and use of power in *any* social situation**, from relationships within or outside the family (at a 'micro' level of analysis) to how countries can be affected by financial institutions, war or environment problems (at a 'macro' level of analysis).

What are the key debates in power and politics?

There are six key debates that examiners are keen to explore when setting exam questions.

1. Competing theoretical views about the nature and distribution of power
2. Competing theoretical views about the role of the modern nation state
3. Competing theoretical views about the role of elites in society
4. The relationship between social class and voting behaviour
5. Conflicting explanations over the nature of democracy and political participation including the role of political parties and social movements
6. The role of globalisation in power and politics.

What are the key ideas we can use to think about power and politics?

- You will need to understand, from a theoretical view, conflicting definitions of power and its relationship to authority, the state, micro and macro politics, postmodernism and globalisation.
- You will need to explain what democracy is (a system of government that involves some form of election of the government by the people) by referring to pressure groups, new and old social movements, totalitarian and non-totalitarian states, and different types of political participation.

- You will need to understand and explain changes in patterns of **voting** behaviour.
- You will need to discuss how concepts of globalisation (the increasing dependency and interaction that societies share on a worldwide scale) have affected the way we understand the power of the nation state.

What does the exam board say about power and politics?

The AQA examiners will expect you to know about:

- different definitions of power and how it is distributed through society
- the definition and role of the nation state
- the relationship between political ideology and political parties
- democracy, political participation and changes in voting behaviour
- the relationship between the mass media and the political process
- new social movements, pressure and interest groups.

The exam for this unit (Unit 4) will be 1 hour and 30 minutes and will be composed of two short data response questions (worth 8 and 12 marks) and one essay (worth 40 marks).

As with all of the AQA units, you have to show competency or ability in the assessment objectives of AO1 (*knowledge and understanding* and *presentation and communication*) and AO2 (*interpretation and analysis* and *evaluation*). For AO1 you need to show *knowledge and understanding* of the names of sociologists and their case studies; the relevant theories; the key concepts (such as globalisation); evidence to support the claims sociologists make and show a keen awareness of the research methodologies used by sociologists of power and politics.

For AO2 you need to show how you can actually *interpret and apply* this knowledge when putting forward a particular argument and *evaluate* continuously throughout any answer you are writing. There is a greater emphasis placed on AO2 at A2 than at AS. This might mean that you choose to draw on the ideas of a theory or case study that was carried out thirty years ago and see how it might (or might not) be relevant to an area of power and politics today. You might also identify trends from the past and see to what extent that particular trend is present today.

It will also help if you learn to draw out links with the synoptic topics of 'Crime and deviance' and/or 'Stratification and differentiation'. You must also examine this topic area in relation to the two core themes:

1. socialisation, culture and identity
2. social differentiation, power and stratification.

Key points to remember

- The six key debates that examiners use when creating questions.
- The exam lasts ninety minutes in which time you will answer two shorter questions and one longer, essay-style question.
- Power is at the heart of all sociology and therefore when studying power and politics try to automatically make connections to your chosen synoptic unit.

How do power and politics link to the AS course?

66 99 Key Definition

By **stratification** sociologists mean the way that societies are hierarchically organised, i.e. those on top are perceived to have more power than those on the bottom. The way different societies are stratified can be based on certain social characteristics such as the possession of wealth, or membership to a certain religion or possession of a particular skin colour. Those on top of the system tend to have greater access to scarce resources, such as land, water, money, than others.

∽ Classic Study

In the classic book *Violence Against Wives* (1979), Dobash and Dobash reported research carried out in Scotland, which focused on women who were or who had once stayed in refuges for battered women. They noted that female victims of violent assault are usually married and that the aggressor is usually the male partner. In this sense they argue that the institution of marriage is the most likely site for violence, psychological abuse, rape and in some cases murder.

Global politics and local powerlessness – an example of where macro sociology meets micro sociology. Farmers in many parts of the world have to purchase seeds from one of the multinational gene technology producers rather than produce the food they really desire or need. Many multinational companies possess significant power over some nation states, which in turn affects the livelihoods of the farmers and their families.

Why are links to AS sociology important for A2 sociology?

Sociology is all about studying the nature and distribution of power and as such focuses on the inequality and **stratification** that exists in most societies. Below are just some of the ways you can connect power and politics to the AS units you might have covered.

What links can be made to family and households?

Many politicians (mainly those holding Conservative or New Right views) blame the break up of the 'traditional' family for the rise of civil unrest and crime in modern societies. Increasing family diversity in the 21st century is regarded by some as something to fear rather than celebrate. Such views offer a convenient scapegoat for failing government policies by diverting attention away from politicians themselves to an 'idealised' version of the family. On a more 'micro' perspective what does the division of labour within the family unit tell you about who does and does not hold power in the family?

What links can be made to health?

At first it seems unlikely that the health of the individual can be related to those that have power in society and those that do not. Yet why is it so difficult to find 'health shops' in inner city areas, but so easy to find them in more expensive parts of the city or town? Politicians increasingly ask those who have money to pay for private healthcare while queues for hospital beds, doctors' appointments and hip replacements grow for those who earn less. Healthier organic foods are out of the reach of many who live on lower incomes. Drugs that are not allowed to be consumed in many western societies are sold or 'offloaded' to other parts of the world desperately in need of medical care despite risks associated with them.

What links can be made to mass media?

Many politicians have the power to choose what programmes or newspapers they wish to voice their opinions in. The newspapers themselves often project the views of a particular political way of thinking (for example, the 'Conservative' voice of *The Daily Telegraph* or the *Daily Mail*). Some argue that the realities we experience via the media are constructed by advertisers, spin-doctors, and marketing people to reflect the views of politicians, civil servants and leading members of legal and religious institutions. In a democratic society such as multicultural Britain, you might challenge the idea that the media truly reflect the variety of opinions that exist.

What links can be made to education?

You might wish to question to what extent education is empowering in the first place. In an increasingly competitive society in which politicians have created league tables and performance targets that guide the views of heads, principals and boards of governors it is not surprising that many people feel marginalised, disempowered or 'left out' within the UK education system. If you are black, female, working class, gay, or come from one of the less established religions you might challenge how the education system meets your needs. You might also question what education is and why politicians are only concerned with one particular type of education – one that prepares pupils for the world of work.

What links can be made to work and leisure?

So much of our identity, i.e. who we are, is tied to the job that we do. In many western societies the concept of having a 'job for life' is now transforming into one in which many teenagers go into the job market for the first time knowing that they are entering a world of diversity and insecurity. The UK economy has transformed from a manufacturing economy to one in which the leisure and service sectors dominate. In such a world, job opportunities come in the form of short-term contracts in which people can be hired and fired by firms. This coincides with the current political view that unions 'get in the way' of making profits. Thus many people find themselves disempowered, either working for cheaper rates of pay or not being represented in the work place.

Key points to remember

- At its most large scale (sociologists refer to this as 'macro' sociology), power and politics is concerned with a study of wars between nation states and the ways in which the views of politicians shape and determine people's lives.
- At a smaller macro level, power struggles exist between politicians, bureaucracies and political pressure groups.
- Of equal concern to sociologists, however, are the smaller scale or micro power struggles concerning people at work, at home, in the playground or in the pub. The successful sociology student will always remember that macro political issues always have micro consequences, such as politicians making decisions about educational policy may well determine how much time you spend in the playground!

☀ Key Ideas

- Connections can also be made between power and politics and the area of wealth, poverty and welfare. For some (those on the political left) the welfare state with its free medicine, social welfare provision and housing programme is seen as the high point in the development of capitalist societies. However, others (most notably those on the New Right) view this as an expensive luxury that many countries cannot continue to fund in the way they do. Many Marxists argue that although the provision of welfare *does* help those in poverty it *does not* help change a system that works in the interests of those in power. They argue that welfare provision helps maintain the belief that the system is fair and stops a revolutionary change occurring.

- Many feminists also challenge 'malestream' methodology. They argue that many sociologists disempower those that they research by taking and using their ideas, their time and their commitment without offering something in return. Furthermore, much that takes place behind closed doors in the private political world of the family cannot be accessed through many of the research methods that exist. This still means that many of the power struggles that exist within the family are never uncovered by sociological research.

∞ Methods Link

You can also make connections between power and politics and methodology. A researcher may have a particular point they wish to prove or disprove and will choose a particular method of research to make this point. This can be seen in the way governments use statistics to show how successful they are in the policies they pursue. For example, Dan Finn (1993) shows that if a government wishes to show that unemployment is dropping when in fact it is rising, they might change the definition of unemployment, something that has been done over fifty times since 1979! This tells you that a method alone cannot guarantee the information produced is valid. You therefore need to know how the data was gathered and what the researcher meant by their definition – sociologists call this 'operationalising their concept'.

2.3 | How can we find out about the sociology of power and politics?

How have sociologists tried to measure power and politics?

You can approach this unit from a macro perspective (i.e. attempt to discover the structures that empower or disempower individuals in the whole of society). You can also study this unit from a micro perspective and examine close up the everyday power struggles that take place, sometimes behind closed doors, referred to by some as 'micro-political' power struggles. However, some sociologists such as Anthony Giddens and Derek Layder combine both macro and micro elements in their research as you shall see when reading this chapter.

You will already have learned in your AS year that 'methodology' refers to research methods and reasons why those methods might be used. Sociologists can gather quantitative data, i.e. data that is statistical and that can be used to make generalisations (for example, questionnaires and surveys). Alternatively, they can choose to gather qualitative data, i.e. data which tends to be in more depth (for example, observations, interviews or the study of diaries). Apart from their own particular theoretical interests, sociologists choose their methodology as a result of issues that include:

- the nature of the research problem (for example, are you researching documents or people, is the research 'covert' or 'overt' or is the researcher looking back over time and comparing past with present?)
- the traditional research strategies, methods and data sources thought to be appropriate for a particular problem (for example, studying voting turnout figures in an attempt to explore whether people are losing interest in politics)
- how available or accessible is the data that the sociologist requires (for example, how easy is it to explore power issues within the family?)
- the resources at the researcher's disposal (for example, funding, time, equipment and assistance).

Values also determine how a sociologist approaches a particular research area. While these values can vary depending on whether the sociologist is a Marxist, feminist or symbolic interactionist they can also vary depending on whether the sociologist is male, female, black, white, middle or working class.

Such values can also determine whether or not the sociologist is gathering quantitative data or qualitative data. This might depend on whether the researcher considers themselves to be 'positivist' (i.e. 'scientific') or 'interpretivist' (i.e. more interested in how the respondent feels about what is being researched) in their approach to research in general.

✓ Top Exam Hint

What do sociologists mean by 'unstructured' interviews? How often is an interview really unstructured? The moment a sociologist explores a particular issue in an interview then there is automatically some sort of structure. Tell the examiner that most interviews are structured to a certain extent because they reflect the interests and values of the researcher. One of the few examples of truly unstructured interviews would be when a patient is talking to a psychiatrist or counsellor about their problems. This means that in power and politics *all* interviews will vary between being 'semi-structured' and 'structured'.

What methods do sociologists tend to use to study power and politics?

Methods vary depending on what the sociologist is trying to find out. Questionnaires that are highly structured provide useful broad-ranging data although their completion rate is low. They also do not allow respondents to 'open' up and give a full response. Observation is time-consuming and the presence of the researcher can change and/or affect what she/he is looking at. Interviews allow the researcher to probe and follow particular trains of thought but then people may decide to 'lie' to the interviewer in order to create the impression they feel the interviewer wants.

These are three sociologists who have used a variety of methods to study power and politics.

- Butler and Stokes (1969) carried out in-depth quantitative analysis of voting patterns in an attempt to show how class loyalty affected voting behaviour.
- Sturmer (1993) in a mixture of content analysis and semiotics, shows how the media can often cater for the needs of those with more wealth and better living standards than those without.
- Holland et al (1998) used interviews to get young people to talk about sex and their relationships and how these are formed within a male-dominated idea of what heterosexuality means.

What problems with definition are encountered in power and politics?

Problems exist when sociologists carry out research in any field and then have to explain the findings from such research to other sociologists. Remember that whatever definition (or 'operationalisation') we use to start our research will then affect what we look for and what we uncover as a result.

To start with the word 'power' itself is problematic. There are a variety of definitions of power and ways in which power can be seen to work. Unless you confirm which type of power you are talking about, it can be confusing for others who read and interpret your work. Equally, as this chapter will show, politics is not just confined to the world of television, the corridors of power and No.10 Downing Street. It is also present in the day-to-day interactions that take place with friends, families and colleagues. Sometimes it takes sensitive research to uncover obvious power imbalances in everyday life and an awareness of how different types of power operate differently in different cultures.

In these unsettled modern times, many politicians across the globe argue that their political systems offer an ideal which others can follow. Such messages can be very confusing, however, if we do not first fully understand the different types of voting systems, patterns of behaviour and opportunities for people to express their views in the variety of different political systems that exist.

Key points to remember

- There are a variety of reasons why sociologists choose the methods they do; these must be learned for the exam.
- Memorise not only the key names associated with this unit but also the method of research these sociologists adopted.
- Don't forget the importance of 'definition' or 'operationalisation' when discussing any research that takes place. Evaluating somebody else's research is impossible unless we know what they mean.

✓ Top Exam Hints

- Technology has come a long way in recent years and has provided extremely sophisticated software. Despite what many textbooks say, questionnaires, observations and even interviews can all generate quantitative data that can be analysed in extremely sophisticated and efficient ways. Make the examiner aware of this but be careful – do not imply that quantitative data is *better* than qualitative data. Each has its own specific uses for the sociologist.

- When you are evaluating writers and research it really helps to remember the concept of 'historical perspective'. This means that what one thing means in one culture at one point in time, may have a completely different meaning in another culture at another point in time. The concept of democracy a hundred years ago in Britain would have a very different meaning to that of modern British democracy or even democracy in Rome 2000 years ago.

Why is power so difficult to define?

What does this mean?

The concept of power is by no means isolated to the macro world of public politics. It is evident in everyday private or micro situations involving family, the work place and even recreational activities with friends (for example, who owns a particular board game may well decide who takes first turn). However, it is often hard to understand the difference between 'power' and 'authority'.

To this point, you have learned that power is the ability to bring about a change in somebody else's behaviour even if they had not wished to bring about such a change. Sociologists often refer to three different types of power.

- Economic power – based on who owns the means of production. Such power allows influence to be 'bought'.
- Political power – based on the power of elected/unelected leaders or politicians. Such power means that vital decisions can be made concerning the state, with or without the agreement of the population.
- Ideological power – from ideological institutions such as religion or the media. These have the ability to 'agenda set' what should/should not be.

We can look at the use of the English words 'you can' and 'you may' when trying to see the difference between 'power' and 'authority'. 'Can' refers to the *ability* to be able to do something whereas the use of the word 'may' implies that there is some outside body which *allows* this action to be carried out (for example, a mother may allow her daughter to go out with friends). It is to this latter relationship that one can apply the word 'authority'. The ability to do something in part explains the difference between 'power' and 'authority'.

Some of the attempts to define power and authority

This chapter will uncover a variety of different theoretical approaches to power and authority. Here are just some of the writers who have tried to clarify these enormously over-simplified terms.

D. Raphael (1970) makes a distinction between three types of power.

1. **Ability** – nothing more than the notion of being able to do something.
2. **Power in a social context** – the capacity to make others do what you want them to do (through persuasion, trust or by way of rank or a particular form of office).
3. **Coercive** – in which a threat is used; it is on the assumption that something bad will happen if the other party carries out the wish against their will.

For Max Weber (1921) power is the ability to make somebody do something which you want them to do. However, he makes a distinction between power that is illegitimate, i.e. not authorised, which he refers to as 'coercion' (using

Hugely influential 20th century Marxist social philosopher, Louis Althusser (1918-1990).

☞ Who is this person?

Neo-Marxist, Louis Althusser (1918–1990), reached the height of his influence writing in the 1960s and 1970s. Passionately re-working much of Marx's writings he asserted that societies are '*ordered combinations of economic, ideological, and political practices*' all of which take equal importance in shaping the whole of society. This view challenges the 'economic determinism' that argued that societies can be explained purely on the basis of who owns (and who does not) the means of production.

✳ Key Idea

One particular debate about the nature of power is whether it is 'constant' or 'variable'. Max Weber (1947) argued that there is a 'fixed' or 'constant' supply of power available to all and therefore those that hold power do so at the expense of others. This idea or notion of power is referred to as a **constant-sum** concept of power. However, functionalist Talcott Parsons (1937) argues that rather than a fixed amount of power, power is 'variable' i.e. the total amount of it can increase or decrease. This functionalist view of power is referred to as a **variable-sum** concept of power.

force), and power that is legitimate, i.e. power that is authorised (winning the hearts and minds of the people). Such power he refers to as 'authority'.

Max Weber defines three types of authority.

1. **Rational-legal** – relates to the types of bureaucracies that exist in most states and their right to give rules and regulations and have these obeyed.
2. **Traditional authority** – stems from those whose power is handed down to them over generations, such as tribal chiefs, and the rules by which they govern are obeyed without question.
3. **Charismatic authority** – relates to those individuals who command authority by their own making (for example, Ghandi, Mohammed, Christ, Churchill and even Hitler).

Barbara Goodwin (1984) makes six different distinctions when she talks about power within politics.

1. **Authority** – where she refers to power being attached to a particular office, such as prime minister or major.
2. **Power** – where power means the ability to influence others.
3. **Powers** – are the rights of the various office holders within society.
4. **Coercive power** – the ability to make people do things and punish them if they do not.
5. **Force** which is unlike coercive power in that it does not take place within any framework and is used, for example, in 'revolutions'.
6. **Violence** which are acts carried out by people who do not have a specified role within the state, such as acts of terrorism.

Conclusion

- It is possible to make a distinction between power and authority but it is first necessary to accept that there is more than one interpretation of power.
- It is clear then that power is the ability to bring about a change in someone else's behaviour and a change that would not have been brought about had they been left alone.
- The rest of this chapter will focus on the variety of theories, both macro and micro, that discuss and analyse not only what power is but how it works both for and against significant groups in society.

For consideration

1. What different forms of power struggles can you see taking place within the school or college where you study?

2. How might you separate explanations for these power struggles using the terms 'macro' and 'micro'?

- For Talcott Parsons (1960 and 1967) power is something that is generated by the community and based upon mutual agreement and collective decision making. Power is not 'fixed' somewhere in society or held by a group or person and kept by them. Power flows from group to group, from decision to decision. Power refers to the ability to use resources to achieve collective goals – power is about doing and achieving. Elected leaders manipulate the power given to them by the community. This idea has been influenced by the general functionalist idea of **value consensus** – the belief that people in society have a 'collective outlook' on the goals of their society, and all work towards these common, shared goals. 'Authority' is the social status that gives groups and individuals the right to use power.

- Remember that word 'ideology' from your first year. It refers to how systematic sets of beliefs can serve the interests of specific social groups in society (for example, patriarchy serving male interests or capitalism serving the interests of the bourgeoisie). This is also a form of power.

⌘ Classic Study

Erving Goffman (1971) produced a micro theory of power concerning the political nature of everyday life adopting a 'dramaturgical approach'. He compared social life to the theatre, arguing that individuals are social actors following scripts and adopting roles to give performances. While the scripts may well be written for us, we have the choice to 'interpret' them in any way we desire. Power is achieved through 'impression management', i.e. we manipulate the impression of our self, which we then give to other social actors. This micro theory of power forms much of the backdrop that comes under the new sociology of politics. Goffman's work has influenced sociologists of race and gender and is an invaluable form of analysis when discussing micro politics.

What is the classical Marxist view of power?

A child working in a garment factory in Bangladesh. Are the ideas of Marx (see below) outdated today?

☀ Key Idea

In today's global economies we wear or possess items that come from nearly every country on the planet. Such items can depend on the **immiseration** of those working and living in other parts of the world. Many of the classical sociological theories, Marxism, functionalism and Weberianism, were developed during periods of immense social change such as during the Industrial Revolution. It was Marx who described the process in which the working classes are alienated and experience poverty and hardship as immiseration. The immiseration thesis describes a process today in which people in western economies have high standards of living at the expense of those living in abject poverty worldwide. Such high standards of living are based on cheap foreign labour and cheap foreign goods bought from overseas countries where the labour costs next to nothing. Many writers are convinced that society today is undergoing enormous political, economic and social changes and are therefore re-evaluating the impact of the writings of Karl Marx.

What does this mean?

When Marxists talk of political power there is an inseparable connection between political power and economic power. Remember the relationship between Marx's economic base/infrastructure and how it determined the superstructure? For Marx, this meant that those that own the means of production (such as land, finance, machinery) shape and determine institutions (such as education, the media and the family) in their own interests.

Therefore, for Marxists economic power gives political power to the class that owns the means of production, i.e. the ruling class. Economic power *is* political power. It is therefore impossible to separate economic power from 'class power'. Capitalists wield economic power by owning the means of production. As such, they own and control the economy which therefore means that they have political power.

What do we mean by Marxism?

Debates about what Marxism is not only exist between Marxists and non-Marxists but also among Marxists themselves. However, crucial to all forms of Marxist analysis is the notion of class and class conflict.

In the book, *The Communist Manifesto*, Marx and Engels (1848) argued that the history of all society (after the very most primitive level) is a history of class conflict. There are different classes being formed within any economic system. With the development of capitalism what emerges is a class that owns the means of production (i.e. the capitalists or 'bourgeoisie') and the working classes or 'proletariat' who own and sell their own labour. The former has power over the latter and, in Marx's view, will lead one day to a revolution in which the working classes take control over the means of production to produce the communist society that he and Engels prophesied.

What did Marx mean by capitalism?

Marx was writing in the mid- to late-19th century at a time when there were a number of developing capitalist countries or economies. Marx was fascinated by the way capitalist economies went through boom and slump phases, i.e. that sometimes there were periods when a country's economy performed brilliantly and others when it did not. At times when the economy was doing badly this meant that the economy was producing too many goods for too few customers. The power of the nation state (see Section 2.17) is such that whenever such economic problems struck, Marx noted a number of possible reactions by individual states.

1. The search for new markets: a state can search for (and conquer) other parts of the world. This in turn provides a new supply of raw materials and a new market to sell goods to. Some Marxists refer to this as a form of 'imperialism'.
2. Sack the workers: when competition at home becomes intense, Marx noted that firms had no problem in making workers redundant.
3. Substitute machinery for workers: another method that capitalist economies deploy when times get tough (and another way of adding to unemployment).

Factors that lead to Marx's revolution

- Marx was excited by the idea that, as unemployment figures start to rise, so do the number of people who are unsatisfied with the government and ultimately the system of capitalism that allows such circumstances to exist.
- Marx used the term 'alienation' to describe the process that industrial production inflicted on those that worked in it. People no longer made things for themselves but for other people and as such felt removed from the creative process involved. Consider the difference between a carpenter who makes a table for his family and a worker working in a production line who just feels like a cog in a machine.
- Marx argued that this whole process would grow and grow with the working classes becoming more 'politically aware'. Instead of a 'class *in* itself' Marx argued that the working classes would become a 'class *for* itself'. In so doing it would form trade unions that would push for a revolutionary movement. Newspapers and a transport system would create a way of connecting different workers from different parts of the country (perhaps the modern day equivalent might be the mobile phone and Internet!). This 'communist' revolution would be a full social revolution carried out by the proletariat. It would take time but eventually produce a 'classless society' where power was shared by all.

Conclusion

- Although Marx accepted that force was the reason that states maintained power he was against the kind of reactionary violence that took place in the French Revolution.
- He argued that, if the economic conditions were right, then you should not require 'terror' to exert power over the oppressors. It would be inevitable that the proletariat would come to power because of the conditions described above.
- In Marx's, *Communist Manifesto*, there exists a 'utopian' notion of the perfect classless society where power is equally distributed.

For consideration

1. What evidence can you find to confirm that any communist regime (past or present), fulfilled the conditions that Marx said would need to apply for his 'revolution' to take place?

✓ Top Exam Hint

Learn and use the following quote to show the examiners how there are both macro and micro elements contained within the writings of Karl Marx.

'Men make their own history, but they do not make it just as they please; they do not make it under circumstances chosen by themselves, but under circumstances directly found, given and transmitted from the past. The tradition of all the dead generations weighs like a nightmare on the brain of the living…'

Karl Marx 1954 (originally 1852)

The macro side of Marxist theory is deterministic (i.e. it argues that economic structures shape the identities and lives of people in societies). However, the micro side of Marxism, as the quotation shows (*'men make their own history'*) accepts that people have agency or free will to act as they choose.

◆ What, when and why?

Feudalism refers to societies that are strongly hierarchical, depending on an individual's relationship to the possession or non-possession of land. Although this can be used to refer to Europe in the Middle Ages, many writers use the term to describe societies today that fulfil certain criteria. These can include land owned by a monarch who gives grants to nobles or 'aristocracy', who in turn can lease or rent the land to 'serfs'. Serfs pay for their land by offering shares of what they produce or, in some cases, by acting as land armies for those in power. There is little chance for social mobility in such societies.

✳ Key Idea

Marx argued that, as in previous revolutions, the communist revolution would take time and need to be one that was naturally occurring. He argued that this was what had happened in the transition from feudalism to capitalism. Any attempt to rush the process would, Marx thought, be disastrous. Just as feudalism took time developing into capitalism and producing a middle class, so the same would happen with the developing of an emerging working class that would lead to the economic conditions that would make them the dominant class.

What is the Weberian view of power?

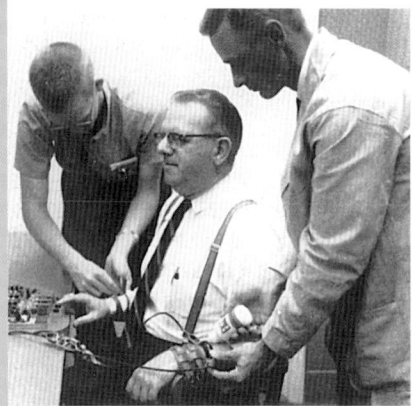

Here a 'teacher' holds a 'learner's' hand onto a shock plate to receive an electric shock, in Milgram's obedience study. Milgram's classic experiment shows how Weber's notions of power, authority and 'legitimation' can sometimes lead to surprising and horrific consequences (see below).

⇨ Classic Study

Milgram (1974) shows how the concepts of power, authority, methodology, deviance and conformity can all be connected. He attempted to test his hypothesis that cruelty was not committed by 'cruel' people but by 'normal' people who, under certain circumstances, feel that it is acceptable to do so. Tricking his volunteers into believing they were giving electrical shocks to other 'volunteers' (in reality no such shocks were administered) his work was inspired by the events of the Holocaust and how those in authority can, under certain circumstances, convince those lower down in any hierarchy that their actions are justified.

What does this mean?

Although Max Weber started writing over a hundred years ago, his ideas are still being read, picked up and adapted by new scholars today whether they are in politics, economics, or sociological fields. The most recent of the classical sociologists (he died in 1920), Max Weber was not only a highly influential social scientist but he was also a key politician within the German government. His ideas on power influence much of how the concept is thought about by other scholars. He also manages to combine macro and micro ideas of sociology in his concepts of power based on class, status and party.

Power, authority and legitimacy

Max Weber makes a broad distinction between the following three seemingly similar terms.

- **Power** – as force, coercion, domination and repression.
- **Authority** – i.e. winning the hearts and minds of people under the threat of force. This type of power is longer lasting. Power is used by superiors with the consent of their subordinates; force should not/is not necessary but everybody knows of its existence.
- **Legitimacy** – the process by which power is granted to those in authority, either freely or under pressure.

Economic and political power

Central to the writings of Marx was the notion that power was fundamentally an issue to do with the economy. Those that held economic power held power in *all* other areas of society. In this sense, power *is* economic power. Max Weber disagreed with this view, arguing that it was possible to make a distinction between economic power and political power.

Weber described modern governments as rational and bureaucratic, i.e. large organisations with rules, regulations and chains of command. People give orders; others follow them. The people who give orders are highly trained, educated experts. In this sense politics becomes a system of power that can bring about change not because of the economic conditions of key individuals but rather because of the status they hold. He claimed that there were three dimensions to domination of any group by another: class, status and party.

Weber's distinction of these three types of power rests upon the following definitions.

1. Class: Weber's idea of class is much wider than that used by Marx. Weber focuses on class both as a social group of people in similar economic circumstances, but also as a more individualistic category since peoples' 'life chances' can vary according to their access to a wider range of sources for economic power. For example, Weber takes into consideration how some

property is more valuable than others, and that some amounts of capital might add up to more wealth than some smaller forms of property ownership.

2. Status: this refers to how an individual or group, such as teachers or doctors, is viewed and valued by others in society. Some groups may enjoy more privilege than others since they are seen in the eyes of society as having special characteristics that afford them more honour than others.

3. Party: by this term, Weber means not just what we call political parties but any organisation devoted to obtaining power for its members, for example, trade union organisations such as the National Union of Farmers.

Max Weber on state power

Max Weber defined the state as *'a human community that successfully claims the monopoly of the legitimate use of physical force within a given territory'* (Weber 1921). Max Weber was in no way a critic of the state or state power. He was also not a radical theorist but rather pointed out what he thought was an important element within state power. People obey the state because the power of the state rests on the ability to use violence against people who do not comply with its wishes, i.e. the state can do nasty things to people who do not obey it (for example, flog, stone, imprison, or execute).

Weber used the phrase 'iron cage' to describe his fears of an all powerful bureaucracy that might emerge in any state. His belief in democracy, politics, and politicians was based on the idea that they should be able to exert their influence on those officials that abuse their power. For Weber the power of officials in bureaucracies needed to be kept in check by a system of checks and balances built into any government structure.

Conclusion

Postmodernist Bauman (1989), writing about the Holocaust, can be used to extend/criticise Weber's idea of bureaucratisation (i.e. the idea that as societies modernise they are increasingly being run by hierarchical organisations in which power flows in a top-down direction). *'The Nazi mass murder of the European Jewry was … the organisational achievement of a bureaucratic society. Hitler's 'final solution' did not clash at any stage with the rational pursuit of efficient optimal goal implementation.'*

Bauman argued that it was the very process of 'modernisation' or 'rationalisation' that gave rise to the conditions that produced the mass extermination of the Jews. The automatic following of orders from an 'unseen official' along with modern technological facilities were enough to produce the appalling events that took place.

For consideration

1. What evidence in recent current affairs highlights Weber's concern over the need for the power of bureaucratic officials to be kept in check?

2. To what extent are you concerned by the idea that other famous sociologists 'interpret' the works of Max Weber, Karl Marx and many others?

✓ Top Exam Hints

- Not many people know that Max Weber's written work was first translated by the American functionalist Talcott Parsons. This has, in the past, meant that other writers have criticised the *interpretation* of Max Weber's ideas and therefore the ideas themselves. Mention this in the exam and point out the importance of knowing whether or not the ideas of *any* writer are in their original form, or are an interpretation of somebody else's. Remember that many sociologists that you are studying about were not English speakers and therefore their works have all been translated. By questioning this you will immediately be gaining evaluation marks from the examiners.

- Weber's use of the term 'authority' is very similar to neo-Marxist Louis Althusser's ideas on how ideology can be far more successful as a way of dominating people than force alone. Referring to how capitalism has lasted so long, contrary to the predictions made by Marx, Althusser argues that if you win the hearts and minds of the people, then an ideology such as the success of capitalism will dominate for a far greater period of time. Mention these similarities in these two writers in the exam to gain high evaluation marks.

⌘ Classic Study

Weber notes that the three sources of power, (class, status and party,) overlap with each other. '*Classes, status groups and parties are phenomena of the distribution of power within a community*' (Weber 1948, page 181). This puts the ideas of Weber in opposition to a great deal of traditional Marxist thinking which identifies only 'class' as a basis for one group to have power over another. It also combines the macro side of Weber's writings with the micro side. Weber accepts that life chances are determined to a certain extent on the amount of wealth that you posses (macro explanation). However he also accepts that certain identities can be interpreted (the micro side of his explanation) by people differently depending on somebody's status (for example, teacher, lawyer, doctor, road sweeper) and that such *interpretations* can account for who has greater or lesser power in any community.

What are elite theories of power?

Key Definition

By **elites** sociologists refer to small groups that may exist at the top of any social group be it state, government, community, tribe or clan. Various debates exist in sociology as to the power, authority and influence that such elite groups possess.

✳ Key Idea

Weber disagreed with the Marxist idea that the state is dominated purely by the bourgeoisie. The political sphere was, in Max Weber's eyes, freer or possessed more 'autonomy' than Marx claimed.
Challenging the economic determinism of Marx (i.e. that all explanations about power could be accounted for by who owned the means of production), Weber believed the domination of any society was based around class, status and party. This therefore means that Weber offers a broader explanation for who has power and how it operates than that offered by Marx.

✓ Top Exam Hint

The New Right is a perspective that draws on Conservative ideas and was extremely popular in the 1980s and 1990s. Although not traditionally viewed as an 'elite theory', impress the examiners with your evaluation skills by arguing that it too could be viewed as elitist. It values the freedom of the individual and emphasises the role of the market in allocating resources (think about educational league tables and the 'farming out' of medical services to private companies). However it is also a theory that stresses the importance of 'moral values' (many New Right thinkers blame single parent families for the rise in crime statistics). This theory can be described as elitist because of its views on a strong centralised state (despite claims to the opposite) while at the same time arguing that the 'moral values' we adopt should be white, middle class and Christian.

What does this mean?

Elite theories of power which you will look at in this chapter challenge many of the ideas that pluralists and Marxists hold. Elite theorists hold that democracy is a 'myth'. However, it is important to note that there is no one 'elite' view but rather a range of views of which two are classical elite and radical elite theory.

Classical elite theory

This view holds that there is a small organisational elite or oligarchy at the centre of all states, either democratically elected or not. An 'oligarchy' is the undemocratic rule by a small group, an elite or leadership.

There are four points that classical elite theories share.

1. Equality is impossible in political terms as human beings are unequal in terms of skills, intelligence and wealth.
2. Throughout history, the 'few' have always dominated the 'many'. This is seen as a natural order and beneficial to the health and stability of society.
3. The masses are irrational, apathetic, stupid and gullible. Hence they are incapable of governing themselves, holding any sort of power or authority, or participating in government to a large degree.
4. The classical elite theorists were mainly concerned with resisting the spread of socialism and revolutionary ideas especially as promoted by Marxists. They had different ideas about the precise nature of the ruling class.

The key classical theorists are:

- Niccolo Machiavelli (1469–1527) who argued in his book, *The Prince,* that elites use two types of power: rule through legal means and rule through force. Effective leadership should mimic the traits of two different animals i.e. the cunning of the fox and the strength of the lion. He called these qualities, combined with courage and boldness, '*virtu*'.
- Gaetano Mosca (1858–1941) who argued that elite rule is natural, inevitable and normal. Strongly influenced by Machiavelli, he suggested that elite rulers are different and separate from the masses because they possess special characteristics, such as organisational skills, which greatly contribute to their being/becoming powerful and successful leaders.
- Vilfredo Pareto (1848–1923), whose theory, although classical elitist, is one that can also be used to account for how political parties/rulers change. Arguing that there was a 'circulation of elites' rather than one that was fixed, he said that even for ruling elites with cunning and strength there will come a time where they are replaced by another elite. Elites are easily corruptible and give way to a life of power and pleasure allowing for elite rule to circulate and another set of elites to rise to power and take over.

Radical elite theories

While classical elite theorists are fearful of democracy, radical elite theorists argue in favour of democracy, but claim that elites dominate most forms of society. This group of theories at first glance seems similar to Marxism except that the elite nature of society that radical elite theorists write about is *not* class based. Two theorists are:

- C. Wright Mills (1916–1962) whose book, *The Power Elite,* argues that unelected elites dominate American society. These unelected elites are those based around business, the military and the government and share the same social background. Capitalism is governed in the interests of these three groups. The power elite offers influence and power in a relatively stable set of elite positions.
- Floyd Hunter (1953), identified the existence, in Atlanta, Georgia, of a narrow group of elites exercising power over the masses, making decisions to benefit themselves and others like them. He studied groups involved in a community's decision-making processes, in order to identify the existence of local elites who, taken together, ruled over large sections of the city. Their interests were always business orientated.

Conclusion

Always remember that writers often write over a long period of time, and this means that their ideas do not remain constant but often change. An example of this is Mosca, a classical elite theorist, who later changed his negative views about democracy, arguing that the election process was a vehicle for the 'circulation of elites' he wrote about.

This version of elite theory is called 'democratic elite' theory and has been backed up by Dahl (1961) who argues that many elite groups compete to influence government policy. He argues that power is not concentrated but revolves around decision-making processes and 'issue areas'. Like Mosca, he argues that it is the election process which restrains elites from gaining too much power.

For consideration

1. To what extent do you think the theories in this section are applicable to all countries or states?

2. How do these theories add to your understanding of how power is distributed throughout society?

66 99 Key Definition

Marsh (1983) refers to **fragmented elites**. Explaining this in research that concentrates on the influence of interest groups, he argues that there is a 'plurality of interests' with some groups having more power than others. Groups occupying high positions in the economy (e.g. the elite of the civil service, key trade union members, powerful business concerns and key politicians) have most power and their decisions directly affect the economy and consequently the government's prospects of re-election. However, these elite groups are highly 'fragmented'. They do not 'share' power or rule but are in conflict with each other. However, such competition occurs within a consensus about the 'rules of the game'.

✍ Coursework Suggestion

Test Floyd Hunter's ideas about the influence of groups in local society. Carry out research within the local community of shops, offices etc. Try to access the owners of these local businesses and ask them who are the key 'movers' within the community. Try to establish whether influencing local elites is more important than gaining influence at government level.

✓ Top Exam Hint

Use the very different approaches of Lindblom and Lukes (1974) to back up the claims made by radical elite theorists. Neo-pluralist Lindblom accepts that some groups do indeed possess more power than others, referring to 'veto group pluralism'. He argues that there are some groups that have the power to 'veto' (close off or stop) certain policies made by government.

Lukes (1974) argues that, when analysing how much power groups possess, the 'three dimensions to power' need to be considered. The first dimension is decision making whereby a group may possess the power to take and make decisions. The second dimension is non-decision making in which some groups possess the power not to take decisions (for example, a group of civil servants may decide to ignore bringing to the attention of MPs a certain type of policy or complaint). The third dimension is the ability to shape decisions i.e. influence the views of others, for example, via the press.

2.8 | How does neo-Marxism help you understand power?

✳ Key Idea

What neo-Marxists try to do is to update the ideas of Marx and make them relevant to today. Marx's ideas went through enormous changes, with his earlier writings focusing on the importance of ideology and culture and stressing the ability of individuals to change their own circumstances. This is sometimes referred to as 'humanist'. His later work tended to be far more structural or 'economically deteministic', i.e. it stressed how economic conditions shape or determine our lives. Contrary to what one might expect, many 'neo-Marxists' quite often draw on the earlier ideas of Marx rather than his later writings although it is possible to see both humanist and structural elements in Marx's writings in the writers mentioned in this spread.

☞ Who is this person?

Antonio Gramsci (1891–1937) grew up in poverty to become an influential journalist, head of the Italian Communist Party and ultimately a political prisoner who died in one of Mussolini's jails. His *Prison Notebooks* are the source of the ideas that social scientists today quote so much from. Gramsci was not only famous for his concept of **hegemony**, but also for the term **'Fordism'** that has become so popular and part of the theoretical tradition known as 'post-structuralism'.

What does this mean?

Marx died in 1883. Despite the success of his political ideas in the former USSR and other parts of the world, he did not become fashionable as a sociological theorist until the 1970s when many of the writers below adapted his theories.

Marx predicted that, under what he considered to be the right circumstances, a revolution would take place in which event the power of the ruling classes would be transferred to that of the proletariat. Those who have power in society are not a ruling elite for Marx, but a ruling class whose power is based upon economic ownership and the control of the means of production, i.e. land, resources, capital and machinery.

Neo-Marxism in its many forms attempts to update these ideas *and* analyse why the capitalist system seems to be so successful in halting the revolution that Marx predicted.

What do sociologists mean by ideology?

The sociological use of the word 'ideology' refers to anything that might not be 'truthful' but is held to be true by those in power. Different ideologies compete to become dominant ideologies such as patriarchy or the belief in the fairness of capitalism. Neo-Marxists believe that in order to possess the social control of any society, i.e. maintain power over it, a dominant ideology must exist.

Ralph Miliband

Critical of elite and pluralist theories, neo-Marxist Ralph Miliband (1973) argues that the state is an instrument in the hands of the ruling class. All actions are determined by the state and people compete for the support and power it offers, making them political beings whether they know it or not. Far from being neutral, he argues that the state consists of a ruling group in society that persuades everybody that the values of the system are necessary to preserve it. Every day terms such as 'profitability' and the 'market' reflect capitalist values that actually serve those who have power and influence in society over and above those that do not.

Antonio Gramsci

Antonio Gramsci (1929–1935) argued that the capitalist or ruling class maintains leadership through repressive and ideological means. The state allows the ruling class to justify and maintain its dominance winning the active consent from those it rules. He argues that the state is composed of two areas: *political society* (the use of force or domination by the state) and *civil society* (the use of ideological means to secure hegemony). By **hegemony** he was referring to the ability of the state to persuade the masses into believing or consenting to the rules and values of the elite that dominates them.

Louis Althusser

Louis Althusser (1971) argues that the state ensures the compliance of its citizens through two sorts of apparatus.

1. The ideological state apparatus which works through the media, education and religion (for example, the Catholic Church in Britain and the role that Islam plays in Iran).
2. The repressive state apparatus which is designed to 'keep people in check', for example, the army and the police.

Although Althusser argued that ideologies had 'relative autonomy', i.e. religious ideologies and educational ideologies might seem to be working separately, in the long run they both serve the interests of the ruling classes.

For the state to be successful in maintaining power, according to Althusser, it should not be seen to be in a situation where the people challenge its power. However, if the state faces challenges, its power becomes much more overt or visible, that is it will act. Examples of this include the Tiananmen Square massacre of students in China in 1989 and more recently the thousands of civilians killed by the Iraqi regime under Saddam Hussein.

Conclusion

Neo means new but it would be wrong to assume there is just one set of ideas that is neo-Marxist. Rather there is a wide variety of views that attempt to update or revitalise the ideas traditionally held by Marx himself. The following four points represent a variety of neo-Marxist ideas.

1. Neo-Marxist ideas focus on the variety of power sources used by the ruling class, not just the ownership of the means of production but the control of capital, technology and the work force.
2. Neo-Marxists refer to a 'power bloc' rather than a ruling class which is made up of the state, owners of capital and controllers of labour.
3. Neo-Marxists argue that there is a rise of a new managerial class possessing more power than the masses and with limited power over the work force.
4. Neo-Marxists argue that ruling class power is maintained through hegemony rather than through ideology. Working class groups in society see through ideology and can develop an awareness of class inequality in society, but end up resigned to such inequality, feeling powerless, accepting capitalist rule as inevitable.

For consideration

1. If one person possesses more power, then does it automatically mean that somebody else possesses less?

2. Is power associated with a person, an office (title) or a structure?

✳ Key Ideas

- Embedded within the writings of Marx are two ideas that neo-Marxists develop. Marx referred to the state as an instrument of the rule of the capitalist class. But Marx also spoke of a more complicated relationship between the ruling class and the state, arguing the state has a *relative autonomy* from the ruling class. Neo-Marxists believe that the state is not always seen necessarily as the direct puppet of the owners of the means of production. Instead, it can sometimes have a degree of 'relative autonomy' making its own decisions that might directly contradict the interests of capital. However, in the long run, the state is still viewed as indirectly as well as directly serving the needs and desires of the ruling class.

- Rosemary Crompton (1993) argues that all known societies are stratified or differentiated (usually in a hierarchical fashion) according to one or more principles of classification whether by age, class, gender, religion or ethnicity. Neo-Marxists still argue that the study of 'class' is as important as it always was. Neo-Marxist theories help to show how wealth and power have contributed to the inequalities in capitalist societies that cause social stratification.

● Synoptic Link

Power itself is a difficult phenomenon to see in social life but the effects of *power differences* are obvious. J. Scott (1996) argues that while people are now less likely to identify themselves in class terms this does *not* mean class relations as objective realities have disappeared. Social stratification still exists as people are forced into a system of social strata that are distinguished from one another by their differing life chances and lifestyles.

What is the pluralist view of power?

How might pluralists argue that George W. Bush and Tony Blair have represented the voice of the people over the 2003 Iraq war?

✳ Key Idea

Functionalism is a strong influence on the ideas of many pluralist thinkers. Durkheim (1938) argued that the state offers an effective system through which the masses convey their wishes to the rulers. Providing social solidarity and collective moral values Parsons argued that power is something to be shared among all in any society albeit at different levels.

✓ Top Exam Hint

While there are similarities between the functionalist and pluralist perspectives on decision making and the operation of power, there are also differences that you can highlight. Functionalists look at the collective decisions of the whole community, i.e. the collective goals that have been decided through a process of 'value consensus'; this view is supported by Talcott Parsons. Pluralism, however, looks at competition and compromise within consensus. For pluralists there is a general collective agreement regarding the goals of society and how the democratic process should work, but within this agreement there are lots of disagreements over the precise direction society should move in to achieve the goals. This view is supported by Dahl.

What does this mean?

You have already learned from your AS year that functionalists hold what is considered to be a consensus view of the world. When analysing power, pluralist theories develop much of functionalist thought and attempt to portray democratic explanations of how some societies work or function. 'Plural' means many and implies there are a wide variety of groups that influence the decision-making process.

Marxist and elite theories of power argue that there is a fixed amount of power, i.e. those that have it do so at the expense of those that do not, but pluralists challenge this view. Talcott Parsons argued that if some societies had more institutions there would be a greater amount of power to go around and if there were fewer institutions there would be less power. Pluralists argue that the role of the state is to balance the competing claims and opinions of different groups in society for the benefit of all of that society.

What is pluralism?

All pluralist theorists believe in the following ideas.

- They reject Marxist ideas of economic determinism and the inevitability of class conflict and argue that capitalist systems are able to operate successfully on the basis of participation and democracy.
- The state is expected to provide for the health and welfare needs of its citizens, as well as more traditional provisions, such as law and order.
- The state must not degenerate into authoritarianism such as in Nazi Germany (i.e. when a state dictates what it wants to the people without consulting them), so it encourages a series of intermediary groups to act as 'buffers' between the state and the masses. These pressure groups or social movements forward demands from the masses to the authorities and defend the individual or minority group against excessive control by the state.
- The role of the state is seen as maintaining an equilibrium or balance between the demands of competing groups, reconciling conflict and acting as a go-between to ensure that public policy is fair.
- Ideology in a pluralist system should employ methods of persuasion and compromise rather than coercion and manipulation to achieve its aims.

What is classical pluralism?

The decision-making process in modern democracies works on the basis of different competing interest groups attempting to represent the case of others to those in power or to the public at large. *Any* individual or group has the *possibility* of influencing the decision-making process and therefore possessing some degree of power. Polsby (1963) argued that society is fractured into hundreds of tiny interest groups with overlapping memberships and a multitude of different techniques for exercising influence on decisions relevant to them.

What is neo-pluralism?

Neo-pluralism tends to be more sophisticated and updated in its analysis of democratic systems. It is also more critical about the level of democracy that does exist in society although it still argues that it exists in most western states. Neo-pluralism is concerned with the way that modern **bureaucracies** distort or restrict the voice of individuals. Focusing on the role that pressure groups play in politics, Grant (1989) argues that there are **insider** and **outsider** interest groups and the state itself decides who it will give positions of influence to.

Writers such as Richardson and Jordan (1979) identify an 'elite pluralist' position, an updated version of the now more classical pluralism offered within the writings of Dahl. The decision-making process in modern democracies works on the basis of different competing **elites** who compete for power whether they are political or social elites. They argue that some interests are represented more than others are. Elite groups such as businesses or middle classes are more likely to be listened to than trade unions or the working classes. So although everyone *does* get their say, the balance favours some over others in an unequal competition.

Galbraith (1969) showed how many large corporations use advertising to shape the wishes of consumers. Lindblom (1977) showed how businesses make decisions not on the basis of markets but rather in the interests of the company directors who lead them. Neo-pluralists therefore warn against the powerful voice that businesses can exert on democratic processes and argue that reforms need to be brought in by the state to recognise this weakness in the system.

Conclusion

Paul Hirst (1988), himself a neo-pluralist, is critical of much pluralist thought, arguing that pluralists possess a *'misdescription of the realities of power'* and that they disregard inequality of income and wealth. He argues that pluralists focus on the surface aspects of the political system, i.e. the way decision making takes place, but they ignore deeper issues such as class in power-based relationships.

If you agree that Britain is a democratic society then it is probable that you will identify with a lot of pluralist ideas. However, many other sociologists, such as feminists, Marxists and the variety of elite theorists, challenge the pluralist perspective of society.

For consideration

1. What empirical evidence is there to back up the variety of pluralistic theories on offer in this spread?

2. How might you apply Lukes' idea to your decision to buy a CD or an item of clothing?

66 99 Key Definitions

Insider groups are groups that tend to have regular contact with the government both in order to bring about pressure for change and to supply the government with information (for example, Amnesty International).

Outsider groups tend to focus on a single issue such as environmental concerns but may not be powerful enough or have enough financial resources to gain the attention of key people within government.

⌘ Classic Study

One example of classical pluralist writing is a study of local politics in New Haven in the United States by classical pluralist Robert A. Dahl (1961). He argued that rather than elites dominating political decision making, the wider community did so through various pressure groups representing their views and interests. The official government were forced to listen and consult the community when making decisions, so the interests of the wider community were engaged in the democratic processes of conflict, competition and compromise.

※ Key Idea

The theory of postmodernism recognises that there is diversity and choice in modern societies and that identities can be multiple, taking on board class, gender, age, ethnicity, sexuality, religion etc. Postmodernists also recognise that individuals today are in a position where they may have a variety of conflicting choices. They may wish to vote for one party on one issue but for another party on a completely different issue. All of this allows you to accept that in some cases there is a strong similarity in postmodernist ideas about power and politics and pluralism. Classical pluralism accepts the idea that in a democratic state competing interests generate the democracy they claim exists. Point this out to the examiner to gain evaluation marks.

How do feminists challenge traditional concepts of power?

Friedrich Engels (1884) argued that the cause of patriarchy, i.e. the disempowerment of women, can be identified in the history of capitalism. He identified the cause of inequalities between men and women in his *Origins of the Family, Private Property and the State*. Taking the traditional line that men were hunters and women were responsible for domestic affairs in primitive society, he nevertheless argued that these two areas were not considered hierarchical, i.e. one more valued than another. Men did not dominate (have power over) women and there were no restrictions on the amount of sexual partners either gender could have. As a result, the male parentage of children was uncertain and with little property in existence at the time what did exist was handed down through the maternal line.

❝❞ Key Definition

Malestream sociology is a description of sociology used by feminists who argue that much of the subject has been written by male sociologists and represents men's interests rather than those of women. Remember that the classical sociologists (Marx, Durkheim and Weber to name but a few) lived and wrote in cultures and at a time when male attitudes prevailed. The concept 'malestream' also highlights a key difference between the 'old sociology of politics' and the 'new sociology of politics' mentioned at the beginning of this chapter. Feminist theories focus much more on private political struggles rather than those that take place in public and under the analysis of the classical sociologists, who are, themselves, male.

What does this mean?

The variety of feminisms that exist represent one aspect of the new sociology of politics discussed at the beginning of this chapter. Feminist theories also combine macro and micro sociologies in that, from a macro perspective, they focus on the structures within societies that shape and determine women's lives. However, most research that explores the experience of being a woman is done from a micro perspective.

Feminists make a distinction between the 'public' and the 'private'. One look at history in the United Kingdom and you will notice how women have been and are publicly under-represented in key positions in society. This ranges from the political sphere in parliament, the political parties, and the judiciary to the media and even the academic world (much of sociology has been accused by feminists of being **malestream**). However, the hidden private world of women is also a world where power imbalances exist but are much harder to research. Different 'feminisms' seek to offer different analyses for how such a situation might be interpreted and changed.

What is politics in the eyes of feminist theories?

Politics in general focuses on the dynamic of power relations within any society. Traditionally politics takes place in the public sphere. Issues of common and public concern have been categorised as 'political' and are therefore the subject of state interest. This view accepts that there is also a 'private sphere', but it is not considered 'political'. For example, the state has no area of interest in family relationships. Feminists challenge such views on what politics is all about.

There are a variety of feminisms that you can refer to, some of which are mentioned here.

Liberal feminism

This branch of feminism broadly focuses on improving rights and opportunities for women. Not overtly critical of society itself, these feminists argue for greater representation within society as we experience it today, along with an equal distribution of power. Examples include greater demands for equal pay, educational opportunity and promotion within the work place. Examples of movements said to reflect 'liberal feminist' ideas are those of the suffragettes, a call for equal opportunities and anti-sexist legislation.

Marxist-feminism

The capitalist system places significance on success within the economic sphere of public and private life – both at the cheapest possible price. The work place subjugates women into lower positions or forces them into the home entirely. Women are responsible for producing future members of the work force, namely children.

Radical feminism

This attacks the very nature of patriarchal society. Radical feminists attempt to bring 'private' issues such as rape, sexuality, and reproduction out of the private and into the public domain. Radical feminists also 'celebrate' women's essential difference to men in terms of the creative and nurturing aspects of femininity.

Black feminism

Many black feminists are critical of the way that ethnicity is not taken into consideration by much of the feminist movement. With a diverse set of viewpoints, black feminists are interested in the western 'ethnocentric' views that white writers have about black women both in their own countries and from around the world, and are highly critical of their contributions.

Dual-systems feminism (also called 'socialist feminism')

This theory criticises how Marxist-feminism focuses on the relationship between capitalism and patriarchy. For Marxist-feminists, capitalism is the more powerful form of inequality, and patriarchy serves capitalism. However, for dual-systems theorists, class and gender, capitalism and patriarchy are as important and are interconnected.

Triple systems theory

Sylvia Walby (1990) argues that race, class and gender all have to be taken into consideration when analysing what is meant by 'patriarchy'. Patriarchy exists in six spheres of society: paid employment, violence, sexuality, culture, the household and the state, all of which are linked. 'Patriarchy' refers to male dominance over women and the state is seen as a patriarchical institution as it operates to legitimate male domination and power in society to the exclusion and oppression of women.

Conclusion

Critical of many of the viewpoints expressed above, post-feminist Catherine Hakim (Hakim 1995) talks of the 'myth' of partriarchy. This post-feminist perspective argues that feminists have often exaggerated their views in order to prove their point. Many of the conditions that women find themselves in today, such as the labour market and motherhood, are largely as a result of choice on their part. In other words they are empowered to choose their own way of life.

For consideration

1. To what extent do you think our lifestyles in England have a negative effect on women from other countries, both in this country and abroad?

2. Identify how many of the variety of definitions of power could be applied to the concept of patriarchy for women living in Britain today.

The 'myth of patriarchy'? What has changed in the 21st century?

✴ Key Idea

Kate Millett (1970) argues that 'the personal is the political' meaning that politics is about the structured relationships in which one person is controlled by another. In this respect, all aspects of human existence are about politics in the sense of power. In the area of relationships between the sexes, Millet argues that sexual domination (men over women) is the most deeply rooted ideology of western cultures. Society is a 'patriarchy', that is ruled by and in the interests of men.

◖◗ Methods Link

Many feminists argue that quantitative or positivist research methods (that try to be 'scientific') are 'research as rape'. They argue this because researchers use the people they research for their own interests and then cast them aside once the research is over. Often no attempt is made to help them to change their lives in any way. Many feminists wish for a feminist-only form of research and knowledge that seeks to help those it studies in an intimate way. Such research methodology needs in some way to give back something to those that are under study.

How does postmodernism help an understanding of power?

◆ What, when and why?

The period of modernity stretched from the late 18th century through to the 1970s. Many writers argue that life during this period was far more predictable than it is now. Science seemed to provide some of the answers that in previous times only religion could address. By the 20th century, scientific theories and other theories were used in the hope that the quality of life would improve. Post-modernists argue that this 'golden' age started to come to an end from the 1960s onwards.

✳ Key Idea

Postmodernists often talk about how our lives today are fundamentally different from times gone by. They often use the terms 'Fordism' and 'Post-Fordism' to explain this. **Fordism** (a term coined by neo-Marxist Gramsci) takes its name from the Ford Motor Company which pioneered mass-production of cars on assembly lines. Throughout much of the 20th century, Fordist methods of production meant that people were trained in a particular skill and then gained jobs that were quite often on a production line or associated with one particular way of working. The expectation was that these were 'jobs for life'. Nowadays, the concept of a 'job for life' no longer exists. '**Post-Fordism**' is the idea that production methods change to meet the needs of consumers/customers whose tastes quickly change from one fashion to the next. Associated with such methods of production are the lack of expectancy of a 'job for life', more women in the work place and an end to the association of a type of politics with a particular type of job (for example, miners and their traditional support for the Labour Party).

What does this mean?

By 'modernity' most sociologists refer to the period of the 18th, 19th and early 20th centuries, a period after the so-called 'enlightenment' which was characterised by industrialisation and the widespread belief that science contained the answers to some of the 'big' questions. These questions included 'why are we here?', 'what is the purpose of human existence?' and 'can scientific theory (or any other type of theory) lead to an improvement in the human condition?' Such thinking lay behind the old sociology of politics discussed at the beginning of this chapter.

Towards the end of the 20th century, a number of writers challenged many of the assumptions held during the period of modernity. Part of the new sociology of politics, postmodernist writers such as Jean Baudrillard (1983), Jean-François Lyotard (1984) and Zygmunt Bauman (1990) have inspired many to believe that we are in another type of world altogether. This world is a 'postmodern' world where none of the accepted theories or 'truths' or 'narratives' can be relied on.

Really big 'narratives' (postmodernists call these 'metanarratives') are the political ideologies of Conservatism, socialism and other mainstream political beliefs. At a time when many people are becoming disillusioned with politics (sometimes referred to as 'voter apathy') postmodernism offers sociologists a variety of viewpoints that help explain why such disillusionment exists.

What claims do postmodernists generally make?

- The idea that science is a force for liberation is untrue. The deaths of Jews in the gas chambers, chemical warfare and increasing health scares prove that scientific theory has not 'liberated' the human condition.
- As a result, no theory, story or set of ideas can offer a reliable explanation for how the world is.
- In a world where consumerism becomes much more important than production, what we 'consume' becomes increasingly a part of our identity.
- Old explanations about identity, such as those built around class, are meaningless in a world where we can 'pick 'n mix' clothes, music, food and even political parties.
- Where once we believed in 'purpose' and a sense of why we are here, postmodernists argue that we have become 'de-centred'.
- In what some postmodernists argue is 'hyperreality', the media has such a powerful influence on all our lives that fashions, beliefs, debates and ideas come and go. In fact we can no longer really distinguish between media reality and fiction.

The death of politics in a postmodern world?

- Jean Baudrillard (1983) argues that the death of politics has occurred. Disillusioned with politics, the masses have become *silent majorities* who have lost the ability even to be interested in power, let alone fight for it.
- Jean-François Lyotard (1984) argues that power is expressed through language in a 'language-game' in which communication becomes a 'battle field'. Language is flexible but the power that institutions have over individuals restricts these 'language-games' by shaping the rules of language. Think of the different ways that politicians, doctors, lawyers and teachers speak. Consider how you might feel 'disempowered' when dealing with such professionals.
- Zygmunt Bauman (1991) argues that postmodernity consists of a new type of politics made up of 'tribal politics' based around identities. These identities are often nationalistic, such as Welsh nationalism, or Christian and Islamic fundamentalism and, in some cases, can lead to the annihilation of particular groups of individuals (ethnic cleansing). On a more local level, tribal politics can also be seen in the variety of gangs that exist within inner city areas. Bauman also refers to the 'politics of fear' based around issues such as BSE, ozone depletion etc., and 'the politics of certainty', i.e. the loss of trust in so-called experts replacing the modern, post-enlightenment notion of trust in scientific explanations.

Conclusion

- If there are no longer 'right' or 'wrong' pieces of knowledge as postmodernists argue, where does that leave the status and power of politicians who are supposed to be entrusted representatives of the democratic process? Postmodernists believe that this accounts for the reason why there is an increasing distrust and lack of interest in politics.
- Surely postmodernism is itself a theory that attempts to offer an explanation for current events? Remember, postmodernists argue that all theories are just stories (they call them 'narratives'). Does this not equally make 'postmodernism' a narrative or story? Use this in the exam as a way of evaluating postmodernist claims.
- As societies become increasingly fragmented and diverse in make up, traditional institutions such as the family and religion have gone through immense changes over the last fifty years. Single parent families make up almost half of all families in Britain. Gay couples are becoming accepted in mainstream society. In a 'postmodern' world what implications might this have for the future of political parties in the UK? Postmodernists argue that these changes, associated with a postmodern world, account for the growth in pressure groups and new social movements over the last twenty years.

For consideration

1. Is the existence of a variety of political parties, pressure groups and new social movements evidence of a 'postmodern world' or confirmation of the pluralist belief that democratic politics exists?

2. Examine the 'rhetoric' of politicians. Do their changing ideas and interpretations of truth confirm the idea of a 'meta-narrative'?

✳ Key Ideas

- Postmodernist claims that the media is increasingly powerful in our lives make sense when we read stories about politicians in sex or drugs scandals. Such immediacy with events that take place has the effect of *pushing* people away from mainstream politics. One example of this was the disillusionment that many people in the UK felt over the war in Iraq in 2003. With a variety of conflicting stories being published in the newspapers, along with conflicting explanations from politicians, many people were *pulled* to other sources of political action, such as the anti-war march in central London. This '*push-pull*' effect is met by the wide variety of political parties, pressure groups and new social movements that they can pick'n'mix' from. This is evidence of the diversity that many postmodernists write about.

- Hebdige (1989) argues that there has been a collapse in the 'economy of truth'. By this he means that any particular theory or 'expert knowledge' is in fact a 'meta-narrative' or big story. Such stories cannot claim to be a 'truthful' portrayal of how the world actually is. Knowledge is just a social construction, i.e. something that powerful groups in society say we should know. Evidence of this 'distrust' in expert knowledge can be seen in the way that many people no longer hold the same trust in doctors or priests as they once did.

⬤ Synoptic Link

Postmodernists challenge traditional explanations of stratification based on class, gender and ethnicity and the accounts that such explanations offer regarding who holds power. They argue that while these old-fashioned concepts belonged to an era when 'production' was what defined an identity now it is what we consume that defines who we are – therefore these old labels are no longer appropriate. This *seduction of consumerism* also means that without the traditional notion of 'class' that was associated with which side of the production process you were on (owner or worker), class-based politics and allegiances no longer apply. Hence Blair's 'third' way politics, which is a political stance between that of socialism and conservatism.

How does post-structuralism help an understanding of power?

The Panopticon (all-seeing) has many of the design features found in modern prisons (see below). Surveillance was a strong feature of Foucault's writing and features in much of post-structural theory.

⟶ Classic Study

Foucault describes a particular type of prison design invented by the English philosopher, Jeremy Bentham, called the Panopticon. While the actual design was never fully incorporated into British prisons, many features were, including towers where prison wardens could see all prisoners most of the time. Lighting was also designed in such a way that wardens could see prisoners but prisoners could not see the wardens. This is a similar concept to the 'two-way mirrors' sometime used in penal institutions today.

The crucial aspect of the design for Foucault was the fact that prisoners would moderate their own behaviour even though they could not be sure they were being watched all the time. In this sense, power did not flow 'top-down' from the wardens to the prisoners, but rather the prisoners themselves changed their behaviour because they *believed* they were being observed. This idea of self-surveillance, i.e. that people moderate their own behaviour in light of some 'unseen' observer, is a key concept in post-structuralism.

What does this mean?

Whereas Weber was very concerned with asking the question 'who has power?', Michel Foucault (1967) was not interested in who has power but rather *how power circulates*. He argues that power is found in all social relationships, including relationships between individuals, institutions and the state. Although his writings cover a wide variety of topic areas, a common theme running through his writing is the relationship between the state and the individual and how power circulates between the two. He argues that the state has the ability to classify (i.e. 'sane'/'insane', 'employed'/'unemployed') and exercise power over its population as a result of such classifications. However, he also says that power is not something that you can easily detect but rather that it 'flows' through discourses.

What are discourses?

By discourses, Foucault referred to '*practices that systematically form the objects of which they speak*' (Foucault, 1967). Let us see how Foucault might apply this to educational policy. The 'object' being formed might be pupils or students. For example, if I believe that discourses in education revolve around words that include 'competition', 'large classes', 'league tables' and 'assessment', I might accept that this is exactly what education means and I might *not* question that perhaps there might be alternative and better ways to teach young people in school. Equally, those pupils that fail to fit into the systems and practices mentioned above might be disempowered within the education system.

The idea that power can be a product of shifting and overlapping discourses, such as those surrounding the family, education, law and religion, allows for a much more sophisticated explanation of power than that offered by other sociological theories. A concept that is associated with post-structuralism and linguistics, 'discourses' can refer to 'structures' of generally accepted ways of thinking that restrict people in seeing alternative forms of action. So who creates these discourses and who holds power?

What is the relationship between power and knowledge?

Foucault argues that throughout history the state has had the ability to develop new types of knowledge that in turn allows it to collect information and, as a result, control its citizens. He argues that the development of psychiatry in the 19th century allowed the classification of groups of individuals as 'sane' or 'insane' for the first time. This medical 'discourse' in turn brought about a building programme creating hospitals for the 'insane' along with experts that could perform such classification. So who is 'empowered' or 'disempowered' by these discourses?

Foucault argued that the discipline of psychiatry *created* the insane where before no such group existed. By doing so it gave power to those that had the knowledge to carry out such classifications as 'sane' or 'insane' along with a set of rules and regulations that reflected government interest at the time, i.e. its concern with rising unemployment and an increasing desire for law and order.

Punishment

Look back at Mel Gibson's tortured execution (racked, disembowled while still alive and finally beheaded) at the end of the film *Braveheart*. This typified the nature of punishment discussed in Foucault's early analysis in his book *Discipline and Punish* (1975). This kind of punishment was normal up to the 17th century, but by the end of the 18th century most public executions had ended and hangings took place behind closed doors.

In the 19th century the focus of punishment moved away from the body to a restriction in freedom, that is the growth of prisons and prisoners. As discourses have grown in number, so too have the creation of new crimes (for example, 'white collar crime') or indeed new explanations for crimes and criminals. Foucault argued that throughout the 19th and 20th centuries the solutions to crime grew as a result of the expert knowledge that existed in psychiatry, education and prison welfare. Each of these had their own set of discourses; each discourse a source of power for some and a source of punishment to others.

Conclusion

The post-structuralists below argue that 'government discourses' have the ability to *disempower* certain groups in society.

- Sharon Gewirtz (2001) argues that globalisation as a discourse allows states to justify changes and cutbacks to welfare state provision under the banner of 'international economic competition'. Such discourses allow states to 'privatise' their provision rather than increase the level of public spending. The poorest suffer as a result.
- Stephen Ball (1995) argues that government discourses in education (for example, those that include the language of 'market forces' and 'competition') generate multiple inequalities with the marginalisation/ disempowerment of working class and ethnic minority pupils as a result
- In the same way that Foucault's Panoptican regulates people's behaviour, surveillance cameras, clocking-in machines, timetables and the setting of work-related targets all monitor and shape the way we act and behave.

For consideration

1. How does post-structuralism differ from Marxism in its views about how power controls people in society?

2. To what extent do you think you can 'contest' discourses that operate against your interests?

✳ Key Ideas

- Post-structuralists argue that surveillance plays an increasing role in the world of work and education by monitoring and controlling the way we function. 'Surveillance' does not just have to refer to being 'observed' by the human eye. With performance-related pay and target setting, workers are under pressure to perform to their highest levels on the basis that they will be 'appraised' at the end of the year by their line manager. Pupils are monitored from an early age; think of the SATs tests at 7, 11 and 14 that children have to sit. Teachers are increasingly being paid according to their results. These are all examples of a type of surveillance that has the effect of altering our behaviour without the need for somebody to actually 'watch over us'.

- Foucault often links the concepts of power and knowledge together. '*We should admit that power produces knowledge ... that power and knowledge directly imply one another; that there is no power relation without the correlative constitution of a field of knowledge, nor any knowledge that does not presuppose and constitute at the same time power relations*' (Foucault 1991, page 27). Foucault terms this relationship 'power-knowledge', suggesting that those who have the ability to define and determine what we think and say are seen as the 'specialists' or 'experts', for example, doctors or teachers. They control how we think and speak and control the discourses that we use. For Foucault '*... power produces; it produces reality; it produces domains of objects and rituals of truth*' (Foucault 1991, page 194).

Why is democracy so difficult to define?

Suffragettes call for votes for women. Ian McLean (1996) attacks the idea that Britain in the 19th century could ever have been called a democracy despite claims to the contrary at the time. He notes that even before the first women were 'enfranchised' in 1918, less than half the adult population of the United Kingdom had the vote, making any such claims of Britain being 'democratic' ludicrous.

◆ What, when and why?

Political theorist, Jean-Jacques Rousseau (1712–1778), argued that *'the people of England think they are free. They are gravely mistaken. They are free only during the election of Members of Parliament'*. This quote of nearly three centuries ago is an idea that many sociology students might like to use in the introduction to any question that raises issues about democracy or voting systems. The quote is easy to remember and raises issues about the nature of democracy and to what extent people have control over their lives. It is also important to note, however, that at the time Rousseau was writing, no women could vote and the only men who had the power to vote were those who were wealthy and owned property. Even by the year 1884, this accounted for only 24 per cent of all men over the age of 21.

What does this mean?

Democracy refers to a form of government in which people rule. It conveys the idea that within the state which claims to be 'democratic' there is a type of political equality among people. Unfortunately, what is meant by the words 'rule', 'rule by' and even 'the people' is open to question depending on where, when, and who is involved in the discussion.

Most nation states and indeed most leaders claim to be democratic; the word comes from the Greek meaning 'rule by the people'. (The word *demos* means people and the word *kratos* means rule in Greek.) If you claim to be democratic it can somehow give the impression of legitimacy even if no such legitimacy exists. One might, for example, question the extent to which Britain can claim to be democratic when the party in power rules the country with two-thirds of the people not voting for it.

The three democracies

Social scientists broadly classify 'democracy' into the following categories.

- Direct/participatory democracy: originally found in Ancient Greece, this refers to decisions about public affairs being made directly by the citizens.
- Liberal/representative democracy: this is where 'elected officers' represent the interests and views of citizens (for example, US, UK, Germany, Japan, Senegal).
- One party democracy: a single party is viewed as being the legitimate expression of the overall will of the community; voters choose from a variety of different candidates rather than a variety of different parties (for example, the former Soviet Union, Cuba).

Three criticisms of the three democracies

1. The direct/participatory democracy that existed in Ancient Greece excluded women and many other marginalised groups, including the enormous slave community that existed at the time. As such it worked in an extremely tight community. It is therefore debatable whether such a system could exist in the modern nation state that exists in many parts of the world today.
2. Those calling for the increase in liberal or representative democracies would argue that it is desirable in the large populations that exist in nation states today to have a system of institutions to promote discussion, debate and competition among competing groups. Such a system requires new social movements, pressure groups and political parties with leaderships to help push the views of the variety of different peoples that exist in any one nation state (see Section 2.17).
3. Those calling for the existence of 'one party democracy' would argue that while there *seems* to be a greater degree of democratic voice in the liberal

version above, the *reality* is somewhat different. Liberal democracies offer formal rights, such as the right to vote, but what 'actual rights' do most people really have, for example, in an education system that treats all people in the same way? What role do liberal democratic states play in the inequality and poverty that many people experience in so called 'liberal democracies'? Critics of liberal democracies argue that power is disproportionately focused within the leadership of the variety of parties that exist, rather than being spread throughout the party system.

Understanding British politics

So-called 'democratic politics' in Britain involves the use of 'universal suffrage' i.e. the ability of most adults in the country to vote for elected representatives (Members of Parliaments or 'MPs'). The MPs are usually candidates for a particular party although some can stand as 'independents'. The political party with the majority of seats after a general election makes up the 'representative' government that, many argue, works in the interests of the country. The government is not a dictatorship and thus not allowed to become 'all powerful' or 'autocratic'. The public has the right to freedom of speech and every citizen in the country has the right to some form of representation or affiliation.

Conclusion

Is there not a tension between the idea of 'democracy' and 'freedom'? If the *majority* vote for an issue that a *minority* do not desire then surely it is impossible to talk of freedom or liberty for the minority in question. Consider the rising number of Muslims in the United Kingdom. What political voice do they have and to what extent would they approve of the many laws passed, such as British licensing laws for alcohol? To what extent can we consider regions like Northern Ireland or countries like Israel truly democratic when there is widespread persecution of minority groups? Consider also the 'non-combatants' taken prisoner in Afghanistan and Iraq by the United States and held prisoner without trial in Guantanamo Bay.

For consideration

1. What minimum proportion of adults would you consider is required to vote before a state can be described as 'democratic'?

2. Why is it legal in England to have sexual relations with somebody at the age of 16 but only legal to vote for a political party at the age of 18?

◆ **What, when and why?**

The global commitment to democracy claimed by many states is actually only a recent phenomenon. From Ancient Greece (c.500 BC to c.300 BC) to the Europe and America of the 18th centuries, little such commitment existed. Democracy today has really only existed over the last one hundred years. Indeed the very mention of the word democracy in the 19th century was thoroughly frowned upon! Democracy is an evolving and changing concept highlighted by the turmoil experienced in Russia under communism and Europe under fascism during the 1930s and 1940s. The worldwide anti-Iraq war demonstrations in 2003 have once again raised the issue as to what democracy means and indeed whether it exists in the states that claim to be 'democratic'.

✴ **Key Idea**

While the idea of direct democracy seems unrealistic in today's densely populated nation states, some postmodernists might argue that with the increase in technology and the domination of the media in society, there is now a *greater* opportunity for people to play a direct role in participating in local and national politics and have a greater say in what goes on. Don't forget that local and national elections are increasingly using mobile phone texting and portable computer terminals where people can vote. In addition to this, think of the possibilities that 'armchair' viewing on television gives to pass opinions; is this not a form of 'direct democracy'?

✓ **Top Exam Hint**

There are a number of issues that you could bring into any exam question that focuses on whether or not democracy can be said to exist. You could discuss:

- to what extent women participate in the voting system, but also to what extent they may or may not be exploited within the home or work place, i.e. to what extent they have a 'voice'
- pressure groups and the role they play in the democratic procedure
- what role does direct action such as riots play in democracies
- voter apathy (i.e. the unwillingness of people to vote) and Baudrillard concept of the 'silent majority' (see Section 2.16).

What is a political system?

❝❞ Key Definition

The word **ideology** has two meanings, the first is the one that you have looked at so far in this chapter and has a negative perception attached to it. However, social scientists also use the word ideology in a second sense. It can also mean political worldviews held by political parties.

✳ Key Idea

Dearlove and Saunders (1991) describe the English system in the following quote. *'Britain can be characterised as a two party system (in the Commons); as a multi-party system (in the country) and as a dominant party system (in the corridors of power) because of the electoral system.'* By this they mean that despite the fact that there are more than two parties across the country, within the House of Commons power has remained with either the Conservatives or New Labour depending on who won the election. At first glance one would argue that the English system can be said to be a two-party system although during the 20th century the Conservative party was in power for the majority of the century.

▢ Key Fact

The only members of the British population that cannot vote are:
- members of the House of Lords
- children under 18
- convicted prisoners
- people compulsorily detained in psychiatric hospitals.

What does this mean?

The beginning of the 21st century is an incredibly exciting time to be analysing politics both nationally and internationally. Political **ideologies** and systems, which were perceived to be 'solid' during much of the 20th century, have collapsed, for example, the end of the 'cold war'. Many claims are being made by world leaders about how one type of political system may be more just or democratic than another. Social scientists use a variety of concepts to describe political systems and how they are made up.

What do we mean by a party system?

By 'party system' social scientists refer to the combination of significant parties, their interactions, and the particular electoral system, voter loyalties and type of leadership produced. There are four easily identifiable models.

1. The single party system: all alternative parties are banned apart from the party that holds power. This party puts up candidates to be voted into power. However, all the candidates are from the same party and therefore such a system is viewed as undemocratic and authoritarian. An example of this was the Nazi National Socialist Party.
2. The dominant party system: there are many parties but only one usually wins or becomes the largest in a series of coalitions. An example of this is the post-war Japanese Liberal Democratic Party.
3. The two party system: two parties compete on an equal or near equal footing. Other parties may win a few seats but exercise little or no power. Many argue that the American and English systems fall into this category.
4. The multi-party system: more than two parties compete on an equal or near equal footing. Power can alternate between the various parties or it can be shared in coalitions, such as in the German system.

The functions of political parties

1. Forming the government: some parties can form governments although not all parties share an equal chance in doing this (consider the difficulties that the Liberal Democrats face in the UK when attempting to compete against the Conservatives and New Labour). Parties recruit politicians and develop programmes of action (their 'manifesto').
2. Forming the 'opposition': the party that is the official opposition to the government, alongside all other parties that are in opposition. In 2003 the official party of opposition was the Conservative Party even though there are other parties that 'oppose' New Labour, such as the Liberal Democrats.
3. Representation: parties are the most important form of representation. The whole electoral process rests on the existence of parties that organise the electorate and allow choice by providing 'labels', that is voters vote for parties rather than candidates. Parties communicate ideas from the government to the public but also shape the ideas from the public

(sometimes via 'pressure groups') and communicate these back to the government.

4. Parties are the main 'agencies of political participation', from voting in the elections, to becoming an MP. The system allows people to assert their political identities, i.e. parties can represent groups according to their class, ethnic group, region, economic interest or ideology.

Changing political ideologies

Before the 1970s, the main political parties could be identified with either the middle class (Conservative) or the working class (Labour) and voting was assumed to be relatively stable – any voter not voting in line with their class interests was seen to be deviant. Two developments in modern UK political ideologies have changed this. These are the rise of the New Right in the UK and the 'modernisation' of the UK Labour Party in the light of four successive election defeats since 1979.

The term 'New Right' is most associated in the UK with the Conservative Party under the Thatcher governments since 1979. In the New Right view, the social problems of rising juvenile crime, massive unemployment and crisis-point state spending are the result of liberal ideas, socialism and the introduction of the welfare state that has allowed immorality and laziness to continue.

Marxist-influenced Stuart Hall (1984) argued that the traditional working class moved to vote for the New Right polices of the then Conservative government. Thatcherism offered a strong sense of leadership and identity. This happened at a time when the Labour Party was generally seen to be discredited due to internal fighting.

Jürgen Habermas (1988) has suggested that during the 1980s the welfare state was seen to cost more funds than the government could or wanted to afford. As a result the media presented a picture of a 'state overload' – a crisis that needed to be managed by reducing state spending at all costs before the crisis point became unmanageable.

Conclusion

The ideologies of the New Right paved the way for the transformation of the Labour Party into the New Left. With the change from 'old Labour' to 'New Labour' a number of left-of-centre thinkers and politicians have started to speak of a 'new way' or rather a 'Third Way' in politics: a political ideology that moves beyond traditional left-versus-right political debates. Most notable among these advocates of a Third Way are Tony Blair, and sociologist Anthony Giddens (1998 and 2000).

New Left advocates such as Giddens point out that the key difference is that the New Right do not seem to care if inequality persists and perhaps feel that those who suffer disadvantage are seen almost to deserve it, whereas for the New Left inequality must be tackled and reduced.

For consideration

1. To what extent do you believe that the political parties have a 'democratic' voice in English politics?

✳ Key Ideas

- Devolution refers to the situation that has taken place in recent years in Scotland and Wales where powers are being 'devolved' from central government in London to each country giving them a degree of autonomy or freedom from the government in Westminster. However, the Scottish parliament has considerably more power and wealth allocated to it than the Welsh parliament. At the time of writing, talks for the creation of a Northern Ireland Assembly, the equivalent of the Scottish parliament, have once again been postponed. In all cases, however, it is the parliament in Westminster that dictates the terms and conditions under which 'devolution' takes place.

- New Right political ideology consists of ideas that include:
  - privatisation of business away from centralised state control
  - the introduction of economic competition through the 'free-market'
  - a desire to return to 'traditional family values', and a criticism of homosexual and single-parent families
  - the removal of state spending on welfare to compensate for the 'nanny-state' of the welfare system that spent too much money and as a result has caused a situation of 'state overload'
  - zero-tolerance policing
  - the view that poverty and unemployment are the fault of the 'lazy' individual.

What are voting systems?

What does this mean?

Any discussion about the extent to which a nation can be considered democratic would be incomplete without reference to how people can/should vote in the country they inhabit. In Britain a system of voting referred to as 'first-past-the-post' (FPP) exists. However, an alternative system exists in many other countries known as 'proportional representation' (PR). In both cases the argument for each system rests on whether or not you believe that government should be a 'representative' or 'decision-making' body.

First past the post (FPP)

FPP takes its name from horseracing, i.e. the winner of the race is the horse that is first past the post. In politics it is the name of the 'majoritarian' system of voting that exists in the United Kingdom (and Canada). You might argue that this system is more associated with a decision-making government. The country is divided up into smaller areas known as constituencies. The election winner of each constituency becomes the Member of Parliament (MP) who goes on to represent the constituency in the House of Commons (i.e. is voted in to represent that area in parliament).

Although the FPP system is supposed to encourage a variety of parties, in practice it encourages a two-party system such as that in England where either Labour or the Conservatives are the only viable election winning parties. In most cases the government is voted in with little more than 40 per cent of votes cast to the winning party. Ian McLean (1996) notes that such systems give absolute majorities to parties with considerably less than 50 per cent of the vote.

One of the advantages of the FPP system is that it tends to provide extremely stable governments where there is little chance for small 'extremist' parties, such as the British National Front, to affect policy making. However, this voting system can also be criticised for not allowing new parties, such as the Green Party, to enter the political system with the effect of bringing about considerable social change. It is therefore possible to describe the British political system as one that is 'stagnant' or 'non-dynamic'.

Proportional representation (PR)

An alternative, and some say far more democratic, system of voting is proportional representation or PR. This exists in most European countries and is seen to be more representative. PR refers to any system which seeks to ensure that any political party is represented in proportion to the number of voters that voted for it. In other words if 20 per cent of the population vote for party

A, 30 per cent for party B and 50 per cent for party C, then parties A, B and C will gain 20 per cent, 30 per cent and 50 per cent of the seats respectively.

While there are many critics of such a system of voting, many argue that it allows for what can be referred to as a multi-party system. This is where more than two parties are represented in government thereby offering a more healthy and dynamic political arena to pursue and challenge new government policies.

Single transferable vote

A variation of the PR system described above can be found in Ireland, Malta and Australia. In these countries when going into the election booth you will be given a list of candidates from the various parties that you have to list in order of preference. Those candidates that gain the required 'quota' or specified number of votes are elected and the remaining votes are passed onto choice number two. Candidates with the fewest first choices are eliminated. This process will be repeated until all available seats are allocated.

Alternative vote

This refers to a system of voting that selects any candidate from a particular party that commands a majority. As with the single-transferable vote, the voters rank the candidates. All first preferences are counted and any candidate who receives more than 50 per cent first choice decisions is elected. In the case where no such candidate exists then the one with the fewest first choices is eliminated from the results with their votes being redistributed until a candidate wins more than half of the valid votes cast.

Conclusion

'Which came first – the chicken or the egg'? The argument *against* a proportional representation system of voting is that it is not required when there are very few parties, as is the case in England and the United States. However, the FPP system in England effectively rules out the possibility for newer or alternative parties to change the political scenery. In addition to this, despite the fact that New Labour have *said* that they are interested in changing the system, it is in the interests of *both* New Labour and Conservatives for such a system to remain in place. In other words, by eliminating the competition it virtually guarantees that no other party can win the election other than either New Labour or the Conservative Party.

For consideration

1. Which do you think would have the greatest impact on bringing more voters back to the ballot box, the increased ease that technology brings or a change in the system of voting?

2. How might Marxists and feminists attack the FPP system that exists in England?

◆ What, when and why?

The origins of proportional representation in Europe date back to the 19th century when the variety of political parties representing groups such as peasants, industrialists, nobility, workers and religions made the notion of FPP seem impractical.

✴ Key Idea

In countries where PR exists and where there are multi-party systems as a result, voter participation is far higher than in British and Commonwealth countries where FPP still exists. Sweden and Germany do have a 5 per cent minimum threshold that, in effect, stops very small (and in some cases extremist) parties from entering the political arena. This means that if a party gains less than 5 per cent of the vote then it will not gain any seats in government.

How might we understand the changing nature of voting behaviour?

At the 2001 general election, only 59.1 per cent of voters turned out to vote, compared with 71.4 per cent of voters in the previous election in 1997.

※ **Key Ideas**

Sociologists refer to models of voting, the key ones being:

- a consumer theory of voting, developed by Himmelweit et al (1981), where a 'rational' choice is made by 'consumers in a market place'. Voters see themselves as little valued within this market place only to be used by the politicians at times when their political lives require them (at elections).
- tactical voting which occurs when, according to Heath et al (1991), voters vote not for a party of their *choice* but rather it is by voting for a particular party that another party might suffer as a result. This is more associated with countries that use the first past the post system. For example, a Liberal Democrat voter who believes her/his party may not win a constituency may vote either Labour or Conservative depending on which party she/he definitely does *not* want to win.
- pocket-book voting which refers to the idea that individual voters only vote with their own economic interests in mind, i.e. voting for the party which they feel will make them more financially secure. Heath et al (1987) argue that rather than individuals voting this way, in fact 'class allegiance' exists where entire classes vote for a party which they consider acts broadly in their own economic interest.

What does this mean?

Psephology is the study of voting behaviour and patterns. Writing in 1969, Butler and Stokes argued that predicting votes was relatively simple in that people tended to vote in line with their particular social position. Using terms such as *alignment* and *partisanship* they argued that people showed a particular bias to a political party and/or voted in line with their class position. They argued that primary socialisation in the family meant that manual workers socialised their children into becoming Labour voters while members of the middle classes socialised their children into becoming Conservative voters. But how appropriate is such an analysis in today's political environment?

How important is class when discussing voting behaviour?

Ivor Crewe (1992) argues that new working classes *can* be identified in the changing social structure. The widespread home ownership that the working classes now share is a long way from the lifestyles that Charles Dickens wrote about in books such as *Oliver Twist* and *Great Expectations*. According to Crewe, working class people vote 'rationally' in the same way that they go shopping in a supermarket picking and choosing what is in their interests. Crewe argues members of the working classes vote on the basis of issues rather than their class 'consciousness'.

Three features of the changing nature of voting behaviour

1. Deviant voters refers to those voters that seemed not to vote in line with their class positions in the way that Butler and Stokes might have expected. Many middle class voters may not vote Conservative because they work in the public services such as the health service and education, an area traditionally associated with Labour support.
2. Dealignment refers to the idea that from the 1970s individuals are no longer aligned to their traditional class and party. Instead they become what is referred to as floating voters, changing their mind from one election to the next on the basis of self-interest rather than party or class interests.
3. Volatility refers to the idea that predicting voting behaviour today is extremely difficult. In fact, the very term 'deviant voter' is problematic in that most voters are deviant. For example, the long-term success of the Conservative Party was largely based on its popularity with the working classes. Equally, New Labour has gained power largely by capturing the Conservative vote. Social background is no longer a clear indication of which party you might vote for.

Voting behaviour today

- Lash and Urry (1987) argue that, in a globalised economy, multinational companies have shifted their manufacturing operations to less developed nations, where labour power is cheaper. This has drastically altered traditional voting patterns because of the loss of traditional working class jobs and the significance on traditional working class movements such as trade unions. As a result this has caused a decline in class politics.
- Thrift and Johnson (1996) argue that traditionally people were socialised within the values and attitudes associated with a particular class background, whether working class or middle class, and voted accordingly. However, they argue that people are now free in their choice and are no longer determined by their class, values, attitudes and expected behaviour or restrained by the previously rigid boundaries.
- For Giddens (2001) the 'Third Way' describes New Labour's response to how the world has changed and how parties of the Left must bring their *'classic concerns about social justice in health, education and welfare into line with the demands of this changed world'* (Giddens 2001, page 30). Taking ideas from both the Left and Right of the political spectrum 'third wayism' is about the creation of a 'social investment state' where social exclusion and segregation is excluded (for example, the New Deal). In what some would consider to be cynical attempt to capture votes, this is an extremely convenient set of ideas for New Labour to attract both traditional Labour and Conservative voters.

Conclusion

- Postmodernist Baudrillard (1983) describes the *'development of the silent majorities'* who, in today's *'media saturated world'*, are disillusioned with politics and politicians, and have lost the ability to be interested in who has power and who has not.
- For Baudrillard, this silent majority have lost the will to fight for change, and are indifferent to party politics; they no longer have a desire to vote.
- However, this disillusionment with the political, on the behalf of the masses, is seen as a *'fatal strategy'* by Baudrillard since it leads to an increasing inability to be truly represented by those political leaders claiming to be doing so, and thus paving the way for more authoritarian or dictatorial forms of government.
- However, while political apathy (no longer caring about politics) might be a modern-day media concern, a review of the increasing amounts of direct action, pressure groups and new social movements would seem to challenge the idea that the masses are apathetic.

For consideration

1. To what extent do you think New Labour have successfully fulfilled the criteria spelled out by Andrew Gamble?

2. Using the ideas on this page, how would you describe the sets of influences that would draw you into making a decision in the ballot box?

⁕ Key Ideas

- Andrew Gamble (1994), writing before the success of New Labour, analysed how the Labour Party would have to reinvent its election strategy in the light of four election defeats at the hands of the Conservative Party. He argued that renewed focus needed to take place on:
  - the ability of any party to attract new voters (by age, gender, class and ethnicity)
  - the structure and organisation of any political campaign
  - the party's public image as represented by the media.

- When attempting to explain why people vote, writers who represented the old sociology of politics would have looked primarily for class-based explanations. Under the new sociology of politics, explanations for voting need to take into consideration all the following: class background, educational experiences, parental views, occupation, trade union membership, views of friends and families, media opinion and bias, political campaigns run in the media by the parties themselves, party literature and canvassing, and financial considerations.

✍ Coursework Suggestion

Devise your own criteria on a questionnaire and, choosing your sample carefully, carry out coursework that investigates how patterns of voting have changed over time in the area where you live. Choose people that voted in the 1950s and who vote now to assess which model of voting is applicable to these two historical periods.

What is the modern nation state?

Some multinational companies are more financially powerful than many nation states.

◆ What, when and why?

Over the last twenty years, many social scientists have argued that there has been a decline in the power of the nation state. Other larger 'supranational' organisations have come into existence such as the European Union that, some argue, overshadow the powers of individual nation states. In addition to this, large multinational companies can turn over more money in one week than some nation states do in a year. For example, the American giant corporation, Walmart, the parent company of ASDA, has a weekly turnover of £4 billion!

⋇ Key Idea

To what extent can all states exercise the national sovereignty that is associated with being a nation state? If we consider that relatively small, weak states exist in a system in which there are much stronger powers, then how much sovereignty do they actually possess? Certainly we cannot talk about all small states in the same way. How much power a state has may depend on its geographical location or what the ambitions of bigger states are in the same area. It could also depend on whether the smaller state has some major economic resource that it either controls or that others desire control over. It could also depend on how much united support there is for the state to be independent, or what alliances it holds with other more major powers.

What does this mean?

Max Weber defines the nation state in the following quotation.

'The primary formal characteristics of the modern state are as follows: it possesses an administrative and legal order subject to change by legislation, to which the organised activities of the administrative staff, which are also controlled by regulations, are oriented. This system of order claims binding authority, not only over the members of the state, the citizens, most of whom have obtained membership by birth, but also to a very large extent over all action taking place in the area of its jurisdiction.' (Weber 1978, page 56)

Attempting to define what we mean by 'nation states' is tricky. There have been attempts to define nations in terms of language, religion, culture, territory, historical tradition and race. Some of these do actually come together in most nations but not necessarily in a clear-cut way. Social scientists often make references to 'nations', 'states', and 'nation states' without necessarily agreeing about what these terms actually mean.

What do social scientists mean by the state?

- A 'state' refers to the political organisation that displays **sovereignty** both within geographic borders and in relation to other sovereign entities. The state is, according to Max Weber, an 'iron fist in a velvet glove', that is the central defining feature is its *legitimate* right to use coercion or violence within its defined territory.
- A 'nation' used to refer loosely to a 'people' although that people may not necessarily be associated with a geographical space, such as the Palestinians. A 'nation' may share the same language, culture and ethnicity.
- 'Democratic states' are states in which there is an election process, a variety of political parties and where human rights are given priority.
- 'Totalitarian states' are states in which there is one party that dominates the state and limited freedom exists for those that live within its boundaries.

Language can play an enormous role in how we define nations. However, this becomes difficult with countries such as Switzerland, which is divided into German, Italian and French speaking regions. Talking about a 'Jewish' nation can be problematic when the vast majority of Jews live outside Israel. An American 'nation' becomes equally problematic with many different groupings speaking different languages and possessing different religions.

Most social scientists, however, would agree that the term 'nation state' applies to any country that can make its own laws, operate its own economy and maintain economic power within its own territory. Nation states also wish to determine their own foreign policy, having their own defence and military capabilities.

What is nationalism?

'Nationalism' is one of those terms that everybody believes they know the meaning of but it is actually a hugely complex term. Many people associate nationalism with fascism and/or racism, i.e. they think of it in negative terms and probably associate it with 'right wing' thought.

It certainly is true that nationalism can assume these qualities but it is misleading to suggest that it is the only form in which it appears. If you think of the demands that some people have for national self-determination against some kind of repressive rule, then nationalism takes on a completely different meaning. It can, in this sense, be associated with demands for political pluralism and tolerance.

Anthony Giddens (1981) argues that the nation state *'exists in a complex of other nation-states, is a set of institutional forms of governance maintaining an administrative monopoly over a territory with demarcated boundaries (borders), its rule being sanctioned by law and direct control of the means of internal and external violence'* (Giddens 1981, page 190). Like Weber, Giddens also argues that a key feature of the state is its ability to use legal or legitimate violence against those within its political and geographical boundaries. Giddens argues that for a state to successfully maintain power it needs:

- centralised organs or institutions of government such as the House of Commons
- a centralised government that is associated with claims to legitimate territorial control
- a distinct dominant or elite class, having definite modes of training, recruitment and status attributes such as the 'high fliers' within the civil service.

(Giddens 1993, page 193)

Conclusion

Remember your micro sociological perspectives? Rather than being determined by forces beyond its control, **state centred theories** assume that a state has interests of its own. In other words, states are like social actors (they possess agency) that can influence the environment around them, that is other states. This theory challenges the idea that the nation state is a product of capitalism or of the class relations that exist within the state. This view also challenges the macro explanations offered by many of the globalisation theories that argue that nation states are shaped and determined by other forces such as international capital and supranational organisations.

For consideration

1. To what extent do you think education contributes to the sense of belonging to a nation state?

2. What role has the media played in creating a sense of either 'harmony' or 'threat' within the state?

66 99 Key Definitions

- By **sovereignty** sociologists refer to the ability of a nation state to operate the right to self rule, govern its own affairs, possess legitimate legal authority over its citizens, all within a specific geographical area or territory.

- **State centred theories** are theories that attempt to describe states almost as 'social actors' that act independently to fulfil their own interests. Theda Skopol (1979) argues that the way a state develops depends upon how well organised other groups are in society. A powerful state can mould the actions of all such groups in its interest. She also argues that the extent to which a state can achieve its own goals is determined by:
  - having a clear territorial base
  - having a reliable source of income
  - recruiting a significant proportion of the academic and social elite.

⁂ Key Ideas

- Friedrich Engels argued that the state is needed to protect and preserve the ruling class's unequal rule gained through economic ownership. Once class distinctions were developed, the state controlled class conflict, resulting in the ruling class being dominant in terms of power and within politics giving them more power to exploit the oppressed class.

- Nordlinger (1981) argues that the state wields power by:
  - concealing its methods of decision making
  - manipulating the honours system, i.e. honouring key public figures in return for their increased loyalty and service
  - offering funding of particular contracts to particular client groups such as the military
  - increasing the role of the media (spin-doctoring).

How do sociologists see the role of the modern state in society?

American soldiers raise the American flag over a statue of Saddam Hussein in Baghdad. Social scientists and political commentators will be closely watching the many processes of nation building that will be taking place over the next decade in Iraq following the 2003 war to depose Saddam Hussein.

What does this mean?

Stjepan Mestrovic (1994) voices the fears that many social scientists express when he refers to the 'Balkanisation of the West'. Using this phrase he argues that the world is becoming less cosmopolitan, less global and less 'rational'. In recent years, many countries have broken up into smaller independent states, for example the break up of Yugoslavia and Czechoslovakia in the 1990s. With states being broken up or re-formed, understanding different views of the *role* of the nation state helps sociologists understand the many complex processes involved.

Competing explanations about the role of the nation state

- Pluralist theories believe in the idea of a democratic state and see the role of the state as an 'honest broker' that negotiates between the competing interests of a variety of different interest groups and parties. The state is 'neutral' in this decision-making process.
- Elite theories are critical about any notion of 'democracy' although accept that it is possible to generate common 'norms and values' (reflecting functionalist ideas). The state should be powerful and reflect the interests of those in power.
- 'State centred' theoretical approaches argue that the state is a very strong 'social actor' or 'agent' that has the autonomy or freedom to act as it best wishes. It uses foreign policy and domestic policy to serve its own interests.
- 'Traditional' or 'orthodox Marxism', itself a confusing term, relates to the early branches of Marxism based on the more 'economic deterministic' explanations contained in some of Marx's writings. The key idea is that ownership of industry and finance gives political power to the bourgeoisie.
- Structural Marxists agree with traditional Marxists in arguing that while the state is important in shaping the nature of society, it is the form of economic ownership it takes (i.e. which class owns what) that is the key factor. Therefore the state is an instrument of the class that owns the means of production and therefore serves its interests.
- Humanist Marxists agree with much of what structural Marxists claim. However, they argue that at times the state *does* have relative autonomy to act in its own interests rather than in the interests of the ruling classes when deciding policy issues. Capitalism, however, is established through the state's ability to manipulate and organise the masses. In what humanist Marxists refer to as 'ideological hegemony', the workers accept the ideas of the ruling classes as being 'natural' and 'right' often through the state's ability to manipulate the media. Nevertheless, the ultimate outcome always serves the interests of the ruling classes.

✓ Top Exam Hint

The term 'neo-Marxism' can be confusing to students and it helps to remind the examiner that the term itself is problematic. There is no one branch of 'neo-Marxism'. What neo-Marxists try to do is to update the ideas of Marx and make them relevant to the 20th and 21st centuries. It is also important to remember that Marx himself went through enormous changes in ideas during his time of writing.

- Weberianism turns the ideas of Marx upside down. Max Weber argued that it was not capitalism that had produced the bureaucratic state but rather the other way around. The success of capitalism and its ability to grow so quickly throughout the 19th century was due to a bureaucratic, rational state that was only too willing to promote the riches that it could generate.
- Postmodernists represent a wide variety of viewpoints, but globalisation, fragmentation and 'glocalisation' are key themes. The state ceases to have centralised control. Decentralised or devolved government appears, such as the Welsh and Scottish assemblies rather than the House of Commons dictating economic policy for the entire United Kingdom. Politics are no longer influenced by traditional indicators such as 'class' but rather by 'lifestyle' with the masses less easily manipulated by a state.

Conclusion

Ralph Miliband (1973) is critical of elite and pluralist theories about the state. He believes that these theories neglect the fact that the interests of the state are the same as the interests of capitalism – the proliferation of profit for the ruling classes. As such, all state institutions operate in the interests of those who own the means of production.

☀ Key Ideas

- Humanist Marxists refer to two types of power being used:
  1. political power: the state's ability to use coercion with the threat of force if necessary
  2. civil power: the ability to gain ideological consent from the masses through media propaganda and a wide variety of other strategies such as religious and national ceremonies designed to bring people together under the banner of one nation.

- Structural Marxist Nicos Poulantzas (1980) argues that the state is not governed by the ruling class but by the government. The state has a degree of 'relative autonomy' from the ruling class but the state always works in the interests of those for whom capitalist society is structured. Elites are by their very nature always going to serve the interests of capitalism.

For consideration

1. Using Iraq as an example, how might you use the above theories to explain how it has been 'rebuilt'?

2. How might you argue that Britain can be described as a 'social actor' using state centred theories?

Do we have a ruling class, ruling elite or power bloc?

Connect the ideas of Scott on power elites to those of radical elite theorist C. Wright Mills (1956) who shares a great deal in common with more contemporary neo-Marxist writers. Mills suggests that a narrow ruling elite makes the decisions in society and that other groups have little if any potential to be able to influence these decisions. *'By the powerful we mean, of course, those who are able to realise their will, even if others resist it'* (Mills 1956, page 9). Mills identifies three elite groups in American society, although his work is seen to apply to western societies in general, which he refers to collectively as the 'power elite'. These groups are:

- military leaders
- political leaders
- business leaders.

Talking about the power elite Mills writes *'The conception of the power elite and of its unity rests upon the corresponding developments and the coincidence of interest among economic, political and military organisations. It also rests upon the similarity of origin and outlook, and the social and personal intermingling of the top circles from each of these dominant hierarchies. This conjunction of institutional and psychological forces, in turn, is revealed by the heavy personnel traffic within and between the big three institutional orders...'* (Mills 1956, page 292).

What does this mean?

The notion of an 'upper class' consisting of landed gentry and commercial and manufacturing elites has, for many writers, seemed a crude classification in light of developments in many post-Second World War capitalist societies. However, in the work of John Scott (1991) we see the two theoretical approaches of Marxism and radical elite theory drawing together in an analysis of power in contemporary society which holds that an upper class still exists.

Upper class or ruling class?

Scott argues that the concept of upper class has changed. Whereas traditionally the upper classes owned land, financial capital and machinery, today's upper classes are in possession of financial assets, pension funds and insurance schemes. But Scott makes a distinction between the terms 'upper class' and 'ruling class'. He believes that those who hold power in society, the ruling classes, still come from the upper classes.

Scott argues that for an understanding of the notion of a ruling class *'this requires that there be a power bloc dominated by a capitalist class, a power elite recruited from this power bloc, in which the capitalist class is disproportionately represented, and there are mechanisms which ensure that the state operates in the interests of the capitalist class and the reproduction of capital'* (Scott 1991, page 124).

Scott states that power blocs refer to those who can hold power over the population for long periods of time. He argues that a power bloc is *'an informal coalition of social groups, often under the leadership of one group, which actually holds the levers of political power in society'* (Scott 1986, page 7).

The power elite comes from the power bloc and is made up of people who hold key positions within the nation state, i.e. *'the various parts of the state elite: cabinet, parliament, judiciary, civil service and military are recruited disproportionately from among the dominant upper class...the upper class and the political elite show a similarity of social background and are, in many cases, the same people'* (Scott 1987, page 7).

What does Scott mean by 'the same people'?

Scott argues that most members of the British cabinet come from public schools, with many going to university at Oxford or Cambridge. The 'elite' of the civil service, i.e. the so-called 'high fliers' who act as policy advisors to the government, are also recruited from public schools and Oxbridge. Therefore they share many of the ideals, values and norms associated with a privileged public school education.

It is important to realise that the civil service is not voted in but rather consists of permanent secretaries who, once in, tend to remain in service for all of their working lives. This is highly significant because while politicians come and go through the ballot box, it is civil servants who advise incoming politicians, regardless of the political party they represent.

This leads Belini (1982) to argue that *'the shape of Whitehall things to come has already been determined by the civil service career structure, for that carefully chosen intake of the 1970s will provide the heads of government departments for the year 2010'* (Belini 1982, page 178). The idea that new civil service recruits today in their early twenties might be around in forty years time advising future politicians, while at the same time having only ever experienced the privileges that Belini writes about, is a worrying thought for many sociologists. It highlights the elitist and conservative nature of government rather than one that is dynamic and democratic.

Conclusion

A ruling government is perhaps a difficult concept to grasp when one considers the work of Scott. With little production evident within the British 'service sector' economy, many sociologists argue that governments are at the mercy of the financial markets and therefore the interests of the so-called 'finance capitalists'. Such 'elites' are interested in short-term gains with little long-term investment. Whether we talk of 'ruling class', 'power bloc' or 'ruling elite', few Marxists or radical elite theorists would argue that any of these three have the *long-term* interests of the *majority* of the population in mind.

✳ Key Idea

The term 'corporatism' refers to both employers and employees playing a key role in the decision-making processes of the state. In the UK the former is represented by the Confederation of British Industry (CBI) and the latter is represented by the Trades Union Congress (TUC). This relationship between government and the CBI and TUC dominated much of the post-Second World War political scene in Britain.

However, it was brought to an abrupt end under the premiership of Margaret Thatcher and her Conservative government. Influenced by ideas taken from the New Right with its interest in a decrease in government intervention, Thatcher set out to weaken the role and influence of the trade union movement during the 1980s and as a result destroyed much of the 'corporatism' that was said to exist.

For consideration

1. To what extent do you believe that the nature of the elites that Scott writes about is so very different from that of the 19th century?

2. How useful is it to have a civil service that is *not* elected but remains in Whitehall regardless of whichever political party holds power?

What are new social movements?

What does this mean?

Reflecting the difference between the old sociology of politics and the new sociology of politics discussed at the beginning of this chapter, there is a substantial difference between what are now referred to as 'old social movements' (OSMs) and 'new social movements (NSMs). Old social movements tended to be class-based organisations such as trade unions in which the role of the state was the focal point for change.

Paul Bagguley (1993) argues that old social movements are influenced by economic factors, for example the trade union movement pushing for higher wages. He argues that old social movements tend to be supported by working class people whereas new social movements tend to have a more middle class membership.

Examples of new social movements are the feminist, anti-racist and environmentalist movements along with the Civil Rights Movement. The term is also sometimes used to describe new religious movements such as the Moonies and also non-political groups such as new age travellers. More recently the direct action taken by groups has come from movements as diverse as the rave scene in the 1990s, the new age travellers and the anti-capitalist movement.

How do new social movements differ from pressure groups and political parties?

- Movement from the 'public' to the 'private': while parties and pressure groups generally focus more on public policy issues, NSMs focus more on prejudice and inequality associated with marginalised groups.
- Movement away from elitist bureaucratised organisations: Hallsworth (1994) argues that there are few full-time officials in such organisations with the structures of NSMs being more informal than those found in pressure groups or political parties.
- Diversity and fragmentation is one quality associated with NSMs where no central leadership exists to coordinate the movements.
- Non class-based issues: Mario Diani (1992) argues that NSMs are 'networks' that focus on lifestyles and identity rather than class-based issues. Individuals, groups and organisations (including pressure groups) fall under the 'umbrella' term of new social movement. Change can be fought for outside the normal accepted avenues of political institutions and usually through some sort of collective action (for example, the 2003 anti-war demonstrations in many cities across the world).
- A focus on post-materialism: Hallsworth (1994) argues that NSMs focus on concerns over quality of life rather than improving material living conditions. Such concerns can only be addressed in societies where the

Direct action? Protesters undertake guerilla gardening in Parliament Square at the May Day 2000 Reclaim the Streets event.

✳ Key Idea

Sociologists tend to group new social movements into two issue areas: those that focus on the *social environment* and include pressure groups such as CND, and Greenpeace, and those that focus on *human rights* issues such as those surrounding race, women's rights, gay rights, and disabled people's rights.

✍ Coursework Suggestion

Carry out a detailed study of one old social movement and one new social movement. Compare and contrast the two organisations to discover whether the distinctions between the two described in this spread are so easily identifiable.

basic requirements for day-to-day living have been met and therefore the assumption is that NSMs are to be found in western or industrialised nations.

Why do some people join new social movements?

- Julian McAllister-Groves (1995) says that new social movements recruit on the basis of an emotional response by their members and that such responses cannot be found in the members of old social movements. The ability to show emotions within new social movements is a 'pull factor', particularly when such a response outside the movement would not be acceptable (for example, farmers in tears over their slaughtered cattle during the foot and mouth crisis).
- Day and Robbins (1992) focus on how teachers and other professionals who joined the Campaign for Nuclear Disarmament (CND) and the peace movement in the 1980s did so out of economic self-interest rather than as a result of any emotional commitment. In other words, if a war broke out teachers and other professionals would lose their jobs.
- Echoing the earlier concerns of Max Weber, Jürgen Habermas (1973) argued that NSMs attempted to defend the quality of life that the rationalisation of modernity was eroding.

Conclusion

- Touraine and Melucci (1989) connect the rise of new social movements to the growth of a 'post-industrial society' in which structural and cultural changes are taking place. Individuals develop their own view of the world where class conflict is no longer the issue. Instead a *principle of identity, a principle of opposition and a principle of totality* exist and classes disappear.
- Such ideas represent an attack on 'modern' notions about 'old politics' which are said to share the key features of party support from particular classes, elite based structures within government, and a nation state which is the central focus of political activity and power.
- Postmodernists like Crook et al (1992) argue that new social movements represent what they refer to as 'new politics' characterised by a lessening of the importance of class based politics, a greater concern with moral issues (for example, the 2003 anti-war demonstrations), and a movement away from politics of the state towards politics of civil society (for example, the anti-capitalist marches in Seattle).

For consideration

1. How effective are new social movements in determining changes in society?

2. How does your knowledge of new social movements and direct action on the one hand, and increasing voter apathy on the other, contribute to Baudrillard's idea of the *'death of politics'*?

◆ **What, when and why?**

'Direct action' refers to any form of political action taken outside the normal formal political process, i.e. that of voting. It includes demonstrations, squats, and other forms of more violent action such as the bombing of animal laboratories to protest against animal experimentation. The following is a quote taken from the May Day Guerrilla Gardening protesters. *'Direct action is about taking control of the very aspects of our own lives, the homes we build, the food we eat, the way we travel, the culture we enjoy, the games we play – it's not just about the occasional protest but about taking power away from the politicians, businessmen and bureaucrats and participating immediately and directly in radical social and ecological change.'*

Reflecting concerns over damage to the environment and the growth of capitalism being its main cause, the May Day event took place in 2000 using non-violent direct action to reclaim the streets. It consisted of a variety of groups ranging from Christian and Jewish organisations to environmental and anarchist groups. The direct action they employed included spray painting Winston Churchill's statue as a Green mohican, the vandalisation of a McDonald's store and the mass planting of plants in various public places including Trafalgar Square and Westminster.

∞ Methods Link

Sociologists use collective terms like new social movements to describe many different types of groups, such as the feminists and new age travellers. This raises enormous methodological issues for researchers or readers of research. We simply do not know, unless the sociologist tells us, what she/he might mean when using such terms. You might wish to raise this issue in the exam as a way of questioning the usefulness of such categories in the first place.

What are pressure groups?

A protest against the common agricultural policy at the European Parliament in Strasbourg, France. Pressure groups have increasingly turned their attention to the European Parliament not only in terms of funding but also as a voice for their concerns if they feel that their voice is unheard in their country of origin.

✳ Key Idea

Elitist theorists, like the New Right, argue that pressure groups hinder both democratic politics and economic growth. Their views are that pressure groups get in the way of what they view as a successful democratic system of elected politicians.

What does this mean?

Bill Coxall (1997) defines pressure groups as *'any organisation which, normally working through lobbying rather than standing for office, seeks to influence public policy and decision making at the local, national and European levels, usually with a particular, quite limited sphere'*. Globally, nationally or locally, pressure groups (or interest groups) tend to be concerned with single issues or a set of issues and are not interested in seeking election or a position in running the country.

Social scientists divide pressure groups into two types namely 'protective', those that seek to preserve the interests of a particular group of people, such as trade unions, and 'promotional', those that seek to promote a particular cause, such as Friends of the Earth. Discussions about pressure groups raise issues about the nature and existence of democracy in many western states where interest in politics has been in decline and when political parties are, according to Grant (1989), increasingly similar in their views about politics and running the economy.

Pluralists and Marxists hold two conflicting views about the importance of pressure groups. Pluralists argue that the existence of pressure groups and political parties is proof that democracy works. Marxists are extremely critical of such claims.

The pluralist argument in support of pressure groups

- Both government and individuals gain from the existence of pressure groups. Trade unions are a prime example of an 'occupational pressure group' where the union acts in the interest of its members. However, trade unions also provide valuable input into the government in the form of trade unions' opinion over government policy. It is therefore possible to see some pressure groups caught in a two-way process of, on the one hand, serving the interests of their members while on the other, serving the interest of the government.
- Pressure groups provide representation according to sets of beliefs, for example, the Campaign for Nuclear Disarmament (CND), Greenpeace, Amnesty International and the RSPCA. Such groups provide a collective voice for like-minded individuals and, according to pluralists, prove the idea that, with such a system, democratic politics exists.
- Pressure groups monitor government power or, in some cases, prevent governments from acting in illegal or unjust ways (for example, the role that Amnesty International has played in recent years). Quite often it is the ability of pressure groups to carry out research and work closely with the press that can bring about changes in government policy.

A Marxist critique of the democratic contribution that pressure groups offer

- Political parties use pressure groups to further their political aims. As already stated, governments can use pressure groups as 'sounding boards' to test policies that may or may not be unpopular.
- The membership of a particular group may not be in proportion to its influence. The Amenity Movement, for example, is concerned with the protection of traditional landscapes and towns but its membership tends to be middle class, and often has an interest in maintaining high local property prices. Compare the membership and influence of this group to that of Help the Aged which has a far greater span of interest and membership but proportionately fewer resources at its disposal.
- Most pressure groups themselves are not democratic institutions. Pressure groups themselves may or may not be democratically organised. Members have little say in the running of many groups despite the fact that the group is supposedly representative of its members' interests.

Conclusion

- A pluralist perspective would argue that pressure groups do help and contribute to the concept of democratic politics by continually ensuring that the government is kept abreast of contemporary opinion and that the minority view (which may have been overlooked) is represented. Pressure groups may only represent certain groups or sections but there is a pressure group available for everyone to join and thus be represented.
- Marxists argue that within an undemocratic system pressure groups have little to offer. Pressure groups are themselves largely undemocratic institutions and, perhaps more importantly, give the impression of a democracy that in actuality does not exist.

For consideration

1. How might the existence of pressure groups be evidence that postmodernist ideas about power and politics are correct?

2. To what extent are classifications like **insider** and **outsider** problematic for social scientists, methodologically speaking?

✓ Top Exam Hint

Remember that distinction between the old sociology of politics and the new sociology of politics? In the exam remind the examiners that the focus has changed in how sociologists view pressure groups. Remind the examiners that the old sociology of politics associated pressure groups and social movements with class-based issues and those of economic interest; for example, the way that trade unions fought for higher wages and better living and working conditions for the working classes. Today pressure groups, although largely single issue, focus on a variety of issues including the environment (Friends of the Earth) and AIDS (the Terrence Higgins Trust).

✳ Key Idea

Pluralists would also argue that pressure groups take a long-term view of political issues, in comparison with political parties whose short-term views are geared towards winning the next election.

❝❞ Key Definitions

Examiners will expect you to be able to refer to **insider** and **outsider** groups. According to many Marxists, the existence of insider and outsider groups proves the inequality of the system. It is easy to imagine that all pressure groups are the same size or share the same degree of influence. However in reality, some groups have access to large amounts of resources, represent powerful groups in society and have the 'ear' of the government. Such insider groups like the larger trade unions (for example, the National Union of Farmers) represent large memberships and have more opportunities to organise themselves or influence others. Smaller 'cause' groups are often outside government interest, have little influence over it, are poorly financed and rely on the charitable donations of others.

However, such a viewpoint would be challenged by neo-pluralists such as Grant (1989), who would argue that the state itself should decide on who it should give influence to or not, i.e. who should be classified as an 'insider' or 'outsider'.

How does globalisation affect the nation state?

Cross and Moore (2001) argue that social structures in cities are changing as a result of the migration that has been caused by global events. Is social mobility the same for all migrating groups or does it depend on class, ethnicity, religion and gender? What *has* changed?

✓ **Top Exam Hint**

Remember that the concept of *empirical adequacy* is a useful evaluative tool in the exams and refers to the evidence that researchers use to back up their claims. Lee and Turner (1996) report that many researching academics complain that authors often make claims about the direction all societies are supposedly heading in as securely established fact when in fact they have no empirical support to back up their claims. In other words their claims are 'empirically inadequate'.

❝❞ **Key Definition**

National sovereignty is the idea that the state is actually in charge of all key elements in domestic policy – law, economic policy, foreign policy and military control. In other words, the state is in charge of the internal and external life of the country. **Supranationalism**, on the other hand, suggests that it is not the state that controls these elements but rather something above and beyond the state (such as the European Union's ability to dictate some aspects of economic policy to its member states).

What does this mean?

Globalisation has become one of the key themes for discussion in the social sciences in recent years. Two debates inform much of what sociologists are concerned about when analysing the nation state.

1. Are nation states becoming increasingly different, similar or adopting values of the dominant 'superpower' of the time, i.e. the United States (sometimes referred to as 'Americanisation' rather than globalisation)?
2. To what extent are nation states free to act as they choose or constrained by '**supranational**' forces?

Globalisation as uniformity?

Reflecting New Right ideas, Francis Fukuyama (1992) argues that a global consensus will occur based on **liberal democracy** creating a new political system where different political ideologies no longer exist. According to Fukuyama, this '*new world order*' will be based upon the triumph of capitalist economics around the globe and consensus politics will emerge between the once opposed East and West blocs.

George Ritzer (1993) offers an alternative on Fukuyama's dream, referring to '*The McDonaldisation*' of society. The way in which the hamburger chain prepares food for consumption is used as an analogy for modern lifestyles in western economies that are increasingly adopting American lifestyles and business principles. This analogy provides a picture of a product that is cheap, quickly produced and identical wherever you go. Globalisation in this sense becomes an 'Americanisation' rather than the equal spread of ideas from countries all over the globe.

Lash and Urry (1987) argue that in a 'globalised' economy, multinational companies have shifted their manufacturing operations to the newly developing countries in South East Asia and South America, where labour power is cheaper. Thus a two-tier form of globalisation takes place producing a 'bourgeoisie' in the West and a 'proletariat' in these developing countries.

Is the nation state shaped and determined by the forces of globalisation?

Many writers argue that, in the same way as structural forces can shape and determine peoples lives, globalisation acts as a deterministic 'structure' that shapes the nation state. Some of these arguments are that:

- nation states can no longer control their own economies. Giddens (2001) argues that political decisions are no longer taken by the state or governments. Instead, he argues that the world system is influenced by several sets of processes '*associated with the nation state system, co-ordinated through global networks of information exchange, the world capitalist economy and the world military order'* (Giddens 1985, page 290).

- international bodies such as the World Bank reduce the power of the nation state. Favid Held (1992), following a Marxist line of thinking, argues that many international institutions (for example, the World Bank and the International Monetary Fund) determine what takes place within a country's own borders. He also argues that many of these organisations represent the interests of the most economically powerful rather than the 'global interests' they claim to represent.
- the myth of globalisation is created by multinational companies. Doreen Massey (1999) argues that the 'deterministic' and negative image of globalisation is in fact a myth. The myth is created by multinational companies in an attempt to legitimate economic and social policies that serve their interests rather than the countries in which the policies originate.

The nation state as a social actor

Far from conceding that the nation state is the victim of globalisation forces that shape, determine or 'structure' nation states, some branches of international relations theory assume that the nation state is the most powerful organisation in society. Viewed as a 'social actor' it is self-interested and has the ability to influence events beyond its borders.

N. Ginsburg (2001), using two countries in close proximity with each other, shows how the forces of globalisation *do not* always force countries into similar actions. He compares the Irish and UK government responses to the forces of globalisation. Under the banner of 'social partnership', the Irish have attempted to expand public spending while the UK government has chosen to cut public spending and encourage private investment in an attempt to boost competitiveness and make efficiency gains. These are two very different policy reactions from two different states, and as such, bring into question the 'deterministic' views about the power of globalisation forces over the nation state.

Conclusion

- Social scientists are concerned whether, at the beginning of the 21st century, the power of the nation state is decreasing or increasing during what many refer to as the period of 'globalisation'.
- Sharon Gewirtz (2001) argues that globalisation is not a singular process but is the product of multiple processes, i.e. economic, political, social and cultural, all of which are in tension with each other.
- Some sociologists argue that in reality globalisation is nothing new. Many parts of the world were affected by the 'globalised economy' produced under the Roman Empire. Consider too the impact of printing in the 14th century and the subsequent spread of Christian ideas with the publication of the Bible.

For consideration

1. To what extent do you consider globalisation to be a new phenomenon?
2. Taking the Internet as one key factor in speeding up the processes of globalisation, what other factors can you think of?

❝❞ Key Definition

Liberal democracy is a system of beliefs based upon freedom of the individual. It would be wrong, however, to assume there is total agreement about what this term means. Some common elements include the right to private property, the free exercise of religious beliefs, claims of minimum intervention by the state in matters of public policy, and a belief that markets are the best way of allocating scarce resources via a value system that believes in competition. One example of such thinking is the introduction of educational league tables as a way of allocating education on the basis of choice and competition.

✔ Top Exam Hint

Can you see the similarity between George Ritzer's analogy of the hamburger and Max Weber's ideas of 'disenchantment' within a modern rationalised world based on scientific management and bureaucratic procedures? Bring this similarity to the examiners' notice to be awarded high marks for your evaluation skills

✳ Key Ideas

- J. Clarke (2001) offers a negative perspective on the relationship between globalisation and the state. He talks *'of a transformed global economy in which hyper-mobile capital rampages around the globe, collapsing time and space on its travels, and undercutting both nation states and their welfare systems'* (Clarke 2001, page 19). Clarke highlights how fragile national economies are in the face of big multinational companies and how difficult it is for nation states to determine their own policies. This challenges the view that nation states possess the power that national sovereignty implies.
- Hirst and Thompson (1999) argue that many of the generalisations associated with the term 'globalisation' assume that all states are hit equally by globalising forces. Challenging this generalisation, they argue that there is still evidence to show how the international economy is to a certain extent managed, albeit tentatively, by individual states. They argue that rather than an inevitable process, economic globalisation is a consequence of political decisions made at a national level and therefore can be controlled at a national level.

How can we make power and politics synoptic?

A juvenile delinquent? Who decides when it is legal to carry guns and why?

66 99 Key Definition

By using the phrase **cultural transmission** you can refer to how one culture can be *transmitted* or passed on from one generation to the next. This can happen via institutions such as the family, education, the media and/or through the various ideologies within capitalist or patriarchal structures.

⁑ Key Idea

Feminists might argue that any dominant culture is 'patriarchal'; Marxists might argue that any culture is 'capitalist'; sociologists writing about race could argue that the dominant culture in the western world represents white, middle-class values. Whatever dominant culture you care to discuss, this immediately allows you to talk about how some people will be 'empowered' or 'disempowered' depending on who possesses more or less of the dominant culture.

Why is synopticity important for power and politics?

Power and politics provides an ideal chapter to use when revising your synoptic unit. Power is a key synoptic concept and examiners reward students who can combine one area of sociology with another when discussing a particular sociological issue. For example, is it really possible to talk about racism in the UK without including discussions about the region where you live, your gender, your class background, the education you receive and the type of work you do?

How do power and politics link to issues of culture?

By '**culture**' sociologists mean the set of shared values, norms and beliefs of a society or group of people. The word also refers to the shared meanings and symbols, such as language, which people use to make sense of the world in which they live. Students can talk about a dominant culture to refer to the main culture in a society whose norms and values are seen to be the most powerful and generally accepted.

How do power and politics link to issues of identity?

Identity itself is an enormously complex term and yet most social scientists will agree that the constraints, challenges and opportunities you face vary depending on how 'empowered' or 'disempowered' that identity is. Politically, we can ask what happens to people individually or in groups if they associate with a particular 'identity' whether based on class, gender, age, ethnicity, religion or any other variable. You can also see how some political policies, such as those of education or health, affect some of these identities in a positive or negative way.

How do power and politics link to issues of inequality?

Politicians and, increasingly, multinational corporations have the power to determine the life chances of those men, women and children who, on the one hand, need the work that such power relations can offer but, on the other hand, suffer from the exploitation they undergo.

Traditional Marxists argue that economic infrastructure shapes the culture of all classes regardless of gender, age, or race. The jobs, property and money you have determine the life you will lead. The concept of 'globalisation' allows sociologists to reflect that as the West becomes increasingly richer with production carried out in other poorer parts of the world, many of the disappearing western 'working classes' are being re-created in other parts of the world to produce goods for western consumption.

How do power and politics link to issues of deviance?

The social construction of crime and deviance

A 'deviant' is somebody who diverges from the norms and values associated with a particular culture. Any one dominant culture is the culture whose norms and values are seen to be the most powerful and generally accepted. The problem with this is that politicians and those that hold power (even your parents) can see the world in very different ways. If a particular individual happens not to possess those very norms and values she/he may be classified as deviant or criminal depending on how the legal system treats such deviancy.

Crime and deviance can be looked at from a post-structuralist perspective by arguing that elite discourses are sometimes used as the official definitions of crime and deviance, thereby punishing those so defined. The laws can be created/banned or relaxed raising the question 'who decides when an act is considered either legal or illegal and why?'

How do power and politics link to issues of stratification and differentiation?

However you discuss stratification, whether by class, gender, sexuality, ethnicity or nation, it can be linked to issues surrounding power. All you have to do is to be able to identify why and by what processes these different 'identities' possess different levels of power in society. Once you have done that, then any institution, family, education, the media, religion, the political system or the legal system, can be used to explain *how* that might happen.

Key points to remember

- Power is a key synoptic concept that can be used to make connections with *any* area of the sociology syllabus.
- When talking about how society is stratified, it is just as important to look behind closed doors and the micro politics of private life as it is to look at more formal political institutions such as the government.
- Power brings with it the opportunity to define people as criminal, deviant or both. As such you are reminded that both 'crime' and 'deviance' are social constructions rather than 'essential categories'. This allows you to pose the question 'in whose interests is somebody defined as either criminal or deviant?'

✍ Coursework Suggestion

Students often have problems in deciding how they can analyse the data they produce when carrying out primary research. One way to provide an analytical framework is to say openly that you will take synoptic concepts and use these as *sensitising* concepts when interpreting your data. So, for example if you have produced interview data why not use four to five synoptic concepts as the focus point for your analysis. Some key synoptic concepts are: socialisation, power, ideology, anomie, alienation, culture and social control. Why not create headings from four to five of the above concepts and then focus on your interview data in light of those concepts; this would provide a good analytical framework for your results chapter.

2.24 | Pushing your grades up higher

There is no substitute for thorough revision in the weeks leading up to your exams; however, by following the tips below you will boost every opportunity for you to gain those all important A-C grades.

1. Don't forget that not only are you evaluating the *case studies* you talk about, but also the *theories*. Of course you will do this by contrasting one theory with another, for example, a Marxist approach to the issue with that of a functionalist or feminist approach. However, it is also useful to remember three categories when discussing theory.

   - Empirical adequacy, i.e. what evidence is there to support the particular theory being discussed?
   - Comprehensiveness, i.e. can the particular theory be used in all cases under all conditions?
   - Logical coherency, i.e. does the theory 'logically' hold together? One example where perhaps you might argue that a theory is *not* logically coherent is 'postmodernism'. It attacks other theories and 'metanarratives' for offering large-scale explanations. You could argue that there is no 'logical coherency' here because surely postmodernism itself is a theory and therefore subject to its own critique?

2. Show that you are in full command of the various theories when discussing a question. Remember that the theories are 'friends' to be called upon when you feel you cannot write any more. Ask yourself 'how might a feminist, or a postmodernist analyse this particular issue?'

3. Look at the style of writing you use. How do your sentences start? If they just start with 'Postmodernist Baumann' you are losing valuable evaluation marks. Much better to use evaluative phrases such as '*In addition to this,* Postmodernist Baumann …' or '*In contrast to the above,* Postmodernist Baumann …' Do you see the difference?

4. Remember always to back up whatever point you are making with evidence. That evidence *must* be in the form of a case study by a named sociologist.

5. Try to identify the period in which the research was carried out. Of course you are not taking a history exam, but the high-achieving student should be able tell the examiner which decade the research took place in, ideally which half of the decade, and what this means to how useful the study is today.

6. To gain extra evaluation marks try to mention the methodology of the case study you are referring to in the exam, for example, 'adopting a positivist methodology, Durkheim …'

7. When discussing the findings of the case study you refer to, you can then gain extra critical evaluation marks by mentioning whether the research

was 'quantitative' or 'qualitative'. By doing this, you can then link one particular study to another to build up your argument.

8. When an exam question asks you to discuss the 'contribution' that a particular sociologist has made to an issue, it is important to realise that contributions can be both positive and negative. Remember this, as it will then allow you to evaluate fully the work of the sociologist in question.

9. Always remember and use the concepts of 'validity', 'reliability' and 'representativeness' when discussing the work of other sociologists. By applying these terms you will show the examiners that you are extremely critical.

10. Show that you are aware of *where* (geographically) some of these theories and theorists are coming from. For example, if you talk about Talcott Parsons, refer to him as 'the American structural functionalist, Talcott Parsons …'

Key points to remember

- You must offer evidence in support of whatever argument you are making – without it the examiners will not reward your argument with marks.
- You must show mastery of the theories when constructing an exam answer.
- Use sophisticated language when criticising the theory, case study or concept. Make sure you start those sentences or paragraphs with those key evaluative phrases.

Frequently asked questions

Q. What do we mean by 'fragmented elites'?

A. Ian Budge, David McKay and David Marsh (1983) offer a version of an elite theory of power. In it they argue that although elites exist, they are far from being a united group in any society. Consisting of many smaller groups, they compete for power. Such groups are fragmented, quite often with Left or Right wing divisions within them, for example political parties. Therefore 'fragmented elites' consist of MPs, civil servants, industries, unions and members of supranational organisations, such as MEPs. Budge et al argue that as these elites are fragmented rather than cohesive, it is impossible to argue that any one elite holds power in any state.

Q. What do we mean by 'relative autonomy'?

A. When describing the power of the state, the traditional Marxist line is that the state operates to serve the economic interests of the ruling classes. Although also a Marxist, Nicos Poulantzas (1976) challenged this 'economically deterministic' view of the state. He argued that the state was, to a certain extent, free from the ruling class's *direct* influence, that is it was 'relatively autonomous' from the influence of the ruling class.

He argued that if the bourgeoisie ruled directly over the state, its power might be weakened by the internal fighting that often exists within elite structures. Such 'relative autonomy' allows the state to continue the myth that it operates in everybody's interests by, for example, providing a national health service. These concessions do not *appear* to be in the ruling class interests but in fact provide the ideological *justification* that capitalism works.

Q. What are the differences between 'pressure groups' and 'new social movements'?

A. Since the 1960s there has been a sharp increase in the number of both pressure groups and new social movements possibly due to a disillusionment with mainstream political parties. Quite often, social movements (new and old) capture the mood of the times and as a result contain a number of pressure groups that express that mood. Pressure groups are distinct organisations that seek to influence government either directly or indirectly, over specific issues. Examples of such organisations are Shelter or the Campaign for Nuclear Disarmament.

In some ways it is possible to argue that social movements gave rise to what later become political parties and pressure groups. One example of this was the workers' movement of the 19th century that, some argue, gave birth to the trade union movement and the right to vote along with Marxist and socialist parties. More recently the term has been used to describe the feminist movements, anti-racial movements such as Black Power and environmental movements including pressure groups such as Greenpeace.

Chapter 3

Religion

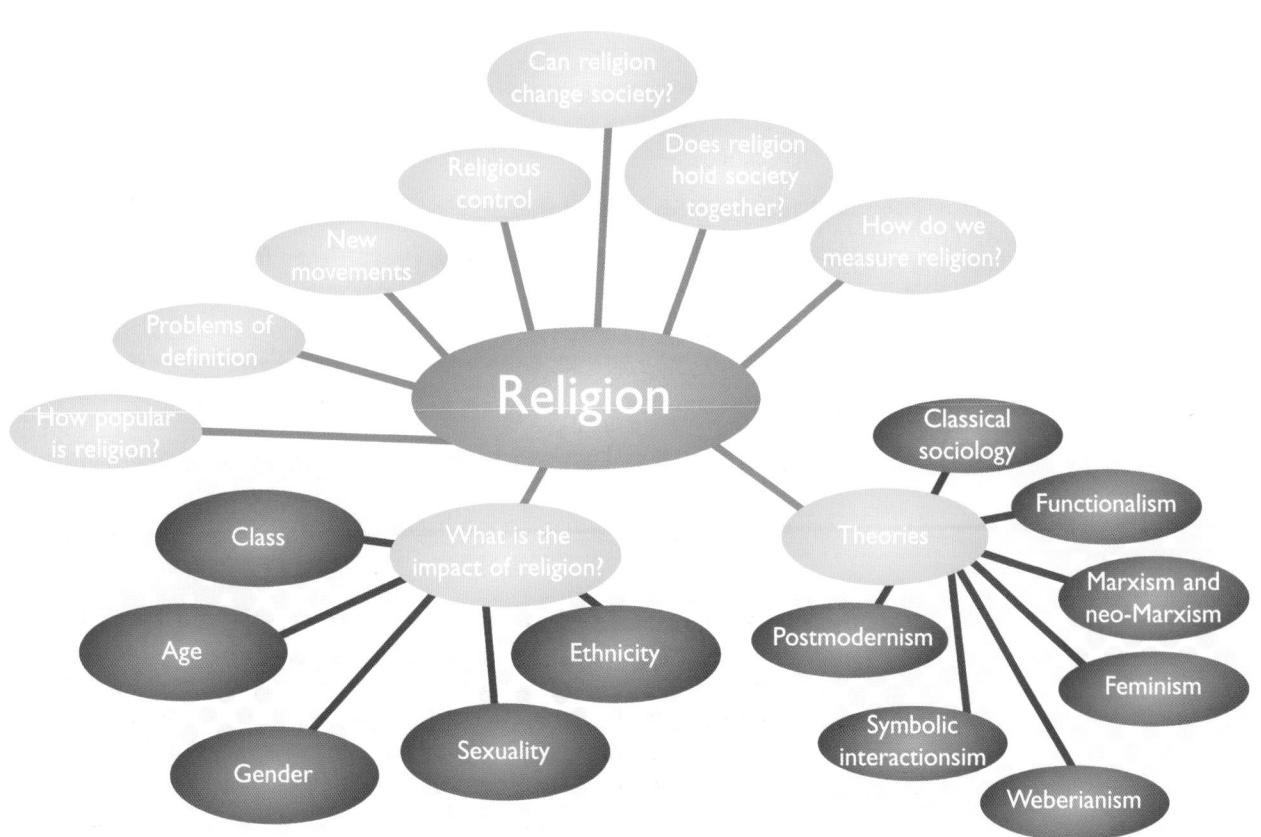

 CD-ROM

3.1

Key issues in the sociology of religion

◆ **What, when and why?**

Remember that the founders of sociology (for example Auguste Comte, Emile Durkheim, Karl Marx and Max Weber) were writing in Europe during the 19th century – a Europe that was by and large Christian and therefore many of their ideas used Christianity as a focus for their research questions. They were not interested in the 'truth' of different religions but the connection between religion and how people were 'socialised'.

● **Synoptic Link**

The sociology of religion can be linked synoptically to both the concept of 'power' and 'methodology'. The concept of 'power' can allow sociologists of religion to examine how religion might be a source of 'power' for some groups and not others; examine why this might be the case and finally explore the effects of that power on different classes, ethnicities, genders, ages and sexualities.

Methodological problems exist when researchers are unclear about definitions. This is particularly difficult with religion because of its personal nature. Religion means different things to different people. This can make researching religion an extremely sensitive area and can create further difficulties when talking about the validity, reliability or representativeness of sociological research.

Why are sociologists interested in religion?

The sociology of religion manages to grab the attention of all types of sociologists – whatever their theoretical background. The founders of sociological theory, for example, Durkheim, Marx and Weber, were fascinated by the role that religion played and we have inherited this interest from them. For some sociologists, religion acts as a way of integrating (and socialising) people into the norms (accepted ways of behaving) and values that are seen to be of importance for a particular society. However, for others, religion is a source of conflict particularly when issues surrounding gender, class, ethnicity, age and, increasingly, sexuality are put under the sociologists' microscope.

What are the key debates in religion?

You need to be aware of *four* key debates that examiners are keen to explore when setting exam questions:

1. Secularisation (to what extent is religion more or less popular than it once might/might not have been and how it has changed over time).
2. Whether religion is (or can be) a means of socially controlling people.
3. Whether religion can (or should) act as a means to cement or 'integrate' people into society.
4. Whether religion is a 'conservative' force (i.e. to what extent religions stop the processes of social change).

What are the key ideas and concepts in religion?

- You need to be aware of the views about religion from the point of view of the classical sociologists, functionalists, Marxists, Max Weber, neo-Marxists, interpretive sociologists and feminists.
- You also need to know about the different ways that we classify religions – the most popular being 'church', 'sect', 'cult', 'denomination' and 'new religious movements'.
- Finally, you need know what role religion might play in any future society. Postmodernist writers offer an exciting discussion about this when they examine the variety of religions that are on offer today and how these might impact on society tomorrow.

What does the exam board say about religion?

The AQA examiners will expect you to know about:

- different theories of religion
- the role of religion as a conservative force and as an initiator of change
- cults, sects, denominations and churches and their relationship to religious activity

- explanations of the relationship between religious beliefs, religious organisations and social groups
- different definitions and explanations of the nature and extent of secularisation.

The exam for this unit (Unit 4) will be 1 hour and 30 minutes and will be composed of two short data response questions (worth 8 and 12 marks) and one essay question (worth 40 marks).

As with all of the AQA units, you have to show competency or ability in the assessment objectives of AO1 (*knowledge and understanding* and *presentation and communication*) and AO2 (*interpretation and analysis* and *evaluation*). For AO1 you need to show *knowledge and understanding* of the names of sociologists and their case studies; the relevant theories; the key concepts (for example 'globalisation'); evidence to support the claims sociologists make; and a keen awareness of the research methodologies used by sociologists of religion.

For AO2 you need to show how you can actually *interpret and apply* this knowledge when putting forward a particular argument and *evaluate* continuously throughout any answer you are writing. There is a greater emphasis placed on AO2 at A2 than at AS. This might mean that you choose to draw on the ideas of a theory or case study that was carried out thirty years ago and see how it might (or might not!) be relevant to an area of religion today. You might also identify trends from the past and see to what extent that particular trend is present today.

It will also help if you learn to draw out links with the synoptic topics of 'Crime and deviance' and/or 'Stratification and differentiation'. You must also examine this topic area in relation to the two core themes:

1. socialisation, culture and identity
2. social differentiation, power and stratification.

Key points to remember

- The four key debates that examiners use when creating questions.
- The exam lasts ninety minutes in which time you will answer two shorter questions and one longer, essay-style question.
- Religion is one of the main institutions of socialisation and, as such, you must try to automatically make connections between this unit and your chosen synoptic unit.

How does religion link to the AS course?

Comedian Aaron Barschak who gatecrashed Prince William's 21st birthday party. Is the picture the British media portrays of non-Christian religions a valid one?

66 99 Key Definition

By **'stratification'** sociologists mean the way that societies are hierarchically organised, i.e. those on top are perceived to have more power than those on the bottom. The way different societies are stratified can be based on certain social characteristics such as membership of a certain religion. Those on top of the system tend to have greater access to scarce resources, such as land, water, money, than others. Religion, like many other institutions, plays its role in the stratification process.

Why are links to AS sociology important for A2 sociology?

Sociology is all about studying the nature and distribution of power and as such focuses on the inequality and **stratification** that exists in most societies. The study of religion plays a major part in this process. Below are just some of the ways you can connect religion to the AS units you might have covered.

What links can be made to family and households?

Debates about secularisation, i.e. the idea that people may or may not be becoming more religious, can be linked to figures on marriage statistics. In 1997, 61 per cent of marriages in the United Kingdom were civil (as opposed to religious) ceremonies. On a different footing, the sanctity of marriage as an institution of religion might imply that families have, in the past, offered the security and socialisation that are associated with mainstream religions. Two factors need to be questioned here. Firstly, many people attended religious ceremonies (including marriages) because it might have been socially unacceptable not to do so. Secondly, the *'dark figure of crime'* shows that women in marriages in the past have suffered violence, both verbally and physically, and yet have been afraid to voice their danger because of the reaction they might receive from their religious community.

What links can be made to health?

Much of what we know about the study of health and illness has, in the past, been associated with magic, religion and science. For people where magic is held to play an important role in society, the causes of suffering either to an individual or community is cured by the *shaman* or witch doctor. When people fall ill, many pray for their recovery even when under normal circumstances they might not consider themselves religious. Mental illness in the past has also been equated with possession by evil spirits and suffering in general can sometimes be perceived (most notably by the poorest in societies) as a test of their faith. Indeed many Marxists argue that, in this sense, religion stops a process of change because many people look to their god or gods rather than wishing to bring about a process of change in the societies they live in.

What links can be made to mass media?

There are huge debates about the role and purpose of the media that some of you may encounter when studying sociology. Issues range from the ownership and control of the media to that of bias in the reporting of certain issues, peoples and religions. There is no doubt that such bias exists and perhaps you might decide to explore this in your coursework in A2. One example of the use of language to determine how people might be perceived has been in the study of war reporting. Phrases like 'Bastards of Baghdad' and 'Crusade' used in the press in the Iraq conflicts show how the press can be used to socially construct images of people at key times. Why, for example, might you have heard of 'Islamic terrorism' rather more frequently than 'Christian terrorism'? – strange when you consider the conflict that has continued in Northern Ireland over the last three decades.

What links can be made to education?

The role religion plays in the national curriculum is a strongly contested one. Those who adopt a 'New Right' perspective might argue that religion enforces norms and values that serve to create stable societies. Unfortunately, many New Right followers would equally argue that those norms and values should come from a Christian form of religion rather than from any of the other mainstream religions. You also need to remember that many religions themselves provide education in the form of Saturday/Sunday schools and thus supplement the education system that exists in England. You might like to explore what values the different religions espouse and attempt to make connections to the variables of class, gender, ethnicity, age and sexuality.

What links can be made to work and leisure?

Max Weber made a powerful connection to religion and work in his *'Protestant Ethic and the Spirit of Capitalism'* (1905), arguing that there was a strong connection between Calvinism (a version of Christianity) and the growth of capitalist economies. However, as a sociologist you have a variety of other possibilities to explore when making the connection between these two seemingly different institutions. Imagine the role that religion plays in the socialisation process when migrant workers move from one country to another with the networks of contacts and friends that exist within religious communities available to them. Explore how different religions might expect different work-related roles from men and women (either in the work place or at home). How might membership of a particular religion restrict leisure opportunities for some women?

Key points to remember

- Good sociology is always synoptic – in other words to gain the highest marks you should always try to make connections from one area of sociology to another.
- While religion as a topic may be new to you, you are already building on and applying all the ideas you came across in AS sociology.
- When working on this chapter, try to make as many connections as you can to your synoptic unit. You could even write them down in a special synoptic notebook and have this ready for your revision.

☐ Key Fact

Christian preacher, John Humphey Noyes, set up a community in 1848 to establish spiritual, economic and sexual equality. As a form of economic communism and group marriage, everyone was expected to contribute to the community. A type of eugenics was also introduced, i.e. only those considered suitable were allowed to reproduce. After birth and an initial time spent with the biological mother, the child was raised by the community.

✳ Key Idea

Post-structuralists argue that knowledge cannot be separated from power. Religion is a special kind of knowledge with a particular kind of language (discourse) that affects the way people understand, discuss and explain why certain norms and values exist. Much depends, however, on who has the power to define what is wrong in the first place, such as Mullahs, Bishops, priests. Remember too that some religions are also 'state religions', such as the Church of England, and can at different times in history reflect the dominant ideology of the government of the time.

↪ Classic study

The Centre for Contemporary Cultural Studies (CCCS) at Birmingham University has researched how ethnicity is portrayed in the British media. Adopting a neo-Marxist position and using a concept known as 'hegemony' (see Section 2.8), they aim to explain media prejudice and the creation of moral panics. Such an idea can be used to explain how different religions are treated in the British press and why.

How can we find out about the sociology of religion?

Politicians are often keen to refer back to a 'golden age of certainty' where the norms, values and everyday actions were said to be more 'fixed' and predictable. These 'certain' times are described in a positive light and are said to have existed until the early 1960s. This 'golden age' is quite often contrasted with what is sometimes referred to as a period of 'uncertainty' that many writers argue exists today. You can question the validity of both claims, i.e. that the past was 'certain' and 'good' and the present is 'uncertain' and 'bad'.

❝❞ Key definitions

By '**quantitative**' sociologists refer to any research method or data that attempts to explain its findings using generalisations, statistics, tables, charts and diagrams. Quite often questionnaires and structured interviews are used to gather such data. '**Qualitative**' research (i.e. data generated from more unstructured interviews, letters, diaries and observations) tends to be richer or 'valid' (i.e. 'in-depth'). Interpretive sociologists prefer this form of data gathering because it represents the 'interpretation' of the respondent's view of the world rather than any 'social reality' that positivist socialists believe exists.

✳ Key Idea

Glock and Stark (1965, 1968) argue for quantitative and qualitative approaches to investigating the sociology of religion by studying:
- the level of belief of the individuals and group
- the personal involvement in religious acts of prayer and celebration
- individual and group *feelings* of super-natural, sacred and spiritual experience
- the knowledge individuals possess about their own religions
- to what extent all of the above influences the day-to-day lives of the researched individuals.

How have sociologists tried to measure 'religion'?

Whether we view 'religion' as an individual activity carried out in private or analyse it from the point of view of a belief system, this area of sociology provides huge possibilities for you to show off your knowledge of sociological methodology. Sociologists choose their methodology as a result of a number of issues that include:

- The nature of the research problem (for example, are you researching documents or people; is the research 'covert' (carried out 'under cover') or 'overt' (carried out with the full knowledge of all concerned) or is the researcher looking back over time and comparing past with present?).
- The traditional research strategies, methods and data sources thought to be appropriate for a particular problem (for example, using church statistics when analysing the popularity of religion).
- How available or accessible is the data that the sociologist requires (for example, how might the lack of written sources of data in some cultures restrict sociologists in determining what religious practices exist or have existed)?
- The resources at the researchers' disposal (for example, funding, time, equipment and assistance).

Values also determine how a particular sociologist approaches the sociology of religion. Are they a Marxist, or feminist or symbolic interactionist, or indeed a Jew, Catholic or Muslim? In all cases the aim or particular focus of their research will reflect the theoretical interest of the sociologist carrying out the research.

Such values will also determine whether or not the researcher is gathering **quantitative** data or **qualitative** data and this might depend on whether they consider themselves to be 'positivist' (i.e. 'scientific') or 'interpretive' in their approach to the sociology of religion.

What methods do sociologists tend to use to study religion?

Sociologists have a wide variety of methods they can use but quite often the nature of the subject being studied will dictate what kind of method can/should be used. Questionnaires are a useful form of data gathering when making broad generalisations although they are not particularly personal – something that religion almost always is. Sociologists also analyse historical documents. However, can we really trust the statistics or the conclusions drawn from them? Here are three sociologists who have used a variety of methods to study 'religion'.

- Feminist C. Butler (1995) carried out interviews with second generation Muslim women in England in order to challenge some of the stereotypical media images associated with women and the Islamic religion.
- Bryan Wilson (1985) used a quantitative approach to religion by analysing church attendance figures to prove that religious thought and practice are in decline.
- Eileen Barker (1984) used participant observation, in-depth interviews and questionnaires in an attempt to explain how and why people joined the 'Moonies' and to discover what kind of people they were.

What problems with definition are encountered in studying 'religion'?

- Remember that whatever definition we use to start our research will then affect what we look for and what we uncover as a result.
- If religion is defined as an organised group of individuals that share a system of beliefs, then how do we include Christians, Muslims and Buddhists under one similar category? The latter is so very different from the first two (both of which are 'Abrahamic' religions). How do we explain differences between Catholic and Protestant forms of Christianity or Sunni and Shi'ite Islamic beliefs?
- Discussions surrounding the 'secularisation debate' (the idea that societies may or may not be as religious as they once were) are confusing if 'being religious' is defined by mosque or church attendance. How do we know that people went or go to church for religious reasons? How many children are 'made' to go to church by their parents?

Key points to remember

- There are a variety of reasons why sociologists choose the methods they do – learn these for the exam.
- Memorise not only the key names associated with the sociology of religion but also the method of research they adopted.
- The importance of 'definition' or 'operationalisation' when discussing any research that takes place – evaluating somebody else's research is impossible unless we know what they mean.

☞ **Who is this pers**

Eileen Barker – a professor of soc the London School of Economics (LSE) was born in Edinburgh and gained her firs degree in sociology in 1970 at the LSE. Her PhD thesis (or 'Doctorate') was published as '*The Making of a Moonie: Brainwashing or Choice*'. Her research focused on the process of recruitment used by the 'Moonies' (members of the 'Unification Church', a 'new religious movement' that was founded in 1954 and attempted to mix western and eastern culture in order to bring about a 'physical kingdom of God'). She was interested in what kind of person would get involved with such a movement. She used a variety of different methods (known as 'triangulation'), including questionnaires, observation and interviews.

※ **Key Ideas**

- Barker's work was inspirational because she rejected the divide between positivist ('scientific' sociological explanations that seek to offer 'cause and effect' explanations) and interpretive methodological approaches ('anti-positivist' approaches that are more concerned about how people 'interpret' their 'social reality') that had characterised debates within sociology for much of 20th century. She argued that to achieve a true understanding of how society worked sociologists must use a variety of methods. This is known as 'methodological pluralism' or 'triangulation'. In Barker's case she produced both quantitative and qualitative research data.

- The term 'Abrahamic' is quite often used to describe the religions of Islam, Christianity and Judaism, which all take as their starting point the religious figure of 'Abraham'. This means that far from these three religions being considered extremely different from each other, they share very strong similarities – something that is quite often over looked by journalists, politicians and in some cases the religious believers of these three faiths.

✓ **Top Exam Hint**

Durkheim's (1912) classic study of religion can be criticised as being 'Eurocentric', i.e. it is viewed from the perspective that European culture is superior to any other culture being discussed or studied. Such a perspective can 'distort' research by producing culturally-biased aims, objectives, hypotheses, analysis, findings and conclusions.

Why is it difficult to define the concept of 'religion'?

What does this mean?

Interactionist Berger (1990) argues that *'definitions cannot, by their very nature, be either "true" or "false", only more useful or less so. For this reason it makes relatively little sense to argue over definitions'*. Sociologists analyse the relationship between religion and society by studying the role that it plays in people's lives. The problem, however, is that everybody (including sociologists) has a different idea as to what religion is and this can create a variety of different theoretical perspectives and research findings.

Difficulties in defining 'religion'

There is no single definition as to what religion is other than a generalised agreement that it is a set of **belief systems**. This makes the job of deciding the 'function' of religion very difficult because this will change depending on what religion we are talking about and where the religion might be taking place. Living as a Christian in an area of famine in Africa and being a Christian in New York will provide two very different 'religious' experiences.

Any discussion about whether religion is in decline or growing (sociologists call this the 'secularisation debate') will depend on what religion we are talking about or indeed how we define religion in the first place. Some sociologists refer to religions as 'ideologies' meaning that they are sets of ideas about the world that embody morals and values.

Useful concepts when attempting to define religion

Animism/Totemism – the belief that natural phenomena (for example, trees, stones, and rivers) are made up of spirits or souls which can affect society.

Atheism – the belief that no one god (or gods) exists.

Agnosticism – neither a belief in, nor a denial of, one god but prepared to believe that a god may exist if enough evidence is produced.

Magic – the belief that by a force of human will, the gods can be made to follow that will.

Monotheism – the belief in one singular god.

Polytheism – the belief in more than one god.

Superstition – the belief that one can be protected from evil events (or bring about positive ones) by a certain of set actions (for example, the crossing of fingers).

Supernatural – the belief that science and modern common sense cannot explain all events that take place.

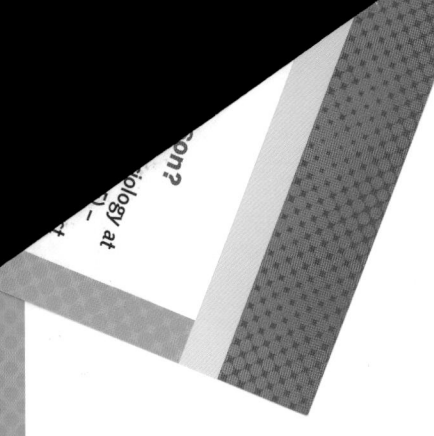

66 99 Key Definition

Polyani (1958) says that any **'belief system'** contains three components.

- A *'circularity' of ideas* – Where each idea within the system is explained referring to another idea (e.g. Mohammed's connection to Abraham in the Islamic religion).
- *Explanations for difficult situations* – If a particular idea cannot be seen to work there will be religious 'reason' for this (quite often this is put down to 'faith').
- *Other belief systems are unacceptable* – A devout Christian will find it impossible to accept a Buddhist interpretation of 'spirituality'.

☀ Key Idea

Polyani (1958) tells us that 'belief systems' are the ideas which we believe to be right and that offer guidelines on behaviour along with justifications for that behaviour. This means that disciplines like politics and science are also **'belief systems'**. In other words belief systems contain norms and values that inform how social interaction can and should take place.

Durkheim offers two helpful concepts in attempting to define religion. The first is 'sacred', by which he refers to aspects of life having to do with the supernatural that inspire awe, reverence, deep respect and sometimes even fear. His second concept is 'profane', by which he refers to aspects of society supposedly not concerned with religion but that instead are part of the ordinary aspects of everyday life.

Of course, what may be 'ordinary' in one part of the world may not be in another. For example, it is quite ordinary in Sumatra, Indonesia, when serving customers in restaurants to stop, go to the corner of the restaurant and offer flowers to a mini-altar. Is this everyday act 'sacred' or 'profane'?

Hammond (1985) argues that it is wrong to associate religion only with the 'sacred'. While religion may well be sacred in modern societies, so too are beliefs of nationalism, science and technology, where the passions for all three can be as strong as any commitment to a 'god' or 'gods'.

The danger of ethnocentricism

Another problem when attempting to discuss and define what we mean by religion is the possibility of placing religions in a hierarchy and implying that some are better than others. Adapting an evolutionary approach that was fashionable at the end of the 19th century, Tylor (1970) charted the course of religious development from 'primitive fantasies' to more 'sophisticated' beliefs in modern times. However, sociologists need to be careful when defining religions that they do not make value judgements about whether some religions are 'higher up' the evolutionary ladder than others, for example, comparing animism with Christianity or Judaism and implying that one is more primitive than another.

Conclusion

When attempting to define religions the classical sociologists were concerned with macro grand theories by which they focused on whole societies and analysed large historical periods in time. Thomas Luckmann (1978) is one of many sociologists who, from the 1960s onwards, have tended to adopt a more micro level on analysis by looking at new age beliefs, the decline in church attendance in some cultures, and the growth in denominations, sects and cults. This is sometimes referred to as 'The New Sociology of Religion'.

❋ Key Idea

Something can be considered to be 'ethnocentric' if it places importance on one cultural set of values over and above others. For example, many textbooks may be written from a white, often male and European perspective which implies that other parts of the world are less sophisticated. This would be the worst example of 'ethnocentric' writing. This idea can be applied to different theoretical views on different religions.

✓ Top Exam Hint

Remember, while you may discover many definitions about religion in this chapter you do not have to know the details of the religions, just the definitions of them. What you must be able to do is evaluate them by 'seeing them in the eyes of other definitions'. If you can do this you will be able to draw out the strengths and weaknesses easily and in a sophisticated way which will impress the examiners.

For consideration

1. Using the concepts of 'sacred' and 'profane', what other examples of 'religion' could you argue fit into these categories?

2. How might your answers to the above point be helpful in building a case for a postmodern approach to religion?

3.5 Why is it difficult to measure the popularity of religion?

Does attendance at religious ceremonies tell us anything about the popularity of religion?

Key Fact

Church membership figures for the 'Trinitarian churches' (Roman Catholic, Anglican, Presbyterian, Methodist, Baptist, Orthodox and other free churches) showed a drop from 9.1 million members to 6.4 million members from 1970 to 1995 (Social Trends 27: 224).

Key Idea

Greeley (1994) refers to the 'myth of the golden age' in which he challenges the idea that older, traditional worlds were safer, more religious places and modern/postmodern worlds are not. Bruce (1996), studying English historical documents, shows how it was quite normal for peasants to be playing cards and firing shotguns in churches during the 18th and 19th centuries. Fink and Stark (1992) point to the American towns of Dodge City and Tombstone as being famous for 'lawlessness, vice and violence' rather than places associated with religious virtue.

What does this mean?

One of the big debates that dominate the sociology of religion is the 'secularisation' debate and we will explore this more fully in the chapter. There is a lot of evidence to show that in western societies the popularity of the mainstream religions is decreasing, although interestingly the popularity of other forms of spirituality (for example, feng shui and astrology) is growing.

However, the term 'popularity' is problematic because we need to be able to look back and see how popular something was at an earlier stage in history. And here lies the difficulty. The evidence that does exist may, on closer examination, not tell us anything about how popular religion was, but perhaps about other roles that religion played in societies.

Finally, the very concept 'religion' means different things to different people. If two sociologists have two different definitions (another word sociologists use is 'operationalisations') for religion, then any research they carry out is going to have different results because of the way they have 'operationalised' the concept of religion.

Why do/did people attend spiritual rituals?

In Europe many people argue that there are fewer people attending church ceremonies now than in the 19th century. While this almost certainly is the case, it does lead to the question 'why do/did they attend in the first place?' Was it ever for purely 'religious' reasons? Herberg (1956) suggested that church attendance in the US was evidence of commitment to the local community rather than an indication of religiousness.

Examine why many people publicly celebrate their religion. There is, for example, evidence that shows that as we get older, we attend more religious ceremonies. Is this out of fear of getting old and perhaps the acknowledgement of an after-life? Could it also be that as we get older it becomes increasingly difficult to meet new people and therefore the local religious organisation (church, mosque, temple or other) can offer a social network that we can belong to?

Other reasons for attendance at religious ceremonies are to do with social acceptance within the community generally. One hundred years ago in the UK, it was considered socially unacceptable if you did not attend 'church'. As a result this could mean you were looked down upon within the community you lived in. The same is true for many communities today.

In addition to this, in the past many people would attend ceremonies if they were about to get married in a church (even if they did not actually believe in the religion). There was also far greater emphasis on religious ceremonies for children (for example, Roman Catholic first communion and confirmation and Jewish Bar Mitzvah) than exists today. More women attend ceremonies as they get older than men. In many cases this is to do with the fact that women live longer than men. Religious organisations can offer many of these women the care and support and social network they desire having lost their partners.

Religion and nationalism

Nationalism refers to the feelings of loyalty that people may have to a particular nation or people. Although the word has a variety of different meanings, in many cases national or ethnic identities of a particular group are bound up with a particular religion.

We can see this in Northern Ireland with the conflict between the Catholics and Protestants still taking place. But we can also see this in the way that the 'West versus Iraq' situation is wrongly being portrayed as a Christian West versus an Islamic East. At such times religious enthusiasm can actually exaggerate the popularity of a religion – particularly if it is considered to be unpatriotic not to celebrate the religion concerned.

Conclusion

In addition to the reasons listed above, war brings about the loss of loved ones and the need for solace and comfort that many religions provide. As a result, during times of war, many religions experience an increase in popularity. This makes the work of the sociologist harder when trying to establish long-term trends in the popularity of any religion.

For consideration

1. What other reasons, apart from those mentioned in this section, can you think of that make religions popular at particular times or with particular people?

2. Why is it more difficult to answer this question when we go back hundreds or thousands of years?

● **Synoptic Link**

You can link religion to social differentiation – it was (and is, in some societies) considered 'deviant' not to attend or be part of a religious organisation. Some religions are 'demonised' by politicians and the media. Islam has faced much negative labelling at the hands of politicians and the media. This tells how 'deviancy' is both a culturally and historically changing concept. Mention this as a sophisticated way of telling the examiner you are aware of the variety of interpretations such terms can have.

✍ **Coursework Suggestion**

Read this chapter carefully but always with a notebook at your side. Every time you come across a reason for why people attend ceremonies, or believe in a particular religion, write it down. By the end of the chapter, your reasons can be turned into questions and thus you will have a questionnaire. Carry out research on a cross-section of twelve people using this questionnaire in order to find out the reasons for their religious belief. Compare and contrast your findings with the writings of other sociologists.

✓ **Top Exam Hint**

One problem that you will encounter in the sociology of religion is the domination of ideas from a 'Christian' perspective. A lot of sociological research has been gathered from Christian organisations. This can be a problem when making generalisations about other religions. As a sociology student, you should mention this point early on in the exam – perhaps in the introduction – and also be prepared to apply some of the ideas to the mosque, temple or other religious place of worship. Remember too, that many of the classical sociologists themselves came from Christian-dominated countries making much of sociological theory ethnoce... by default.

What did the classical sociologists think about religion?

What does this mean?

When the early sociologists were writing, 19th-century religious values were considered to be extremely important in everyday life. Children received their education in many cases from priests; family life revolved around religious customs and the head of the Protestant Church in the UK was the king or queen of England (and still is today). The very structures, constraints and in some cases freedoms that religion offered people were a matter of interest to the emerging discipline of sociology.

Writers such as Comte, Weber, Marx and Durkheim, the latter two both from Jewish backgrounds, stated that rather than 'godly creations', traditions were the creations of 'men' and as such were suitable subjects for sociological inquiry. The enormous wealth of some of the religions (for example, that of the Vatican) also brought into question issues of power and exploitation.

Auguste Comte (1798–1857)

The classical sociologists were interested in the relationship between types of religious beliefs and types of society. Comte divided the history of society into three stages based on the dominant type of knowledge used in society.

- *Theological society* – knowledge is based on a belief in magic, superstition and religion. The emphasis is on blood ties, and the belief in intuition (the ability to 'feel' if something is 'OK' or not).
- *Metaphysical society* – moving away from a belief in a variety of gods (polytheism) to a belief in one god (monotheism).
- *Final 'positive' society* – a 'secular' society where subjects like sociology offer 'scientific' answers to the questions formerly addressed by the religions.

Emile Durkheim (1858–1917)

Durkheim stressed the role of religion as a way of forging common values and a **'conscience collective'** in society (see Section 3.7). The 'profane' world is a world of 'empirical knowledge', i.e. knowledge gathered through the senses. However, for Durkheim there was also a 'sacred' world that inspired 'awe' and 'reverence' and that was considered above the profane.

His work on the 'totem' as used by the Arunta tribe in Australia shows how a sacred (and profane) symbol can symbolise both god and society. In this way he argues that religious ceremonies encourage a sense of common purpose that unites people beyond their own selfish interests. Religion is a force that binds the individual to society.

☀ Key Idea

Comte hoped for a *'priesthood of sociologists'* in what would become the new 'secular religion'. Comte developed the 'enlightenment' tradition of going beyond common sense or tradition as explanations for the commonplace. His sociology was one that was to be rooted in evidence.

66 99 Key Definition

The **'conscience collective'** was for Durkheim the existence of one social and moral order, i.e. a shared set of beliefs and values of the individuals making up traditional societies. He argued that it could act as a force on the individual that in turn produced a consensual society. The problem for Durkheim, however, was that as societies modernised, this 'conscience collective' was weakened.

● Synoptic Link

Use Marx's views on religion to provide a synoptic link between religion and

Karl Marx (1818–1883)

Marx is often described as a 'materialist', meaning that he did not believe in the supernatural. To him, religion was an ideology that helped create and maintain the 'false consciousness' that people lived under – this, Marx believed, hid the 'evils' of the capitalist society. By 'false consciousness' he meant that religion stopped workers seeing that they were, in reality, being 'exploited' by their 'bosses' – the middle classes. An ideology is a systematic set of beliefs serving the interests of a particular social group in society – in this case, the ruling class.

The social order that Marx was so critical about was maintained with the help of religion. By promising a life hereafter and teaching honour and respect for those above, religion helps keep the capitalist system alive. Religion was, for Marx, the ideological tool of the ruling classes.

Max Weber (1864–1920)

Whereas Durkheim and Marx both argued that religion helped maintain the status quo, Weber argued that religion was a force for social change. Calvinism (a form of Christianity), for example, believed that by demonstrating self-reliance and hard work, divine approval would be automatic.

By looking at China, India and Europe he argued that it was the religious beliefs held by Calvinists that hastened the arrival of a capitalist system in Europe. Many of the Eastern religions were 'anti-materialist', i.e. they did not value the possession of goods – essential for the survival of capitalism.

However, this view can be criticised by arguing that it was the other way around. Protestantism developed in countries where capitalism was already starting to develop. In addition to this, other highly capitalistic countries such as Japan do not have a Protestant tradition.

Conclusion

The theories of Comte and Durkheim are referred to as 'teleological', i.e. they explain norms, values and customs by referring to the particular end they serve. Functionalists, for example, explain the existence of social customs by explaining the purpose that they serve, i.e. to maintain society as a whole. These theories can therefore be criticised for assuming that all human action is purposeful, which others might argue is not.

For consideration

1. According to all four writers, what is the social function of religion?

2. In what ways are the classical theories expressed above both similar and different to the contemporary sociological theories?

✳ Key Idea

By taking Weber's idea that there is something 'religious' in the everyday act of work it is possible to make links with both the New Right and New Left government approach to policy. Both views stress the 'moral' aspect to living life on a day-to-day basis, 'hard work' and 'sensible' investment. These components were, according to Weber, a vital component within the Calvinist tradition – a tradition that Weber argued was responsible for the success of capitalism.

By New Right, sociologists refer to those ideas associated with the right wing of the Conservative party who stress the need for individual freedom and responsibility. This also means that they believe that the government should play less of a direct role in the lives of its citizens. The New Left has its origins in the growth of the variety of movements that developed from the 1960s involving students, hippies, women and the black community. Today the term is used to describe those on the 'left of politics', who believe in an extended welfare state while combining the ideas of the 'free market'. Tony Blair has been strongly influenced by such thinking.

✓ Top Exam Hint

Point out the similarities between Marx and Comte. Both theorists argue that there is a 'historical' or 'evolutionary' pattern to society. Comte talks about the three types of society (see this section) and Marx talks about the five stages of history (primitive communism, slavery, feudalism, capitalism and communism). Both view history as a set of 'stages' that societies move through.

What is the functionalist view on religion?

Aboriginals from Australia have their rituals – what 'rituals' do you have?

What does this mean?

Durkheim was convinced that religion played a crucial role in how societies worked. Remember that Durkheim was a consensual sociologist who believed that shared norms and values were essential in 'functional' societies ('consensual' meaning that societies and individuals in general were not in conflict). Since 1912, other functionalists have adapted and developed his ideas to examine the role that religion plays as one of society's biggest institutions.

What functions does religion fulfil?

1. Durkheim (1912) argues that religion demonstrates the moral superiority of society over the individual.
2. Functionalist Malinowski (1954) argues that the function of religion is to bond the community together at times of stress or danger.
3. American sociologist Talcott Parsons (1977) argues that religions provide 'core' values which in turn produce social solidarity. Parsons' version of functionalism in the 1950s was referred to as 'structural functionalism'.

How does Durkheim argue these functions are fulfilled?

Durkheim argued that religion was a social construction. He said that religion reinforced the 'collective conscience' by providing regular opportunities to establish and reinforce shared values and moral beliefs. Durkheim said that social life can be split into the 'sacred' (things to do with religion) and the 'profane' (things which are not). By bringing people together in the shared experience of religious ceremonies, the sacred affects the profane because people recognise the benefits of the social group (and society) and their dependence upon it. By doing this people automatically accept the importance that society has over them.

Durkheim argued that the symbols or '**totems**' that most religions use (for example, statues, carvings, and pictures) help make the process of this continuous shared experience an easy one. Durkheim studied the Arunta, an Australian Aboriginal tribe. He showed that totems were seen as sacred, i.e. considered religious by the clan, but also as profane by being clan emblems. This combination of both sacred and profane served to unite members of the tribe into a form of collective unity.

How does Malinowski argue these functions are fulfilled?

While many functionalists argue that religion at all times helps to sustain social solidarity some argue that this only happens in times of transition and stress.

Functionalist Malinowski shows this in his 1954 study of the Trobriand Islanders. These South Pacific fishermen had a number of prayer rituals they would perform before going out in the open sea. However, they would not perform these when sailing in the safety of the lagoon. Malinowski argued that the danger these fishermen faced by fishing in the open sea was a threat to the stability of the community, hence the prayer rituals.

How does Parsons argue these functions are fulfilled?

As a structural functionalist Parsons agrees with much that Durkheim said. Writing in 1950s America, he argued that religion provided core values and enhanced social solidarity. It also set up a framework for human action by which people's conduct could be judged. By combining concepts of the sacred and the profane the norms and values of the American political and social system were heavily informed by a framework that reflected Protestant values (for example, 'God Bless America' is a chant quite often heard at the beginning of American baseball matches).

However, he also agreed with Malinowski that religion 'comforts' people in times of stress. For those who are close to death or who know people that have died it promises an afterlife (or a chance of reincarnation). Religious places have served as important destinations to gather in times of war or threat to the community. In the former Soviet bloc countries, churches were quite often used as meeting places to discuss courses of action by those being oppressed. In London, during the Second World War, people would often gather in local churches during the Blitz. Social solidarity in both these cases was strengthened as a result.

Conclusion

Drawing on the ideas of Durkheim some sociologists argue that the 'sacred' still exists today albeit in a wider form. Interpretivist Bellah (1967) and interactionist Luckman (1967) both argue that religion is being transformed rather than in decline. With the concept of 'transformation' they are able to argue that while 'public' forms of religion may well be in decline, personal belief and individual practice lives on in 'private' (whatever variety of forms that may take).

66 99 Key Definition

For Durkheim the most elementary form of religion is '**totemism**', referring to the belief that animals and plants have supernatural powers. In his study of the Arunta tribe he found that their totems were the lizard, caterpillar, rat, cockatoo and plum tree. The totem symbolised both 'god' and the 'clan' of Aborigines, i.e. being both 'sacred' and 'profane'. Talking about the totem Durkheim writes '*if then, it is at once the symbol of god and of society, it this not because god and society are one and the same thing?*' (Durkheim 1912 in Stephens et al 1998, page 407).

✓ Top Exam Hint

Score high evaluation by recognising that the word 'religion' can be interpreted in a number of ways. Interpretivist Bellah's (1970) concept of 'civil religion' shows the different interpretations of the word. His reference to 'Americanism' as a 'civil religion' with values rooted in the Protestant religion indicate that whatever 'godly' religion people believed, faith in the American way of life came above other beliefs they had. Refer to this in the conclusion as a sophisticated way of evaluating the concept 'religion'.

✳ Key Idea

Functionalist Robert Bocock (1985) refers to 'civic rituals' in which he argues that it is not just religion that provides us with ways to reinforce cultural values. If we are to take sporting events, theatre, cinema and even 'shopping', we can provide examples of how a 'sense of belonging' to society is culturally reproduced other than through religious means. This idea can be used to criticise the importance that some sociologists place on religion as the main source for cultural values.

For consideration

1. Functionalist argue that the rituals in religions reinforce cultural values and provide a sense of belonging. What other non-religious rituals do the same thing?

2. How might the American flag be argued to be both sacred and profane?

What is the Marxist view of religion?

● Synoptic Link

Highlight the role that religion plays in maintaining the class system, something that most Marxists and neo-Marxists would agree with, e.g. Althusser. Marxists argue that religion not only acts as an ideological tool of the state but also allows people to live a 'false consciousness', i.e. to forget they are living in a class-ridden society. According to some Marxists, the promise of an 'afterlife' that many religions claim exists can mean that people are prepared to 'suffer in silence' rather than change the nature of the society they live in.

❝❞ Key Definition

The Marxist term **'alienation'** refers to the idea that modern conditions at work, i.e. mechanisation, have resulted in repetitive tasks that are no longer satisfying to the worker but are boring and breed resentment. The worker who lacks dignity makes no profit and only has their own worth to sell on an hourly, weekly or monthly basis. The worker is separated from what was once the 'skill' of the job, for example they are no longer a craftsman but a production line worker. For Marx it is the capitalist/ruling class that has placed the worker in this situation.

Princess Diana's funeral – religious mourning or a celebration of British nationalism?

What does this mean?

Marxist sociologists concentrate on the ways in which religion reinforces the status quo. They argue that it acts as a conservative force, in that it upholds (or conserves) the ruling class and maintains the social and economic order through ideological control.

Why was Marx critical of religion as an institution?

Marx (1857) said that *'Man makes religion, religion does not make man . . . Religion is the sigh of the oppressed creature, the heart of the heartless world . . . It is the opium of the people'*. You can use the quotation and apply the following points of evaluation in the exam.

- Marx argued that the capitalist system **alienates** and exploits people and that religion, rather than challenging the capitalist system, allows people to escape within their own beliefs.
- In most religions people are taught that if they suffer in this world their reward will come in the next – this view also stops people from challenging the capitalist system.
- By preaching words like 'honour', 'respect' and 'obey', religion can be seen as a method of social control whereby people accept rather than challenge the status quo.

How can religion challenge the idea of democracy?

Marxists argue that religion is an ideology, i.e. a system of thoughts and ideas that works in the interests of those in power. Until the enlightenment period of the 17th and 18th centuries, kings and queens in many western European countries reigned by 'divine right' (i.e. with God's consent). The acceptance of this ideology has been used by Marxists to show how religion legitimised both the oppression of the working classes and the privileges of the ruling classes. The automatic assumption that people are, by the right of God, allowed to rule over others is, for Marxists, a direct challenge to the meaning of democracy.

A distortion of real class relations

Marxists argue that an important ideological function of religion was to distort or hide the true nature of the division between the classes. The injustices of the capitalist system can be 'hidden' by the 'false consciousness' experienced when ruling and subject classes come under one roof in a place of worship. The illusion created is one in which there is a unity when, in fact, there is division based upon exploitation and alienation.

Even the tradition of the 'holy' institution of marriage is, for Marxists, a way to maintain property rights from one generation to another. By automatically accepting such traditions, Marxists argue that we fail to see an alternative where property might be shared communally.

A Marxist Utopia

Religion was, for Marx, an agent of social control in that by creating 'gods' and the belief in an afterlife, people ceased to realise the exploitation that the capitalist system created. Any thoughts of rebelling against any state system could be threatened with 'eternal damnation'. Marx wanted a revolution that would change the nature of society as he saw it. He argued that the religious afterlife that many religions wrote about where all humans could be treated fairly could be created today on earth once the capitalist system had been overthrown. He called this new society 'Utopia'.

Conclusion

Can religion alone bring about social change? If you are a Marxist then the answer to this question is 'no'. Marx argued that infrastructural change, i.e. changes in the economic structure of any society (most importantly, from one epoch to another) will carry with it superstructural change (family, legal system, educational system, religion, and so on). In other words, for Marx, profound social change always has an economic base and that the superstructure (for example, religion) can only, at best, attempt to fit in with or reinforce the necessities of the economy.

Key Ideas

- Neo-Marxist Althusser (1971) categorises religion as an 'Ideological State Apparatus' i.e. an arm of the state to maintain power of the ruling class over the rest. Althusser would argue that belief in this power is strengthened by the media portrayal of royal weddings and royal funerals, sanctioned in both cases by the church. As a result the 'authority' of the aristocracy is legitimised by these church ceremonies. The extraordinary media coverage of Princess Diana's funeral is evidence of this viewpoint.

- **Hegemony** is a neo-Marxist term coined by Gramsci (1891–1935) that refers to the idea that members of the working class 'consent' to the control imposed upon them by those in power. The institutions that were best able to 'win this consent' were those of the family, trade unions and 'the church'. By teaching words like 'honour' and 'respect', while the working classes recognise that middle-class ideas may not necessarily be in their interests, there is an 'acceptance' that this is 'the way things are'.

For consideration

1. What recent events in the media have had a religious connection?

2. How might Marxists argue that these events have been used to maintain the capitalist system?

What does Weber say about religion?

☀ Key Idea

Max Weber argued that as societies 'modernised', i.e. transformed from a mainly agrarian/farming way of life to the more industrialised way of living associated with cities, they became more 'rational'. 'Rationalisation' for Max Weber meant that societies increasingly use logic to solve problems whereas before traditional societies may have used religion and traditions to solve day-to-day problems. Weber used the German word '*zweckrational*' to describe this process and this type of thinking.

❝❞ Key Definition

For Weber, the '**spirit of capitalism**' is the pursuit and renewal of profit together with the application of calculation and rational bookkeeping. Such 'rationalism' was something that, he argued, Calvinists have been extremely good at. Calvinism, a version of Christianity, stressed values of hard work along with a contempt for squandering money on trivial items. Therefore, as a large body of people, Calvinists were far more likely to become economically successful than other groups that did not possess such an everyday approach to life.

Can the ideas of classical sociologist, Max Weber, be applied to societies today?

What does this mean?

Max Weber saw religion as an agent for social change. In his book *The Protestant Ethic and the Spirit of Capitalism* published in 1905, Weber took the transition from the feudal system to the capitalist system as a case study to look at the importance of religion and ideology to the creation of major social change.

Why was Weber so interested in the Protestant religion?

Weber identifies all of the earliest capitalist countries as Protestant ones, rather than Roman Catholic, Islamic, Buddhist, or any other particular religion. He deduces from this that there must be something about Protestantism which makes it 'fit' capitalism and which encourages capitalist ways of looking at the world and acting within it (he calls this the '**spirit of capitalism**' and it is perhaps worth noting that even as a sociologist he was using words that reflected the highly religious influences of his time). Weber focuses on a particular type of Protestantism, Calvinism, because in countries which demonstrated western capitalism the entrepreneurs and skilled workers were Calvinists.

How did this work?

Weber claimed that there are a number of factors within the Calvinist tradition that helped accelerate the processes of capitalism. The belief that hard work was rewarded by God was known as the 'work ethic'. The old expression '*the devil makes work for idle hands*' summed up the idea that hard work was rewarded by God and this meant that people worked efficiently and did not waste time. The Calvinist concept of vocation meant that work was a 'calling' and had to be done for the greater glory of God.

Calvinists also believed that they must work as hard as they could in this life to look for signs of God blessing them with (material) success. However, they also believed that it was wrong to spend money on frivolous objects and this meant that the money they earned was usually reinvested in ways that would generate more wealth later on, for example, in land, machinery and tools. The belief that lending money at interest was not sinful combined with the relatively high literacy rates of Calvinists (Bible reading was considered essential to the religion) went hand-in-hand with the essential skills required for the entrepreneur.

What was Weber's methodology?

Weber was a historian who looked at the documentary evidence left from the past, but, as a structuralist sociologist, he attempted to find underlying patterns rather than simply deal with unique historical events. By using 'verstehen' sociology Weber attempted to understand what it was like to be a typical Protestant and how this type of person would differ from somebody from a different religion. His 'ideal type' of Protestant was not any specific real religious group, but rather consisted of generalisations that included aspects of every different Protestant group. He intentionally created a 'model' to help analyse aspects of the Protestant way of looking at the world.

What do sociologists learn from Weber?

Weber's research shows that religious forces are important in their own right in creating very significant socio-economic change. It also shows how ideological factors shape economic and other behaviour. While Weber agreed with much of Marx's writings, he challenged a lot of the 'economic determinism' of Marx, i.e. the way that the economy shapes our institutions (for example, the family, religion and the media) and our individual actions. However, it is not just the economy that shapes people's lives for Weber – his work has been taken to show that religion can influence social change.

Conclusion

In many societies today there is increased pressure on workers to work long hours as they fear being seen by bosses as shirking responsibilities if they arrive or leave on time. For Weber this type of uniform lifestyle is a characteristic of the standardised organisation and reproduction of capitalism and its ever-continuing pursuit of profit.

66 99 Key Definition

The concept known as 'verstehen' has always been associated with the work of Max Weber and is the attempt to understand the world from inside the head of someone else. The sociologist adopting this approach places the interpretation of the person they are studying at the centre of their own research.

✳ Key Idea

Do people of the same religion share the same religious experience (i.e. do all practising Jews have similar thoughts, feelings and experiences of being 'Jewish')? Max Weber challenged this idea with the notion of 'theodicies of privilege and non privilege' ('theodicy' is a set of religious ideas which explain why people are in a certain social position). Religion is a set of ideas and beliefs that explain the existence of god/s. But the 'theodicy' of the rich will be very different from the 'theodicy' of the poor. While the rich have little to 'complain' about, the poor will see their religion as a way of justifying their unhappy existence.

● Synoptic Link

Use Max Weber's concept of 'theodicies of privilege and non privilege' to make a synoptic link between religion and stratification. Some groups may develop a theodicy of disprivilege. For example, the Jews historically have seen themselves both as the 'chosen people' and subject to persecution. Quite often historically they have been placed in the lower strata of society (e.g. in ancient Egyptian times and more recently during the Nazi era). The poverty that they endured was made bearable by what they perceived was 'salvation' in the next life – such salvation was seen as 'compensation' for the hardship they endured.

For consideration

1. In what other ways can religion be connected to the growth of capitalism in the 21st century?

2. How does Weberianism differ in its approach to religion compared with functionalism and Marxism?

What is the neo-Marxist view on religion?

Friedrick Engels (1820–1895) – co-founder of Marxism and inspiration for many branches of modern feminism.

☞ Who is this person?

Friedrich Engels (1820–1895) was born into a wealthy family of mill owners in Germany. This influenced his critical outlook on life that was later to develop with the working relationship he had with Marx. In their many writing partnerships, some argue it is difficult to tell who wrote what. Involved in the European revolutions of 1848, they went into exile in England where Engels helped build the German socialist movement. An inspiration to feminists, Engels also wrote much on the subordination of women in modern societies.

What does this mean?

Marxist ideas argue that conflict exists between those who own the means of production and those who don't (and therefore have to sell their own labour to stay alive). Marx argued that the capitalist system is oppressive and class-based and religion helps people not to realise this. By 'neo-Marxism' sociologists refer to any theory or form of sociological analysis that takes and develops these ideas – the ideas of Karl Marx and Friedrich Engels.

Humanist and materialist forms of Marxism

When trying to classify different types of neo-Marxist writers it is helpful to recognise the different strands to Marx's writings, from which other writers have drawn their influences. Humanist Marxist approaches tend to focus on the importance of ideology and individual 'consciousness', whereas materialist forms of Marxism are more concerned with universal laws that can be applied to all types of society. Both approaches are helpful when looking at the sociology of religion. Many neo-Marxists draw on both branches of Marxism to inform their writing.

A dominant ideology?

Abercrombie, Hill and Turner (1980) question to what extent religion acted as a 'dominant ideology' controlling people in the interests of the ruling classes in the way that Marx (1845) had argued. They stress that economic and repressive control was far more effective than religion as a way of controlling the masses. Neo-Marxist Turner (1991) also argues that the nature of capitalism has changed. Whereas once it was possible to identify exploitation at the hands of individual members of the elite class, he argues that now business corporations dominate capital. Arguing that secularisation is taking place, he says that religion is no longer the social or moral force that it once was.

However, Turner also challenges many orthodox Marxist writers on the role that religion has actually played in the shaping of ideas. Taking Christianity in Europe as an example, from the period of the Middle Ages onwards, many peasants practised far older religions than the state-determined forms of Christianity (for example, Catholicism and the Church of England). If that is the case, Turner argues that religion could not possibly have had the ideological effects that some Marxist writers claim.

Goods not gods

Neo-Marxist Marcuse (1964) argues, like orthodox Marxists, that religion acts as a source of oppression of the working classes, stopping them from resisting the exploitative nature of the capitalist system. However, in an argument that supports the secularisation thesis, he argues that 'commodity fetishism' (the idea that we are obsessed with buying new products regardless of whether we really need them) will bring about a new 'god' that will replace the older religions – the god of 'consumerism'.

Marx argued that commodity fetishism is an inevitable capitalist process where goods take on a worth that is unrepresentative of the labour that went into it. For example, the price of a box of chocolates in one part of the world can be the same as an emergency trip to the doctor in another. Marcuse argued that as we become hungry for consumer goods, the older religions will cease to have meaning. Through institutions such as the media, this new religion will once again stop the working classes from realising the exploitative nature of capitalism.

Liberation theology

This is one example of where Marxist ideas have been developed alongside a religious set of beliefs. This blend of South American Catholicism with Marxism argues for social change. Christ is pictured as a 'revolutionary' who wished liberation for all people who were oppressed.

Attacking government corruption and exploitation, some of these Catholic revolutionaries supported the notorious rebel Sandinista movement against the government in Nicaragua in the late 1970s. Liberation theology is therefore one example of a religious movement committed to social change. A second example can be seen in Poland during the 1980s where the Catholic Church was often used as a meeting place for those wishing to bring down the communist government.

Conclusion

The ideas of Max Weber can be used to criticise both Marxists and neo-Marxists, who generally agree that religion does not bring about social change but rather is a force for conservatism. By looking at the development of capitalism in the aftermath of Protestantism (Calvinism) Weber argued that religion can bring about social change under the right conditions. By using the example of liberation theology and pointing to leaders like Gandhi in India, and the events in Poland where the communist government was overthrown, neo-Marxist ideas can be criticised showing how religion can act as a powerful force for change.

✳ Key Idea

Turner (1991) was also interested in the ways religion controls sexuality and gender roles through inheritance of property and property rights through institutions such as marriage. Remember that until recently males (rather than females) in most societies inherited property. This meant that female gender roles were being socialised into norms and values that gave little or no material rights to women. The church sanctioned these extraordinary male powers with the words 'love, honour and obey' that the woman would have to repeat in the church marriage service.

◆ What, when and why?

A western movement of thought that generally started after the Second World War, Neo-Marxists developed the ideas of Marx and his followers in the 19th century. They started from analysing why the 'revolution' that Marx predicted did not/has not yet taken place. Two strong branches of neo-Marxism are identifiable: those influenced by the 'Frankfurt School' (a group of German Marxists who argued that the capitalist ruling class use the mass media and popular culture to shape society's thinking), who focus on the importance of 'culture' in maintaining middle-class 'hegemony'; and structuralist ideas that focus on how 'structures' of language, thought or institutions maintain middle-class hegemony.

✳ Key Idea

Steve Chapman (2002) argues that the fact that liberation theology was disowned by the Catholic Church is useful in lending support to the Marxist idea that the church and mainstream religions in general can be ideological tools of capitalist states.

For consideration

1. To what extent do you believe that neo-Marxism is very different from orthodox Marxist approaches?

2. Think of as many religious leaders as you can. How many of these would have been described as 'revolutionaries' in their time?

What is the interpretive view on religion?

What does this mean?

Structural (or 'macro') approaches to religion tend to argue that religion as an institution shapes or determines the way we are. However, interpretivist sociologists Berger and Luckmann (1967) argue that throughout human history religion has played a major role in how social actors (people) shape, determine and make sense of the universe around them.

Rather than seeing social actors (or humans) as being shaped, interpretivist sociologists focus on the meanings that religion has for its many different followers. In particular they focus on the meanings of certain symbols, rituals, beliefs and religious experiences. They are also interested in the sense of community provided by many religious organisations and the way that they contribute to a socially constructed reality.

The importance of symbols

Many religions use symbols, for example, the cross (Christians); the crescent moon and star (Muslims); the Star of David (Jews). We have already seen how Durkheim stressed the importance of symbols to indicate what was to be considered sacred. Symbols are also used to separate the sacred from the profane. Daniel Bell (1973) argues that individuals create religious meaning because it meets fundamental and ever-present emotional needs that all human beings possess. Philosophical questions such as 'What is mankind?' and 'Who am I?' are answered relatively easily if one has strong religious beliefs.

Berger and Luckmann (1967) argue that individuals create, socially construct and develop reality by searching for meanings. For them, religion represents a means of constructing a social framework of meaning for people (i.e. a set of ideas and related values that allows them to make sense of the world). Interpretive sociologists argue that humans attach meanings to objects and events which they then use to communicate with others.

Interpretivists are particularly interested in the feelings of awe, reverence or hatred that such symbols evoke. We need to remember that many images, while worshipped by one group, can also symbolise the oppression of one religion by another (for example, many Palestinians will not have the same meanings attached to the Star of David that most Israelis share). Either way, such symbols are a 'shorthand' that convey shared knowledge about the customs and traditions of the religion, culture and identity of the person worshipping the particular symbol in question.

The importance of rituals

It is not only physical objects like the cross that can be described as symbols. Many religious rituals such as Jewish circumcision or kneeling in front of religious statues symbolise the feeling of reverence and respect for the deity in question. These rituals follow on from the particular beliefs of a religion that are often made up of values that are designed to show how people should lead their lives.

Remember that many interpretive sociologists argue that religion provides cultural meanings and a way for people to construct their identities (for example, 'I am a Muslim'; 'I am a Sikh'). Interactionist Berger argues that a meaningful world is created for social actors by the use of mutually understandable symbols and rituals that create the sense of shared community found in many religions. By doing this, religions create order and meaning in people's existence.

A bleak outlook

Berger is however quite pessimistic about the role that religion plays in today's world. With the growth of technology, science and the media, traditional religion is plunged into a crisis of credibility, i.e. people no longer accept that religion offers answers to problems in the way that it once appeared to.

He goes on to argue that the loss in certainty and the fear of a loss in identity causes (and here he draws in the work of Durkheim) feelings of 'meaninglessness' or 'anomie'. He concludes that religion, for so long a way of giving meaning to life, no longer has the power to do this.

✓ **Top Exam Hint**

Evaluation marks can be gained in the exam if you make sure that you draw out the similarity between functionalists and interpretivists and their interest in symbols as a significant element of study within the sociology of religion.

∞ **Methods Link**

Remember to use the concepts 'reliability' and 'validity' (see Theory and methods) when talking about interpretive sociological research. Because so much interpretive sociology is about individual, subjective meanings, it is very difficult for the sociologists who practice this to claim their work is 'reliable'; however, they may well wish to describe it as 'valid'. Students will gain evaluation marks for simply stating this in the exam. For a sophisticated conclusion mention these points there.

For consideration

1. Why do you think many churches are extremely tall with high ceilings?

2. How might a sociologist analyse the use of the word 'crusade' by American President, George Bush, after 11 September 2001?

What is the feminist view on religion?

What does this mean?

Feminist sociology has two major concerns when focusing on religion.

1. What roles do women occupy within the various religious institutions?
2. What role does **patriarchy** play within religion?

Many feminists argue that religious institutions and beliefs help legitimise gender inequality. By studying these institutions and movements we can examine to what extent women's role and status is constructed by religion and to what extent religion oppresses women.

Women, witchcraft and medicine

The witch hunts were a 17th century phenomenon particularly strong in America where many women were tortured and burnt because they were believed to be witches. It seems strange that many women were burnt as witches for their ability to heal others. One argument for this is that the power women demonstrated threatened the newly emerging 'sciences' that were, at the time, dominated by men. Post-structuralist Michel Foucault (1990) argued that during the 19th and 20th centuries even women's bodies were, through the discourse of medicine, subject to male control (for example, gynaecology) because the doctors were male. By 'discourse', Foucault meant the collection of related statements or events which define what we take for granted within a particular area of knowledge.

Women, Christianity and Islam

Grace Davie (1989) argues that not only do more women than men attend Christian services but they also view 'God' differently. Whereas men view their God in terms of power and control, women view God in terms of love, comfort and forgiveness. Many churches forbid the priesthood to women and Christian churches generally do not endorse either abortion or female homosexuality and bisexuality.

The popular (but very controversial!) conception of women within the Islamic religions is one of oppression due to the wearing of the veil, the tolerance of male to female violence (but not vice versa) and women's inferior legal status. However, such views are typically ethnocentric. Many Islamic feminists argue that the veil is liberating as it frees women from the predatory gaze of men. The wearing of traditional clothing is also seen as a cultural resistance to the effects of globalisation and/or westernisation.

66 99 Key Definition

The traditional concept of 'patriarchy' refers to divisions in status that occur as a result of gender. Early feminists argued that women had less power than men did in most types of society. While it is important to realise that there is more than one type of feminism (e.g. liberal, black, Marxist and radical) – they all share and use the notion of 'patriarchy' to indicate how women are 'exploited' by males – either individually or within the institutions that they work in.

⤏ Classic Study

Walby (1990) argues that patriarchy consists of six social structures.

1. *The patriarchal mode of production* where women's labour is exploited within the household by men.
2. *Patriarchal relations in paid work* where women are segregated and paid less.
3. *Patriarchal relations in the state* where the state operates in the interests of men rather than women.
4. *Male violence against women* through rape, sexual, emotional and physical assault.
5. *Patriarchal relations in sexuality* where men's sexuality is viewed completely differently from that of women.
6. *Patriarchal relations within cultural institutions* and the creation through religion, the media, and education, of masculine and feminine identities.

Fundamentalism and gender

Diversity and change can bring about fear and uncertainty and therefore, in some cases, a desire to return to traditional values. In rapidly changing times fundamentalists (for example, Christian and Islamic) are attracted to (and find comfort in) the idea of women and men who have clearly defined norms, values and roles. The fear of change leads to a widening of the gender boundaries as a result.

A word of warning. While many writers argue that 'fundamentalism' (for example, Christian and Islamic) has a negative effect on women (reducing many of the freedoms won by feminists during the course of the 20th century) good sociologists will appreciate that this view can be criticised for being ethnocentric. Such views are often held by white, middle-class academics and are therefore often biased. Many fundamentalists are themselves women who believe in the 'liberation' offered by the religious choices they have made.

Women and religious movements

Women have played a decisive, yet historically understated, role within the development of religious movements. Mary Wollstonecraft, one of the first feminists, wrote *A Vindication of the Rights of Women* in 1792. In the 19th century, it was Ellen White who set up the Seventh Day Adventists and Elizabeth Fry had enormous influence within the Quaker movement with her work on prison reform.

Writing about more recent 'New Age' movements, Bruce (1995) argues that there is a gender divide evident in the types of movement that women and men play a part in. He argues that women play a major role in complementary medicine (for example, homeopathy) whereas men tend to be more involved in parapsychology (for example, seeking causal explanations for poltergeists).

Conclusion

State-endorsed religious institutions (such as the Church of England) tend to emphasise the 'traditional' role of women within the family, for example by stressing the 'natural' maternal role of the woman (this reduces the opportunity for paid employment for women). We have also seen that many religions exclude women from key positions within their organisations, for example, the Catholic priesthood. Finally, the emphasis on marriage and monogamy (having only one relationship) that most religions have, tends, historically, to be harder on women than men (i.e. women are judged more harshly than men if they have another relationship outside of marriage).

Does traditional dress liberate Muslim women, or seek to control and oppress them?

☞ Who is this person?

Mary Wollstonecraft (1759–1797) was an early champion of women's rights. A teacher, governess, translator and then literary advisor, she famously wrote the *Vindication of the Rights of Women*, which was a publication that argued for equality between the sexes. She was a strong supporter of the French Revolution and her ideas have been influential to the history of the liberal feminism movement.

✓ Top Exam Hint

Show the examiners excellent evaluation skills by applying the ideas of Anthony Giddens to the term 'fundamentalism'. 'Fundamentalism' is used to describe forms of religion that take literally the words of the scriptures (e.g. those of both Christians and Muslims). Christian and Islamic fundamentalists share a fear of change which often results in a non-acceptance of other viewpoints. Giddens argues that fundamentalist ideas are a way of rejecting modern society.

For consideration

1. How does religion support the ideology of family life?

2. How might religion support the notion of female obedience to their husbands?

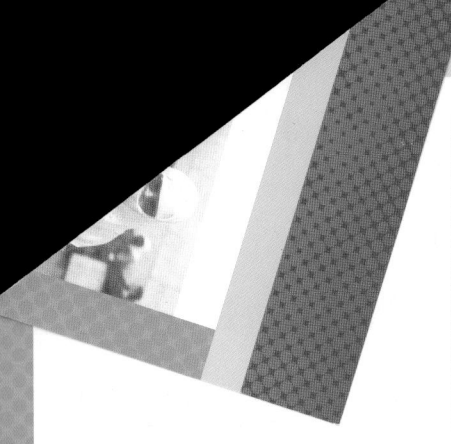

What are churches, denominations, sects and cults?

What does this mean?

Sociologists differ in their views as to what 'churches', 'sects', 'cults' and 'denominations' are. However, providing you explain what you mean by these terms, the examiners will evaluate your work and award you marks according to your interpretation.

What is the difference between churches and denominations?

- Although definitions vary, most sociologists agree that by 'church' we are referring to a large organisation quite often linked to the state, for example, the Church of England. Members of churches tend to 'conform', i.e. go along with the norms and values of the society the church is in.
- Stark and Bainbridge (1985) describe denominations as 'diluted' churches. While denominations are separate from the state, they do not reject ideas held by the majority of society. However, while still highly bureaucratic and following many of the ideas of the established churches, they are open to new ideas and less inclined to follow the strict ceremonies associated with churches, for example, the Methodists.

What are sects?

While often associated with a more deviant image, sects are generally what are called 'world-affirming' new religious movements, i.e. they do not challenge the way things are in the world. While often critical of other religious movements, nevertheless they tolerate their existence.

Some sects are described as being 'millenarian' movements, which means that followers believe at some point the world will end (referred to as 'Armageddon') and that God will save them while not saving other groups of religious believers. Examples of these are the Jehovah's Witnesses. Other sects can be described as 'reformist', i.e. they want to reform or change society, but not in any radical or revolutionary way. One example of this type are the Quakers.

What are cults?

Cults are 'world-rejecting' religious movements or protest groups who are highly critical of the more established religions, churches and denominations. They tend to be quite small and elitist with highly committed members who often reject societies' norms and values. Members are usually asked to cut ties with family and friends. Like sects, some are described as being 'millenarian' movements. Examples include the American People's Temple where approximately 900 members took part in mass suicide in Guyana in 1978.

Some cults are 'manipulationist', i.e. they tend to be led by charismatic individuals that promise to 'unlock' spiritual powers, and, quite often through the use of meditation, promise increased personal awareness and ability. The Scientologists are one example of this.

Why do sects and cults grow?

- Weber argued that those who felt marginalised (left out) in society could be drawn into either a cult or sect. The close-knit networks of support these organisations offer can provide marginalised individuals with a feeling of belonging (as well as offering food, comfort and in some cases shelter).
- Some individuals join either sects or cults because of the so-called 'exclusivity' they offer. If on joining individuals are made to feel they are special (some organisations require donations of money) then this feeling can quite often make up for the poor status that individual may have felt they had prior to joining the movement.
- The *Church–Sect cycle theory* can be applied to how some sects and cults are created. For churches to remain popular over long periods of time they have to make compromises (for example, the growth of female Anglican priests over the last ten years). Such changes upset members of that particular church. Some members then decide to break away and form a new organisation. The new organisation (cult or sect) attracts recruits who come from economically poor backgrounds. This poverty is something that is seen in a highly positive light by the movement they join. The sect (or cult) grows in membership and the circle is completed when the sect takes on church-like characteristics. According to this theory the process will start again as new sects are formed as a result of some members leaving when disillusioned with the new organisation. The Methodist Church has been described as a sect.

∽ Classic Study

Three evaluations you can use in the exam to describe religious groups come from the three classifications of Roy Wallis (1984).

1. *World Rejecting Groups* whose members are *hostile* to the world around them.
2. *World Accommodating Groups* whose members largely *ignore* the world around them.
3. *World Affirming Groups* whose members largely *accept* the world but try to focus on making individuals feel better and more successful within the world they operate.

✳ Key Idea

There are two possible problems that some sects or cults may face.

1. Reliance on a charismatic leader can mean that once that leader has died then so too does the organisation.
2. Those 'millenarian' organisations, which predict that the world will end, weaken their legitimacy if that prediction is believed to be unfounded.

For consideration

1. How easy is it to use Wallis's categories to describe all th different religious groups you can think of?

2. What does this tell you about using such categori

What are new religious movements and why have they grown?

What does this mean?

The term 'New Religious Movements' is used by contemporary sociologists to recognise the enormous variety of religious organisations that have come into existence in recent decades. This has occurred at the same time as membership of much large-scale, mainstream religions has declined.

Indigenous and imported new religious movements

Roy Wallis (1984) describes indigenous new religious movements as those movements that drew on Judaeo-Christianity, but developed into extremely enthusiastic and distinct versions of the original. One example is the 'Jesus People' popular with young people in the USA in the late 1960s. Imported new religious movements draw on distinctly different religious traditions quite often from Asian countries. One example popular in most western cities is the familiar Hare Krishna devotees (usually dressed in white or orange and with shaven heads), followers of Krishna, who developed a form of Hinduism.

● **Synoptic Link**

A theory associated with crime and deviance, Merton's (1946) Strain Theory offers five ways people respond to the 'strain' of living in modern societies. You might like to apply these to the religious movements you learn about:

- *Conformity* where no form of deviance takes place.
- *Innovation* where the failure to succeed in society draws individuals to commit criminal or deviant acts.
- *Ritualism* where pe~~

How ~~~~e new religious movements influenced by

~~ a form of self-help psychotherapy, has now finally been ~~rch' in America. Popular in the 1970s, Scientologists ~~t a cost of several thousand pounds, in order to get back ~~at humans once possessed many centuries ago. ~~he ability to function better at work and the reduction ~~re the promised benefits of Scientology.

~~minars Training (EST) drew on the ideas of Freud. ~~ollective ritual or worship it was designed as a way ~~ their full potential and promised '*to transform your* ~~ Popular today with some of the 'Hollywood set', ~~ directors and successful film makers, such ~~ and are run more as multinational businesses ~~ious lines.

Religion

~~ld accommodating new religious

~~ described as 'world affirming', i.e. they do ~~ctually works. Wallis offers two more ways of analysing new religious movements: 'world rejecting' and 'world accommodating'. By 'world rejecting' he refers to those new religious movements that reject the 'corrupt' world around them. As separate communities that believe in Christ, they anticipate some sort of spiritual revolution. One such group is 'the Children of God'.

By 'world accommodating', Wallis describes groups that do not wish to separate themselves from the rest of society but rather their religious practices allow them to carry on normal family and work life. Neo-Pentecostalists are one such group who are committed Christians who believe that the more orthodox religions (including mainstream Christianity) have become bureaucratised in modern times and have lost some of the vitality and spirituality that religion, in their eyes, should have.

Who joins new religious movements?

Norman Cohn's study *The Pursuit of the Millennium* (1970) argued that many religious movements were most likely to emerge during times of famine or war. Members were recruited from the 'dispossessed poor' and believed that their lives would change for the better as a result of joining the movement. Max Weber suggested that religion helped the underprivileged in a society cope with their situation by giving meaning to people's suffering. Weber termed this *'the theodicy of non-privilege'*.

However, while popular opinion might suggest that new religious movements are made up predominantly of marginalised people, some research suggests otherwise. Eileen Barker's study of the Moonies and Wallis's study of Scientology, for instance, both point out that the typical member of these new religious movements is middle-class, young, fairly well educated, and predominantly female.

Conclusion

In what Max Weber would refer to as a *'disenchanted world'*, modernity brings with it 'fragmentation'. By this he means that in more traditional societies the family would work together on the land in what were closer forms of community life. In today's competitive world fragmentation happens when children are separated from adults in schools and colleges and couples have separate professional careers. As a result some middle-class professionals search for their 'real selves' and join a new religious movement to counteract their feelings of 'disenchantment'.

For consideration

1. What are the differences in the functionalist concept of *anomie*, the Marxist concept of *alienation*, and the Weberian concept of disenchantment?

2. How could you apply these concepts when discussing why people join new religious movements?

☐ Key Fact

The members of Sun Myung Moon's 'Unification Church' (the 'Moonies') believed that it was down to the 'Moonies' to bring about a 'physical kingdom of God'. A synthesis of western and eastern culture, it was founded in 1954. Members would abandon homes, families and friends. Eileen Barker's (1984) study argued, however, that brainwashing did not occur. Those joining were individuals interested in religion and spirituality, and did not often need much convincing to join. Membership rates indicated a rapid turnover of members, i.e. a succession of people continuously joining or leaving the organisation.

✳ Key Idea

Stark and Bainbridge (1985) argue that organised religion offers 'compensators' to those who do not achieve great health, wealth or happiness. People who are materially satisfied but who are relatively deprived (psychologically, spiritually) might need compensators to help deal with this. When mainstream religions become more secular, people turn to other religious groups in order to gain the benefits of 'compensators'. New religious movements are able to fulfil this function, and it is the relatively deprived who are most likely to join such groups.

A Moonie mass wedding. Eileen Barker explored reasons why people joined the sect known as the Moonies.

| # What is religious pluralism?

Religious plurality or religious intolerance? Until the 1980s the turban stopped the employment of Sikh males in the police force.

What does this mean?

Religious pluralism refers to the different forms of Christian and non-Christian beliefs along with all other types of religion that we have looked at in this chapter, for example, Scientology, animism, and so on. Closely associated with the secularisation debate, the idea of 'religious pluralism' assumes that the mainstream religions (for example, Christianity, Islam, Judaism) no longer appeal to all members of society. Instead what is in place is a 'market place' of different religions where we are at liberty to pick and choose in the same way a consumer might do. This choice could be referred to as spiritual shopping.

Classical sociology on pluralism

Sociologists a hundred years ago did not predict the religious pluralism that exists today. While the opinions of the classical sociologists varied enormously about religions, they generally agreed that as societies modernised and became more 'rational' and science offered more tangible reasons for why things took place, religions would eventually disappear.

However, with the growth of new religious movements and the expansion of older religions such as Mormonism and Pentecostalism, combined with the increasing fundamentalism that flourishes throughout the world, it is hard to disagree that religious pluralism is not a reality.

A plurality of beliefs and ideologies

Berger and Kellner (1981) argue that before the period of industrialisation, religion provided societies with a *'fixed universe of meaning'*, i.e. one single set of core beliefs that people understood and felt secure in. Interactionist Berger (1990) used the word 'nomos' to describe the feeling of meaningfulness that religion helps bring about. Berger and Kellner argue that, with the process of industrialisation, values and ideas are subjected to a number of influences (for example, the media, the work place), which come into conflict with the traditional beliefs contained within most religions and which functionalists would argue brings about *anomie*, i.e. the feelings of meaninglessness and the opposite to nomos.

As a result this *'plurality of beliefs and ideologies'* leads to what Berger and Kellner refer to as a *'collapse in certainties'*. In other words, people start to question many of the claims that religions have made, leading them to question to what extent the traditional religions offer acceptable forms of knowledge and guidance. This leads to either the secularisation process, where some argue that a decline in religious belief is taking place, or a move into one of the many new religious movements. Postmodernists ironically refer to this as *'shopping for God'*.

✷ Key Idea

Interpretivist Bellah (1970) argues that far from living in a society where religion is in decline, it provides us with the freedom to choose what we believe in. This is in sharp contrast to more traditional societies either in the present or in the past where the main religion *stopped* people from making a choice about what they believed. He calls this freedom to search and choose *'individuation'*.

Civic religions

It is not possible to answer any question on religious pluralism without talking about 'civic religion'. While the growth in most major religions (apart from Islam) has ceased, what does not seem to have stopped growing are the rituals that historically belonged to orthodox religion. If we think of the number of state ceremonies that can be watched on television, for example, royal funerals, royal weddings and events like Remembrance Day, there is, according to some sociologists, a sacred element to these events. We can refer to 'civic religions' as those that celebrate the citizenship of the nation state. As such it forms part of the religious pluralism discussed in this section.

Conclusion

Living in multicultural Britain it is not difficult to see how, or why, at the beginning of the 21st century churches such as the Church of England or the Roman Catholic Church are struggling to maintain congregation numbers. With its multi-ethnic population, most parts of Britain have populations that celebrate a variety of faiths: the Islamic and Jewish communities, Hindus, Sikhs and West Indian Pentecostalists to name but a few.

However, while the idea of a 'market place' where one can pick and choose whatever religion one desires may sound convincing, sociology students need to be highly critical of such thinking. With the storming of a mosque by police in early 2002 (a family of suspected illegal immigrants was arrested and deported to Germany) and again in January 2003 (this time in the fight against 'international terrorism'), the sacrilege laws that exist in the UK to defend the Christian churches do not protect believers of other faiths.

● Synoptic Link

Some religions 'socially stratify' and 'socially differentiate' certain individuals as deviant or 'untouchable'. The Hindu caste system is one example of religious stratification. The system does not allow people from different castes to marry.

✍ Coursework Suggestion

Carry out coursework that analyses secondary data (get permission first from your coursework tutor). Gather attendance statistics from one of the religious communities in your area. This might be difficult but you could try approaching religious leaders of local communities where such religions are practised. Gather statistics at two points in time, perhaps five years apart. By comparing the statistics over time you can apply some of the ideas looked at in this chapter to account for the changes in attendance that you have discovered.

For consideration

1. To what extent do you think that the national curriculum subjects you have studied reflect the notion of 'religious pluralism'?

2. What type of evidence could you gather to show that many so-called 'minority' religions are actually growing in numbers?

What is secularisation and has it happened?

What does this mean?

Bryan Wilson (1966) argues that the process of secularisation is one in which religious thinking, practices and institutions are said to be in decline and losing their social significance. The 'secularisation debate' is one in which this process is hotly contested by some sociologists.

What has the Enlightenment got to do with secularisation?

Before the 17th century, traditional 'sacred' beliefs meant all explanations about the weather, love or war could be explained in terms of how 'God' or 'the gods' wished it to be so. In today's world, however, natural disasters are no longer explained in terms of the divine punishment of God but through scientific and rational explanations.

Classical sociologists such as Marx, Durkheim and Weber were writing about the effects of this new 'modern world' (remember Weber's concept of 'disenchantment', i.e. the loss of 'magic' in the world). Associated with the Enlightenment has been the so-called 'modernity thesis', which maintained that as societies developed, the desire for religious beliefs would decrease.

What evidence is there to show that there is a decline in religion?

- The argument at first appears a strong one if we look at evidence based upon the Christian religions. There has been a decline in religious baptisms, confirmations and church marriages, traditionally major events in the lives of many Christians. Stephens et al (1998) state that 65 per cent of all babies in the UK were baptised into the Anglican Church in 1900. By 1993 this figure had dropped to 27 per cent.
- The traditional function of the church as a centre for community support, news and advice has declined in Western Europe with the growth of social services and the media.
- There has been a sharp drop in church attendance during the 20th century. At the beginning of the 20th century, over a quarter of the adult population in the UK were regular churchgoers. However by the late 1990s, only 1.5 per cent of the adult population attended Church of England services and only one-third of Catholics in England and Wales went to church.
- Over the last decade it has been increasingly possible to shop and to buy alcohol on Sundays – something that was inconceivable in the 19th century. This development shows how the Church has lost much of its political power, although, as we shall see below, not all of it.

☐ Key Fact

The 'Enlightenment' refers to a period in European thought in the 17th and 18th centuries when, because of the developments in science, there was widespread disillusionment with religious and traditional explanations about the world. In particular the natural sciences (e.g. chemistry, physics and biology) could now offer explanations about how the world functioned. These beliefs severely challenged the authority of many religions. The Enlightenment referred to how these ideas were expressed through the arts, science, politics and philosophy.

❊ Key Idea

American functionalists Stark and Bainbridge (1985) talk of the 'reorientation rather than demise' of religion. By this they mean that the many religious movements that are springing up on both sides of the Atlantic Ocean are a direct response to a more 'secular' society. The idea of secularisation is itself far too simplistic a term and fails to describe the complex sets of processes that take place: 'in the future, as in the past, religion will be shaped by secular forces but not destroyed. There will always be a need for gods' (pp. 527–8).

Is there evidence to show religion is not in decline?

- If, however, we look beyond the Christian religions then there is evidence to suggest that religion is growing. Many of the ethnic minorities in the UK have a variety of religions that members strictly follow.
- Hamilton argues that survey research in 1998 revealed that only 10 per cent of the population in Britain do not believe in God (although their definitions of 'god' varied from individual to individual).
- While the political power of the church may be said to be in decline (people cite the changes in the licensing laws as an example), the Queen is still head of the Church of England and the charter of the BBC still requires it to transmit religious programmes albeit on a limited scale.
- The growth in alternative New Age religions challenges the idea that we are an increasingly secular society. Robert Bellah (1970) argues that with the increasing disillusionment with traditional medical and religious doctrines/ideas comes renewed interest in astrology, the occult, oriental religions and more recently feng shui.

Conclusion

We should perhaps remember that while people may not be attending ceremonies, they may well be practising some sort of religion in the privacy of their own home. It is also hard to believe that religious beliefs are in decline with the growth of Christian fundamentalism in the USA and Islamic fundamentalism in many parts of the world today.

Whose house is this? Many churches today are being converted and sold off as luxury homes.

 Coursework Suggestion

Carry out a small number of in-depth interviews (five or six would be appropriate) with different religious leaders from the local community where you live, e.g. a Catholic priest, Jewish rabbi, and so on). Explore with them, in the interviews, the debate over secularisation, and see to what extent they believe the processes of secularisation are taking place within their communities. Compare and contrast your findings with existing sociological theories.

For consideration

1. To what extent do people attend churches, mosques, temples or any other religious establishment for religious purposes, i.e. if they did not, would they be looked down upon within the community?

2. What activities could be considered to be replacing religion today?

How might secularisation be a problem for methods?

What does this mean?

Gather quantitative data (for example, church attendance figures) and you might be forgiven for assuming that religion is in decline. Gather qualitative data (for example, through in-depth interviews) and you might equally be forgiven for saying the opposite, i.e. that religions of all types are growing. However, as this chapter shows, such discussions are far more complicated and in this section we examine more closely some of the methodological problems researchers face when examining secularisation.

'PETS' as a form of evaluation

PETS stands for 'practical', 'ethical', 'theoretical' and 'sensitive' issues that must be considered when evaluating anything to do with methods or methodology. You can identify a number of problems associated with secularisation by applying these concepts. Here are just some examples of ways you can do this.

- *Practical problems* – To what extent can sociologists access reliable records from previous centuries that accurately tell us how popular religion was? Comparatively few people could read and write and therefore we have no real way of knowing to what extent they were 'religious' nor what they meant by the word.
- *Ethical problems* – Is it acceptable to question people about their own (often very private) spiritual beliefs? Is it then equally acceptable to publish the findings of research on the basis of what other people have told you about their beliefs?
- *Theoretical problems* – We know that quite often values of researchers drive the research in a particular direction, for example, feminists, Marxists and functionalists will be looking (and arguing) for different things when researching secularisation. Sampling strategies, research methods and operationalisations of concepts may all differ depending on the theoretical approach of the researcher.
- *Sensitivity* – Issues to do with secularisation must be handled carefully by sociologists. How representative, reliable or valid the research data is likely to be considered may well depend on how sensitive the researchers were when carrying out their studies.

Reliability, representativeness and validity

Good sociology (and therefore successful exam answers) means that any question to do with methods or methodology must be answered by referring to the following three concepts.

1. *How reliable is the research data?* This refers to whether the same results could be achieved if the research were repeated at a later point in time,

carried out by different researchers or using different methods and samples. Researching secularisation becomes problematic in this case because of the periods of time involved (we cannot interview people who lived over a hundred years ago); the way statistics are gathered, calculated, recorded, and interpreted differs greatly from one region to another; and the way that the concept of 'religion' culturally and historically changes.

2. *How representative is the data?* This concept is more associated with quantitative methodology rather than qualitative research and refers to the ability for generalisations to be made from the sample used in the study. Weber's research has been challenged on this issue because of the claims he has made about capitalism developing as a result of Protestant religious values. Looking at the highly successful capitalist economy of Japan, where no similar religious tradition exists, his work is criticised for not being representative of all capitalist economies.

3. *How valid is the data?* Despite many textbooks arguing that this concept is only associated with qualitative research, it actually refers to the ability of research data (both quantitative and qualitative) to reflect the true nature, attitudes, behaviour or characteristics of whatever the researcher claims is the case.

Remember at all times to question the methodology in any data that you are reading about using PETS and reliability, representativeness and validity. The following case shows how official statistics can be very deceptive. Most Germans pay a 'church tax' that is collected by the state and used to support many church organisations and the work that they do. While the tax itself is quite small, it does come out of the weekly or monthly pay cheque of German workers. Many Germans who attend church services will, however, not claim they are church attendees in order to avoid the tax. This means that if a sociologist is working from the tax figures in order to investigate church 'popularity', there will be fundamental flaws in the research.

Conclusion

As you can see, the secularisation debate throws up many difficulties for sociologists. Just because fewer people (in some religions) attend religious ceremonies now than in earlier times, may not mean they are less religious. The reverse of this statement also may well be true.

Do packed churches mean a secular society? Functionalist Will Herberg argues that while 40 per cent of adult Americans attend church, they do this to express commitment to the community rather than for 'religious' reasons.

✓ Top Exam Hint

Three evaluations you can use in the exam are:

1. the empirical adequacy of the data on offer, i.e. is there sufficient and reliable data provided by the claim or theory?
2. the comprehensiveness of the theory or claim, i.e. can the theory or claim be used in all situations?
3. the logical cohesiveness of the theory, i.e. does the theory 'make sense' and fully explain the cause or effect of the situation being described?

For consideration

1. Using PETS as a method of evaluation, how might the concept of religiosity be criticised?

2. How might religiosity be evaluated in terms of reliability, validity and representativeness?

Can religion be a source of social control?

What does this mean?

All macro or deterministic theories would argue that to a certain extent we are socially controlled through the various institutions, for example, the family, education, the media and of course religion. By 'social control', sociologists refer to the social processes by which the behaviour of individuals or groups is regulated.

However, while functionalist and New Right theories see elements of this control in a positive light, Marxist and feminist conflict theories are highly critical of the way in which religion determines people's lives.

Three ways religion can socially control people

1. *Ideological control* – the ability to shape ideas, values and attitudes through institutions such as the media, the family, education and religion.
2. *Repressive control* – the ability to force people to carry out actions both by physical and ideological means.
3. *Coercive control* – the ability to make others carry out actions against their will by threat of alternative action or fate.

What questions do sociologists ask when exploring issues of social control?

Gordon Marshall (1997) argues that there are four questions that all theories should address.

1. By whom is control exercised?
2. What techniques of control are used?
3. How far can individuals or groups resist processes of social control?
4. In whose interest does such control work?

By applying each of these questions to any theoretical approach, sociologists can evaluate to what extent religion can be used as a means of social control.

How can theories help?

- *Functionalists* see social control as a vital element to the maintenance of social order. Religion and religious beliefs are a source of control in society because they give us our norms, morals and values (for example, through the Koran and the Bible). People are united by a common set of beliefs which are often linked to national identity. For example, in Britain the Queen is the head of state and head of the Church of England. People have been executed in the past for breaking away from state religions – the act itself was considered treason.

✳ Key Idea

Cohen's concept 'moral panic' can be applied to the way women were 'controlled' during the 16th and 17th century witch hunts. Feminists argue that by accusing women of evil acts members of the church who had vested interests in the progress of medicine were acting in self-interest. Many of these accused women were skilled herbalists whose ability to cure threatened the newly emerging science of medicine. By creating 'moral panic' many religions control and persecute other minority groups.

The execution of Guy Fawkes and the Gu[n]... Plotters. Guy Fawkes led the ... blow up the English ... nd King James I in 1605, ... park a Catholic uprising.

- *Marxists* argue that women and men have created religion and then have allowed it to dominate them. It becomes a form of ideological control that stops people from realising they live in an exploitative society. It controls people by providing rules and examples of how to live life and promises an 'afterlife' to anybody who follows the norms and values contained within that particular religion. As such it stops people from questioning all that may be wrong in any society they live in ('false consciousness').
- *Marxists* also recognise that religion has been imposed by conquering nations in times of empire building (for example, the British and Spanish empires). The conquering nations used religion as a tool to keep people in their places by forbidding certain religions. The British often sent Christian missionaries out to developing countries during the Victorian era. By teaching English, building churches and schools, and establishing trade connections, such missionaries without realising it aided the colonialisation of many of these countries.
- *Feminists* also argue that religion can be seen as a mechanism of social control. The patriarchal structure in most religions (male mullahs, bishops, priests and rabbis) enforces the notion that women should remain in the home and not concentrate on professional careers – despite the fact that they often make up more of the congregation than men do. Many religions are also hypocritical in the punishments they offer men and women for love affairs outside marriage, with women being judged more critically than men (for example, the stoning to death of women in Nigeria).
- We can apply the post-structuralist ideas of Michel Foucault (1982) to the 'controlling' nature of religion. Through 'mechanisms of control' he argues that the human body is under continuous surveillance. By this he means that through institutions such as education, the legal system, medicine and, of course, religion individual identities are constrained. Applied to religion this means that humans will 'internalise' religious rules that dictate the actions of that individual – without the need for outside observers. Foucault refers to such processes as 'hidden forms of control'. In this sense humans police themselves through their beliefs in morals and the promise of a life hereafter.

Conclusion

All the above theories show how religion can be a source of social control; however, not all theories say that it should be. With the exception of functionalist theory the remaining theories are critical of the role that religion plays in controlling members of society.

For consideration

1. To what extent does the institution of religion have more control over you than other institutions such as education or the legal system?

2. How might you argue that new religious movements socially control people?

● **Synoptic Link**

By applying post-structuralist ideas, a synoptic link can be made with religious power and state power. Religion acts as a control mechanism that changes our behaviour as a result of the 'internalisation' of religious rules, e.g. the Ten Commandments. In much the same way, the increased 'surveillance' through CCTV and speed cameras changes our behaviour because we 'internalise' the rules and regulations that these forms of surveillance are set up to govern. In this way both technology and religion act as powerful forms of social control without the need of external supervision.

✓ **Top Exam Hint**

Evaluate post-structuralism by drawing on its similarities to Marx's earlier work where he focused on consciousness and ideology (referred to as 'humanist' Marxism). This idea is similar to the 'internalisation' process that post-structuralists write about – they argue we create ideas such as 'competition' and 'success'. What we then do is 'internalise' these ideas and allow them to shape how we think, act and react to those around us. In both cases, the theories say that we 'constrain' or 'control' ourselves. Mention this in a conclusion and be awarded high evaluation marks.

3.19 | Can religion be a source of social cement?

What does this mean?

This section asks you to examine to what extent religion acts as a unifying force on society, i.e. how (if at all) does it bring about 'social cohesion'? In fact the word religion comes from the Latin *religare* which means 'to bind'. However, as we also know, religion has been used as an excuse for conflict both in the past and sadly in the present. In the exam you must be able to offer a balanced argument that offers evidence on both sides.

How does theory help answer this?

- Functionalists argue that religion forms part of the social 'cement' that binds the structure of society together. The strong moral codes of behaviour that religions offer provide the norms and values of society through religious traditions and ceremonies. We develop a strong sense of social obligation around us through collective worship.
- When social cohesion is threatened, religion can be used to help bind societies in times of danger or insecurity. We know from the work of functionalist Malinowski (1954) that the Trobriand Islanders used religious rituals before fishing in the dangerous open waters but did not do so in calm water.
- We can apply the ideas of Weber by arguing that religion cements groups together by providing meaning to individuals through collective forms of practice and worship. Whether such forms of practice are shared through orthodox religions such as Christianity or Judaism or through 'civic religions' such as 'Americanism' is not important. Weber argued that the values of Calvinism provided the consensus needed for successful capitalist economies to work.

Karma and Dharma

The Hindu religion offers an example of how religion cements society together. The highly stratified (and often criticised) Hindu system referred to as 'caste' means that the social position you are born into often becomes the one you remain in, through marriage, work and childbirth. The religious concepts of Karma and Dharma help explain how such a system remains unified.

Karma ('fate') is the acceptance that whatever existence you have is either reward or punishment for behaviour in a previous life. Dharma ('acceptance') is the belief that the more virtuous you are in this life, the better your next one will be. The belief in these two concepts cements this socially stratified system.

n question: can Judaism and the state of Israel?

How do sociological variables help answer this debate?

If we take three such variables, namely class, gender and sexuality, then the issue of religion cementing society together becomes immediately more complicated.

- Marxists would certainly question to what extent working-class and aristocratic families 'worship' their religions in the same way. Does the church really 'cement' these groups together with the same sets of shared values that some functionalists claim exist?
- Feminists would question to what extent religion cemented men and women together. They would consider issues surrounding abortion, female sexuality and employment within religious organisations and freedom for women generally. Many feminists argue that most religions have been highly oppressive on these issues.
- Finally, to be gay or lesbian is still viewed by many religions as 'deviant'.

It would seem therefore that the social cement does not necessarily stick to all groups all of the time.

Conclusion – thinking like a sociologist

In some cases religion is used as an excuse by governments and people to engage in conflict. Some sociologists argue that we draw our sense of identity from the culture we live in. In some cases, where national identity is concerned, religion is a core part of that culture, for example, being Irish can also mean being Catholic or Protestant or Yugoslavian can also mean being Muslim or Eastern Orthodox Christian. However, sometimes purely looking at religious reasons for conflict is far too simplistic (for example, the Israeli/Palestinian conflict which is as much to do with conflict over land and resources as it is with religious beliefs).

◆ **What, when and why?**

- The idea that religion can be 'social cement' can be challenged by using the example of former Yugoslavia, a country torn apart by civil war during the 1990s, which was composed of Serbian, Croatian, Albanian and Bosnian ethnic groupings. These different religious traditions were a source of social conflict rather than 'cement'. Serb identity is mainly made up of Eastern Orthodox Christianity; Croatian from Roman Catholic Christianity; Albanian from the Islamic tradition; and Bosnian also from the Islamic tradition. Yugoslavia collapsed *partly* as a result of the conflict between these traditions.

- The division of Ireland into two separate jurisdictions took place at the beginning of the 20th century because of the differences between Protestant and especially non-conformist Protestant Irish (often of Scottish descent) largely grouped in the North, and the Roman Catholic majority mainly grouped in the South. This division has caused intense conflict between the two religions in Northern Ireland ever since.

For consideration

1. What examples can you offer to back up the argument that religion does act as social cement?

2. What examples, other than the ones in this section, challenge this view?

How is religion a conservative force?

Has the attack on the New York World Trade Center on 11 September 2001 forced social change or just strengthened and 'conserved' existing prejudices?

What does this mean?

Both functionalists and Marxists agree that religion can be seen as a set of beliefs that offer resistance to change. Both theories accept that religion is a conservative force that attempts to 'conserve' many of the existing structures in society. Certainly there is strong evidence to support the argument that religion helps maintain existing values rather than acting as a force for change.

The functionalist argument

Functionalists argue that religion is a conservative force that holds society together for the good of all. It also acts a force of social integration by reinforcing the norms and values of society.

By applying the ideas of Durkheim we can argue that religion exercises a 'regulation' role, maintaining existing values and providing rules for common behaviour. Durkheimian approaches would see this in traditional societies, for example that of the Australian Aborigines where the totem is a focal point by which people can express collective respect for the values in that society.

In some cases religion can force the individual through coercion or persuasion into the acceptance of particular codes of moral behaviour (the threat of 'fire and eternal damnation' can be very persuasive!). Durkheim argues that once these values and norms have been internalised, habit takes over and these ideas become resistant to change.

The Marxist argument

Marxists argue that religion is only ever a conservative force that seeks to enforce the dominance of one class over another. They argue that religion is part of the ideological superstructure of any society and part of its purpose is to 'mystify' the real nature of the exploitative relationship between the classes.

As a conservative force we can see how the church plays its part in this process when we look at how Church of England schools in the 19th century taught children from extremely poor backgrounds. At that time most of the clergy were members of the middle classes who helped reproduce the idea of a hierarchical social order by teaching respect and obedience to those 'above' them.

The feminist argument

Many feminists would also agree that religion acts as a force for conservatism in that it helps conserve the patriarchal systems found in many societies. The persecution of witches; the refusal of many religions to accept women as religious leaders; religious perceptions of the role of women within the family; and in some cases the particular forms of dress and segregation in some ceremonies – all of these point to a particular type of conservatism that wishes to conserve the subservient role of women that many religions endorse.

Conclusion

The idea that religion is a conservative force has been challenged. In Weber's *Protestant Ethic and the Spirit of Capitalism* (1930), he argued that religion could act as a force for social change and that such ideas can change the course of history. Yinger (1970) also argues that *'religion cannot be understood simply as a force that blocks or retards change'*; in other words, religion can conserve social stability or can be seen to challenge it.

One example of Weber's force for change is the way that some churches in other parts of the world have helped educate children to challenge many of the ideas pushed forward by the state, for example, the role of Catholic schools in South Africa in contesting the apartheid system there.

A second example is that of liberation theology (see also Section 3.10). This is a Latin American movement within the Roman Catholic Church where progressive clergy (especially but not exclusively Jesuits) have become aligned with progressive and socialist movements, for example, in Nicaragua where a Roman Catholic priest was a member of the revolutionary socialist Sandinista government.

In South Africa, between 1978 and 1985, Archbishop Tutu played a key role in the way Anglican and other Christian churches were involved, alongside communist and other radical groupings aligned to the African National Congress, in the liberation struggle against apartheid.

✓ Top Exam Hints

- Evaluate the argument that religion is a conservative force by criticising it. Offer examples to show that this is not the case and that, in fact, religion can be seen as a force for change. Apart from those examples offered in this spread you can also use: Martin Luther King; Gandhi; the early Christians, and currently al-Qaeda.

- While the big changes described here brought about by religion challenge the argument that religion is a force of conservatism, Marxists would be critical of this. They argue that although religion might bring change in some countries, this is not significant compared to the economic shifts from one historic period to another, e.g. the huge economic change that took place as a result of the change from feudalism to capitalism.

For consideration

1. Should religion act as a conservative force in society?

2. Do 'the ends justify the means' where religious conflict is concerned?

How might secularisation be a feature of the postmodern world?

What does this mean?

By 'modernity' most sociologists refer to the period of the 18th, 19th and early 20th centuries – a period after the so-called Enlightenment which was characterised by industrialisation and the widespread belief that science contained the answers to some of the 'big' questions. Such questions included 'Why are we here?'; 'What is the purpose of human existence?'; or 'Can scientific theory (or any other type of theory) lead to an improvement in the human condition?' (See also Section 3.16.)

Towards the end of the 20th century a number of writers have challenged many of the assumptions held during the period of modernity. Postmodernists writers like Jacques Derrida (1991), Michel Foucault and Jacques Lacan (1977) have inspired many to believe that we are in another type of world altogether – a 'postmodern' world where none of the accepted theories or 'truths' or 'narratives' can be relied on. One really big narrative (postmodernists call these 'metanarratives') is that of religion.

What claims do postmodernists make?

- According to postmodernists the idea that science is a force for liberation is untrue. The mass extermination of Jews in the gas chambers, chemical warfare and increasing health scares prove that scientific theory has not 'liberated' the human condition.
- Equally, no one theory, story or set of ideas can offer a reliable explanation for how the world (or 'afterworld') is.
- In a world where consumerism becomes much more important than production, what we consume becomes increasingly a part of our identity.
- Old explanations about identity – such as those built around class – are meaningless in a world where we can 'pic'n'mix' clothes, music, food and even religion.
- Where once we believed in purpose and a sense of why we are here, postmodernists argue that we have become 'de-centred', i.e. a product of discourses, religious or otherwise.
- In what some postmodernists argue is '**hyperreality**', the media has such a powerful influence on all our lives that fashions, beliefs, debates and ideas come and go. In fact, we can no longer really distinguish between media reality and fiction.

A pluralisation of lifeworlds

In pre-industrial societies, religion tended to provide one set of ideas that

Ali Mosque in Cairo, Egypt.
does the growth in Islam as
gion challenge postmodern
isation?

explained the universe – a set of core beliefs centred around a particular religion. Referred to as lifeworld by interactionist Berger (1990), this became 'lifeworlds' during the period of industrialisation as people increasingly became involved in a number of conflicting 'core beliefs', for example, family values, work-place values, capitalistic values, religious and scientific values. This is referred to by Berger as a 'pluralisation of lifeworlds'.

Conclusion

- The dissatisfaction that many people are increasingly feeling towards so-called 'expert' opinion is having its effect on religions. Decreasing church attendance figures are evidence of this. People are becoming 'relativist' in their religious views, i.e. adopting the position that one claim may be as valid as another. This means that while somebody may call themselves Christian or Jew, they may also seek advice from astrological sources, medication from complementary medical practitioners or Chinese feng shui.
- Postmodernist claims that the media is increasingly significant in our lives make sense when we read stories such as the involvement of priests in the US in child-sex scandals, which has the effect of pushing people away and pulling them to other sources of religion. This 'push-pull' effect is met by the wide variety of religions that people can pic'n'mix' from. The growth in new religious movements is evidence for the diversity that postmodernists write about.
- Churches are trying to respond to decreasing numbers by marketing themselves in the community, for example, hiring out church halls for public events; providing music at church ceremonies; and putting on local community events such as raffles and 'bring 'n'buys'. Meeting the needs of the consumer is yet more evidence that identity is no longer based on religion, class or any of the other significant variables – but rather, as postmodernists claim, the wishes and desires of a hungry consumer.

66 99 Key Definition

Hyperreality means being more 'real' than real.

✓ Top Exam Hint

When postmodernists claim diversity, choice and decreasing church numbers, point out that this depends on historical, cultural and regional circumstances. Where wars are being fought in the name of religion (e.g. Ireland, Israel and India), be highly critical of 'academic' explanations not taking into account the circumstances at the local level. Remember Weber's 'theodicy of non privilege' argues that people experiencing poverty and hardship will have a different 'take' on what their religion means to them.

For consideration

1. To what extent do you believe that postmodernists are guilty of over-generalisation?

2. If we are, as postmodernsits claim, so dominated by the media, how do you explain the diversity of ideas, images and identities that exist?

What is the future of religion according to sociology?

What does this mean?

First, to what extent can sociologists ask such a question based on their research and on the work of some of the writers looked at in this section? Second, what lessons can we learn (if any) and what predictions can be made? Most sophisticated conclusions will probably make reference to these issues.

The danger of predictions

There are dangers for sociologists when attempting to predict future events based on past events. It was Karl Popper who argued that so-called scientific claims about future events cannot be scientific if they are not open to being disproved (of course you may wish to debate about whether sociology should be considered 'scientific' in the first place).

Certainly, if, and only if, postmodernists are correct, there is widespread disillusionment with many traditional religions that offer so-called 'truths'. In addition to this, many interpretive sociologists would argue that religion along with science and all other 'disciplines' are all 'social constructions' and therefore religious claims are really just reflections on social experience.

Where does that leave sociologists?

- Science and education have not stopped the human search for some of the 'big' questions. The discipline of philosophy shows us that human beings never stop asking: 'Why are we here?'; 'Is there an afterlife?'; or 'Is there a God'? Religions in different ways provide possible answers to these questions and it is difficult to imagine human beings stopping their search for such answers.
- Sociology cannot answer these questions above. Sociology cannot carry out objective tests to see if 'God' exists. Neither sociology nor the natural sciences can explain the purpose of life. Sociology can also not offer any proof of a life after death despite the claims made by many religions that this is the case. While many religions imply a moral superiority it is not the job of sociology to determine what is or what is not morally acceptable.
- While sociology or any other discipline fails to come up with the answers to such questions, it seems likely that in future religions will grow, shrink, change form and multiply in much the same way as this chapter has attempted to portray. Sociology in the meantime will watch, analyse, discuss and debate all issues that concern power, culture and identity that go hand-in-hand with all the debates covered in this chapter.

Karl Popper, considered one of the greatest philosophers of science of the 20th century.

☞ Who is this person?

Karl Popper (1902–1994) was an Austrian philosopher who worked for most of his life at the London School of Economics. Professor of logic and scientific method, he was knighted in 1965. His contributions to the philosophy of science are enormous and you will probably study his work in your second year of sociology. For Popper, the job of the social scientist was to attempt to falsify concepts and theories rather than to prove them correct. Popper argued that for theory to be taken seriously then it must be open to falsification. Therefore any theory that makes predictions about the future (and therefore is not open to falsification) cannot be held to be scientific.

Are we moving towards a secular world?

The secularisation debate looked at in this chapter provides many sociologists with enough evidence to show that the belief in religion is far from over. While many of the processes of industrialisation have been said to lead to secularisation, religion is still popular today.

Associated with the secularisation debate is the notion that we are moving within a period described as 'religious pluralism', i.e. the development of a culture characterised by widespread diversity of religious expressions. What sociologists can do is to continuously examine to what extent this is the case and help politicians create an environment that really is multicultural.

In changing times

One popular sociological issue, globalisation, must be taken into consideration when talking about any future direction for the religions. However we choose to define globalisation, we have to accept that many societies across the world are becoming increasingly interconnected. Economic, political, technological or cultural connections must have an impact on any discussion that takes place over the future of religion.

Conclusion

This chapter has examined the way in which religion can act as both a conservative force and a force for change. For functionalists, religion 'cements' individuals together through dominant norms and values within a meritocracy. Both feminists and Marxists challenge the meritocratic idea arguing that religion helps maintain exploitative societies. Max Weber has argued that religion can act as a 'motor' of social change under specific circumstances. Postmodernists argue that the variety of different belief systems on offer is just evidence of the postmodern society they claim we all inhabit.

There have been many examples of all these ideas and sociologists will continue to examine what religion does and how it does it in the future – and to whom. However, what religion also does for some in troubled times is to offer support. Perhaps even sociologists need to remember that in their many theoretical discussions either praising or damning the role religion plays in human interaction.

● **Synoptic Link**

By considering the future of religions in general, many synoptic links can be made with stratification. By taking class, gender, and ethnicity and placing a sentence in your conclusion about possible future developments, the examiners will recognise that you are interpreting, applying and evaluating concepts in a sophisticated fashion. Always remember to start your sentence with: 'Synoptically speaking…'

For consideration

1. Do you consider the history of religion to have been one that progresses in a historically straight line or are the new religious movements really just different versions of earlier religions?

2. What kind of developments can you predict for women in the next twenty years within the mainstream religions?

3.23 How can we make religion synoptic?

Why is synopticity important for religion?

Examiners reward students who can combine one area of sociology with another when discussing a particular sociological issue. Religion provides an ideal topic to use when revising your synoptic unit. By using the synoptic concept of 'power' you can use religion to show that it might be a source of 'power' for some groups and not others.

How does religion link to issues of culture?

By 'culture' sociologists mean the set of shared values, norms and beliefs of a society or group of people. The word also refers to the shared meanings and symbols, such as language, which people use to make sense of the world they live in. Students can talk about a 'dominant culture' to refer to the main culture in a society whose norms and values are seen to be the most powerful and generally accepted.

How does religion link to issues of identity?

Identity itself is an enormously complex term and yet most social scientists will agree that the constraints, challenges and opportunities you face vary depending on how 'empowered' or 'disempowered' that identity is. Religion can play a major part in this process. Think about the various identities that can be said to exist, such as those identified with class, gender, age, ethnicity and sexuality. It is easy to discuss how different religions encourage or discourage certain types of behaviour associated with these identities and, in some cases, the identity itself (usually those based around homosexuality).

How does religion link to issues of inequality?

Traditional Marxists argue that the economic infrastructure shapes the culture of all classes regardless of gender, age, or race. From this viewpoint alone, you can argue how religion itself reflects the dominant ideas of any society, i.e. the ideas of the ruling class. Experiencing religion from poverty rather than from a position of wealth will drastically affect your religious views. These ideas were enhanced by Max Weber when he talked about 'theodicies of disprivilege' (see Section 3.14). Remember too that just believing in a certain religion may well place you in a disempowered position in society (for example, think about the Jews in Nazi Germany and the Palestinian Arabs in Israel today).

How does religion link to issues of deviance?

A 'deviant' is somebody who 'deviates' from the norms and values associated with a particular culture. Any one dominant culture is the culture whose norms

66 99 Key Definition

By using the phrase '**cultural transmission**' you can refer to how one culture can be *transmitted* or 'passed on' from one generation to the next. This can happen via institutions such as religion. Remember that religion plays a significant role not only in many families in the UK but also through the school system (remember that many schools have strong religious ties). Norms and values that existed in one country or one generationcan be transmitted from country to country or generation to generation via the many customs associated with most religions.

and values are seen to be the most powerful and generally accepted. Deviance can be looked at from a post-structuralist perspective by arguing that 'elite' discourses are sometimes used as the official definitions of crime and deviance – thereby punishing those so defined. In many societies, religious leaders hold significant power in defining what is considered to be either criminal or deviant (for example, the burning of witches in this country and the stoning of women in Nigeria).

How does religion link to issues of stratification and differentiation?

However you discuss stratification, whether by class, gender, sexuality, ethnicity or nation, it can be linked to issues surrounding religion. All you have to do is to be able to identify which theory best associates one of the above variables with religion. For example, you might wish to use Marxism and discuss how religion and class are intertwined or you could use feminism to focus on the way in which many religions stratify women in society. Do not forget, however, to choose another theory to evaluate the one you have started with (for example, how might functionalists criticise the Marxist explanation about religion and class?).

Key points to remember

- Religion can be used to make connections with any area of the sociology syllabus.
- When talking about how society is stratified, remember that religion, like many other institutions, plays a significant role in this process.
- You are reminded that both 'crime' and 'deviance' are social constructions rather than 'essential categories'. This allows you to question 'in whose interests somebody is defined as either criminal or deviant' and why different religions might have an interest in playing a part in the constructing process.

☀ Key Idea

In many societies religion and culture go hand in hand. Feminists might argue that any dominant culture could be 'patriarchal' and that this is reflected in the religious values that exist within that culture; Marxists might argue that any culture could be 'capitalist' and that as an institution religion reflects the infrastructure to which it is attached; sociologists writing about race could argue that the dominant culture in the western world represents white, middle-class values and therefore how followers of Islam might be perceived in such cultures. Whatever dominant culture you care to discuss, this immediately allows you to talk about how some will be 'empowered' or 'disempowered' depending on who possesses more or less of the dominant culture.

✐ Coursework Suggestion

Students often have problems in deciding how they can analyse the data they produce when carrying out primary research. One way to provide an analytical framework is to say openly that you will take synoptic concepts and use these as *sensitising* concepts when interpreting your data. So, for example, if you have produced interview data why not use four to five synoptic concepts as the focus point for your analysis. Some key synoptic concepts are: socialisation, power, ideology, anomie, alienation, culture and social control. Why not create headings from four to five of the above concepts and then focus on your interview data in light of those concepts – this would provide a good analytical framework for your results chapter.

Pushing your grades up higher

What do I need to do to get a good grade?

1. Employing a historical perspective when writing about other sociologists will push your grades up: for example, if you talk about Malinowski's research, identify it as being carried out in the 1950s.

2. Show that you are aware of where (geographically) some of these theories and theorists are coming from: for example, if you talk about Talcott Parsons, refer to him as 'The American structural functionalist …'

3. Mention the methodology of the case study you are referring to and the type of data it produced, i.e. 'adopting positivist methodology, she …' or 'the qualitative data he produced …'

4. Your paragraphs (and if possible your sentences) must start with evaluative key words (for example, 'Following on from this …' or 'In contrast to this …' or 'From this we can see that …').

5. Remember always to back up whatever point you are making with evidence. That evidence must be in the form of a case study by a named sociologist.

6. You will always be given credit for knowledge of contemporary issues that you can link to the sociology of religion. That means you must in the final weeks before the exam be listening to/watching the news and buying a broadsheet newspaper (for example, *The Times*) on a weekly basis.

7. When you see the word 'contribution' in the exam, this can be both positive and negative. You will be rewarded for commenting on the positive contributions that Marxists have brought but you also need to be able to offer negative ones, i.e. what do Marxists not focus on (for example, 'in the sociology of religion, Marxist contributions tend to be deterministic whereas interpretive sociologists argue from a more individualist perspective …')

8. Always remember to use the concepts 'validity', 'reliability' and 'representativeness' when discussing the work of other sociologists. By applying these terms you will show the examiners that you are extremely critical.

9. Learn to use the language of sociology; if used properly it is not jargon but rather it shows that you know what you are talking about. Make sure that you know and understand terms such as: agent, structure, determinism, validity, reliability, representativeness, operationalisation and methodological pluralism. Use the terms frequently in your written work. If you are using the terms appropriately it will show that you have developed a good understanding of sociology.

10. Consult your specification carefully. Theory and methods is an 'integral element' of your specification. This means that it is relevant to all the topic areas you study. Use every opportunity to show your theoretical and methodological understanding. It demonstrates that you are thinking like a sociologist.

Key points to remember

- You must answer every question from a theoretical perspective if you are chasing the highest grades.
- Theory is not enough. You must have evidence in the form of the findings that other sociologists have written about.
- Do not forget to use 'sophisticated' language when criticising the theory, case study or concept. Make sure you start those sentences or paragraphs with those key evaluative phrases.

Frequently asked questions

Q. Why does the sociology of religion focus mainly on Christianity?

A. The word 'ethnocentric' means analysing other societies in terms of one's own cultural assumption or bias. The classical sociologists who explored the sociology of religion tended to come from countries where Christianity was the mainstream religion. Although sociologists throughout much of the 20th century tried to avoid such claims, it is only relatively recently that textbooks (with a lot of help from postmodernist theorists and theorists of new social movements) have recognised the enormous diversity of religions.

Q. Do the classical sociologists help me understand contemporary religion?

A. Yes! To understand fully the theories used by sociologists today we have to understand the ideas that these theories have developed from or, in some cases, challenge. Theories, like fashion accessories, can be popular, become dated, be recreated or re-emerge albeit in a sometimes more refined form. The classical sociologists wrote about industrial society at a time of immense social, political and economic change. Many commentators argue today that, with all the varieties of globalisation processes that exist, huge changes are once again taking place. It is therefore no surprise to see that classical theory has some of the answers to the questions that sociologists pose.

Q. Do I need to know all the variety of different religions to answer well in the exam?

A. No. In this exam you are not being tested on your knowledge of religion. You are, however, being asked to assess the role that such an institution has in the many socialisation processes that exist. In order to do that successfully you need to be able to show that 'religion' is an extremely widely-contested concept and therefore it will help to be able to draw on some examples from the variety of religions that exist.

Chapter 4

Theory, methods and methodology

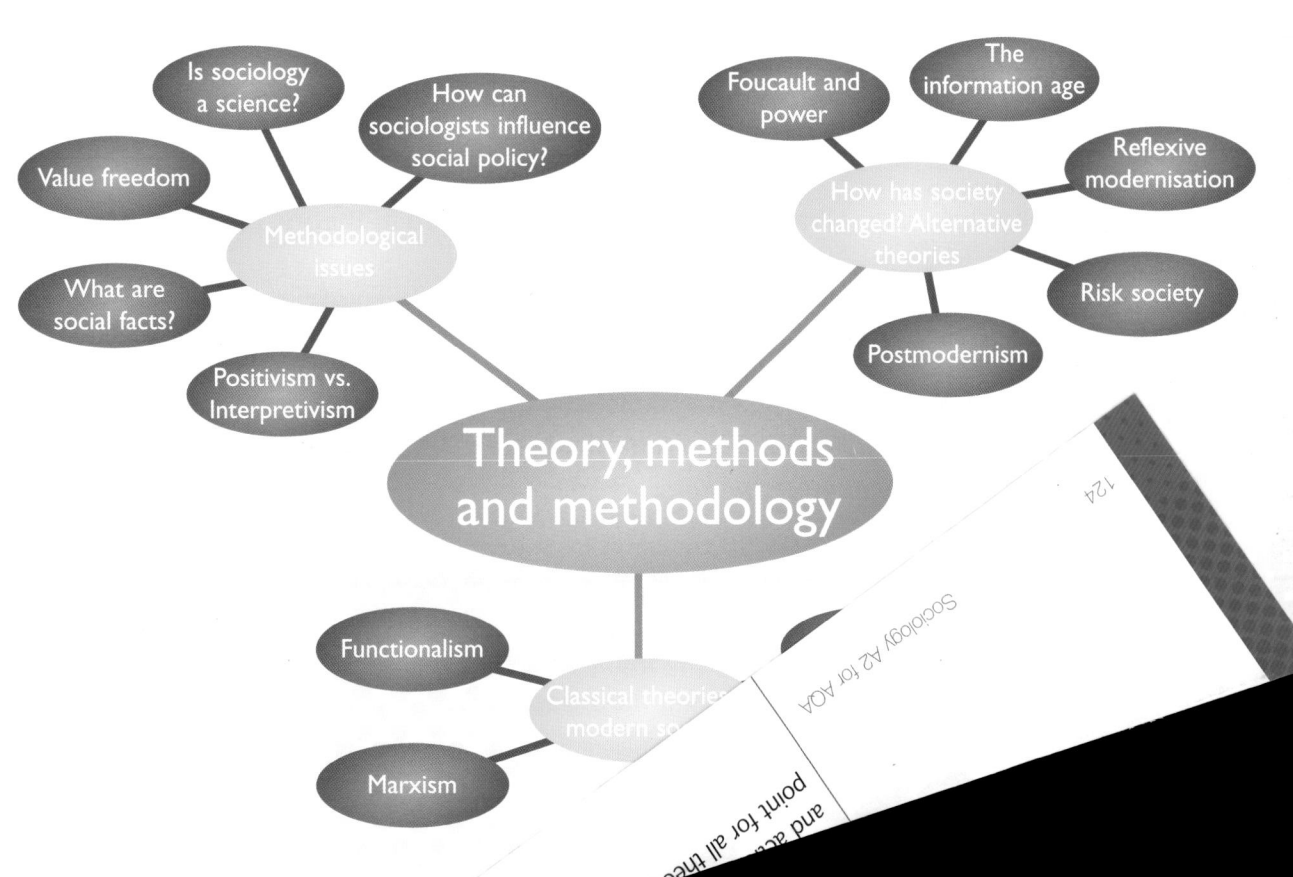

 CD-ROM

4.1 Key issues in theory, methods and methodology

What are the important issues in theory, methods and methodology?

The aim of sociology is to produce valid explanations and descriptions of social processes and phenomena. This means that researchers have to decide what questions to ask, what evidence to gather, and how to interpret the results. In making these choices, researchers have to make assumptions about the nature of the thing they are trying to research and the best way to study it. Two key issues in theory, **methods** and **methodology** are therefore as follows.

- What is the nature of society? Sociologists will be influenced by one or more theories of society. Whichever theory they choose will influence what they decide to research and the questions they ask. It can also, of course, mean that they rule out some issues or questions as being unimportant.
- How do we best learn about society? Sociologists have the choice of two different approaches on this issue. They may take a positivist view and believe that they can study society scientifically, or they make take an interpretive view and believe that more qualitative methods are more appropriate to studying people and society.

The focus of this chapter is on **sociological theories** and methodology as opposed to sociological research methods, which have been dealt with in *Heinemann Sociology AS for AQA*.

Why are sociologists interested in theory, methods and methodology?

Sociologists are interested in theory, methods and methodology because these issues have a tremendous influence on how they go about doing research. There are several key questions which always arise when theory, methods and methodology are considered.

- Has the sociologists' choice of research topic been influenced in some way by their theoretical view of the nature of society? Has the theoretical approach taken led to any biases?
- Has the research methodology influenced the findings? Would an alternative methodology reveal a different picture or give a different answer?

What are the key ideas we can use to think about theory, methods and methodology?

There are many different theories and methods and two approaches to methodology. This leads to a variety of debates between the competing viewpoints. There are two basic types of sociological theory: structural theories [and ac]tion theories. There are other theories but these two are the starting [point of theo]rising in sociology.

- Structural theories, such as Marxism and functionalism, claim that all social behaviour is shaped by social structures.
- Action based theories, such as interactionism, argue that in fact people are more creative (have agency) and have more freedom than structural theories assume.

In terms of methodological approaches, sociologists will take one of two approaches. They will either adopt a positivist approach, which mainly involves using quantitative methods, or they will take an interpretive approach using mainly qualitative methods.

What does the exam board say about theory, methods and methodology?

Although many students do not take an exam on theory and methods, this topic is still very important for several reasons.

- You need a deep understanding of theory, methods and methodology to evaluate sociological research findings thoroughly and critically.
- Throughout your work you are expected to be able to demonstrate an awareness of theoretical debates in sociology.
- You will need to demonstrate that you understand the connections between sociological thought, methods of enquiry, and the various topic areas that you have studied. The key area where you can do this is in the synoptic paper (Unit 6, either Crime and deviance or Stratification and differentiation). Section 4.2 discusses this in some detail and throughout the chapter suggestions will be made as to how you can make relevant links.
- If you complete a piece of coursework, it will be vital that you demonstrate a good understanding of theory, methods and methodology throughout your work.

What are the key problems in theory, methods and methodology?

The key problems in theory, methods and methodology are as follows.

- Is society best seen in terms of structural theories or action theories?
- What is the best way to study society? Should we take a positivist or an intepretivist approach?
- Can we study society without being biased by our own theoretical and methodological viewpoints, and our experiences and social background?

Key points to remember

- There are two basic types of methodologies, and these shape the findings sociologists generate.
- There are two key approaches in sociological theory which make different assumptions about society, and these shape the questions which sociologists ask.
- In sociology empirical findings on their own are not sufficient because findings always have to be interpreted. This can only be done by looking at them in a theoretical perspective. Theory and methods always go together in sociology.

✳ Key Idea

The debate between structural and action theories is a key debate in sociology. Structural theories take the view that our actions are strongly shaped and influenced by society. Action theories suggest that we have much more control over our own destiny than this implies. According to action theories, people have agency, which simply means the ability to act.

How do theory and methods link to the AS course?

✳ **Key Idea**

The word **synoptic** means to summarise or form an overview. It is part of the nature of an overview or summary that it shows the links between different ideas or events. This is exactly what synopticity in sociology should do. In sociology you cannot fully understand topics such as Families and households or Crime and deviance, unless you also have a good understanding of theory and method, so you will have to use your knowledge synoptically, and show how it illuminates our understanding of a particular topic area.

Why are links to AS important for sociology?

At A2 level your examination in Unit 6 (where you will study either 'Crime and deviance' or 'Stratification') will involve **synoptic** questions. The word synoptic simply means that you will be asked to make links to the topics you studied for AS sociology, such as 'Families and households', 'Education', 'Media', 'Health', 'Work and leisure', or 'Wealth, poverty and welfare'.

However, you will also have to demonstrate your understanding of the links between the topics you have studied in Unit 6 for A2 and sociological theory and sociological research methods.

- One question will ask you to make links between either 'Crime and deviance' or 'Stratification', depending on which topic you do for A2, and your knowledge of sociological theories.
- Another question will require you to make links between the Unit 6 A2 topic you have studied and your knowledge of sociological research methods.

Examine your specification carefully and you will see that theory and method are described as *'integral elements'* of the course. This means that in order to develop a good understanding of sociology you need to have a good knowledge of theory and method. This is essential for the deeper understanding that is expected at A2 level.

Why are theory and method so important in sociology?

Of course these are sound practical reasons why you need to have a good knowledge and understanding of theories and methods, but these don't explain why these topics are considered to be so important by the examiners in the first place. There are several reasons why theory and methods are so important in sociology.

- If sociological research is to be considered authoritative and rigorous it must be based on sound methodology that reveals an accurate picture of society.
- However, there are debates about which methods and methodological approaches are most adequate, and even about whether it is possible to do any meaningful social research. If you are going to be able to evaluate research findings adequately, you must have a good knowledge of these debates.
- Sociologists also need to use theories in order to make sense of research findings. Theories help us to see the connections between different parts of society, and to identify what causes social processes. Theories also provoke

us into asking more and different questions about the nature of society and how it works.

What links can be made to theory and method?

The importance of theory and method can be seen in all the topics which you have studied at AS level.

- In the topic of 'Families and households' there are key issues about operationalisation and questionnaire methodology in the study of conjugal roles, for example Young and Willmott.
- In the education topic, Willis' *Learning to Labour* has met with criticism because not only was the study small scale and unrepresentative, but it also presents a good example of 'interviewer' or 'Hawthorne' effect.
- In 'Wealth, poverty and welfare', the measurement of poverty involves researchers having to define what they mean by this concept. One of the key issues raised is whether it is possible to do this without making a value-judgement.

Theoretical issues also abound in AS topics. In 'Families and households', the issue of who has most power and who most benefits from family organisation, which is a key theoretical debate, runs through the whole topic. 'Education' raises interesting questions about structure and action in the context of examining explanations of educational attainment. In both topics there is also a continual theoretical question being raised about the construction of identity. How are gender identities constructed? Sociologists cannot avoid discussing the structure/action debate in trying to answer questions like this.

This should serve to underline the point that the better your knowledge of theory and method, the better your understanding of sociology as a whole, and the better your ability to evaluate sociological arguments in detail.

Key points to remember

- You will be tested on your knowledge and understanding of theory and methods by the synoptic questions in Unit 6.
- A good understanding of theory and methods is vital in order to demonstrate a deeper understanding of sociology
- The methods sociologists use are important because they shape the sort of information we gather and the theories are important because they shape the way we interpret the information and make sense of it.

∞ Methods Link

In the examples discussed here you can see how some debates in topic areas such as 'Families and households', 'Education' and 'Wealth, poverty and welfare', are really methodological debates. How concepts are operationalised, for example, is a key issue. How sociologists operationalise particular concepts will depend a great deal on the theoretical and methodological perspective they take. The debates on conjugal roles (see *Sociology AS Chapter 3, 3.3 and 3.14*) are a good example of this.

∞ Classic Study

The Hawthorne experiment was conducted by American academic, Elton Mayo (1975, originally 1933), in the GEC Hawthorne factory. Mayo created an 'experimental group' among the workers, whose working conditions were regularly changed, in order to see which working conditions maximised production. Other workers acted as a control group and worked under normal conditions. The study showed that whatever treatments the experimental group were given their production increased. It was concluded that being observed changes people's behaviour. This shows the difficulties that researchers face in observing natural behaviour, since the researcher's presence may change the behaviour of the research subjects.

✓ Top Exam Hint

Read through the notes you made while studying AS Sociology. Use a highlighter to mark up important references to theory and methods. Look out for key theoretical debates, summaries of the most important theories, and examples of studies where methodological issues arise.

Why do we need to know about theory and methods?

Why do sociologists need to use methods?

Sociology has to use rigorous research methods because it aims to find out the truth about social life and behaviour. There are critics of sociology who try to argue that sociology is simply common sense and that society does not need people called 'sociologists' to tell them what everybody already knows. There are several serious problems with such arguments.

- Once it is examined carefully, it seems that 'common sense' varies tremendously between different people and between different places, times and cultures. If it really was 'common' then this would not happen.
- Common sense gives us no criteria for solving disputes between these differing answers and explanations. Whose common sense is the correct common sense?
- There seems nothing to stop common sense being a veil for bias and prejudice.
- We cannot generalise from our own experience of social life as it may not be typical. This means we cannot assume that our own culture, our own time, or our own social background provides us with a picture of what is typical behaviour.

Since its beginnings in the 19th century, sociologists have argued that there is a way to gather valid knowledge of society and social processes. That is by the rigorous use of sociological research methods. These methods may be quantitative or qualitative, and they enable evidence to be gathered systematically. Researchers and the public can then examine evidence, evaluate it, and reach conclusions. If there are disputes, then it is possible to have a reasoned debate about what the evidence is, how it was collected, and how it should be evaluated. This does not mean that debate is always easily concluded, but it does mean that there are at least some clear criteria or standards by which judgements can be made, and against which evidence can be assessed. The same cannot be said for the idea of 'common sense'.

Why do sociologists need to use theories?

If sociologists can develop and use rigorous research methods, perhaps a bit like scientists, it should then simply be a question of collecting the evidence and then working out the results. The trouble is that the results of any sort of research always have to be interpreted. Many sociologists would agree with the view that 'the facts never speak for themselves'. Those who believe that the facts do speak for themselves are called empiricists. The word **empirical** simply means that something is known through the evidence of our senses. In

66 99 Key Definition

Empirical evidence is gained through observation or experiment. Empirical knowledge is based on experience and is something we know because we have seen it, rather than being just a theoretical idea we might have of something.

☀ Key Idea

Empiricism is an example of a theory of knowledge, or what sociologists often call an epistemology. Empiricism is an old theory of knowledge, but it became particularly important in the 18th century. It is associated with the development of ̶science and for a long time was seen as a ̶ful way of gaining knowledge. ̶ ̶tly sociologists and ̶ ̶ave concentrated on the ̶ ̶theory.

other words, we have to be able to see the evidence in some way, for example by looking at tables of statistics, reading interview data, or by having observed it. Sociologists make several criticisms of empiricism.

- It assumes that our senses are accurate.
- It neglects the fact that we may be biased in some way.
- It ignores the role of values and the idea that we may have reasons for selecting some evidence or seeing some evidence as more important.

Despite these criticisms or weaknesses of empiricism, sociologists still need to do empirical research and gather data. However, these weaknesses do serve to remind sociologists that the evidence which they gather always has to be interpreted. A mass of evidence has to be made sense of in some way, and theories enable sociologists to do this.

Theory is therefore used in sociology to:

- identify which findings may be significant
- explain the relationships between different parts of society
- develop **hypotheses** and models about what causes certain social processes or phenomena to occur
- raise questions for research.

Key points to remember

- We cannot learn about society simply by generalising from our own experience and our own society.
- Sociologists have to use rigorous and systematic research methods.
- Research findings can only be understood by using theory to help us identify the connections between different aspects of society and the causes of social processes.

✓ Top Exam Hint

You can use the ideas in this section to evaluate all sociological studies. Always try to identify the theoretical and methodological approaches which a study is based on. Also remember to apply concepts such as reliability, representativeness, validity, and operationalisation. How was a piece of research conducted? What methodological and theoretical assumptions did the researcher make?

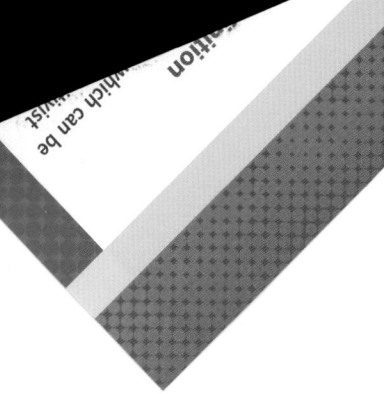

How do sociologists think about society?

What does this mean?

What this means is that all sociologists will have different opinions and views about the basic nature of society – about what it is, how it works, and how it is best understood. In sociology this fact means that there are different approaches to methodology and theoretical perspectives.

What is methodology?

When sociologists use the term 'methods' they are referring to the different research methods that can be used, such as questionnaires or interviews. Methodology on the other hand refers to the assumptions being made about the nature of society and human beings by different approaches to sociological research. There are two key approaches, **positivism** and **interpretivism**.

- **Positivists** believe that sociology can be a science and that sociology should therefore involve the use of *quantitative data* and methods similar to those used by scientists. Positivists believe that the task of sociology is to uncover the laws which govern social behaviour.
- **Interpretivists** believe that it is more appropriate to use *qualitative data* and methods, such as interviews and observation, to study society. This is because they believe that people are more complex than other aspects of nature (such as atoms and chemicals). The key thing that makes people different is that they are reflective and have reasons for acting they way they do. The job of sociology is to find out these reasons. This, the interpretivists argue, is much more easily done by using qualitative research methods.
- These two methodologies reflect two very different ways of studying sociology. Positivists adopt a *macro* approach. They suggest that the best way to understand how society works is as a system. Interpretivists, on the other hand, recommend a *micro* approach. For them society can only be understood by examining social relationships on a smaller scale.

In addition to these differences, sociologists also differ in their views about what society actually is. They have very different perspectives.

What are theoretical perspectives?

Sociologists, just like other people, have different views about what the nature of society is – about what society is like. To be sociological, though, involves trying to think systematically and critically about these views. It also involves trying to create theoretical models of society which can explain social events and processes. It also means testing these theories by critical examination and supporting them with empirical evidence. The first sociological perspectives to be developed when the subject was founded in the 19th century are known as

66 99 Key Definitions

- **Positivism** is the theory that society can and should be studied like a science. Positivists believe that sociologists should be able to reveal the laws which govern social behaviour.

- **Interpretivism** is the theory that society cannot be studied using scientific methods. Sociology has to study the meaning which behaviour has for people in order to make sense of society.

☀ Key Idea
Primary and Secondary Data

Primary data refers to data that has been gathered by a researcher for the purposes of their research. This will therefore be first-hand evidence, which is not possessed by any other researcher. So if a researcher does a questionnaire the data gathered is primary data.

Secondary data is information which has been previously collected by another researcher or person for other purposes. So sociologists using official statistics are using secondary data.

the 'classical theories'; they include theories such as Marxism, functionalism, and symbolic interactionism. More recently other perspectives have developed as society has changed, such as feminism and postmodernism.

What is the relationship between theory and method?

In sociology, theories and methods are always closely related. For example, positivists, who take a macro approach to society, tend to use quantitative methods. This methodological approach though tends to be associated with structural theories, such as functionalism or Marxism. The link here is that structural theories tend to see society as consisting of a system, and generally work on the assumption that the task of sociology is to discover how these structures shape our lives.

Interpretivists, taking a micro perspective, tend to use qualitative methods. This methodological approach takes the view that quantitative methods are not the most appropriate way to study society since people have reasons for acting as they do. Interpretivists therefore believe that the job of sociology is to explain how society is created through our own actions. Interpretivists believe that society is socially constructed. This methodological approach is associated with the sociological perspective of interactionism.

These links are important because the different methodologies and theories sociologists use involve key assumptions about what society is like and the best way of studying it. If we understand what these assumptions are, we will be in a better position to assess the validity of sociological research.

Conclusion

Three points to bear in mind for evaluating theories and methods are:

1. that sociologists may be influenced in their methodological and theoretical approaches by their own class, race, gender, age, and culture
2. that researchers do not have to adopt one theory or method, or another; sometimes it may be useful to combine methods
3. if sociologists make their theoretical and methodological assumptions clear it is easier for others to evaluate their research findings.

∞ Classic Study

Durkheim's study on suicide is a classic example of a positivist approach to sociology and claims to show how social structures influence our individual lives. Durkheim used official statistics (quantitative data) to reveal the social structures causing suicide. He argued that the level of social integration (a structure) was the causal factor influencing suicide rates in different societies. Studying social processes by comparing different societies is referred to as the comparative method. Durkheim's study of suicide is discussed in greater detail in Section 4.18.

✳ Key Idea

Most sociologists tend to adopt an approach which leans either towards a macro or a micro approach. However, some sociologists do try to combine both approaches by triangulating methods. Triangulation simply means using both qualitative and quantitative methods. Sociologists using this approach believe it is necessary to look at macro and micro level aspects of society in order to gain a valid picture and to see how the two levels of social reality are connected.

For consideration

1. Is sociology a less valuable subject because there is no agreement about how to study society?

2. Do you agree with interpretivists that quantitative methods are less appropriate to the study of human society?

What is modern society?

Scientific or industrial methods of production have been one of the key characteristics of modern society.

What does this mean?

The term 'modern society' has been used by a number of sociologists to refer to the sort of societies which developed in Europe from the 18th century onwards. Modern societies were seen as radically different from the so-called traditional societies which had existed before. Modern societies and the period called 'modernity' are seen to have been created by the development of urban living and industrialisation. Traditional society, in contrast, consisted of small towns and villages and was largely based on agricultural and craft production.

What are the key features of modernity?

The type of society developing in Europe from the 18th century onwards can be seen as having several key features.

Economically, modern societies were industrial societies, which gradually urbanised and developed sophisticated and powerful economies based on mass production. These produced considerable wealth for the whole population (though it was unequally distributed). Such economies also created the need for a well-trained and diverse range of skills and occupations. This led to the creation of many new opportunities for individuals, and it also led to the creation of a society composed of different social classes. This was very different from the traditional society, where people were born into a particular level of society and many remained there for the rest of their lives. Sociologists would call this a fixed social order, one in which there was little opportunity to move up into higher classes. Modern society, in contrast, offered the prospect of social mobility on the basis of achievement. In political terms, these changes involved the creation of modern nation states, often created by people from different regions or ethnic cultures. Philosophically or theoretically, modern society saw the growth away from religious belief and towards the ideas of science and progress.

What do modernist theorists say about identity?

Modernist theorists do not all share exactly the same views about identity, but there are some common ideas. As Anthony Giddens (1990) argues, modern society is seen as creating a break with the constraints of the society that existed before it, i.e. traditional society. In traditional society, according to many social theorists, identity was largely fixed and **ascribed**. This meant that gender roles, and class and status were hard to change. Differences between racial groups were believed to be the result of natural differences and seen in terms of a strict and unchangeable hierarchy. In modern society these ascribed differences and statuses gradually came to carry less force. Increasingly identity came to be something which was **achieved** rather than imposed.

What does modernist sociology say about methodology?

Sociology itself was a product of modern societies and the pioneers of the subject (such as Marx, Weber and Durkheim) were firmly committed to the philosophical values of 'the Enlightenment' (see above). This involved a belief in the power of scientific methods of research to continually increase human knowledge and the mastery of nature. It also involved the belief that human beings could reason. People had the ability to reflect and to think critically; by doing this they could determine the truth about the world. In terms of methods, therefore, modernist sociology has been particularly associated with one methodological tradition, positivism.

- Positivists assume that sociology can generally adopt the methods and rigour of the natural sciences.
- This usually involves the adoption of quantitative methods.

However, not all modernist sociologists were positivists. Some, like Weber, while they shared a belief in the ability of social scientists to identify the true causes of social processes and events, held that sociology had to be an interpretive discipline.

Intepretivist sociologists believe that sociology has to use qualitative methods. Since people think and reflect, and have reasons for acting as they do, qualitative methods are sometimes a more appropriate way of studying society. This is because qualitative methods enable people to explain their actions and beliefs; sociologists can therefore come to understand the meanings which actions have for people.

Conclusion

1. Modernist thought, like all ideas, reflects a certain time and place. Were modernist thinkers right to be so optimistic about the possibilities of progress?
2. This picture of historical change is generalised. It may exaggerate the extent and scope of social change.
3. Modernist thinking views scientific reason as a superior form of knowledge. Is it objective?

For consideration

1. Can scientific reason lead to the mastery of nature?
2. Are modernists right to see identity in modern society as achieved rather than ascribed?

❝❞ Key Definitions

Ascribed status means that status (position, prestige) is fixed at birth, whereas **achieved status** means that a person gains prestige by doing something such as setting up a successful business.

✓ Top Exam Hint

When discussing classical sociological theories (the works of Marx, Durkheim, and Weber), point out that all of these take a modernist view of society and of knowledge. This can allow you to contrast them with postmodernist writers who have a very different view of society and of knowledge (see Section 4.12).

Is society based on conflict? Marxism

❝❞ Key Definition

The base-superstructure model
Marxists see society as a system composed of two parts. The base is the economy (or economic base), and everything else in society, such as political system, culture, is called the superstructure.

What does this mean?

Marxism has been an important theory which has attempted to explain modern societies. Marxists believe that society can only really be understood if we focus on the fact that capitalist societies are based on conflict. Marxists say that conflict arises because capitalist society consists of two classes who have very different aims in life. It is important to realise, though, that this conflict can be expressed in different ways. Conflict may be expressed in many ways, for example through poor working relationships or by high crime rates.

Karl Marx and his colleague, Friedrich Engels, argued that the most important characteristic of modern capitalist society was conflict between different classes. Marxism has also become well known because of the attempt to put some of its ideas into practice in the Soviet Union. However, sociologists aim to use Marxist ideas sociologically to explain society, not necessarily to promote their own political views.

What are the key features of modern society according to Marxism?

Marxists claim that modernity was brought about by the development of capitalist society, and that this formed a decisive break with previous forms of society. Marxists see capitalist societies as involving three key components, a **base** and a **superstructure**, and two classes. These three elements are linked together in a relationship characterised by conflict.

- There are two classes of people in capitalist societies; the bourgeoisie and the proletariat. The bourgeoisie are the owners of land and factories. These are the means of producing wealth and Marxists call these the means of production. The proletariat, or the working classes, are all those people who do not own the means of production, and who therefore have to work for the bourgeoisie in order to survive.
- These two classes exist in a relationship which is very tense and where there are continual conflicts. These conflicts arise because each group has very different interests; workers want to increase their wages and get the best payment for the least work, and the owners want to maximise their profits. Marxists say that these two sets of desires (or interests) are contradictory. This means that they want completely different things; obviously, it is not possible to have both. Therefore conflict arises as the two sides struggle. Traditional Marxists would say that this struggle will continue forever, until the capitalist system is overthrown by revolutionary change.
- The Marxist word for the economy is the base or the means of production. This is because they see it as a sort of base or foundation upon which everything else in society is built. In capitalist society the means of

production, or base, is the capitalist system of production. Marxists say that the economy (or the base) shapes everything else in society.

- All the other parts of society, such as the political system and the cultural system, are shaped by the economy. Marxists claim that these other parts, which are called the superstructure, inevitably reflect the interests and desires of the dominant class, the bourgeoisie. Society is therefore seen as a system. This view of society is called the base-superstructure model.

What does Marxism say about identity?

Marxists claim that the identity of people in capitalist society is distorted and that capitalist society alienates us from our true nature. In literal terms alienation means that *we become strangers to our selves*'. Marxists claim that capitalism dulls our senses and oppresses us by making us all slaves to work. All relationships in capitalist society become defined by market relationships, so people are seen in terms of how much money they earn or their position in the division of labour, instead of in human terms as the sort of person they are. People even come to be seen as, and indeed come to see themselves as, commodities – things which can be bought or sold to the highest bidder.

Conclusion

Here are three points to use in evaluating Marxism.

1. Marxism has been accused of making the assumption that the needs of the economy shape everything else in society. This is called economic determinism.
2. Marxism is a structural theory which makes people look like puppets with no free will.
3. Marxists have addressed these sorts of criticisms by adapting the theory. Neo-Marxists such as Gramsci (see Section 4.7) argued against economic determinism and said that capitalism was maintained by cultural domination.

For consideration

1. Is Marxism now an irrelevant theory?
2. Why does Marxism have so little to say about race and gender?

⊙ Classic Study

The Communist Manifesto was written as a political pamphlet in 1888, but nevertheless it provides a brief and simplified insight into some of Marx's views about the essential nature of capitalist society. The following quotations highlight two of Marx's chief concerns.

'*Society as a whole is more and more splitting up into two great hostile camps, into two great classes directly facing each other – bourgeoisie and proletariat.*' (Marx, page 80)

'*The executive of the modern state is but a committee for managing the common affairs of the whole bourgeoisie.*' (Marx, page 82)

⋇ Key Idea

Some of the main points about alienation are summed up by Marx in the following quotation.

'*In what does this alienation of labour consist? First, that the work is external to the worker, that it is not part of his nature, that consequently he does not fulfil himself in his work but denies himself, has a feeling of misery, not of well-being, does not develop freely a physical and mental energy, but is physically exhausted and mentally debased. His work is not voluntary but imposed, forced labour. It is not the satisfaction of a need, but only a means for satisfying other needs.*'

(Marx, *Economic and Philosophical Manuscripts*, 1844)

∞ Methods Link

Marx's views on methodology are complex, but he essentially argued that his theoretical views were scientific. Many sociologists have, therefore, seen Marxism as involving a tendency to be a positivistic theory. However, other Marxist-influenced sociologists have tried to develop Marxism into a more qualitative or humanistic approach, for example, Paul Willis in *Learning to Labour* (see Section 4.2).

Is society based on conflict? Neo-Marxism

Max Horkheimer, a member of the Frankfurt School. Neo-Marxists have adapted Marxism in order to counter some of the criticisms directed at Marxist theory.

66 99 Key Definition

Relative autonomy is a term Althusser uses to describe the relationship between the three levels of social structure. He means that the economy does not determine everything else in society. The different levels are linked but all have a degree of freedom (autonomy).

☀ Key Idea

'For Gramsci hegemony means the ideological subordination of the working class by the bourgeoisie, which enables it to rule by consent.'

(P. Anderson (1976/7). *New Left Review*, page 100)

What does this mean?

Like all theoretical perspectives, Marxism has been adapted and changed in response to criticism. There are many different versions and interpretations of Marxism. Two of the most important have been Louis Althusser's structural Marxism and the humanistic Marxism developed by Gramsci and also by the Frankfurt School sociologists.

What is structural Marxism?

Louis Althusser tried to create a more elaborate version of Marxism which could avoid the criticism of economic determinism. Althusser argued that the structure of capitalist societies was best thought of as consisting of three different levels of structure; political, economic, and ideological. All of these levels were interrelated and influenced each other. Althusser claimed that no one level determined or shaped the others, though one level might be more dominant in a particular historical period. Althusser concluded that the different levels existed in a state of **'relative autonomy'**. This concept allowed Althusser apparently to solve the problem of economic determinism because of the view that economic structures never act independently of political and ideological structures.

What is humanistic Marxism?

There are two main strands in humanistic Marxism and both focus on the role of culture and ideology. Both of these interpretations of Marxism show how sociological theories also reflect the time at which they are developed.

Gramsci was a political activist working in Italy in the 1930s. He was very aware that the working class in most European countries had not become the sort of revolutionary force which Marxist thought had suggested. Gramsci's concept of hegemony attempted to explain why this was so, and why capitalism was so stable.

- Hegemony means leadership or dominance. Gramsci argued that Marx had been wrong to focus almost exclusively on the role of economic structures.
- Gramsci argued that elites could not rule just by economic domination. An effective system of domination has to involve the consent of the people who are dominated.
- Gramsci claimed that the cultural hegemony of the elites meant that it was their values and ideas which dominated society, and this made their domination seem natural and fair.

For Gramsci, the arrival of a fairer society would only come about if an elite intellectual group could educate the masses and challenge the dominant cultural hegemony of the capitalist ruling class.

The Frankfurt School

The other strand of humanistic Marxism was developed by the group of sociologists and intellectuals known as the Frankfurt School. Their particular version of sociological theory is also known as critical theory. The Frankfurt School consisted of a number of sociologists, all with their own particular views. However, the ideas of the Frankfurt School focused on the following key points.

- Marxism needed to focus on culture as well as economic factors.
- Capitalism was clearly much more stable and durable than it had appeared to Marx. The Frankfurt School argued that this could be explained by the mass culture which capitalism encouraged. They believed that mass culture repressed and stupefied the population and promoted false needs.
- The shift to focus on culture meant that some members of the Frankfurt School turned their attention away from class politics towards the growth of what they called 'new social movements' in the 1960s. It was felt that these were becoming more important than class based movements (see also Sections 4.12, 4.13, 4.14 and Chapter 2).

What do these theories say about methodology?

The different versions of Marxism discussed here represent different methodological approaches.

- Althusser always maintained that structural Marxism could be scientific and that our lives are determined by structural forces.
- Humanistic Marxists have rejected this view as being excessively structural and positivistic. The Frankfurt School theorists argued against this scientific Marxism saying that it portrays society and social change as if it were a natural process (**reification** – see Key Definition box) which human action could not alter or influence in any way. They also see it as neglecting human agency, portraying people as passive.

Conclusion

Use the following points to evaluate neo-Marxism.

1. Neo-Marxist theories demonstrate that Marxism can be adapted to take other factors, such as culture, into account. However, neo-Marxist theory may still seem to have little to say about inequalities on the basis of race and gender (see Chapter 2).
2. The theories discussed here have widely differing views on key points. Remember that there are often sharp theoretical and methodological disagreements between those who use the same perspective.
3. The differences between the approaches reflect different answers to the structure/action debate (see Section 4.11). Structural Marxism advocates a scientific approach and emphasises the force of structural constraints, and humanistic Marxism argues for a methodology which acknowledges human agency.

For consideration

1. Why do neo-Marxists disagree about methodology?
2. Does mass culture stupefy people and make them accept capitalism?

◆ **What, when and why?**

The Frankfurt School developed in Germany in the 1930s but moved to the USA following the rise of Nazism. Their experience of fascism in Germany and the mass culture of capitalism in the USA influenced their assessment of Marxist theory and led them to conclude that the possibility of human liberation was severely limited due to the pervasive spread of the cultural value of instrumental rationality. This concept drew more from the work of Weber than Marx, and suggests that people's actions in capitalist society are dominated by technical efficiency rather than ethics.

❝❞ **Key Definition**

The term **reify** means that something is regarded as if it is natural and unchangeable, rather than being the product of human action, and therefore changeable.

Is society based on consensus? Functionalism

What does this mean?

Functionalists such as Durkheim and Parsons believed that modern society has to be based on consensus. This just means 'agreement'. Functionalists believe that societies can only hold together, or be integrated and function effectively, if people are united around a core set of shared values and goals.

What are the key features of modern society identified by functionalists?

Functionalists see modern society as being characterised by industrial production on a mass scale. They do not focus on the economic inequalities that this system produces as Marxists do; for the functionalist other features are more significant. Functionalists share with Marxists the idea that modern societies need to be seen as consisting of structures, and they agree that they are very different from previous societies. However, here the similarities end, and functionalists see modern society in a very different light. For functionalists:

- Modern societies are characterised by consensus and shared values, not conflict.
- Modern societies are best understood as being industrial societies. This means that they are capable of mass production using industrial technology. It also means that they have a large and complex division of labour (many different types of jobs and occupations).
- The division of labour in modern societies is characterised by meritocracy. This means that they provide equality of opportunity and people are rewarded on the basis of their achievements and capabilities. There is no discrimination on the basis of class, race, gender or other characteristics.

What does functionalism say about identity?

Functionalists say that the creation of modern society has led to a big shift in the sorts of identity that are open to us.

- They argue that, prior to industrialisation, our roles and identity were mainly ascribed. This means that they were fixed, and could not be changed very easily, and depended on factors like our gender, class and race.
- In modern society, however, functionalists claim that roles and identity are achieved. This means that we can achieve a different identity to that of our parents by, for example, passing exams and gaining access to different jobs.
- The pace of change in modernity can mean that there are periods of great uncertainty when it is unclear what the norms and values are. This can lead to what Durkheim calls 'anomie', or normlessness. Durkheim says that this leads to a situation where people increasingly come to see themselves as

◆ What, when and why?

Critics often see sociology as being primarily concerned with radical (or 'left wing') political ideas, but some of the key founders of the discipline were in fact conservatives. Comte, who first used the word 'sociology', developed his theories in reaction to the French Revolution and Enlightenment philosophy (see Section 4.5) and believed his studies would help prevent anarchy. Durkheim feared that modern society would create disorder and wanted to show how order could be created. Parsons' sociological views have been seen as a reaction either to the economic depression of the 1930s or to the challenge of Marxist theory in the mid-twentieth century.

individuals since there are few social controls on their behaviour. Society is less integrated around shared norms and so people become more individualistic.

However, in modern society we also have multiple roles because we may have many functions or responsibilities. For example, one woman can be a lawyer, wife, school governor, mother and daughter. This can mean that tensions arise as we are pulled in different directions by the demands of our different roles. This process is termed role conflict.

What do functionalists say about methodology?

Functionalist Emile Durkheim was a key figure in the development of sociology. In a classic study on suicide (Durkheim 1897; see also Sections 4.4 and 4.18) he argued that sociology could aspire to the status of a science and that it should take a positivist approach to methodology. Durkheim believed that society consisted of structures, and these had to be thought of as being like objects which are external to us. It is the task of sociology, he argued, to identify these structures (see Section 4.18).

Conclusion

Here are three points to use in evaluating functionalism.

1. Sociologists, working from a conflict perspective, argue that society is not held together by value consensus.
2. Conflict theorists, in contrast, suggest that it is power and force which maintains social order.
3. Conflict theorists argue that there is strong evidence against the meritocracy thesis.

✳ Key Ideas

- Functionalists think of society in terms of the organic analogy (an analogy is a comparison). According to this view, society is best seen as if it were an organism. Just like an organism it has certain needs, such as food and shelter, which have to be provided for. Functionalists call these 'functional prerequisites'. This idea also highlights the point that societies evolve and change over time, as living organisms do.

- The importance of solidarity and integration and their relationship to anomie is summed up well in this quotation from Durkheim,

'If the division of labour does not produce solidarity … it is because the relations of the organs are not regulated, because they are in a state of anomie.'

(Adapted from Durkheim *The Division of Labour*, New York Free Press 1964)

☙ Classic Study

In his study, *The Division of Labour* (1893), Durkheim argued that modern societies are held together by organic solidarity. By this he means that complex industrial societies have to be seen as if they were organisms with many different parts. All of the parts have to work harmoniously if the organism, or society, is to function effectively.

'In order for the division of labour to engender solidarity, it is not, therefore, sufficient that each person has his task: this task must suit also suit him …[where there is] painful wrangling, this is because the distribution of social functions… on which the solidarity is based does not correspond to the distribution of talent.'

(Adapted from K. Thompson, *Readings from Emile Durkheim*, London, Routledge 1985, page 33)

For consideration

1. Is the functionalist perspective on modern society value-free?
2. Does meritocracy exist in modern societies?

| # Is society created by human action? Interactionism

What does this mean?

Interactionism and other theories which are closely related, such as ethnomethodology, argue that structural theories, such as Marxism, functionalism, and feminism, look at society in the wrong way. Interactionists argue that structural theories tend to see people as if they just automatically respond to structures, making them seem like unthinking robots. In contrast, interactionists say that people are reflective and thinking beings, who actively create society. Interactionists therefore say that to understand social behaviour we need to understand the reasons people give for their actions.

What are the key features of modern society identified by interactionists?

Interactionism is composed of a number of distinct theorists, but for our purposes it is possible to summarise a number of key features which characterise interactionist theorists.

- Modern societies are best understood initially by examining them on the micro rather than the macro level.
- Interactionists argue that this is because human action is characterised most of all by the fact that it is meaningful.
- Meaning is generated through symbols and by a process of negotiation. This is best studied on a micro level and by using qualitative methods.
- Social order is the outcome of micro level interaction. It is therefore something which is created by social action, not, as structural theorists such as functionalists and Marxists suppose, something which is imposed upon people.

What do interactionists say about identity?

Interactionists say that people are actively involved in creating their identity in modern society. They make two key points.

- Identities depend both on how we see ourselves but also on how other people see us. This means that there is a process of negotiation. We may try to get people to see our identity in a particular way, but this may or may not be successful.
- Other people or groups of people may succeed in **labelling** us. Labels may be positive or negative and can lead to self-fulfilling prophecies. However, when these labels are negative, we can say that individuals or groups of individuals will have a 'stigmatised identity'.

↪ Classic Study

A classic interactionist study in the field of crime and deviance is Howard Becker's book *Outsiders* (1963). This book consists of essays based on Becker's observational work and argues that deviance is in fact something that is created when social groups create rules and label those who break them as deviants. Here the contrast with structural theorists such as Durkheim is clear, since deviance only exists once it has been defined as such by a social group. If social groups had not created (or invented) the term, people would not be able to use it.

66 99 Key Definition

Label... the idea that the identity of a p... group is stereotyped, ... s in a negative way. ... something ... naccurate

What do interactionists say about methodology?

Interactionists of various types all agree that sociology must progress by using qualitative methods, such as observation (participant and non-participant), ethnographies (studies of the way of life of a group) or by various types of interviews. There are several reasons why interactionists are so keen on qualitative methods.

- Interactionists believe that people always have reasons for their actions.
- The purpose of sociology is to identify and examine these reasons and to study the meaning that behaviour has for people.
- In order to do this, sociology has to use qualitative methods.
- Interactionists also maintain that qualitative methods, although they may be small scale, are more valid than positivist/quantitative research.
- Lastly, interactionists argue that human behaviour is distorted by studying it in the artificial conditions which positivist research encourages. The reality and true meaning of social behaviour can only be obtained by studying people in their natural environment, for example, in schools, at work, in the community. Ethnographies (a study of the way of life of a group or society) and observational methods provide good ways of achieving this.

Conclusion

The following points offer some good ways of evaluating interactionist approaches.

1. Interactionists' unwillingness to discuss society as a system makes it difficult to see where power comes from as there are no structures in this view of society.
2. Interactionists' approach to methods seems to be subjective and easily open to bias. How can we replicate and test interactionist findings?
3. In the structure/action debate, interactionists seem to lean far too much towards the action side. Surely we do not have quite as much freedom as they imply?

✳ Key Idea

The concept of the self-fulfilling prophecy suggests that once a label has been successfully applied it will lead to a process of interactions whereby the label comes to be confirmed. The classic example is Rosenthal and Jacobsen's *'Pygmalion in the Classroom'* study, where it was claimed that labelling of students by teachers created self-fulfilling prophecies leading to either success or failure.

✓ Top Exam Hint

Remember that the methodological criticisms of qualitative research provide a useful way of evaluating interactionist studies and shows that you are thinking synoptically.

For consideration

1. What criticisms would Marxists and functionalists both want to make of the interactionist approach?
2. Can interactionists tell us anything about social control?

Is society based on conflict? Varieties of feminism

What does this mean?

Feminism is a set of sociological theories which all focus on examining society in terms of the relations between men and women, i.e. gender relations. It is quite hard to categorise feminist theory in terms of the usual distinctions made between modern sociological theories, but in many ways feminists reflect a conflict approach.

What are the key features of modern society identified by feminism?

The main feminist theories on modern society are liberal, radical and Marxist versions of feminism.

Liberal feminism has origins which go back to the 18th century, but more recently it was developed by American feminists such as Friedan (1981) and Jessie Bernard (1976). Liberal feminists argue that modern society creates two distinct parts of society, the public sphere (work and politics) and the private sphere (the home and personal life). Women's roles and identity are restricted to the private sphere, mainly by legislation and cultural beliefs. Liberal feminists believe that gradual reform will see women's position improve. Other feminists are more sceptical.

Radical feminists such as Kate Millet (1970) argue that the key feature of modern society is **patriarchy** and, in particular, the way that patriarchy involves the control of women's sexuality. Radical feminists argue that men oppress and control women and reduce them to sexual objects whose sole purpose is to provide for male sexual gratification and to be responsible for the upbringing of children.

Marxist-feminists such as Michelle Barrett (1980) argue against the radical feminists' view that the only key feature of modern society exploiting women is patriarchy. Marxist-feminists claim that women are *also* exploited by capitalism. They therefore see women's position in society as the result of both the cultural values of patriarchy, and the particular economic needs of capitalism (for example, for reproduction of labour power, and a reserve army of labour).

All of these varieties of feminism are referred to as 'second wave feminism', as it is considered that the first wave of feminism was created by feminist writers in the 18th century. Second wave feminists, despite their differences, do have some views in common. They all believe that modern society is sexist and patriarchal, and they all share the slogan that 'the personal is political'.

Sociologist Ann Oakley's groundbreaking studies of housework and medicine have forced sociologists to pay more attention to women's role in society.

66 99 Key Definition

Patriarchy means a society or institution is male dominated.

Some feminists have suggested that capitalism and patriarchy are two distinct systems of oppression and this is termed 'dual-systems theory'.

Sylvia Walby (1990) has written about what is termed 'triple systems theory', arguing that sociologists need to examine how capitalism, patriarchy and racism all connect to create a complex set of structures which influence female identities, status, and position in modern society.

What does feminism say about methodology?

Feminists such as Abbott and Wallace (1990) have argued that feminism was necessary to correct what feminists see as the '**malestream**' bias of modernist sociology. They argue that mainstream sociological interests have always marginalised and neglected gender issues and therefore use a play on words – 'malestream' – to highlight this fact.

What have feminists said about postmodern society?

More recently, there has been a reaction to second wave feminism by black feminists and others influenced by postmodernism and post-structuralism. These feminists have argued that second wave feminism mainly reflected the views of white middle-class women and they argue that the experience of patriarchy and femininity varies tremendously depending upon factors such as class and race.

Conclusion

Feminism has made a great contribution to sociology by forcing sociologists to reflect carefully on whether research methods are biased, and on whether theories are selective. Use the following points to evaluate the usefulness of feminist theory.

1. Second wave feminism tends to see women as passive since they seem to accept oppression and exploitation (it neglects agency).
2. Second wave feminism tends to neglect differences between women, such as class and race.
3. Feminism has contributed some useful insights, but it is only a partial theory of society, and offers a limited range of concepts (for example, patriarchy), borrowing other concepts from other theories.

Methods Link

Feminist points such as those discussed in this section are helpful to use when discussing the ideas of value-freedom and bias in sociological research. Some feminists claim that only women can adequately research certain issues and that there is a need for what they call a 'feminist methodology': feminist ways of doing research (see Sections 4.18 and 4.19).

Key Definition

Malestream is a play on the word 'mainstream sociology', and refers to the normal or most common ways of thinking about sociology. Feminists felt that the mainstream was so male biased that it might as well be called malestream.

What, when and why?

Feminism developed particularly quickly in the USA during the 1960s. This so-called 'second wave' of feminism perhaps reflected the fact that women's role was changing rapidly at this time, with more women going to university and then finding that they were not completely equal to men at the work place. By the 1970s and 1980s there had been further social change, and a third wave of feminism has focused on differences between women in terms of race and sexuality.

For consideration

1. Can men be feminists?
2. Why are there so many different types of feminism?

A game of two halves? The structure/action debate

What does this mean?

There is a debate between the two sorts of theories considered so far, structural theories and action theories, called 'the structure/action debate'. These theories offer contrasting views of society. But we may not have to choose between them; it may be that they both have something to tell us about society.

What is the structure/action debate?

- Structural theories, such as Marxism, functionalism and feminism, claim that our action and behaviour is shaped by structural forces, such as class, race, and gender, beyond our individual control.
- Action theories, such as interactionism, take the opposite view and claim that people actively create and shape their own destiny. The resulting debate between these two theories is known as the 'structure/action debate'.

Clearly, whichever view a sociologist takes will have a big influence on the way that they theorise about society (how they 'see' society) and the sort of explanations they develop for social behaviour.

Are there any solutions to this debate?

Sociologist, Anthony Giddens, has proposed a solution to this debate, termed **structuration theory**. Giddens argues that in fact we need to use both of these sets of theories to understand society fully. His solution takes elements of each side in the debate and creates a synthesis – a combination of points from each side that aims to overcome the weaknesses in both.

Giddens' (1984) resolution of the structure/action debate involves thinking afresh about the way we view the two key elements in the debate: actors (people) and structures. Giddens believes that the way both of these things are defined in sociological theory is inaccurate and unhelpful. Because of these faults, he claims that most sociological theories do not accurately explain how people and society interact. Giddens is particularly critical of views which portray people as passive and incapable of thinking for themselves. According to Giddens, structural theories such as Marxism and functionalism tend to make people appear rather like puppets. Hidden forces appear to be pulling the strings and making people act in certain ways. Giddens' arguments can be summed up in the following points.

- Human behaviour cannot be seen as being determined by structures. People are reflective, i.e. they think (Giddens also uses the word 'reflexive') and always have reasons for acting as they do. Giddens therefore takes a similar view to action theorists.

✳ Key Idea

Structuration theory suggests that the structure/action debate can be solved by the realisation that structure and action are both parts of the same thing. Structures are formed from the actions of human beings; without this, there would be no structures. '*Structure is not 'external' to individuals … Structure is not to be equated with constraint but is always both constraining and enabling.*'

(*Constitution of Society: Outline of the Theory of Structuration*, Cambridge, Polity 1984, page 25)

☞ Who is this person?

Anthony Giddens is a well-known British sociologist. He was, until recently, the Director of the London School of Economics and prior to that was Professor of Sociology at the University of Cambridge. His work has mainly been theoretical. He is well known as the originator of the so-called 'Third Way' policies, which have had a big influence on the New Labour governments of the 1990s and the early years of the 21st century.

- **Reflexivity** means that people think about what they do and that they can monitor their actions. This enables them to change their behaviour in the light of circumstances, knowledge and feedback. This has important methodological implications (see Section 4.14 for more on Giddens' methodology).
- Giddens says that structures should be seen as sets of social practices (ways of behaviour that are continually repeated, such as gender relations or the relationship between education and class) that are repeated time over time, rather than as forces which exist outside of or external to us.
- Crucially, it is people who create these structures through their own activities. One important implication of this is that structures are always changing. Another is that we should not think of structures as preventing us from doing things. Giddens argues that structures are simply the very condition of our lives. Giddens claims that they enable us to do things as well as preventing us from doing some things.

Giddens suggests that rather than seeing society as consisting of structure and action, we should acknowledge that structure and action are really just different aspects of one thing. This means that people create 'structures' through their own activities, but at the same time, our own activities are 'structured' or patterned by these very activities.

Conclusion

You may find Giddens' synthesis very convincing, but there are several points which can be used to evaluate it critically.

1. People may not be as free as Giddens suggests; he emphasises action more than structure.
2. He suggests that everyone has the power to act. However, it is surely important to note that we do not all have the same amount of power.
3. Structure and action are indeed best understood as two different aspects of society. Structures are, in contrast to Giddens' view, external to us.

For consideration

1. How can social institutions be reflexive?
2. Is Giddens right to argue that structures are not external to us? Compare his views with those of Durkheim.

How has modern society changed? Postmodernism

◆ **What, when and why?**

Postmodernism developed in the late 1970s largely as a result of debates in French philosophy and sociological theory. Postmodernists such as Jean-François Lyotard (1984) and Jean Baudrillard (1980) claim that language is the key to understanding social life. This has led them to focus on how language, ideas and society are constructed and to be very sceptical about the idea of social structures. For postmodernists, society is nothing more than the language (or signs) that we invent and interpret.

What does this mean?

Some sociologists believe that society has changed and that it is inaccurate to say that we still live in modern society. Modern societies are seen as having key characteristics such as classes, a nation state, and mass-scale industrial production. Postmodernists believe that society has changed and that all these features have changed. Postmodernists say that we now live in a new period that has followed modernism, called postmodernity.

What are the key features of postmodernity?

Postmodernists say that contemporary society has fragmented. They identify several key aspects of change.

Economic change

There has been a shift from mass production to smaller-scale production for niche markets. In the modern era, production was done on a mass basis. This form of production enabled large quantities of a product to be made, but postmodernists point out that in a more affluent society consumers are bored with identical products and want more individuality and flair. In a competitive market, manufacturers have had to respond to consumers' demands.

Political change

The boundaries between nation states are becoming less important as people are able to move more freely as a result of globalisation. Nation states have therefore become less powerful. Also political parties offer increasingly similar policies and the main differences between political parties is often simply a matter of taste and style.

Social change

Postmodernists claim that social divisions such as class, race and gender are becoming increasingly irrelevant. Postmodernists Pakulski and Waters (1996) argue that class is no longer a significant part of people's self-identity. They also believe that, in a more affluent society, the concept of class is simply not relevant or analytically useful to sociologists.

Cultural change

Many (but not all) modernist sociologists used to see shared culture as a way in which modern society was held together. Postmodernists, though, argue that society is fragmenting. They also claim that cultural boundaries between different groups and styles (see photographs) are blurring, creating a myriad of cultural options. Postmodernists are often interested in the boundaries of

Hotel New York, New York, Las Vegas. The idea that it becomes harder to know what is real and what is imaginary in postmodernity is reflected in the design of buildings and places where different styles and designs are mixed or are playful.

culture in terms of people's interests in art and music, which is another rather different way of looking at culture.

What do postmodernists say about identity?

Unlike modernists, who claim that our identities are strongly shaped by social structures such as class, race and gender, postmodernists argue that we can create our identities in many diverse and different ways. Many sociologists have been influenced by postmodernists such as Connell (1987), who argues that there are many different versions of masculinity and femininity, and Stuart Hall (1992) who observes that there are now many 'hybrid' ethnic identities where people see themselves as partly British and partly, say, African, Indian, or Pakistani. Many sociologists would agree with Harriet Bradley (1996) that the task for researchers now is to understand how factors such as class, race and gender are interrelated and not experienced in the same way by all people.

What do postmodernists say about methodology?

Postmodernists are highly critical of the modernist belief in reason and the idea that we can study anything in an objective way. Postmodernists believe that all knowledge is **relative**. This means that there is no way of obtaining objective knowledge and so it is not possible to find the truth. In fact they believe that there cannot be such a thing as 'the truth', only different subjective versions claiming to be the truth. Critics of postmodernism, such as Anthony Giddens (see Section 4.20), have argued that this must imply that the very attempt to produce objective knowledge about the world, which is what sociology attempts to do, is impossible. Many critics are therefore very hostile to postmodernism as they see it as giving up on the attempt to explain and understand the world.

Conclusion

Here are three evaluation points to use with postmodernism.

1. It may exaggerate social change, for example, the decline of the nation state and mass production.
2. If we do not think about class, race and gender, it does not mean that these structures do not exist. We can say that postmodernism is voluntaristic – this means that it suggests people are able to act freely, unconstrained by social structures.
3. It is contradictory. If we cannot ever know the truth (and sociological accounts are just another alternative), the same point must apply to postmodernism. Why should we therefore privilege postmodernist views as having greater truth than any other account?

For consideration

1. How could we test the claims of postmodernism?
2. Are there any limits to the sort of identity we can create in postmodern society? What implications does your answer have for postmodernist theory?

※ Key Idea

Jean Baudrillard argues that in postmodernity we all live in a state of 'hyperreality' where we can no longer tell the difference between reality and fiction. Our understanding of society consists of 'simulations' or images which we gain from the media. '*Disneyland is there to conceal the fact that it is the "real" country, all of "real" America, which is Disneyland. Disneyland is presented as imaginary in order to make us believe that the rest is real, when in fact all of Los Angeles and the America surrounding it are no longer real, but of the order of the hyperreal and of simulation.*' (Jean Baudrillard, *Simulations*, Semiotext, 1983, page 25)

66 99 Key Definition

If knowledge is objective, it means that it is unbiased and factual. If we say that a belief is subjective we mean that it is just the view of an individual and is not generally agreed to be true. To say that knowledge is **relative** is to deny that there is any possibility of objective knowledge, and to argue that all knowledge and beliefs are subjective. This would mean that truth is relative, or that there is no agreed truth about something. This view is called relativism.

☐ Key Fact

According to postmodernists it is a fact that there are no longer any facts in postmodernity. Like many sceptical sociologists, you may perhaps feel that this view is contradictory.

How has modern society changed? Do we live in a risk society?

☞ **Who is this person?**

Ulrich Beck is a German sociologist who became famous with the publication of his book *Risk Society – Towards a New Modernity* in 1992. He started his sociological career studying the sociology of science and technology and the green movement. His ideas are strongly reflected in Anthony Giddens' work and he is co-author of a book with Giddens and Lash.

What does this mean?

The term 'risk society' was devised by German sociologist, Ulrich Beck, in the early 1990s. Beck uses the term to describe what he views as a range of important social changes. While he believes that there has been considerable social change, he thinks that postmodernists are wrong to say that we live in a period of postmodernity. Beck does not agree that knowledge is always relative and he believes that through reason and research we may find solutions to the problems of our time. Beck believes that the industrial society typical of many western societies in the 20th century is dying out and that we now live in a new phase of modernity where science and technology have the power to change our lives for the worse. For this reason Beck says that what we now live in is a 'risk society'.

What are the main characteristics of risk society?

Beck believes that contemporary society is most accurately seen as beginning to move into a phase where it can be characterised as a 'risk society'. Beck claims that modern society was dominated by industrialism and identities were founded on class. In modern industrial society, a key issue which organised social life and politics was that of wealth, inequalities in wealth and how they could be reduced.

However, Beck claims that in the new society that is now emerging class inequalities are no longer a key issue. He argues instead that it is now what he calls 'risk' that is the main problem in society, while the key issue is safety and how to achieve it. By risk Beck is mainly referring to the tremendous problems of ecological risk, such as greenhouse gases, genetically modified food and science and technology in general. Beck contends that it is modern industrial technology which has created these risks and he uses the term 'the boomerang effect' to express the way that these problems of risk return to the places that have created them, namely industrialised societies.

As class is less important, so Beck maintains, the nature of politics changes. The state has less power because politics is seen as less relevant by people. This is because the state is less and less able to control the risks created by industrial technology. So class politics is dead, and what Beck calls 'sub politics' develops. Beck means that the most effective political movements develop outside of the formal mechanisms of the state. Examples of this would be the green movement, anti-globalisation protestors, road protestors, and animal rights activists.

Is modern society a 'risk society'? Pollution from power plants and factories contributes to greenhouse gases.

This may seem a gloomy view of contemporary society but Beck is optimistic. He argues that people and society are reflexive and terms current processes of social change 'reflexive modernisation' (see Key Idea box). Our ability to act reflexively means that we can learn and come to question risks. Experts can also help us in this process.

What are the implications of this theory in terms of our individual identity?

As already indicated, these changes have a big impact on identity. Beck argues that a process of '**individualisation**' is occurring. People see themselves as individuals to a much greater extent than was the case in modern society. This arises, Beck contends, because people are increasingly free of structural constraints such as class or gender.

What does Beck say about methodology?

Apart from expressing a belief in the modernist idea of reason, Beck is vague in advocating any particular methodological approach. A discussion of Beck's work in a recent edition of *The Oxford Dictionary of Sociology* edited by Gordon Marshall (1998), commented that a concept such as risk society was so abstract that it was '*in principle untestable*'. This reflects the tendency of some sociologists to focus on theoretical issues at the expense of empirical research. It can be argued that this is justified given the complexity of theory. Nevertheless sociologists of a more empirical frame of mind insist that theory is only useful and meaningful when used with methods.

Conclusion

Use the following points to evaluate Beck's theory.

1. What empirical evidence is there to support Beck's claim that class has little or no influence on identity in contemporary society?
2. Beck seems to neglect the idea of structures and perhaps exaggerates the degree of power and choice which individuals have.
3. Beck's views of knowledge, reflexivity and experts should be compared with Foucault's more pessimistic views (see Section 4.16).

For consideration

1. Is the idea that people are reflexive an accurate one? Does being reflexive give us power?
2. Is it industrial technology or capitalism that creates the environmental problems that concern Beck?

66 99 Key Definition

Individualisation means that the importance of collective identities, such as class, race, gender, are in decline, and that people increasingly see and define themselves as individuals, and in turn are seen by others primarily as individuals.

⁑ Key Ideas

- Reflexive modernisation is an idea used by Beck and also by Giddens. The term reflexivity refers to the idea that people think and reflect. Contemporary society, which Beck views as entering a new phase of modernity, is seen as reflecting upon the various economic and technological problems it faces, particularly the risks brought about by technology, and acting to solve these problems.

- Beck argues that we now live in a new form of society which is very different to traditional society: post-traditional society. *'Just as the forms of living and working in feudal agrarian society were dissolved at the end of the nineteenth century, the same thing is happening today to those of the developed industrial society: social classes and stratification, the nuclear family with the embedded 'standard biographies' of men and women, the standardizations of labor, and so on.'* (Beck 1992, page 153)

● Synoptic Link

Link the risk society theory to stratification. Beck's theory and the notion of *individualisation* suggests that class identities are no longer an important aspect of identity. Beck can be seen as taking a rather similar view to postmodernists here, but be careful not to say that he is a postmodernist.

How has modern society changed? Late modernity

What does this mean?

Anthony Giddens argues that postmodernists have exaggerated the extent and nature of social change. He claims that we still live in what is basically a modern society, but at the same time that there have been some important social changes. This point of view is therefore trying to take a middle way approach to the debate between modernists and postmodernists.

What are the main features of late modernity according to Giddens?

For Giddens, one of the key features of contemporary society, which he calls 'late modernity', is globalisation.

- Globalisation, in Giddens' terms, means that we increasingly live in a world that is interconnected. Giddens also refers to the transformation of space and time. By this he means that modern technology has changed our ability to move and communicate across long distances.
- For Giddens, globalisation is a process that has changed social organisation and social relationships. For example, he argues that nation states are less powerful. At the same time, globalisation is something that can influence our personal lives because attitudes about equality for women are now ideas that have an influence across the globe.
- Giddens views the culture of late modernity as undergoing a big change and that late modernity gives rise to cosmopolitanism. This means that there is a great diversity of cultures, ways of life, and also of ethnic groups and social movements. Cosmopolitanism is itself a product of globalisation. However, **cosmopolitanism** in late modernity is accompanied by the rise of **fundamentalism** (see Key Definition box).
- Finally, a key feature of late modernity is that it is characterised by reflexivity. Giddens means two things by reflexivity. Firstly, he means that people think and reflect on their actions. This is a view he shares with interpretivism. Secondly, Giddens argues that reflexivity also works on a social level, which he calls social or institutional reflexivity. This means that institutions and societies are continually reflecting on what they do and monitoring and changing as a result of this. Giddens argues that it is this that has led late modern societies to break away from tradition.

How has identity changed in late modernity?

Identity in late modernity is transformed by these social changes. Individuals are able to develop themselves free of the constraints of traditional society. Giddens maintains that people seek what he terms security by reflexively constructing their own set of goals in their life, which Giddens calls their 'life project'.

66 99 Key Definitions

A **cosmopolitan** is literally someone who is a 'citizen of the world', that is they do not think of themselves particularly in terms of a national identity. Giddens defines **fundamentalism** as an unwillingness to enter into a dialogue about truth. The term is often used to refer to religious groups in a critical way, particularly with reference to extremist groups. However, it is important to point out that there can be Christian fundamentalists as well as Muslim fundamentalists.

✳ Key Idea

The following quotation gives a flavour of why Giddens thinks globalisation is so important.

'Instantaneous electronic communication isn't just a way in which news or information is conveyed more quickly. Its existence alters the very texture of our lives, rich and poor alike. When the image of Nelson Mandela maybe is more familiar to us than the face of our next door neighbour, something has changed in the nature of our everyday experience.'

(Giddens, Reith Lecture 1 1999)

Late modernity is a time of great individual freedom. Intimate relationships are guided by personal fulfilment not the rules of traditional society. Giddens refers to 'plastic sexuality', since sexuality is now something which is mouldable as people search for the 'pure relationship' formed purely on the basis of self-fulfilment. What Giddens terms the 'democratisation of emotions', though, has led to a crisis of masculinity, an uncertainty as to gender roles.

What does Giddens say about methodology?

Giddens is well known for his methodological writing, in a earlier stage of his work, in a book titled *New Rules of Sociological Method* (1976). One of the key arguments in this book is that sociology cannot be seen in a positivist way as uncovering the laws governing human behaviour. In contrast, Giddens makes several important suggestions.

- Sociologists have to acknowledge that people think and reflect.
- People will also think (they are reflexive) and reflect about the activities of sociologists.
- This means that sociologists' research findings can become public knowledge.

This means that there is a two-way relationship between researchers and the public. While sociologists may develop all sorts of explanations about the people they study, these people can learn about and reflect upon sociologists' explanations, and they can change their behaviour. Sociologists must research systematically and rigorously, but this is always an interpretive process and indeed sociologists themselves are part of the very society they study. This is what Giddens means by reflexivity and he argues that this is simply one of the conditions of the existence of sociology. Sociology is difficult and inevitably an interpretive activity.

Conclusion

1. Giddens may be wrong to emphasise the contrasts between modern and traditional society. There is still much continuity with the constraints of traditional society, for example, gender roles, class, status.
2. Tradition can be reinvented.
3. Giddens exaggerates the extent to which people are free; see also the criticisms in Section 4.11.

✳ Key Idea

Reflexivity is the term Giddens uses to describe the fact that people think and reflect on their actions and behaviour. Institutions can also be reflexive as the people working in them and running them make decisions reflexively.

✓ Top Exam Hint

Giddens' view of power is a good one to use for evaluations on many different topics and shows that you are using theory synoptically. Use Giddens either by criticising his views on power (see above) or use his views to help you synthesise two opposing views and resolve a debate.

For consideration

1. Identify the sociological perspectives and other theori~ have most influenced Giddens.

2. Is there a crisis of masculinity in contemporary s

Sociology A2 for AQA

How has modern society changed? Castells and the information age

☞ **Who is this person?**

Manuel Castells (born 1942) is a Spanish sociologist. He was educated in France and was influenced by Marxist theory. His early work was in the field of geography and urban studies. Castells has worked in the USA since 1979 and his current work has moved a long way from his early Marxist views. However, he is still on the side of the poor, and his interest in geography, an important social science subject, remains clear in his concern to highlight the links between social movements across the globe.

❝❞ Key Definition

Globalisation describes the way in which the world is becoming increasingly interconnected and events in far away places can have an impact on our lives.

◆ What, when and why?

The Zapatistas, a guerrilla movement in Mexico, have protested against global capitalism and the policies of the Mexican government, which have dispossessed peasants of land in the Mexican rainforest. Aum Shinrikyo is a Japanese religious cult which was responsible for releasing sarin gas into the Tokyo underground in 1995, killing twelve people. Castells argues that both groups are examples of resistance identity, but also points out that both have utilised the media and the Internet to recruit and publicise their causes.

What does this mean?

Manuel Castells (1996, 1997) argues that in the late 20th and early 21st centuries a new form of capitalism has developed. Castells calls this new form of capitalism 'informational capitalism', and sees the growth of information technology as having helped to create a new and more dynamic form of capitalism. New social identities have developed, and together these changes have created a new sort of society, which Castells calls the 'network society'.

How has modern society changed?

Castells argues that the development of information technology has had profound effects on modern society and its institutions. He reasons that information technology is very different from any previous technological advances. There are several reasons for this.

- It can be used flexibly and has been applied much more widely than other new technologies, such as the steam engine, and has therefore had a bigger impact on society and social organisation. IT is visible everywhere – in schools, shops, at home, as well as in the office or factory. In all of these contexts, it transforms social relationships and institutions.
- It is a technology that promotes reflexivity (knowledge, self-awareness). The product of IT is information and IT vastly speeds up the production and spread of knowledge and information. Castells argues that this means that societies investing heavily in IT develop and innovate much more quickly than competitors.
- It has changed the institutions of work; businesses are now smaller and organised around 'flexible production'.
- It is a global phenomenon. Its flexibility and technical capabilities mean that our views about time and place have changed. We can communicate at any time with people a great distance away from us (compare with Giddens in Section 4.11).

These changes, however, do not lead to equality and harmony. Informational capitalism works on a **global level** to create huge asymmetries of power, but these cannot be understood simply as class divisions.

What forms of identity are created in the network society?

It is not just the development of this informational form of capitalism that leads to the creation of a new form of society, however. Social identity also has a key the process. Although Castells originally worked in the Marxist tradition, this last point highlights a significant difference between Castells' view of informational capitalism and the Marxist tradition. Whereas Marxists would see identity as reflecting social structures (particularly class relations), Castells argues that new social identities are a key factor in structuring and shaping social institutions. Castells identifies three important types of social identities.

- Resistance identity: Castells considers that groups which many would term terrorists can be examples of this sort of identity, for example, the Mexican Zapatistas, and the Aum Shinrikyo group in Japan. Castells argues that these identities are formed as those who are marginalised and excluded in the network society react to their position by creating their own alternative communities to cope with their situation.
- Project identity: This form of identity includes movements such as environmental groups, or gay and lesbian groups such as OutRage! This form of identity reflects what Castells calls the 'end of patriarchalism', arguing that in the network society some marginalised groups will aim at transforming society, rather than just struggling for their own survival.
- Legitimising identity: This form of identity can be thought of as a conventional identity and is the form of identity sanctioned by states (or governments). One of the most important aspects of this sort of identity is the role of the citizen. Castells argues that states introduced this role in order to control populations, but now that the power of the state is in decline such identities are also losing their power. In the UK, for example, this might be used to explain the increased sense of regional identity (Scottish, Welsh, Irish, English), as the power of the British state to unite these disparate groups has declined and other institutions (for example, the European Union) develop.

Conclusion

Several critical points can be considered in evaluating Castells theory.

1. Frank Webster (1995) claims that the theory is technologically determinist.
2. Castells exaggerates the importance of technological development. Perhaps he is over-generalising from his experience of Silicon Valley in California, where he lives.
3. Castells seems to emphasise action rather more than structure. Does identity shape institutions and structures as Castells argues, or is it the other way around?

'Outrage' members at Mardi Gras, London, protest against homophobia. An example of project identity at work in informational capitalism?

☀ Key Idea

Technological determinism is the idea that social change is caused by developments in technology. Most sociologists are highly critical of this idea because they point out that, firstly, technological developments have to be adopted and used by people, and secondly, because technologies can be used in many different ways. Cultural values exert a strong influence on how a technological innovation is used in a society.

● Synoptic Link

Link Castells' theory to your study of stratification. Castells' theory reflects the idea that forms of stratification such as class, race and gender are less important in contemporary society and are being challenged by new forms of social identity.

For consideration

1. Can information technology be a means of oppression rather than a means of promoting reflexivity?
2. In Castells account of identity, how are social identities formed?

How has modern society changed? Michel Foucault and power and language

Foucault's studies of the medical profession and prisons led him to develop the idea that expert forms of knowledge simply became new forms of power, or discourses.

☞ **Who is this person?**

Michel Foucault (1926–1984) was not a sociologist, but his work has had a big impact in a number of disciplines. Foucault as an academic is hard to categorise, but he is perhaps best considered as a philosopher or a historian of ideas. At the time of his death in 1984, Foucault was Professor of the History of Systems of Thought at the Collège de France.

❝❞ **Key Definition**

A **discourse** is just a way of talking and thinking about a subject. Discourses are sets of words or vocabularies which we learn and use in particular ways and contexts.

What does this mean?

Michel Foucault argued that sociologists should look at the way language and ideas shape our action. This is a view he shares with several other thinkers associated with two theories termed post-structuralism and postmodernism. Like all of those writing in these traditions, Foucault thinks that language is an important factor to consider in explaining social life. He is also important for creating a different view of power to that found in many sociological theories.

What does Foucault say about language and knowledge?

Foucault's work is complex and he does not present his ideas in a very systematic way, but he makes several key points about language and knowledge.

- Foucault believes we can only understand the world in terms of the language we use. Foucault calls language 'discourse'. He argues that what we think and how we think are limited by the discourses that develop in any society.
- For example, people would only describe someone as being 'overweight' in a society where we have a word to describe that phenomenon. There have of course been people of various sizes in many societies! In our society though, a particular discourse has developed and this leads us to talk about it and act in certain ways, for example, to go on diets, feel self-conscious etc. The idea of being 'overweight' therefore becomes an important aspect of our reality.
- Foucault argues that the rise of the medical profession was accompanied by the development of a discourse about the body and a 'medicalisation' of the way we think about our bodies. A focus on body image and size and the concept of being 'overweight' is one example of this discourse. In contrast to our own society, some other societies consider being 'large' to be a good thing, since it indicates wealth. Foucault concludes that knowledge, rather than being something which is objective, just reflects discourses. This means that knowledge is relative and is linked to power.

In conclusion, unlike positivists, Foucault thinks that we cannot guarantee the objectivity of knowledge, since what we 'know' is always a result of the discourses (the language) that we use to describe our lives and world. Contrary to the views of many modernist sociologists, Foucault claims that knowledge does not increase our freedom. Knowledge can be used to control us. For this reason Foucault refers to 'power/knowledge' to indicate the link between the two.

What does Foucault say about power?

Foucault's view of power can be usefully explained by contrasting it with a Marxist view of power. Foucault argues that power should not be seen as like an object which a person might have a quantity of. He is also critical of Marxist views of power which see it as something which only the ruling class or the state has, and which comes from economic relationships.

The Marxist view of power suggests that it is best seen as a constraint, stopping us from doing things. Foucault, though, claims that power is more fluid and always involves a range of options. This is a more efficient form of power since it leads people to control themselves rather than to be controlled by others. An example of this would be the way that many people 'want' to go on a diet. Foucault would say that dominant discourses lead us to think (persuade us) that it is good to be thin, so we choose to diet. Remember, **discourses** shape our world and form the options which we believe are open to us. Foucault applies this view of power to many areas including law and order and education.

Conclusion

Foucault provides a provocative view of contemporary society but there are several points that you can use to evaluate his ideas.

1. Foucault neglects the importance of economic structures and instead argues that ideas (or discourses) are more important.
2. Foucault's view of power is too pluralistic – power is everywhere and everybody has some power. Conflict theorists would argue that it is more important to see that some have more power than others.
3. Foucault does not really explain where power comes from, except to say that it comes from discourses. But who decides what discourses are available?

❋ **Key Id**

Foucault links the knowledge together and them as power/knowledge. indicate, in contrast to the modern view, that knowledge does not liberate Foucault believed that social groups would always try to use knowledge for their own benefit and to control others, as the following quotation indicates.

'The judges of normality are present everywhere. We are in the society of the teacher-judge, the doctor-judge, the educator-judge, the "social-worker"-judge; it is on them that the universal reign of the normative is based.'

(Foucault, *Discipline and Punish* 1977, page 304)

For consideration

1. What do you think Foucault's ideas imply for the goal of value-free sociology?

2. Is Foucault right to argue that knowledge always leads to power and cannot be liberating?

What are the strengths and weaknesses of the different methodologies?

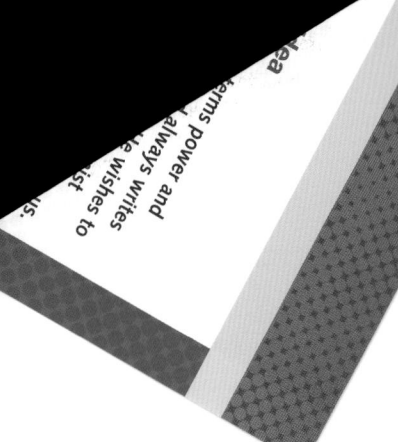

What does this mean?

Both of the two main methodological approaches used by sociologists have faults as well as strengths. There is no such thing as a perfect methodology. This inevitably means that sociologists have to engage in debates about the strengths and weaknesses of the different methodologies.

What are the strengths and weaknesses of positivist methodology?

Sociologists using a positivist methodology argue that we should use rigorous scientific methods to study people in their natural environment, with the view that this will provide valid, representative and reliable data. This approach has several key strengths.

- The rigorous use of quantitative methods should enable sociologists to create large sets of reliable and representative data. The constant emphasis on reliability should also mean that positivist methodology can eradicate bias as results may be re-tested by other researchers.
- Secondly, positivist methods should enable us to identify the **causal relationship**s between different variables.

However, while the goals of reliability, validity and representativeness should not be neglected by any sociologist, there are several key weaknesses with the positivist approach to methodology.

- Firstly, the positivist approach seems to assume that people can be studied in just the same way that chemicals or atoms are studied, and that their behaviour will not be altered by the presence of an observer.
- Quantitative methods also frequently neglect to discover the reasons why people act in certain ways or the meanings that social actions have for them.
- Positivists assume that bias can be easily controlled by testing the reliability of sociological research.
- As Ray Pawson has argued (1999), a key problem with quantitative research methods such as questionnaires is the 'imposition problem' (see *Sociology AS*, Chapter 2, unit 2.4 (pages 62–3).

Interpretivist approaches to methodology offer an alternative view of how sociologists can learn about society and social processes.

What are the strengths and weaknesses of interpretivist methodology?

Those who favour interpretivist methodology argue that it has two main strengths.

66 99 Key Definitions

- A **causal relationship** is where one factor or event (a variable) is identified as causing another. For example, the variable of social class may be considered to be the key variable determining educational success, or, to use the example of Durkheim's study of suicide, the degree of social integration causes suicide.

- **The difference between quantitative and qualitative methods**

  Quantitative methods express data in a numerical form. Questionnaires are therefore a quantitative method. Quantitative methods are favoured by positivist sociologists.

  Qualitative methods gather information which cannot be expressed numerically and is concerned with people's attitudes and motivations. Interviews and participant observation are examples of qualitative methods. These methods are favoured by interpretivists who emphasize the importance of understanding the meaning which participants place on social action.

- It acknowledges that people are **reflexive** and this enables it to develop more meaningful and truthful theoretical accounts of social processes and behaviour.
- Interpretivists argue that this sort of methodological approach is likely to provide a richer and more valid account of social behaviour. It is also likely to avoid the 'imposition problem' since researchers will give the people (the subjects) they research more opportunity to speak for themselves. Interpretivists also argue that this enables them to create more valid theoretical explanations of social behaviour.

However, several methodological criticisms can be directed at interpretivism.

- The characteristics of the qualitative methods such as their small scale and the difficulty of quantifying results can make them particularly susceptible to bias, and hard to replicate. Positivist critics would say that qualitative methods are weak in terms of reliability and validity, and are not representative.
- People may respond to researchers in unhelpful ways. The concept of the 'Hawthorne effect' or 'interviewer effect' refers to the process whereby the respondent's behaviour is changed by the presence of the researcher. Respondents may, for example, alter their behaviour due to the class, race, gender, or age of the researcher.

Which methodological approach is best?

Few sociologists would now claim that they are trying to identify the laws which govern social behaviour. Many sociologists use the technique of **methodological pluralism** or **triangulation** (see Key Definition box). Many professional sociologists now take what is called a realist approach to methodology. This means that they see society as consisting of a number of different levels or layers, including macro and micro levels. Realists argue that sociologists need to adopt a variety of methods, depending on which level of social reality they wish to research.

These approaches have been challenged in recent years by feminists arguing for a 'feminist methodology' and most recently from postmodernism, which has claimed that all methodology is biased and that the hope of objective knowledge is futile. (These will be discussed in more detail in Sections 4.19, 4.20 and 4.21).

Conclusion

Use the following points to evaluate sociologist's methodological approaches.

1. Was the research methodology appropriate for the research aims or has it missed out vital part of the picture?
2. Always use the concepts of validity, reliability, representativeness to analyse a piece of research, a finding, or a methodological approach. Try to identify how key concepts have been operationalised.
3. Try to think how a piece of research would be evaluated by a sociologist who adopts an opposing methodological approach.

For consideration

1. Is it possible to create an objective methodology?
2. Should sociologists always use triangulation?

↪ Classic Study

One of the most well-known observational studies in sociology is William Foote Whyte's study, *Street Corner Society* published in 1943. Whyte's introduction to Chicago gangs came through his friendship with 'Doc' who acted as a 'gatekeeper' allowing Whyte to gain access. As Whyte famously said of this method, '*I learned answers to questions I would not have had the sense to ask*'.

66 99 Key Definitions

- The term **reflexive** is associated with sociologist Anthony Giddens, who was influenced by the German sociologist, Max Weber, who in turn advocated the verstehen approach to social science. Verstehen is the German word for 'meaning' or 'understanding' and is also associated with 'empathy'. Weber argued that society could not be understood as if it were an object or a thing that existed independently of people's thoughts, as Durkheim advocated.

- **Methodological pluralism** means that a researcher uses a variety of methods, both qualitative and quantitative, thereby gaining the advantages of each. This is also called **triangulation**. This approach can be associated with a realist approach to methodology.

What are social facts?

... every way ... able of exerc... ...traint on the individua... ...The Rules of Sociologica... ..., in K. Thompson (1985). So typ... of action such as suicide or crime are **social facts**. For Durkheim these apparently individual actions are the result of social forces which control individual actions.

✳ Key Idea

Durkheim believed that social structures exist 'externally' to individuals. This means that we do not have free will and that these forces will always shape our behaviour. Durkheim states: '*When I undertake my duties as a brother, husband, or citizen and fulfil the commitments that I have entered into, I perform obligations which are defined outside myself and my actions, in law and custom.*' (K. Thompson, *Readings from Emile Durkheim*, London, Routledge 1985, pages 68–9)

A Kamikaze pilot prepares for his suicide flight during the Second World War. Interpretivists say that sociologists ought to focus more on how our definitions of suicide are influenced by social factors.

What does this mean?

The concept of **social facts** was created by Durkheim. Durkheim was a positivist, and believed that the aim of sociology was to identify the general laws governing society, something which involved identifying social facts. Durkheim used the term '*social fact*' to refer to forces which he believed acted to constrain our behaviour, such as social integration. Durkheim famously said that we should '*treat social facts as things*' (Thompson 1985). According to Durkheim these forces are '*external*' to us and we have no control over them. Durkheim's claims have a central place in sociological theory and methodology. Those who follow Durkheim argue that sociology can and should adopt a positivist methodology. However, Durkheim's position is the subject of considerable debate.

What exactly do positivists say about the nature of social facts?

In his study on suicide, Durkheim aimed to show how even something as apparently individual as the decision to commit suicide, was the result of social forces and should be seen as a 'social fact'. Durkheim argued that suicide was caused by the level of social integration. He decided to test the hypothesis that when social integration was high, suicide rates would be low, and that the suicide rate would rise as the level of social integration fell. He chose religion as his indicator of social integration, and hypothesised that in mainly Catholic societies the suicide rates would be lower than those in Protestant societies. Durkheim tested his hypothesis by gathering secondary quantitative data. He found that the evidence did indeed support his hypothesis, and concluded that his hypothesis was proven.

What do interpretivists say about social facts?

Sociologists who take an interpretivist approach to methodology have made a number of criticisms of Durkheim's study and his positivist methodology.

- Durkheim assumed that the official statistics which he used for his research gave a valid picture of suicide in the societies studied. As Douglas (1967) and Atkinson (1978) have argued, all these statistics prove is that there were lower recorded levels of suicide (on average) in different societies. The statistics may not give a true picture of reality.
- Interpretivists argue that Durkheim ought to have considered the social processes by which the courts and legal officers came to classify certain deaths as suicide.
- Interpretivists argue that our understanding of suicide is socially constructed, and is not, as Durkheim argues, something which is external to us. It is, in fact, people who create the idea of suicide and then make judgements as to whether a death should count as a suicide or not.
- Interpretivists conclude that if Durkheim had followed this alternative

methodology he may have found that differences in recorded levels of suicide simply reflect the fact that coroners in Catholic societies are less likely to record deaths as suicide, as suicide is considered to be shameful in a Catholic society. Interpretivists would argue that this is indeed the case.

Interpretivists use this example to argue the case that reality is not an object that is external to us. On the contrary, it is socially constructed, and the best way to understand it is by using an interpretivist (qualitative) methodology.

Why does the debate about social facts matter?

We can see that views on the nature of society and about how sociological research should be done are sharply divided, and can give us radically different descriptions and explanations of the world. The debate about the nature of social facts is therefore important for the following reasons.

- It relates closely to the structure/action debate (see Section 4.11). Positivists follow Durkheim and see structures acting as external constraints. Interpretivists see structures as less rigid and society as socially constructed. This is important because it involves a disagreement over whether we actually have any ability to change our situation or not. Are we free or are we the prisoners of external social forces?
- The debate provides us with two competing views about whether sociology is a science. These are important because they shape our views about what sociology is for and what it can do.

Conclusion

Use the following points to evaluate and draw conclusions from the debate about social facts.

1. Durkheim's positivist approach has the great merit of showing how our world consists of social structures which shape our lives.
2. Interpretivism, however, usefully points out that we have to understand that people have reasons for acting as they do. People are reflexive and have free will.
3. We can synthesise the useful elements from both of these methodological approaches by adopting the methodological approach of realism (see Sections 4.19 and 4.21).

For consideration

1. What does it mean to say that social structures are 'external' to us?

2. Does positivism have a flawed view of human agency?

◆ **What, when and why**

It is important to be able to understand Durkheim's classic study on suicide (1897) in its historical context. The 19th century was a period of tremendous social change. There was also a widely-held belief that social progress was both good and inevitable. Durkheim conducted his study because he wanted to prove that sociology could be as scientific as the natural sciences and could make a great contribution to social progress. Now of course, views on the possibility of social progress and the role of sociology are more sceptical (see Sections 4.12–4.16).

● **Synoptic Link**

The debate about social facts and methodological approaches is one which runs through all topics in sociology. It is particularly useful to use when discussing the validity of official statistics in crime. Positivists follow Durkheim and believe statistics reveal social reality, while interpretivists argue that they just show how crime is socially constructed.

Can sociology be value-free?

What does this mean?

Sociologists aim to provide accurate information about society and to explain social behaviour. However, there have always been debates about whether sociologists can investigate social issues in an objective and factual way, and whether they can put their own values aside when conducting research.

Sociology can be value-free

The idea that sociological research is true, regardless of the values of the researcher, is most clearly associated with positivism. This is because positivists claim that they are able to demonstrate their objectivity through the use of scientific research methods.

However, Max Weber, although not a positivist, also took the view that researchers' values need not bias good research; he believed that sociologists could maintain what is referred to as a 'separation of fact and value'. Weber's chief concern was that sociology teachers and lecturers should not let their own values influence their students and he thought that in lessons and lectures sociologists should stick to the facts. Weber did admit that values would clearly play a role in what researchers selected to study, which he called value-relevance. However, Weber believed that from that point, systematic, empirical procedures had to be used by sociologists to ensure that their own values did not shape or bias the conduct or results of research.

Sociology cannot be value-free

Throughout the 20th century and into the 21st sociologists have continued to debate the role of values in social research and whether researchers are able to be objective. There are two well known advocates of the view that **value-freedom** is not possible.

Howard Becker in a famous article 'Whose side are we on?' (1967) argued that sociologists should take sides. Becker argued, though, that this must mean taking the side of the underdog or the oppressed.

Alvin Gouldner (1968) argued that sociologists cannot claim neutrality and must always make their own values clear. He contradicts Weber on this point and says that lecturers should make their values clear so that their students can identify the values at work and make their own decision about whether they agree with them or not.

Can sociologists be objective?

More recently feminists have made an important contribution to this debate by

66 99 Key Definition

Value-freedom in research means that research has not been biased by the researcher's values and therefore is objective and factual.

⁎ Key Idea

The feminist standpoint approach suggests that people's differing values, experiences, and personal and social characteristics cannot be eliminated from research. Moreover, as long as researchers are rigorous and systematic, such factors can even be helpful in conducting research, perhaps by helping researchers identify with respondents' beliefs, or by sensitising them and enabling them to identify important issues or questions.

criticising the view that sociologists can or should exclude all 'irrelevant' influences from the research process.

Several feminist researchers have pointed out how their own personal characteristics and values have been helpful to them in conducting research. Ann Oakley, for example (in Roberts 1981), has been critical of the supposed neutrality of interview methods given that researchers have to interact with respondents if they are to gain good data. Janet Finch (in Roberts 1981) agrees, arguing that it is impossible to exclude the researcher's own status and identity as an influence on the research process. She conducted research on clergy wives, but notes that the character of her interviews was inevitably influenced by the fact that she was a woman and that her respondents knew that she too was married to a clergyman.

Feminists such as Stanley and Wise (1983) have interpreted findings like this as meaning that only women can do valid research on certain issues and that the experience of women is therefore more valid (or privileged) than that of a male researcher. However, critics contend that this leads to relativism and a situation where it could be argued, for example, that white researchers could not conduct valid research on ethnic minorities. One solution to this debate comes from what is termed standpoint feminism (Cain 1990). This view suggests that women's particular experiences can give them greater insight and sensitivity into some issues and that this can be turned to an advantage in the research process.

Postmodernist-influenced sociologists would take a more sceptical view of this approach and argue that all knowledge is inevitably partial and subjective. Postmodernists such as Lyotard (1984) argue that all truth is relative, and that sociologists are mistaken to claim they can be objective or can separate fact from value.

Conclusion

Here are three points to use in evaluating the role of values in research.

1. Values can determine what scientists consider to be relevant and useful research questions.
2. Experience may sensitise us and lead us to ask new questions, it is not always a disadvantage.
3. When you are evaluating a piece of research, consider whether the researcher's background could have influenced the findings.

Do the social characteristics of the researcher influence the research process?

✓ Top Exam Hint

You can use postmodernists' sceptical views on the possibility of value-freedom to evaluate other sociological views. Remember, though, that while sociologists may not be able to be objective (maybe it is impossible to be completely objective) they can use methods systematically and rigorously, and demonstrate how they reached their conclusions.

∝ Classic Study

Ann Oakley's study of housework, *The Sociology of Housework*, (1974) provides a good example of the way sociologists' research interests are influenced by values. Oakley had tremendous difficulty in getting permission to study housework as a topic for her PhD thesis at the University of London. Her academic supervisors (who were male) could not see how housework could be a relevant topic for sociological study.

For consideration

1. Do you think Weber is right to suggest that values only influence the research problems that sociologists choose?

2. If postmodernists are right, is there any point in doing sociological research?

| # Is sociology a science?

What does this mean?

For classical sociologists, such as Marx and Durkheim, the aim of sociology was to provide a 'science of society'. They wanted to be able to study society scientifically, free from prejudices. This would enable us to solve social problems and lead to a society capable of continual progress.

What evidence is there that sociology is a science?

The sociologists most closely associated with the belief that sociology can be scientific are called positivists. Positivists believe that providing research is carried out in the correct manner, using rigorous empirical methods, then sociology can be scientific. In order to do this, sociologists have to develop and test hypotheses. This process enables them to identify causal relationships and laws.

What evidence is there that sociology is not a science?

Not all modernist sociologists have taken the view that sociology can be a science. Philosophers of science such as Paul Feyerabend (1993) and Thomas Kuhn (1970) have argued that science itself is not as objective as its supporters claim. Thomas Kuhn argues that science always involves value-judgements and that scientists are influenced by many factors in selecting what they see as the most relevant 'facts'. Kuhn says that studying science involves learning a set of key facts and assumptions, which he calls a **paradigm**. These facts and assumptions are not questioned. The result is that many findings which do not fit in with the assumptions of what he calls 'normal science' are disregarded. Eventually these findings may become meaningful when a new 'discovery' is made. This means that what counts as science changes over time, and this casts great doubt over the notion that science provides us with the truth.

It follows that scientists may not be as 'objective' as is claimed. All knowledge is produced in a social context involving assumptions and beliefs about what is relevant. Scientists may be influenced by personal values, religious beliefs, political values, by their own background (gender, race, class age, nationality) and by the desire to win professional acclaim. Lastly, the subject matter of sociology – people – are far more complex than the subject matter of natural science, most of which does not think or talk and whose behaviour remains the same whether it is being observed or not.

What have sociologists said about this debate more recently?

This debate has developed in new ways since the 1960s and 1970s. Realists (sometimes called scientific realists) such as Layder (1994) and Sayer (1984) argue that sociology and science are in fact very similar. Both can be open to the criticism of bias and subjective influences. There are differences in the subject matter of both, but these differences can be exaggerated. Not all of the subject matter of the natural sciences lacks consciousness, but it can be

✓ Top Exam Hint

You can use your knowledge of feminism to evaluate questions on this topic. Many feminists would argue that science is a highly gendered discipline, where what counts as knowledge is shaped by patriarchal attitudes and values. These tend to rule out the role of experience and use what many feminists see as a bogus claim to 'objectivity' and 'detachment' to make claims to knowledge seem more authentic.

66 99 Key Definition

A **paradigm** is simply a set of assumptions and beliefs about something. Kuhn argues that science operates in terms of a set of common assumptions, for example, the belief that the earth is round not flat, and that time travel is not possible. Kuhn calls this paradigm 'normal science'.

harder to study the so-called '**open systems**' of society, where the behaviour of the subjects of research is less predictable.

Postmodernists such as Lyotard (1984) have become well known for presenting the argument that all knowledge is relative and that absolute truth is simply not attainable. Science and sociology are simply alternative **metanarratives** and the only basis on which to choose between them is personal preference.

Anthony Giddens has argued that sociology cannot be scientific because people are reflexive beings (Giddens 1974). This makes sociology very different from a science. Sociological findings actually act back upon society, because people learn about them, and this can then lead to them changing their behaviour. As a result sociology is more like a very sophisticated form of social criticism, rather than a science which allows us to try and control nature.

More recently Giddens has argued that postmodernists' claims that all knowledge is relative are ultimately contradictory (Giddens 1990). Giddens contests that knowledge is always uncertain and always provisional. It is also true that knowledge is always produced in a certain social context. However, Giddens says that the idea of reason is still a useful one. This is because reason is always open to criticism and argument. Through systematic research, debate, and criticism we arrive, not at the absolute truth, but at the closest to it that we can expect.

Conclusion

One way of concluding this debate is to suggest that neither sociology nor science can be absolutely objective and the differences between them are often exaggerated.

1. Scientific and sociological knowledge are both open to bias and both scientists and sociologists have to select and interpret evidence.
2. The interpretation of evidence (whether in a science or social science) will always occur in a social context.
3. The best that we can do is to interpret evidence systematically and rigorously.

For consideration

1. Will complete objectivity ever be possible?
2. What factors might lead scientists to be biased?

How can sociology influence social policy?

What does this mean?

All governments make policies (plans) which map out the main guidelines and principles as to how a particular issue or topic will be dealt with. For example governments have policies on transport, health, education, the economy, and so on. **Social policies** are concerned with the social needs of the population, such as welfare, employment, education, housing, health, and law and order.

Many sociologists want their research to help solve social problems and lead to change. However, to understand how sociology can influence social policy, we first need to know a little about how sociological research is organised and funded in the UK.

How is sociological research organised and funded in the UK?

Sociological research always requires some form of funding, to pay for secretarial staff, research staff, computing facilities, postage and all the other facilities that are needed to collect and analyse data. This means that research is rarely carried out by researchers acting in isolation; they usually need some institutional support to help them in their work.

For this reason most sociological research in the UK is carried out by academic researchers in universities. Most of these academics have to carry out research in addition to teaching duties; a far smaller number are able to devote their time solely to research. Academic researchers of both types though still need funding. One of the biggest sources of funding for research in Britain is the government, in order to inform new social policy.

Government departments often invite researchers to apply for research contracts, but this is a competitive process. Bids are called for (a process termed tendering) and departments appoint those offering the best research package. In this context, 'best' means that the research will deliver the data required quickly and at the right cost. The Departments of Health, Work and Pensions, and Education and Skills, and the Home Office, are some of the biggest users of sociological data. There is also a body called the ESRC (Economic and Social Research Council) which is funded by the government. The ESRC has an annual budget and sponsors a range of projects across the social sciences. Again, researchers have to compete and have to produce the sort of research that the Council wants to fund.

Sociological research can also be carried out, or sponsored, by other institutions, such as think tanks, pressure groups, and local government authorities such as police forces, health authorities, social services departments, or by private companies.

How can sociology influence social policy?

Many sociologists working in the modernist tradition had an optimistic view about the influence sociology could have on social policies. It was believed that sociology could:

- help to provide the solutions to social problems, for example, unemployment, crime, educational failure and poverty by showing how they are caused
- identify ways of improving social services and social policies, for example, the health service, the courts and the criminal justice system.

Are there any problems raised by the funding of research by government and large organisations?

Some sociologists, such as those from the tradition of **critical theory**, have felt that sociology is inevitably compromised by too close a relationship to government and large organisations. This relationship can be difficult for several reasons.

- Funding bodies only want a certain type of research. They often want research which does not threaten or challenge their own basic assumptions. Researchers have to share the institutional definitions of common sense. This can mean that there are some questions which cannot be asked.
- The style and the nature of the research can be shaped by funding bodies. Most large organisations want research conducted very quickly. They also want research reports kept brief, quantified whenever possible, and with clear and simple recommendations for action. A more complex qualitative report might be more truthful but could be seen as less useful.

Conclusion

1. The nature of sociology should caution us against excessive optimism. Sociology cannot provide a 'scientific' solution to social problems. Sociologists can only hope to contribute to social policy.
2. Researchers are also members of society. They too have a variety of political views and values. Sociological views and policy recommendations should be systematic and based on evidence, but they still have to be evaluated and that must involve values.

For consideration

1. If sociology is not a science, what is the point of studying it?
2. Should research which is not considered useful (i.e. not policy related) be funded? If so, who should fund it?

※ **Key Idea**

Critical theorists is the name given to sociologists influenced by Marxism and the work of the Frankfurt School, including Habermas (see Section 4.7). These sociologists believe that the production of knowledge is always a social activity and inevitably permeated by power relations. They believe that the separation of facts and values is impossible and that sociology must challenge oppression. However, in many ways this moves them from a positivist to a more interpretive view of Marxism and of sociology.

● **Synoptic Link**

It is important to see how sociological research in different topic areas could both influence social policies, and be influenced by the demands of policy makers. For example, in much funded research into crime and deviance there appears to be a relative neglect of crimes of the powerful. Try to identify some further links in your topic areas.

✓ **Top Exam Hint**

It is well worth applying Anthony Giddens' idea of reflexivity to evaluate the way that research findings can influence social policy. Giddens argues that sociological findings often end up becoming common sense. This knowledge can then be used by people to change their behaviour, but this can happen in unpredictable ways. For example, sociological research on marital breakdown may lead people to appreciate that entering a marriage is a risky business. This may change people's behaviour and may alter the subject being studied, i.e. family structures, in new and unexpected ways which sociologists cannot predict.

Are sociologists interpreters or legislators?

What does this mean?

Sociologist Zygmunt Bauman (1989) has argued that postmodernism has led to a more fundamental shift in the views we have about what sociology is for and what it can do. Bauman argues that it is now possible to see that there are two main answers to the question of what sociology can do; a modernist answer and a postmodernist answer.

What is the modernist view of sociology?

Bauman says that sociology has been formed by many of the intellectual beliefs of modern society. Bauman is referring to philosophical beliefs, and particularly important are the values of the philosophical movement called 'the Enlightenment'. One of the most important ideas of the Enlightenment philosophers was the idea that knowledge could be generated through reason. This may seem obvious now, but prior to the Enlightenment people had often thought in terms of mystical or religious beliefs. The Enlightenment saw the beginnings of what we recognise as modern science, and the idea that knowledge could be gained through reasoning, rational discussion, and empirical investigation.

Bauman says that these beliefs led to a particular role for intellectuals in modern society. Bauman states, *'The typically modern strategy of intellectual work is one best characterised by the metaphor of the "legislator" role. It consists of making authoritative statements which arbitrate in controversies of opinions and which select those opinions which, having been selected, become correct and binding.'* (Bauman 1989, page 4)

What Bauman says about the role of intellectuals in modern society can also be applied to sociologists. A legislator is someone who makes laws or rules for the rest of the population, and Bauman says that the modernist version of sociology was one where sociologists took the role of legislators. They did this in the following ways.

- Modernist sociologists assumed that they were able to identify the truth by using reason and rigorous empirical methods (whether positivistic or interpretivist).
- This meant that sociologists (like other 'intellectuals') could take the role of expert and make pronouncements upon social issues which they had researched. This also meant that they could help to 'legislate', or to put it more bluntly, join the ranks of those people in society who tell others what to do (cf. Foucault, Section 4.16).

In doing this, modernist sociologists would, Bauman argues, necessarily be making a claim to have knowledge that was universally valid, since it was based on reason.

Zygmunt Bauman is Emeritus (retired) Professor of Sociology at the University of Leeds. He discusses the role of sociologists in his 1989 book, *Legislators and Intepreters.*

✳ Key Idea

The notion of universal truth implies accurate knowledge of the world which [is t]rue at all times and in all places. In [... t]erm relativism suggests that [... so]cially constructed [... differen]t cultures.

What is the postmodernist view of sociology?

Bauman argues that the postmodernist view is that intellectuals and therefore sociologists can only take the role of 'interpreters'. This is because postmodernist thinkers believe that it is no longer possible to entertain the idea that we can objectively identify the truth nor trust **metanarratives**. Postmodernists believe that all ideas about truth vary (truth is relative) between different cultures and knowledge is always socially constructed. This means that all any intellectual or sociologist can do is give their own, socially constructed, account of the truth. In doing this researchers will inevitably be influenced by their own norms and values; it is impossible to escape from these. For this reason, postmodernists argue that those making claims to knowledge can really only offer us alternative interpretations of reality, and not, as modernists would claim, an objective, truthful account of reality.

Should sociologists be interpreters or legislators?

Postmodernism has forced sociologists to reflect carefully on some of their methodological and theoretical assumptions. It has usefully drawn attention to the uncertainty of all knowledge, and to the pervasiveness of power and the difficulty of change.

However, there are good reasons for maintaining our belief in the principles of the Enlightenment. Anthony Giddens (1990) has rejected the postmodernist view that it is not possible to identify the truth, commenting *'Let us first of all dismiss as unworthy of serious intellectual consideration the idea that no systematic knowledge of human action or trends of social development is possible'* (Giddens 1990, page 46). Giddens points out that uncertainty is the normal state of human knowledge, something identified by Popper and Kuhn (see Section 4.20).

Conclusion

You can use the following points to evaluate the methodological debates between postmodernism and modernism.

1. Postmodernists have been right to point out that all knowledge is socially constructed. However, this does not mean that we cannot make judgements about the accuracy of different research findings.
2. Philosopher Jürgen Habermas argues that postmodernists hide their values and beliefs, in contrast to his own work which makes clear his commitment to reason. He also argues that postmodernist approaches to theory and methodology are too general. This makes their claims impossible to test empirically (1981, 1987).
3. Postmodernist claims that truth is relative are contradictory. Presumably if we should have no more belief in metanarratives, we should also include postmodernism itself?

For consideration

1. Do sociologists always know better than non-sociologists?
2. If knowledge is always uncertain, what is the point of sociological research?

66 99 Key Definition

Metanarratives are theories which attempt to explain how society works and claim that they reveal the truth. Lyotard argues that a key characteristic of postmodern society is that we no longer trust such theories. *'I define postmodern as incredulity toward metanarratives.'* (Jean-François Lyotard 1984, page xxiiif)

∞ Methods Link

Modernist sociologists believe that we can use argument and reason to dispute rival claims to the truth and eventually we can reach agreement.

Postmodernist sociologists believe that all of our knowledge is inevitably socially constructed and therefore we cannot identify one truth that all will be able to accept (a universal truth). In fact, postmodernists say that such a truth does not exist, precisely because all knowledge and ideas are socially constructed. The idea of truth itself is a social construct. The idea of truth therefore can only ever be a product of a particular time, place and culture.

How can we make theory and methods synoptic?

Why is synopticity important for theory and method?

It is particularly important to use theory and method synoptically because there are some vital sets of concepts and debates contained in this topic that have implications for all areas of sociology. Key concepts, for example, are power, and social control, and a key debate is the structure/action debate.

How do theory and method link to issues of culture?

Sociological perspectives on culture illustrate the importance of power and social control. For functionalists, culture integrates and holds society together. Marxists see it as a form of power and social control.

How do theory and method link to issues of identity?

Identity is an issue where the structure/action debate is highly relevant. Modernist theories have tended to see identity as a relatively straightforward process of socialisation. Marxists and feminists have particularly emphasised the role of social control in this process. All of these theoretical approaches though have tended to emphasise that identity is the outcome of structural forces, and have tended to see people as rather passive. More recent theoretical views (for example, Giddens, post-structuralists, postmodernists) have seen identity as something which is socially constructed.

How do theory and method link to issues of inequality?

Theoretical debates about what society is like also link up to methodological debates about how we should find out about it. Sociologists measure wealth in different ways and emphasise different types of wealth according to their theoretical background. Marxist sociologists tend to focus on what is called 'productive wealth' (property ownership). This is because their theoretical view suggests that the most important aspects of ownership are those that reinforce the structural position of the ruling class. Here we can see how a theoretical view helps sociologists to interpret, select and order information in a way which fits their theoretical outlook. Another example occurs in the way sociologists define and **operationalise** poverty, which is inevitably influenced by subjective values and theoretical outlook.

How do theory and method link to issues of deviance?

In crime and deviance, methodological issues arise in the study of official statistics. Sociologists influenced by positivism tend to see official statistics as providing a useful basis for research. Intepretivist critics see official statistics as lacking in validity and tend to give more credibility to studies using qualitative

✳ Key Idea

Operationalisation is the way that abstract concepts are turned into something that can be measured and involves selecting appropriate indicators. This is often a contentious area in sociology as researchers often disagree about the meaning of an indicator.

methods. This debate has implications for theories of crime, since many theories of crime tend to assume that most crime is committed by young working-class males, as crime statistics indicate. If official statistics lack validity, however, it may be that theoretical explanations of crime also lack validity. Here we see how theory and method can influence each other.

How do theory and method link to issues of stratification and differentiation?

Sociologists use various definitions of class and operationalise the concept in different ways (see Chapter 2). Marxists believe in a ruling class and, as indicated above, see the ownership or non-ownership of the means of production as a key criteria or indicator of class position. Weberians take a very different approach and argue that there are significant differences, for example in terms of income, between non-owners. These different definitions and operationalisations of class lead to very different descriptions of the class structure and theoretical debates about which explanation is correct.

Feminist sociologists have been highly critical of the 'malestream' definition and measurement of class, which always neglects the class position of women and their contribution to household incomes and life chances. Recently, sociologists influenced by postmodernism such as Ray Pahl (1989) and Pakulski and Waters (1996) have even suggested that sociological measurements of class are meaningless and have little significance in contemporary society.

Theories such as Marxism have been considered 'race blind', and seen as reducing issues of race to class issues. This may reflect the fact that Marxism was developed in a time when ethnic and racial issues were not considered to be as important as they are now.

Key points to remember

- Theory and method always shape the way data is collected, what data is collected, and how it is interpreted.
- Remember to apply key theoretical concepts such as power, social control, or debates like the structure/action debate to all the topics you study.
- To understand a sociologist's work, you have to understand the context in which the work was done, since it will always reflect a particular time and culture.

✓ Top Exam Hint

Methodological issues such as reliability, representativeness, and validity are essential concepts to use when evaluating a piece of sociological research. Discuss them where relevant and show that you understand why the concept is important. You can do this by showing how weakness in any of these points undermines a sociological conclusion, or alternatively how we may have more confidence in conclusions where these factors are convincingly covered.

4.24 | Pushing your grades up higher

66 99 Key Definition

AO1 is about your knowledge and understanding.

AO2 skills are about your ability to identify, analyse, interpret, and evaluate.

What do I need to do to get a good grade?

At A2 level you are expected to have a deeper knowledge and understanding of theory and methods than you did when studying for the AS level. This is reflected in the allocation of marks. More marks are available for **AO2** (Identification, Analysis, Interpretation and Evaluation) than for **AO1** (Knowledge and Understanding). This means that it is not sufficient just to know about theories and methods. You must be able to apply your knowledge appropriately and critically, evaluate competing perspectives and methodological approaches, and interpret data and sociological material.

Whatever level you are working at there are always things you can do to improve your work, so this section is relevant to everybody. There is a range of strategies that you can use to help maximise your chances of improving your work and gaining the best grade possible. The following are just a few tips to get you started.

1. Theories are fun, they challenge received wisdom and give you alternative pictures of the world. Learn to see them like this and you will find them helpful and maybe even liberating.

2. Consult your specification carefully. Theory and methods is an 'integral element' of your specification. This means that it is relevant to all the topic areas you study. Use every opportunity to show your theoretical and methodological understanding. It demonstrates that you are thinking like a sociologist.

3. Use the AS edition of this book to help you find at least five studies using qualitative methods from each of the topic areas you studied in the AS year. Make a list of the strengths and weaknesses of these studies. Do the same for quantitative methods. Follow the same procedure for your A2 topics.

4. Get some past papers and practise writing outline answers. If possible get your teacher to check over your plans.

5. Learn to use the language of sociology; if used properly it is not jargon but rather it shows that you know what you are talking about. Make sure that you know and understand terms such as: agent, structure, determinism, validity, reliability, representativeness, operationalisation and methodological pluralism. Use the terms frequently in your written work. If you are using the terms appropriately it will show that you have developed a good understanding of sociology.

6. Read broadsheet newspapers such as *The Times*, *The Guardian*, or *The Observer*, or journals such as the *New Statesman*, *The Economist*, *Sociology Review*, or *New Scientist* regularly. These will expand your vocabulary and allow you to apply your knowledge of theories and methods. In newspapers and journals, try to see if politicians' explanations

of social problems reflect particular sociological theories. Examine the nature of evidence used in public debate.

7. Work out which theories and methods you find most convincing. Do not expect to be able to identify only one theory or approach as the 'correct' one. You may, for example, lean more towards conflict theory, or more towards a micro view of society. Working out what your own preferences are will help you to evaluate theories and methods more convincingly. List four reasons why you prefer a theory and a method in your own words.

8. Whatever your own theoretical preferences are, identify three criticisms that are made of this theory. Work out how you would respond to these criticisms.

9. Now follow the same procedure in point 8 for your preferred methodological approach. For example, you may be a keen fan of qualitative methods such as participant observation. Work out how you would respond to these common criticisms of this method: its lack of reliability, the problem of the observer influencing events, the lack of representativeness.

10. By this stage in your studies you should be becoming more skilled at extended evaluation. Nevertheless, remember to evaluate theories and methods in detail. Explain why a theory or method is open to a criticism. Also remember that in long answers for 40 mark questions you have to construct a reasoned argument (even if you are a postmodernist). Organise your thoughts into logical paragraphs, link paragraphs with 'signpost' words or phrases, such as 'However', 'In contrast, others argue that…', and end your answer with a good conclusion.

Key Points

- Make sure you learn the key terms and concepts in theories and methods.
- Make sure that you can evaluate theories and methods and take opportunities to demonstrate your sociological imagination.
- Learn at least five studies from each topic you have studied and ensure that there is an even spread of quantitative and qualitative studies.

✓ Top Exam Hints

- Obtain copies of past exam papers and spend some of your revision time planning out (although not writing in full) answers to previous questions.

- Remember to practise how you will set your answers out in the exam. Clearly indicate which question and which part of the question you are answering. It is a good idea to leave a line between each distinct question or part of a question. This enables the examiner to distinguish easily the different parts of your question. This is particularly important in the 'Identify and briefly explain' type of short question.

Frequently asked questions

Q. Why are there so many different theories in sociology?

A. Firstly, because sociologists all have different views on any given matter. They are no different in this respect from anybody else. Secondly, as theories are criticised and new evidence is generated, problems are found with theories. Sociologists are, therefore, frequently modifying theories to try and take these factors into account. Thirdly, theories in sociology are said to be underdetermined by empirical evidence. This means that however much evidence is collected, a theory is never really proved, it just seems more convincing. This means that the number of theories that we have does not shrink as much over time as you might think it would. Lastly as society changes, it becomes apparent that old theories are lacking and need updating, so new ones are created.

Q. Why do some theories get updated?

A. Theories are living bodies of thought and will inevitably change as society changes. For example, those influenced by Marxist thought in the 20th century were constantly adapting and modifying Marxism in the light of social change, such as the absence of revolution in western societies. Sociologists such as Giddens argue that this is simply part of the nature of knowledge and sociological theories (see Sections 4.14, 4.20).

Q. Can a man be a feminist?

A. The answer to this will depend on who you ask. Most radical separatist feminists would say no. Liberal feminists are more likely to say yes. Another way to look at this is to understand that sociology is meant to be an analytical discipline and our personal views are not supposed to bias our observations and explanations. So it could be argued that a man could adopt a feminist perspective sociologically, using its concepts to explain social phenomena. Those who say men cannot be feminists argue that our values and experiences are so strongly shaped by gender that it is impossible for us to understand fully how the world is seen by others. Similar arguments have been expressed about the possibility of whether white researchers can properly study black people, or vice versa.

Part 2 SYNOPTIC SKILLS – UNIT 6

Chapter 5

How to be synoptic

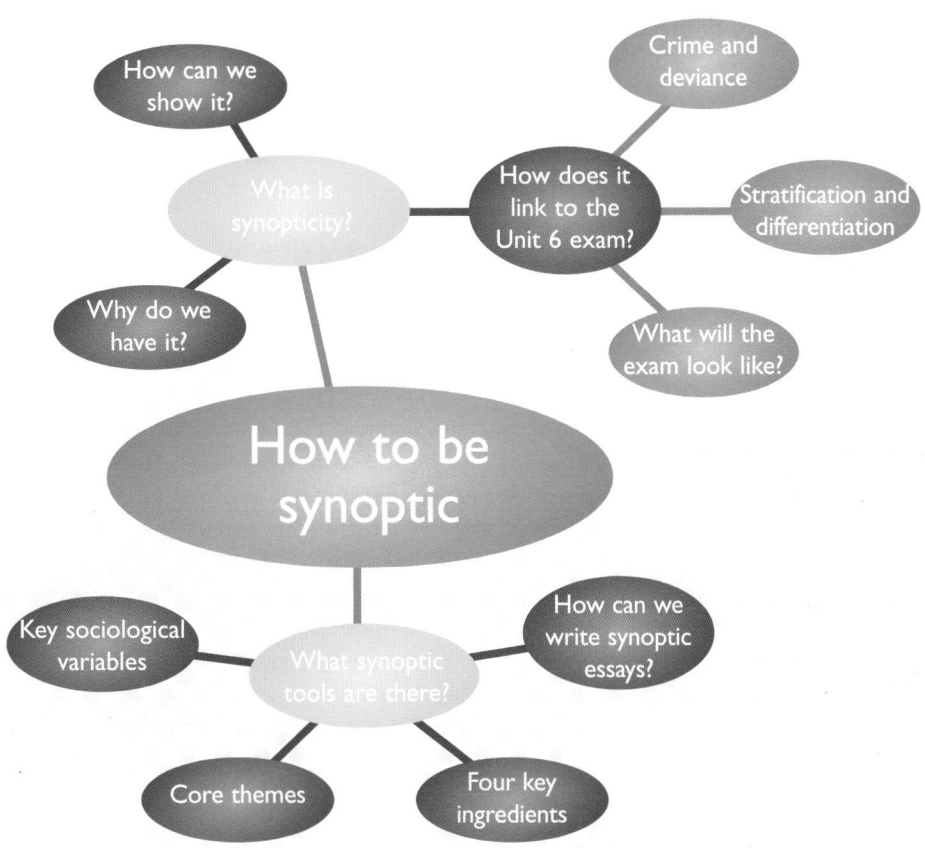

Key issues in synopticity

Synopticity is all about making links between the different ideas, concepts and theories that come up in each of the six units in the two-year course.

∞ Methods Link

Do not forget that of the three questions in the Unit 6 exam, one will be based on making links to theory, one will be based on making links to topics and one will be based on making links to issues of methods.

66 99 Key Definition

Being **synoptic** means being able to tie things together, while summarising at the same time.

● Synoptic Link

Synopticity accounts for 20 per cent of the final grade.

What does synopticity mean?

By being **synoptic** we actually mean *being able to tie the whole course together:* being able to see how the whole six modules over the two years link together.

How can you be synoptic?

The idea of synopticity means that, as a student, you should be able to see that the different units and modules of sociology do, in fact, all link together as a whole. It is about looking at the things that join the individual bits up; looking at connections.

The good news is that sociology has always been 'synoptic', even before we actually started using the word. If you want to think like a sociologist then you are going to have to understand that society is interconnected, and therefore that all the different parts of the course are also interconnected. This is simply good sociology anyway.

- In order to be synoptic, the starting point, as usual for sociology, is theory. Theories let us make comparisons between topics – what a theory might say about one aspect of society, such as family, would then probably affect the thinking about another different aspect of society, such as education or the media. Theories let us see that society is interconnected. Theories encourage us to think about the joined up bits of the course, rather than simply see sociology as a series of unrelated topics.
- The other key synoptic tool we have is methods. Each topic or unit in sociology has case studies that are completed using methods. The same issues and problems of research and data gathering exist in many different topics.

Building up and breaking down

Often, students' perception of school is that different knowledge is taught by different teachers in different rooms and that the subjects all have different names and are located in different 'faculties' or 'departments'. It does not look as if there are any common connections, but there are! Learning about chemicals in science would help you in art. Learning about art history might help you in English literature or in history itself. Teachers often encourage us to break down connections because it is always easier to learn something if it is split up into smaller parts.

This is also true for this book. We are pulling sociology apart to show you how it all works. But, once you have pulled it apart, you then need to re-build it again, otherwise it will not work. This means that being synoptic is really important and useful; it will allow us to see how sociology links together. It has always been the case that good students saw and discussed in exams all the connections between the different ideas in sociology. Now, you get rewarded formally for this too.

What synoptic tools are there to use?

We can talk of synopticity in two main senses.

- **Social synopticity** means seeing the connections between the parts of society, and hopefully using sociological theories and ideas in order to do this.
- **Sociological synopticity** means seeing connections between sociological ideas themselves; looking at what might link together different studies or theories or even debates that sociologists might have.

It makes sense to see these two types of synopticity as related. Since everything in society is connected, then everything in sociology must also be connected. Imagine it like this. You leave your house and you go to school one morning. You talk to your friends on the bus about what you watched on TV last night. Even in this 'normal' example of life we have a lot of connections going on – family, education and mass media. We must also note that culture tells us we must go to school, and so does the law! Class is a factor here, as is ethnicity; these might affect where we live and also what we might actually watch on TV. As you can see, life is one big interconnected whole. In order to do good sociology, you must be aware of this.

In order to try and see how both society and sociology are connected, we can use the following 'tools':

- class
- gender
- ethnicity
- culture
- identity
- age
- location
- globalisation.

These tools will allow you to think about how ideas and theories are connected. You can use them to link studies together or to link theories together, both from within the same topic, or from different topics even across the AS and A2 years. You will find that these 'tools' are key concepts that have a massive relevance to every topic in the whole specification.

At the end of the day, all sociology is about two ideas, which are related to each other.

- **Power**: who gets their way in society, and how and why?
- **Stratification**: how is society divided up?

Conclusion

You will be examined for synopticity at the end of the A2 course in either the crime and deviance module or the stratification module, depending what your school or college teaches. This is the very final exam you will sit, Unit 6.

Key points to remember

- Synopticity is a natural part of the 'sociological imagination'.
- Synopticity means making links and seeing connections.
- There are a number of tools or concepts that you can use in order to be synoptic.

✓ Top Exam Hints

- Students get high grades by showing that they are aware of all the inter-connections between the ideas in each topic. They also get high grades for using theories and methods issues in essay questions.
- Use the synoptic concepts in high-mark questions as a way to show your understanding of how all sociology is connected.

SUBSTANTIVE TOPICS

5.2 | How will your synoptic skills be tested?

What does the specification want you to do? It asks you to be familiar with three things: connections between your Unit 6 topic and other topics; the nature of sociological thought; and how sociologists use methods of enquiry. You will need to use these three things in the exam.

✓ **Top Exam Hint**

It is really important that you familiarise yourself with what the exam paper will actually look like, not just for this Unit 6 exam, but for every exam in every subject. Sometimes just the look of an exam paper can put people off, so know exactly what you can expect before you go into that exam hall. Ask your teacher for a copy of the Unit 6 exam from last year. Make sure it makes sense.

✓ **Top Exam Hint**

As we know that you will always be asked a question about methods, think about this as part of your revision. Make a list of all the ways in which issues of methods, measurement and definition might affect or be affected by the synoptic unit you are studying. Do not let the question surprise you.

What does this mean?

The skill of synopticity is formally tested in the Unit 6 exam, which will either be on crime and deviance or stratification and differentiation and one or more areas of sociology, depending upon what topics your teachers choose. Since this exam paper accounts for 20 per cent of the final A2 grade, synopticity is clearly an important skill.

What will the Unit 6 exam paper look like?

- Unit 6 is what we refer to as the synoptic paper. In other words, even though this paper has a theme or a 'topic', you will also be expected to illustrate how the topic might link to all the other topics you have studied both at AS and A2. This means you will need to show the sociological links between topic 6 and topics 1, 2, 3, 4 and 5.
- The topic of this unit will be either crime and deviance or stratification and differentiation.
- Whichever topic you do, the question paper is similar to those for Units 4 and 5, but with some significant differences.
- You still get an 8-, 12- and 40-mark question (see section 9.1) but you do not this time get a choice for the 40-mark essay. You have to do the one you are presented with.
- The main difference on the Unit 6 synoptic paper is that each of the three questions do something quite particular. One question will link the topic to the previous topics you have studied, one will link it to methods, and the other question will link the topic to theory. This is why the paper is the 'synoptic' paper.
- To guide you, and quite unlike the other exam papers, this Unit 6 exam paper provides advice to you on what the purpose of the question might be, synoptically speaking. Clearly, the exam board is not going to tell you what to write, or how to interpret the question. However, they do tell you on the exam paper what sorts of links they might be looking for in each question. Make sure you pay attention to this advice. It will stand out on the exam paper since it is written in *italics* directly after each of the three questions.

What sorts of things can you be asked to do?

The three questions, as we have already mentioned, each do different things. It is really important to be clear about this, as they want very different things from you. Whether you are doing the crime and deviance or the stratification and differentiation topic, the paper asks you:

- to link your topic to methods issues, debates and problems
- to link your topic to theories and how they differ in the way they see the world
- to link your topic to another topic.

Be careful with this last point. Make sure you read the italicised advice given by the exam board on the question paper very carefully as they usually say what topics they want you to make links to. They will give you a choice though, since they do not know what topics you did for each unit (the exam papers have three possible choices of topic but you will have only studied one).

Think about the options.

1. They might ask you to link Unit 6 to any AS topic.
2. They might ask you to link Unit 6 to a Unit 1 AS topic only.
3. They might ask you to link Unit 6 to a Unit 2 AS topic only.
4. They might ask you to link Unit 6 to your A2 Unit 4 topic.
5. They might ask you to link Unit 6 to any AS or A2 topic.
6. They might ask you to link Unit 6 to a specific combination of AS and A2 topics.

Unit 3 (AS) and Unit 5 (A2) are about theories and methods and are assessed either by exam or coursework. The knowledge you have learned in these topics will also be needed in the Unit 6 exam since you are required to think about how theories and methods link to the issues in this exam.

Do not let the exam paper confuse you. Remember, the exam board will list all the combinations since the paper is sent to all students across the country. Some topics you have not studied. Just look for the ones you have done.

Key points to remember

- The questions require you to do different things: link to theory; link to methods; and link to topics.
- Synopticity accounts for 20 per cent of the final grade.
- You can practice synopticity skills as part of your revision.

● Synoptic Link

As part of your revision, go over all the studies that you have learned over both years of your course. Hopefully you will have these on revision cards. Make sure you know which ones from which topics might link to other topics. For example, studies by feminists in the family topic about domestic violence would also link to both stratification and to crime and deviance, and even to the power and politics topic if you do it for Unit 4. Draw out all these links. They might come in handy for the synoptic exam.

What are the key synoptic tools?

What does this mean?

In order to think more clearly about synopticity and about how we might do it, it is possible to identify a number of key tools that we can use in order to start to build the bridges or links between ideas, issues and topics. We can refer to these as synoptic tools.

What are the key sociological variables?

If you follow the advice given to you in this book you should be aware of what we mean when we talk about the 'key sociological variables'. We often refer to them in margin boxes or in exam hints. These are key ideas in sociology that you can use and apply against any theory or study.

The key **variables** are:
- class
- gender
- ethnicity
- age
- location
- globalisation.

We might use these in a number of ways:
- to show how theories differ or compare and contrast when discussing these variables
- to show how the variables link theories together across topic areas
- to show how the variables link studies together across the topic areas.

The variables are also very useful when trying to think about synopticity. We can use these as tools to help make connections.

What tools can we use?

As well as the key sociological variables listed, there are other important tools or concepts that we must be aware of. The exam board says that there are core themes that exist in everything you do in sociology (see section 5.4). These core themes come up in every topic, and most theories and studies can relate to them. We can therefore use them to explore links in a synoptic fashion (see section 5.4 for ideas on how to use them).

The core themes are:

- socialisation
- culture
- identity
- power
- social differentiation
- stratification.

✳ Key Idea

Key sociological variables are considered to be 'real'; they affect society and are in turn affected by society. They affect the life and the life-course of the individual.

❝❞ Key Definition

As the name suggests, a **variable** is something that varies – something that changes.

⬤ Synoptic Link

Use these variables and apply them to studies. You might try to connect studies from different topics together by using these ideas as a link between them.

⚭ Methods Link

In all sociology, theory and methods are what underpin all sociological thought. They are good ways of making synoptic links, as the exam paper requires. Theories from different topics can be compared with each other, and debates and questions in each topic can be related to the types of methods that sociologists use to find out what they know.

What does the exam board say about synopticity?

The AQA specification uses the phrase 'drawing together' when referring to the skill of synopticity. It says that you must demonstrate in a clear and obvious way connections between theories, methods and topics.

It also says that synopticity involves using the skills that we call AO2 (see section 9.2). Synopticity is not just about knowledge and understanding as such, it is more about what you do with your knowledge and understanding, how you manipulate it. This means that synopticity is about the skills of:

- identification
- analysis
- interpretation
- evaluation.

Key points to remember

- Do not forget the key sociological variables.
- Do not forget the core themes, these could be seen as synoptic tools.
- View synopticity as a process of building bridges between things.

✓ Top Exam Hint

Try to imagine sociology as being made up of four essential ingredients: theory, key words, named examples and the skill of evaluation. It might make it easier to think about the skill of synopticity as a way to manipulate these four ingredients, to show your understanding of them by connecting them together in different and interesting ways.

❝❞ Key Definition

Identification – thinking about what questions mean and responding accordingly.
Analysis – pulling apart the ideas you have learned and questioning them.
Interpretation – taking what you have learned and applying it in different ways to other ideas and to questions set.
Evaluation – assessing the ideas you have learned.

5.4 | How can we make good use of the synoptic tools?

● **Synoptic Link**

The specification for AQA sociology clearly states that there are core themes that must be taught in the two years of the sociology course. The first is socialisation, culture and identity, and the second is power and stratification. Along with these, theory and methods are seen as part of the 'core' of all sociological knowledge. These provide you with a sense of the basics. They are the things you need to use in every exam answer as a way of making sense of the whole of sociology, not just simply thinking about topics in isolation from each other.

✓ **Top Exam Hint**

Use these words, these 'tools' in your essays. Use them for depth and detail, but do not forget to define them within the 'flow of your writing'.

● **Synoptic Link**

Try to be synoptic in your Unit 4 exam essay question. It is a good way of creating a unique and individual answer, and therefore keeping the attention of your examiner. But make sure you do not go off the point. Stick to relevant connections and links only.

What does this mean?

As we have seen from the previous section, it is possible to identify a number of key synoptic tools that run throughout the whole of the two-year sociology course.

The core themes are:

- socialisation
- culture
- identity
- power
- social differentiation
- stratification.

However, it is one thing knowing they might exist, but another to get used to using them in an active fashion. This section of the book will provide a number of hints that you can follow in order to try and develop your synoptic skills further.

What do the synoptic tools mean?

Let us first define each synoptic tool in turn.

- **Socialisation**: learning about your culture
- **Culture**: the way of life of a group
- **Identity**: knowing who you think you are
- **Power**: making others do what you want them to
- **Social differentiation**: structured social inequality and difference between groups
- **Stratification**: the process of creating power inequalities through the social hierarchy.

Now that we know what they mean, how might we use them?

What can we do? How can we develop our skills?

- Try to link the idea of power to both macro- and micro-studies in all topics.
- Try to see power as a major theme throughout sociology.
- Take any two random studies from any two topics – can you see a link between them? Use the sociological variables (see section 5.3) and the synoptic tools to build these bridges.
- Take any of the synoptic tools, and take any two theories. How would the theories compare and contrast over the issue in question? You could link in studies and key words. Try practising writing these things out as if you are doing an exam essay. Practise writing in a detailed fashion.

- Take each topic and link it to every other topic in turn. For each of the above six synoptic tools, try to make a list of five or six ways in which the topics might connect to each other using these tools. If you revise this, it will really help you in the examination for Unit 6.
- Try to get used to using the synoptic words identified in this section on a regular basis in essay answers.
- Practise writing introductions and conclusions to essays where you can use these synoptic words as a way to explore the issue in question.
- Use synoptic tools to connect crime and deviance and stratification and differentiation to other topics.
- Use these synoptic tools to help you evaluate a theory or to compare theories with each other.
- Use these synoptic tools to help you to evaluate a case study. Think about how the tools might affect the process of data gathering and data handling.
- When you revise, use the tools to brainstorm what you know in each topic area. Use them as headings to organise your thoughts while brainstorming.

How can we use theory and methods?

You must get used to using theories and methods not just to write about and describe, but also as ways to make links.

- Try to find similarities between the theories in your Unit 6 topic. What ideas do they have in common with each other?
- Take case studies from different theories and show common ideas or points of similarity.
- Take a theoretical idea from one unit, and link it to what the same theory might say in a different unit. For example, what a theory might say about crime might be linked to what it also says about the family, the media or education, as these things tend to be linked themselves in society.
- Explore the ways that different theories 'see' the same piece of evidence in different ways because they approach it differently. Theories that rely on statistical evidence might draw very different conclusions to theories that rely on more in-depth personal experience that does not lead to generalisation.

Key points to remember

- Try to practise synoptic skills as part of your revision.
- Try to use the synoptic tools in essays for depth.
- Try to use the synoptic tools as a way to organise your thoughts about how topics and studies might connect with each other.

How can we write synoptic essays?

What does this mean?

In Unit 6 of the examination, you will be required to demonstrate your synoptic skills. One of these questions will be a 40-mark essay question, although in Unit 6 you will not get a choice of question, unlike Units 4 and 5. You are going to be required to demonstrate synopticity while writing an essay.

What can you do?

- Do not fall into the trap of making links for the sake of it, stick to the question and make it relevant at all times.
- Do not prioritise showing off your synopticity at the expense of actually addressing and answering the question.
- You can be synoptic in Unit 4 and 5 essay questions as a way of showing more depth, but again, the warning about relevance applies.
- For an essay question, you might take any of the synoptic tools (see section 5.3) and try to use them to explore what theories argue. They all link to both Unit 6 topics: crime and deviance and stratification and differentiation.
- Use the synoptic tools and make links between studies within the same topic. You could use them in order to link together what different people say, and how they might agree or disagree about a particular issue.

To signpost (see section 9.2) to the examiner that you are making links, there are a number of phrases you might like to practise, such as:

- synoptically speaking …
- we can make a link here between XXX and XXX because …
- thinking about this in a broader context, we can …
- there is an important connection here between …
- if we use our sociological imaginations, we can see a link here between …

Think about how you can use synoptic skills as a form of evaluation in essays (see section 9.5) – this would be two skills for the price of one. Try to make connections to other studies in other topics that might support or disprove what someone might say. Spell out the comparison for good evaluation.

Think about how you might weave synoptic skills into introductions in essays. You might like to try to make links and connections as part of the opening to the introduction. Elsewhere in this book (section 9.5), this is referred to as the 'opening seductive sentence'. Can you explore interesting links as a way of capturing the attention of the reader at the very start of an essay answer?

Key points to remember

- Try to weave synoptic skills into essays.
- See synoptic skills as a form of evaluation.
- Always use synoptic tools in essays for depth.

How do theory and methods allow us to be synoptic?

What does this mean?

We have shown that the best way to learn sociology (as with anything) is to break it down into elements. If you can see what the individual parts are, and see how they then link to each other, you will understand quicker and, ultimately, in more depth. To show that you understand, you must be able to manipulate these different elements or ingredients together.

We have identified four main ingredients of sociology (see page 12).
1. Theory
2. Key words
3. Named examples – studies or research examples (case studies based on methods)
4. Evaluation.

Although the ingredients are as important as each other, and each cannot exist without the others, theory does play a special role in sociology. We have tried to show theories as convenient ways to begin thinking about the world and to allow us to put what individual sociologists say into a broader context.

Theory is especially useful for the skill of synopticity. One way of looking at it is to see synopticity as the process whereby you tie together all the different insights that the theories have. How can we do this?

Theory comes up in every topic in sociology, and most if not all sociologists can be linked in some way to a wider theoretical view. Most of the time, the same theories come up in each topic, with a couple of specialised exceptions. Theories tend to talk about the same sorts of things in each topic; after all, no matter what the topic, the theory remains with the same outlook for the whole of society.

We can use theory to link our understanding of the different elements of sociology together.

How can we think about theory in a synoptic fashion?

Do not forget the synoptic tools (section 5.3) to link each theory to each of the tools; what would each say? All theories offer ideas and opinions about these issues. Make sure you understand what they have to say. This will help you gain more depth in the exam, especially in essay questions.

Do not forget the key sociological variables (section 5.3) to link each theory to each of these variables; what would each theory say?

Take any two theories and see how they compare and contrast with each other. Use the tools as bridges that you can build – common ground, or even a 'battle-ground' over which the theories might fight.

To really show your detailed and sensitive understanding of theory, show how theories which might seem or look different are actually very similar. Use the synoptic tools to raise issues over which theories might agree.

How can we think about methods in a synoptic fashion?

Try to get a relevant reference to methods into essay answers. Each 'debate' or 'issue' in each topic usually has a hidden methods issue behind it. The reason why sociologists sometimes disagree is not really over what they say, but how they may have measured or defined or interpreted the thing in question in the first place. The method you use to gather your data will affect what your data looks like, and therefore what you actually find. Quantitative data based on statistics and generalisations will lead to very different answers than qualitative data, which is more about people's feelings.

Key points to remember

- Try to explore different theoretical ideas using the tools available.
- Remember to see sociology as being made up of four ingredients. Try to manipulate these to show your understanding of them by connecting them together in different and interesting ways.
- Practise synoptic skills linked to theory as part of your revision. It is an easy way to get depth and detail into your writing.

✓ **Top Exam Hint**

The key sociological variables are: class, gender, ethnicity, age, location, globalisation. Try to use them.

● **Synoptic Links**

- The synoptic tools are: socialisation, culture, identity, power, social differentiation and stratification. These can best be seen as 'themes' that exist everywhere in every topic. Try to refer to them.

- Do not forget that out of the three questions in the Unit 6 exam, one will be based on making links to theory, one will be based on making links to topics and one will be based on making links to issues of methods.

School tends to give the impression that subjects and forms of knowledge are separate from each other. Subjects are taught by different teachers in different rooms at different times, and they are broken up into little 'segments' or separate 'parcels' of knowledge. This is also true in sociology – we have different topics with different names. But remember, they are all part of a wider whole; they are all linked.

Pushing your grades up higher: what ways are there to demonstrate synopticity?

What does this mean?

This chapter is full of ideas that you can use in order to try to be synoptic. This section is available to print off from the accompanying CD ROM and contains a checklist of the advice elsewhere over the past few pages. Print it off and use it! Try out the ideas; practise them not just for revision but also throughout the course as a whole.

Remember these 'tricks' and use them.

- We can talk of synopticity in two main senses. **Social synopticity** means seeing the connections between the parts of society and using sociological theories and ideas in order to do this. **Sociological synopticity** means seeing connections between sociological ideas themselves and looking at what might link together different studies or theories or even debates that sociologists might have.
- All sociology is about two ideas, which themselves are related: **power**, who gets their way in society, and how and why, and **stratification**, how society is divided up.
- Remember, one question will link the topic to the previous topics you have studied, one will link it to methods, and the other question will link the topic to theory. This is why the Unit 6 paper is the 'synoptic' paper.
- Make sure you pay attention to the advice given on the exam paper about the point of the synoptic questions. It will stand out on the exam paper since it is written in italic writing directly after each of the three questions you have been set.
- It is really important that you familiarise yourself with what the exam paper will actually look like, not just for this Unit 6 exam, but for every exam in each subject. Ask your teacher for a copy of the Unit 6 exam from last year. Make sure it makes sense
- Do not let the exam paper confuse you. Remember, the exam board will list all the combinations since the paper is sent to all students across the country. Some topics you have not studied. Just look for the ones you have done.
- As we know that you will always be asked a question about methods, think about this as part of your revision. Make a list of all the ways in which issues of methods, measurement and definition might affect or be affected by the synoptic unit you are studying. Do not let the question surprise you!

- As part of your revision, go over all the studies that you have learned over both years of your course. Hopefully you will have these on revision cards. Make sure you know which ones from which topics might link to other topics. For example, studies by feminists in the family topic about domestic violence would also link to both stratification and to crime and deviance, and even to the power and politics topic if you do it for Unit 4. Draw out all these links. They might come in handy for the synoptic exam.
- Key sociological variables are considered to be 'real'; they affect society and are in turn affected by society. They affect the life and the life-course of the individual. The key variables are: class, gender, ethnicity, age, location, globalisation. Use these variables and apply them to studies. You might try to link studies together from different topics by using these ideas as a link between them.
- Show how the variables link theories together across topic areas.
- Show how the variables link studies together across the topic areas.
- The exam board says that there are core themes that exist in everything you do in sociology. These core themes come up in every topic and most theories and studies can relate to them. We can therefore use them to explore links in a synoptic fashion. The core themes are: socialisation, culture, identity, power, social differentiation and stratification.
- As part of your revision, take each topic and link it to every other topic in turn. For each of the six synoptic tools, try and make a list of five or six ways in which the topics might connect to each other. If you revise this, it will really help you in the examination for Unit 6.
- To signpost to the examiner that you are making links, there are a number of phrases you might like to practise using.

Frequently asked questions

Q. Is synopticity a new thing?

A. It is new for the examination since it has only been a formal requirement since the relatively recent introduction of the curriculum 2000 specifications. But, in one sense, sociology has always been synoptic. These links and connections have always existed and good students have always seen them and tried to explore them.

Q. Is synopticity hard?

A. It is harder than simply remembering things, yes. But ask yourself, what does simply remembering things actually tell you about learning? Synopticity asks you to use the AO2 skills; to try to manipulate what you know, in order to do more with it than simply repeat it. You could say it is a true test of your sociological imagination!

Q. Why do we have synopticity?

A. Synopticity is now a requirement of all A2 levels. However, it is very sociological for us to have this! As we have said before, sociology has always been synoptic – mainly because society is itself. The connections we see and try to explore are connections that exist in real life.

Chapter 6

Crime and deviance

Key issues in crime and deviance

What are the important issues in crime and deviance?

The sociological study of crime and deviance is a fascinating topic which challenges our 'common sense' views about right and wrong. Sociologists bring their usual approach to studying society to this topic, and aim to ask provocative, searching questions in order to identify the truth about crime and deviance. The following are the sorts of questions posed by sociologists.

- What counts as crime? Do some groups have more power in defining crime and deviance than others?
- How can we measure crime?
- Are some people more likely than others to acquire a criminal identity? Is this the result of natural or social factors? Is it a matter of choice or the result of powerful structural forces beyond individual control?
- Do criminals come from particular social groups? Are men more criminal than women, black people more criminal than white people, and the poor or those from lower social classes more criminal than the middle classes? Alternatively, are some important social processes shaping our picture of crime and criminals?

Why are sociologists interested in crime and deviance?

The study of crime and deviance is currently of great interest to sociologists. Criminology courses (a multi-disciplinary subject, but one which involves much sociological theory and research) are increasingly popular in universities, and crime has a high profile in the media. There are several reasons why sociologists have such an interest in crime.

- We are currently living through a period of great social change. This involves changes in the types and levels of crime. Understanding how crime is changing can help to shed light on how society is changing and vice versa.
- In a period of change, society's rules (its norms and values) change a great deal. Durkheim argued that shared rules are one of the things that hold society together (integrate it). Sociologists are therefore interested in studying crime and deviance as a way of understanding what holds society together.
- In a time of rapid social change, we tend to look back and compare our society with the past. Sociologists are interested in finding out whether crime really is worse now than in the past.
- Whether or not there is now more or less crime compared with the past, it is indisputable that crime is currently a big social problem. Sociologists want to conduct research in order to contribute to solving the social problem of crime.

What are the key ideas we can use to think about crime and deviance?

Some of the concepts, theories and studies you will learn about in crime and deviance will be new to you. Sociological definitions of crime and deviance

◆ What, when and why?

Sociological views and explanations of crime change over time, as do laws and other aspects of society, such as technology. In an article published in 2002, researchers at the Harvard University Medical School (see Denscombe 2003) argued that murder rates in the USA are lower than would otherwise currently be expected, given the high rates of violence, because of improvements in emergency medical care. They argue that this is 'masking' what they describe as an 'epidemic of violence'. This indicates one of the ways in which crime is socially constructed.

✳ Key Idea

Power and stratification are key ideas running throughout this topic. Power is vital because some people have more power than others in defining crime and in enforcing law and order. This is also clearly linked to stratification, so sociologists are keen to investigate how crime and deviance and law and order are linked to differences of class, race, gender and age.

themselves, and the concept of sanctions (rewards and punishments), social order and social control are a few key examples, and they will help you to understand how crime is socially constructed. Other ideas though will be familiar from previous topics and the core themes. Chief amongst these ideas are the following.

- Power and stratification: sociologists aim to find out how the social construction of crime and deviance is influenced by power relations and stratification. This raises the question of whether social rules and the law represent the interests and views of all members of society or of some social groups in particular.
- Stratification also involves gender and ethnicity. Sociologists are interested in whether crime and deviance are gendered, that is, whether defining crime and deviance also involves any processes of differentiation and division on the basis of gender. Similar questions are raised with regard to ethnicity and crime.
- Another useful key idea is labelling theory (see section 6.9), which you will have learned about in education. Sociologists use this theory in a similar way when studying crime and deviance, aiming to see whether criminal and deviant identities are imposed on some people through labelling.

What does the exam board say about crime and deviance?

The exam board identifies a number of areas within crime and deviance, which you are expected to know about, and you can check these for yourself on the specification. Most importantly, though, the exam board says that crime and deviance will be a synoptic topic. This means that in your exam you will be asked questions which require you to link your knowledge of crime and deviance to your understanding of sociological theory, methods and methodology, and other topics (called substantive areas) that you have studied, such as families and households; education; wealth, poverty and welfare; the mass media; health; or work and leisure. This will be discussed extensively in section 6.23 and there will be synoptic link boxes at relevant points throughout the chapter.

The exam for this unit (Unit 6) will be 1 hour and 30 minutes long, and will be divided into two sections: crime and deviance, and stratification and differentiation. This paper will test both your AO1 and AO2 skills but AO2 (identification, analysis, interpretation and evaluation) has more weighting for this paper. You must choose one section and answer the three-part question. The questions will be worth 8, 12 and 40 marks. See Chapter 5 for more details of the synoptic paper.

Key points to remember

- Sociologists aim to challenge commonsense views of crime and deviance and show how these phenomena are socially constructed.
- There are several key ideas to use in understanding crime and deviance, but it is important to remember to link your study of crime and deviance to the core themes of social differentiation, power and stratification.
- Crime and deviance is assessed synoptically so you must make sure that you understand the links with other topics and your study of sociological theory and methods and methodology.

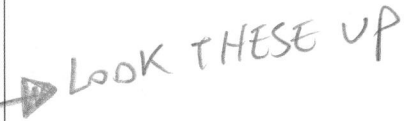 LOOK THESE UP

Synoptic Link

It is vital to show that you can link crime and deviance to other topics and see the connections that exist. Crime can be linked fairly easily to families and households (poor parenting, single-parent families, family poverty) and to education (cultural deprivation, anti-school sub-cultures and educational failure). Do not put your knowledge into separate compartments; appreciate that all the different topics are linked together.

✓ Top Exam Hint

Use CW Mills' idea of the relationship between the public and private to demonstrate your sociological imagination when discussing crime. For example, show how crime and deviance, and the acquisition of a criminal identity, vary depending not simply on the seriousness of the offending behaviour, but on who is carrying it out, and where and when it is taking place.

How does crime and deviance link to the AS course?

Why are links to AS important for sociology?

In order to have a good understanding of sociology, it is important to see how all the parts of the subject fit together. This will take your understanding to a new level. Links to work you did for AS are also important because crime and deviance will be assessed **synoptically**, so you will be asked questions that require you to demonstrate your understanding of these links. This does not mean that you have to remember everything you did last year, or every study. However, you do have to be able to remember some key concepts, and you can pick a few studies or examples that you think demonstrate the links between crime and deviance and the rest of the sociology you have learned.

If you are taking the crime and deviance option, you will have to answer a three-part question in the exam. Each part of the question will require you to make links to different parts of sociology that you have learned previously.

- One question will require you to link your knowledge of crime and deviance to other topics you have studied.
- One question will require you to make links between crime and deviance and methods and methodology.
- One question will require you to make links between crime and deviance and sociological theory, or as the exam board phrases it, 'the nature of sociological thought'.

What links can be made to families and households?

Some theories and studies of the family can provide explanations of crime. For example, Parsons' theory about sex role socialisation, and various studies of conjugal roles, could be used to tell us why crime is a gendered activity. All of these show that female identities are structured towards domestic roles and this is one way of explaining the lower rates of recorded crime committed by women.

Bowlby's theories about maternal deprivation offer another explanation of the link between family and crime, arguing that single-parent families are less stable and lead to higher rates of juvenile delinquency (1946). A study by Farrington (1994) suggests that criminal careers develop within problem families. Such families are characterised by poor parenting skills and consequently children develop an anti-social personality.

What links can be made to education?

Criminal behaviour is often associated with low levels of educational attainment. Therefore, explanations of educational attainment can provide us

with insights into crime. Bernstein's
the various studies on cultural depriv
values such as a focus on instant gra
Paul Willis's famous study, *Learning*
class boys actively create a macho a
prepares them for a life of unfulfilli
anti-school sub-cultures of this sort

How does crime and devian

You must also link your study of crim
will be assessed on this in two of th

- Sociological theory is importan
  study crime and deviance will
  methodological approach that
- A sociologist's theoretical appr
  theoretical approaches to pow
  different approaches to the str
  theories can be categorised in
  has an important influence on
- Methodology is also relevant
  and adoption of either a posit
  to very different types of findings about cr...
- A good example of the importance of methods occurs in the debates
  about the usefulness of official statistics on crime. This draws very much on
  material that you will have examined previously in the debates between
  positivist and interpretivist approaches to methodology, so you will need to
  be sure that you have a good understanding of that part of the specification.

Key points to remember

- You will have to answer one three-part question on crime and deviance
  and link it to other topics, theories, and methodology.
- The concepts, studies, theories and topics you learned about in your AS
  year are relevant to crime and deviance.
- The core themes of differentiation and socialisation are important because
  they tell us about people's social position and identity. This is vital to
  understanding crime and deviance.

66 99 Key Definitions

- **Self-report studies** are usuall
  questionnaires which try to
  whether people have com
  crimes which have not
  by the police.
- **Victim surveys**
  whether peopl
  of crimes th
  to the p
  Both
  of

an we find out
t crime and
eviance?

dentify
mitted
been recorded

aim to identify
have been the victims
at they have not reported
lice.
methods provide a valuable way
trying to estimate the validity of the
recorded crime figures produced by the
police, by providing an estimate of
crime which has not been identified or
reported to the police.

How have sociologists tried to measure crime and deviance?

The measurement of crime and deviance has led to a great deal of controversy in sociology. Sociologists have tried to measure crime in several main ways:

- through the use of official statistics of recorded crime rates
- by using **self-report studies** which invite those who have committed offences to admit to their activities
- by using **victim surveys** which ask a large sample of people to say whether they have been victims of crime and to provide details of these crimes.

There are advantages and disadvantages with all of these methods of trying to measure the extent of crime and deviance (see section 6.15).

What methods do sociologists tend to use to study crime and deviance?

Sociologists have used the methods indicated above to try and measure the extent of crime and deviance. However, measurement is only one aim of sociological research into crime and deviance. Sociologists also wish to find out why people commit crime, how certain actions come to be seen as criminal, as well as how the criminal justice system functions. This means that sociologists may draw on many methods, both quantitative and qualitative, primary and secondary, in order to investigate crime and deviance.

What problems with definition and measurement are encountered in crime and deviance?

Although sociologists are keen to point out that definitions of crime and deviance are socially constructed, there are relatively few disputes in sociology about the meaning of either term, in the way in which, for example, there are disagreements about how the term 'the family' should be defined.

There is, however, debate about how crime is best measured. Official statistics measure recorded crime, which comprises crimes that are known to the police, either because they are detected by the police or because other people report the offence to the police. Clearly this means that crime statistics cannot give a comprehensive picture of all crime in any time or place, and do not tell us how much crime is unreported. While all sociologists recognise the limitations of official statistics, there is disagreement as to exactly how useful official statistics are.

What other problems are there in studying crime and deviance?

There are several other methodological issues in this topic which concern sociologists. Three main issues stand out:

- the value of qualitative methods in studying crime and deviance
- ethical concerns
- the issue of bias in sociological research.

Qualitative methods have been used extensively in studying crime and deviance by researchers who have taken the view that the reality of crime can only be understood by taking an **interpretive** approach. However, such methods have received widespread criticism for their alleged lack of validity. It can be argued that people participating in criminal activity have an interest in exaggerating and glorifying their activities, or in concealing the true nature and extent of them, or in rationalising (defending) their activity. All of this may mean that researchers do not gain a true insight into crime. The other common disadvantages of the method, such as the Hawthorne effect, also have to be considered (see section 4.17).

Ethical issues are important in all sociological topics, but there are perhaps some especially difficult issues in crime and deviance. The British Sociological Association advises researchers to keep to the principle of informed consent and to avoid deceiving respondents and participants wherever possible. Nevertheless there are well-known cases where sociologists have not obeyed these principles, such as James Patrick's research (1973) into gangs using covert participant observation, and Laud Humphreys, who deceived participants by not revealing his identity as a researcher. Researchers are also put in a difficult position if they are aware of crimes which have been committed.

Lastly, but perhaps most important of all, some sociologists have claimed that the dominant approach in sociology which depends on quantitative (positivist) methods, has led to the incorporation of systematic biases into the sociological study of crime. Marxists, for example, have argued that positivist sociology most commonly identifies criminality with the working class, and crimes committed by other social groups are relatively (but not completely) neglected (Sutherland 1933). Feminist sociologists have argued that our views of crime are strongly gendered, and that the dominant view of crime in sociology reflects a malestream approach (Abbott and Wallace 1990). Finally and more recently, some researchers have argued that the dominant view of criminals in contemporary society is also highly racialised and is the result of a form of racism called institutional racism (Fitzgerald and Hough 2002, see section 6.19).

Key points to remember

- Official statistics provide details of the extent of crime, but they only measure recorded crime.
- Sociologists can also use qualitative methods to study crime, but these raise issues of validity.
- Research into crime and deviance raises especially difficult questions about research ethics.

DARK FIGURE OF CRIME

- **Qualitative methods** are concerned with people's attitudes and motivations, and gather information that cannot be expressed numerically. Interviews and participant observation are examples of qualitative methods. These methods are favoured by interpretivists who emphasise the importance of understanding the meaning which participants place on social action.
- **Interpretivism** is the theory that society cannot be studied using scientific methods. Sociology has to study the meaning which behaviour has for people in order to make sense of society.

⚭ **Methods Link**

These examples illustrate how sociologists' theoretical views and methodological approaches have a strong influence in shaping what they see when they investigate crime and deviance. Try to show these links in your own work.

⚲ **Classic Study**

James Patrick's *A Glasgow Gang Observed* (1973) is a classic example of a covert participant observation study. Patrick gained access to a gang of delinquents and observed their activities over several months. Several of the boys were suspicious of Patrick. Critics might suggest that Patrick's presence changed the behaviour of the boys (Hawthorne effect), and that the resultant study was an unrepresentative and highly-subjective view of just one gang.

✓ **Top Exam Hint**

Do not forget to use and discuss key methodological concepts such as validity, reliability operationalisation, and representativeness, when you are evaluating studies on crime and deviance.

What is crime, what is deviance?

Which of these people is committing a crime? Which acts are deviant?

What does this mean?

Sociologists think about **crime** and **deviance** in ways which are subtly different to those used in everyday conversation. It may seem unnecessary to agonise over what we mean by these terms, but sociologists argue that they are more complex than we realise. Looking at crime and deviance in a more sociological way enables us to raise important questions about who defines crime and deviance and who benefits, thus raising important questions about power and stratification.

What is crime and what is deviance?

Crime can be simply defined as any act which breaks the law, and deviance can be defined as any action which departs from 'normal' behaviour. Sociologists make several critical points about these definitions.

- To say that crime is any act which is against the law is a circular definition, and it just tells us that crime is anything that the law says it is. This certainly describes crime, but it does not explain how and why certain acts become defined as crimes, and it seems to carry the implication that crime is a natural and universal category.
- To define deviance as any behaviour that departs from normal behaviour immediately begs the question of what normal behaviour is and how (and by whom) it can be identified and defined. Furthermore, the idea of normal behaviour is usually made in contrast to behaviour which is 'abnormal'. Abnormal behaviour is often considered to be a sign of disease or illness. Are we to define crime and deviant behaviour as a type of illness?

Sociologists are highly sceptical of the ideas that crime and deviance are natural and universal, or forms of illness.

Can sociologists offer anything better?

Sociologists argue that crime and deviance are both socially-constructed concepts. This means that our ideas about crime and deviance vary between different cultures and different periods in history. Neither crime nor deviance are natural or universal categories. This means that our views of what is criminal or deviant behaviour are influenced by the values and norms of the society we live in and which we have absorbed through socialisation. The evidence from cross-cultural studies and historical studies of our own society shows instead that views about what counts as criminal or deviant are remarkably flexible.

- Homosexuality, for example, was a criminal offence in the UK until 1963, whereas in 1994 the age of consent for homosexual relations was reduced to 18. Michel Foucault's historical study of sexuality (1977) is one of many studies which have mapped out changing attitudes to sexuality, showing

66 99 Key Definitions

- A **crime** is any act which breaks the law and can lead to official punishment.
- **Deviance** encompasses any act which breaks social norms.
- **Situational deviance** includes acts which are deviant in a particular social situation.

that homosexuality and other practices have been tolerated in different societies at different times.

- Steven Box (1983) points out that our own society does not have entirely consistent views about the criminality or deviant nature of killing. He argues that only some types of killing are counted as murder. In other cases where death results from human actions, such as drink driving or work-related fatalities due to inadequate safety standards, the actions are not defined as murder.

Deviance can also depend very much on the situation where actions occur. Ken Plummer (1979), for example, distinguishes **situational deviance**. For example, walking about naked is deviant in a shopping centre, but not in a sports centre changing room.

Lastly, it is important to understand that some actions can be criminal but not deviant, and some may be deviant but not criminal, such as smoking cannabis or shouting in a library. The fact that these distinctions can occur, reinforces the notion that crime and deviance are socially constructed, and therefore that relationships of power are important in determining whether an action is deviant or criminal.

How are definitions of crime and deviance maintained?

These social definitions of crime and deviance are upheld through the process of social control. Sociologists argue that all of our behaviour is subject to **sanctions**. Sanctions are responses to our behaviour, but they may be rewards or punishments. The general idea is that people are less inclined to act in ways which are punished and more likely to follow rules when they are rewarded in some way.

There are two types of sanctions, formal and informal. Formal sanctions are imposed by governments or legitimate political authorities, whereas informal sanctions are imposed by other groups, such as friends or neighbours. Thus all our actions are locked into a web of relationships which guide our behaviour in terms of society's norms and values.

Conclusion

- Crime and deviance are socially-constructed categories.
- Crime and deviance are not universal categories of behaviour. They change according to time and place.
- Power relationships determine which actions are defined as criminal or deviant.

For consideration

1. Which social groups have the power to define actions as criminal or deviant?

2. Many young people now smoke cannabis. Does this mean it is not deviant?

✳ Key Idea

It is vital to grasp the idea that crime and deviance are socially-constructed categories. Sociologists argue that crime and deviance vary considerably between different societies and different times. This indicates that crime and deviance must be seen as being defined by social judgements and reactions to people's actions, rather than to any universal quality of the nature of an action. This concept allows sociologists to distance themselves from moral judgements about crime and deviance.

66 99 Key Definition

A **sanction** is either an imposed order (i.e. imposed trade sanctions) or an approval or formal permission.

● Synoptic Link

To fully understand how sanctions are applied you must link these concepts to stratification and power. The study of stratification shows us that society is composed of different groups with differing access to power. The reason why some groups or individuals are more likely to have negative sanctions applied to them is related to their position in the stratification system. Law and order is created and maintained by those with more power; the higher social classes, dominant (white) ethnic minorities, and adults.

▢ Key Fact

According to the 2002 British Crime Survey, 52 per cent of all people between the ages of 20 and 24 have smoked cannabis.

Are criminals born or made?

1. Trococéphale violateur, de Ravenne.

2. Voleur milanais, condamné 13 fois.

Lombroso started a long tradition in criminology which maintained that criminals were abnormal, and either psychologically or physiologically different to 'normal people'. This view is no longer considered as offering a satisfactory explanation of crime.

☞ Classic Study

Lombroso's study, *L'uomo Delinqente*, was based on phrenology – the belief that character could be assessed from the shape of the skull. The study aimed to show how abnormal features were linked to criminal behaviour. Lombroso believed that criminals were less evolved than 'normal' people, and even argued, for example, that female prostitutes could be identified through the possession of prehensile feet (the big toe widely separated from the other toes).

☐ Key Facts

- Mednick's sample consisted of 14,427 adoptions in Denmark between 1924 and 1947.
- Lombroso's sample included some 3839 living criminals, and he examined the crania (skulls) of 383 dead criminals.

What does this mean?

It has been argued that some people are naturally inclined to be criminals. This means that it is part of their nature, or that they have a 'criminal gene'. An alternative view is that people are shaped much more by the environment that they are raised and live in, and it is this which will determine whether they turn out to be a criminal. The debate between these two views is called the 'nature/nurture debate'.

What evidence is there that criminality is innate?

A study published in 1876 claimed that criminality was the result of biological factors and could be identified through characteristic physical features. This research was conducted by an Italian doctor, Cesare Lombroso, who studied a large sample of prisoners as well as anatomical samples. Although this might seem far-fetched and old-fashioned, the idea that biological factors are important in determining whether a person will exhibit criminal behaviour persists today. Psychologist Sarnof Mednick (Mednick et al 1987) has argued that studies of adopted children appear to show that criminality can be inherited. Mednick argues that findings from his study of adoption in Denmark show that adopted children's behaviour shows more similarity to their biological parents than to their adopted parents, especially where there is persistent offending behaviour.

What criticisms have been made of this evidence?

Several important methodological criticisms have been made of these research studies.

- Lombroso's study used a sample drawn from the prison population. This cannot be used to generalise on the wider population. There may have been similar proportions in the wider population with the physical features which Lombroso identifies and associates with criminality, and this would mean that the association was a false one. Lombroso's study therefore cannot be said to be representative of either the whole population or the whole criminal population.
- Mednick's study provides some interesting findings, based on a very large sample. However, this only measures the relationship between parents and children in terms of recorded crime rates. It may therefore not provide a valid measure of criminality, since many crimes go unrecorded.

Are criminals born or made?

In trying to answer this question, it is worth noting that Mednick's views have sometimes been distorted in textbook accounts of his work. Mednick has commented that an understanding of 'biological factors **and their interaction** *with social variables* may make useful contributions to our understanding of the causes of criminal behaviour' (1987: editorial emphasis page 91). This comment indicates that both biological and social factors have a role to play in explaining crime and deviance.

As geneticist Steve Jones has argued, genes should not be seen as determining our behaviour (1994). Genes are complex sets of 'chemical instructions' which shape (rather than determine) our lives, our physical characteristics, and our behaviour; but they do this in interaction with the environment. Individuals may have genetic coding that predisposes them to be taller than other individuals, or likely to develop certain diseases, but precisely how tall they will grow, or whether a disease will develop, will also depend on environmental factors.

Steven Rose argues that biology, psychology, and sociology offer different levels of explanation (1984). Biology and psychology can tell us about why particular individuals are predisposed to commit crime. Crime, though, is socially defined and constructed, and to understand how this happens we have to examine social factors, and not see crime as just the activities of unusual, abnormal, or sick people, nor reduce it to an individual phenomenon. These characteristics may typify some crimes, but not all, nor are they exclusive to certain social groups. What sociologists emphasise is how an action, such as killing, can be seen in very different ways depending on when and where it takes place, and who commits it.

Conclusion

- Crime is clearly caused by both biological and social factors.
- The task for sociologists is to examine how crime and criminals are socially constructed.
- Explaining crime only in terms of individual factors is reductionist.

Key Ideas

- Reductionism (see al... form of explanation which ... causes of an event down to on... Sociologists are highly critical of the idea that the cause of crime can be reduced to an explanation in terms of the discrete characteristics of an individual, for example, 'he was insane', 'he cannot control his temper'. This does not explain the regularity and structured nature of what we know about crime, for example, the relationships between different groups as indicated by crime statistics.

- The nature/nurture debate is crucial to understanding a sociological approach to crime. Sociologists generally claim that human behaviour cannot be reduced to and understood in terms of biological drives or instincts. Any such influences of biology are always developed in a culture or a social context. Therefore, attempts to explain human behaviour only in biological terms will never provide a complete answer.

For consideration

1. If criminality is innate, what are the implications for the punishment of criminals?

2. Are biological explanations of the relationship between crime and gender, age and ethnicity, convincing?

The functionalist approach to crime and deviance

(handwritten annotations: "SUICIDE" with arrow; "BELIEVES CRIME HEALTHY & ACTS AS DETERRANCE")

What does this mean?

Functionalists say that we should look at society as an organic system. This means that all the components or parts of society fulfil a particular function, which helps the whole society to work efficiently and effectively. The classical sociologist, Emile Durkheim, argued that crime actually plays a useful role in maintaining social order, provided it does not reach a harmful level.

What does Durkheim say about crime and deviance?

Durkheim argued that crime increases during periods of rapid social change characterised by anomie (no norms, normlessness). Durkheim therefore suggested that we can best understand crime and deviance by seeing how it is linked to social order. Durkheim claimed that all societies require social order if they are to function effectively. Social order requires rules, laws, and shared norms and values. However, Durkheim recognised that social order is a fragile thing. It would be impossible, he felt, to imagine a society where social order had reached a level such that nobody ever broke the law. Durkheim therefore believed that crime and deviance are inevitable. However, Durkheim also believed that a society without crime would not be very desirable, and he saw crime as having several useful functions in society.

- All societies respond to the breaking of rules and laws by attempts to enforce formal sanctions (punishment), and this leads to collective ideas about social morality being reinforced. This sends out a strong message, which helps to reinforce shared norms and values, and therefore social order.
- In societies where there is very little crime or deviance, there will be little challenging or questioning of social order. Durkheim argues that this is bad, because it can prevent questions about social order and morality being debated and discussed. It also means that social change is less likely, since societies change by responding to challenges and questioning the existing social order.
- Crime and deviance can be seen as providing society with a safety-valve; too much crime and deviance indicates that social integration is too weak, while too little indicates a society where the forces of integration are so strong that they will prevent the challenging of social order and the innovation needed for further evolution.

Durkheim took the view, therefore, that both crime and the punishment of crime were necessary to maintain a healthy society.

✳ Key Idea

Durkheim's belief that crime and deviance are closely related to the regulation of social integration is clearly reflected in this quotation from his book *The Division of Labour in Society*.

'We can say, without being paradoxical, that punishment is above all designed to act upon law-abiding people. For since it serves to heal wounds inflicted upon the collective sentiments, it can only fulfil this role where such sentiments exist and to the extent that they are active.'

Source: *Readings from Emile Durkheim*, K Thompson (ed and transl), London, Routledge, 1985, page 45.

STRAIN THEORY

What does Robert Merton say about crime and deviance?

Not all functionalists would agree completely with the following view of crime and deviance. Robert Merton (1949) argued that functionalists need to pay more attention to inequalities in society. Merton's so-called strain theory, argues that as a result of inequalities, not all social groups will have the same ability to achieve the common cultural goals of a society, so there is a strain (tension) between the cultural goals of a society and the means of achieving them. Merton claims that some groups will have less access to the means of achieving cultural goals by, for example, not having an equal chance of gaining entry to higher education and top professions.

Merton contends that this means that social groups will adapt or respond to cultural goals in different ways, and he identified five main adaptations to common goals.

- Conformists accept the goals and the means of achieving them.
- Ritualists lose their belief in the goals, but stick to the means or rules in society.
- Retreatists withdraw from society having given up on the goals and the means.
- Innovators accept the goals but reject the means.
- Rebels reject the means and the goals and replace them with alternative means and goals.

Merton says that crime and deviance are therefore likely to occur when there are unequal opportunities to the means of achieving common social goals. Merton's idea of strain reflects his functionalist approach, since he is claiming that crime and deviance are the result of a lack of balance between goals and the means of achieving them during periods of social change. This reflects the functionalist idea of the **organic analogy**, and the idea that societies have to be based on consensus and harmony if they are to function effectively.

Conclusion

- Functionalists assume that society is based on shared values.
- It is possible that the law could benefit some groups more than others.
- Functionalism neglects actors' reasons for committing crime.

☞ **Who is this person?**

Robert K Merton (1910–2003) was strongly influenced by functionalists such as Durkheim, and was taught by Talcott Parsons at Harvard University. Merton had a wide range of interests; students may be surprised to learn that he was the originator of the idea of self-fulfilling prophecy (often thought of as an interactionist concept). Merton argued for a more complex notion of functions, including dysfunctions and manifest and latent functions, the last referring to the unintended consequences of actions.

❝❞ Key Definition

The functionalist concept of the '**organic analogy**' means that we should examine society as if it is an organism or living being. An analogy is a comparison. Crime can therefore be seen as a disease. However, just as a small amount of a disease can be used to innoculate a body against further infection, so a degree of crime can be useful.

✓ Top Exam Hint

Durkheim's analysis of crime is important, even to sociologists who are not functionalists, because it suggests that crime is created by society. Durkheim shows us that crime is related to social order and social integration, and it varies with them. Crime is therefore not 'natural', it is socially constructed. Other sociologists, for example Marxists, may disagree about how crime is constructed, but they would agree with Durkheim that it is socially constructed.

For consideration

1. Is there a consensus on which crimes help reinforce social order and which do not?

2. What assumptions does Durkheim make about power?

The Marxist approach to crime and deviance

The Marxist approach to crime and deviance

What does this mean?

Marxist views of crime and deviance, unlike other theories, put a much greater emphasis on the role of economic inequality and inequalities of power in creating crime and deviance. Marxist theory therefore prompts sociologists to examine the political structures and institutions responsible for maintaining law and order, and to raise the question of which social groups control these institutions and which groups benefit most from capitalist law and order.

How does Marxism explain crime and deviance?

In order to understand how Marxism can be applied to explain crime and deviance, it is worth reminding ourselves of some of the key ideas in Marxist theory.

- Marxists argue that capitalist society consists of two classes with opposing interests. This means that class conflict is an inevitable feature of capitalist societies.
- Marxists claim that the state in capitalist society always works in the interests of the capitalist ruling class (bourgeoisie).
- The dominant ideas of society are always those of the dominant class (the bourgeoisie).

Taken together, these points lead Marxists to argue that law and order in capitalist society reflects the ideas of the dominant class, and that it is their definitions of crime and deviance which are the dominant ones. Marxists therefore argue, in contrast to functionalists, that law and order does not function to the benefit of everyone in capitalist society. On the contrary, it reflects the interests and views of the dominant social class. It is in fact a form of social control, which enables the bourgeoisie to control and coerce the working class. In the 1970s, Marxist-influenced theories of crime and deviance were particularly popular, and a number of American studies elaborated Marxist views.

Does the law reflect class interests?

David Gordon (1976) argues that law and order fulfils a number of vital functions for capitalist society. Gordon argues that crime comes to be associated with the working classes, and this helps the bourgeoisie to control the working class. Crime is seen to be a working class 'problem' and this helps to justify the need to control them and imprison those who break the law. It also justifies the need for a strong police force and the use of force where necessary. Law breaking in capitalist society is therefore seen to be the result of 'bad' or 'unruly' members of the working class. Gordon argues that this also helpfully distracts attention from the misdeeds of the bourgeoisie.

Key Facts

The National Prison Survey (Walmsley 1992) found that the prison population of the UK was disproportionately working class:

- 41 per cent of male prisoners had unskilled or partly skilled jobs before coming to prison
- the proportion of the general UK population with unskilled or partly skilled jobs is 18 per cent
- 13 per cent of male prisoners were homeless before going to prison.

William Chambliss (1976) and Frank Pearce (1976) echo these views. Chambliss investigated organised crime in Seattle in the 1960s, and argued that most organised crime was controlled by a small elite group that included senior members of the business and political communities and even reached into the police force. While this was going on, though, Chambliss argues that most police time was spent dealing with minor public order offences. Pearce also studied organised crime in the USA and claimed that such crime was conducted on a bigger scale than crimes committed by working-class offenders.

Steven Box (1983) has argued that the implications of views such as these for the way we must view crime are radical. Box argues that law and order in capitalist societies is applied in a highly selective way. Selective law enforcement means that those identified as criminals tend to be predominantly young, male, working class, and, disproportionately, black. Box argues that law and order in capitalist society is a process of mystification, whereby the evils of society are seen to emanate from a small and relatively powerless group. This mystifies the mass of the population, precisely because it identifies crime in such a selective way, while carefully neglecting the crimes of the powerful. This process is one which criminalises certain sections of the population. Crime therefore is ideologically defined, in a highly-distorted way, which acts as a powerful mechanism of social control.

The idea of 'criminalisation' refers to the way that particular activities come to be defined as criminal. The term can also be applied to the activities of particular groups of people. Box and others influenced by the Marxist approach, consider that it is the working classes and many of their activities which are criminalised in capitalist society. Their cultural values are also likely to be criminalised, and the identities which they can construct are more likely to be stigmatised criminal identities. Those from other social groups committing similar activities are less likely to be criminalised (for example, dope smoking in inner cities areas such as Brixton has been policed quite strictly, whereas this activity taking place in middle-class suburbs or student halls of residence does not receive similar police attention).

Conclusion

Use these points to evaluate Marxist approaches to crime and deviance.

- Marxist theory is economically **reductionist**.
- Marxism neglects race and gender.
- Consider what empirical evidence there is to support the Marxist approach.

✶ Key Idea

The idea of criminalisation acknowledges that crime is socially constructed, and suggests that members of some social groups are likely to be seen by others as more prone to having a criminal identity. Marxist-inspired sociologists have argued that the criminal justice system criminalises the working class, and others, such as Hall, suggest that it also criminalises ethnic minorities. Criminality can therefore also be 'racialised'.

● Synoptic Link

Marxism is a structural theory, so in evaluating this approach you need to remind yourself about the importance of the structure/action debate. You can consider whether Marxist accounts need to give more weight to the explanations people give for their actions and to the idea that people have agency (freedom). Apply these points to the studies discussed here and those in section 6.8, such as Hall's.

66 99 Key Definition

The term **reductionism** refers to arguments which reduce complex social processes to one or a limited number of causes. Marxism is thus often criticised for 'economic reductionism', that is, reducing the cause of crime to economic inequality.

For consideration

1. Identify working-class activities that have been criminalised.
2. What is the evidence for selective law enforcement?

How is neo-Marxism different from Marxism when discussing crime?

What does this mean?

Marxism has been criticised for appearing to say that all crime has an economic cause and is related to the persistence of economic inequality and class conflict. Marxism was also criticised for its economic determinism – the idea that all our actions are caused by economic factors and that people have no free will. These criticisms have led some sociologists to try and overcome the weaknesses of Marxist explanations of crime.

How have Neo-Marxists explained crime?

A group of sociologists based at the Centre for Contemporary Cultural Studies at the University of Birmingham have argued that Marxists need to pay much more attention to factors such as culture and ideology. Stuart Hall's study, *Policing the Crisis* (1978), is one of the most well-known examples of this version of neo-Marxism.

These sociologists have been strongly influenced by the ideas of Italian Marxist Antonio Gramsci. Gramsci was aware of the need to address the criticism that Marxism was economically deterministic. He developed the idea that capitalism did not simply depend on the use of force or economic power to prevent the working class from rebelling. Instead Gramsci argued that the role of ideology and **hegemony** was crucial in legitimating the capitalist system. In capitalist society, the dominant or hegemonic ideas are capitalist ideas. These ideas are therefore widely accepted by the working class.

Hall used Gramsci's theory of hegemony to argue that the moral panic over 'mugging' that arose in the 1970s was amplified by the media, and was in fact a reflection of the economic crisis at the time (during the 1970s Britain's economy declined following the long post-war boom). The moral panic soon took on racial undertones following a focus on certain stories in the press, so that mugging became linked with black youths. The panic distracted the mass of the population from the economic crisis, found another social problem to concentrate on, and blamed a group that was politically weak for the existence of that problem. The whole process therefore worked as a sort of ideological smokescreen, distracting people's attention from the more serious issues, and created a 'myth' of black criminality (see section 6.19).

Gramsci argued that there are always struggles over ideas and culture in capitalist society, and ideas are always being contested. Sociologists such as John Clarke (1975) have further developed these views, arguing that working-class crime and deviance is best seen as an oppositional sub-culture, as those in marginal social positions respond to their position by rejecting some of the values of the wider, capitalist society.

 **Key Definition**

By **hegemony** Gramsci was referring to the ability of the state to persuade the masses into believing or consenting to the rules and values of the elite that dominates them.

How else has Marxism been developed in order to explain crime?

In a book entitled *The New Criminology* (1973), Ian Taylor, Paul Walton and Jock Young tried to adapt Marxist views to changing circumstances in the 1970s. They attempted to maintain Marxism's emphasis on the importance of economic factors, but also wanted to argue that criminals were free to choose whether to commit crime or not. They believed that it was important to consider the role of non-economic factors. Thus they contended that there were several key elements of any sociological explanation of crime:

1. Inequalities in wealth and power
2. The factors and circumstances leading to the decision to commit a crime
3. The meaning that deviance has for the person committing the act
4. How other members of society react to the deviant act
5. An understanding of which social groups have the power to make the law
6. The effects of labels and labelling.

Points 3, 4, and 6 are drawn from interactionism, while points 1, 2, and 5 reflect the Marxist approach to crime and deviance. The New Criminology (sometimes called 'critical criminology', see section 6.9) aimed to provide a complete theory of crime and deviance by combining the strengths of both Marxism and interactionist theory. In doing this, the 'New Criminology' approach argued that sociologists had to be critical of the established capitalist order that created the conditions which allow crime to develop – that is, social inequality and deprivation. The New Criminologists were arguing that criminals were, in a way, rebelling and protesting against an unequal society, where there was one law for the rich and another for the poor. They argued that this allowed the crimes of the powerful to be neglected.

Conclusion

Use these points to evaluate neo-Marxist theories.

- What evidence is there for interpreting crime as a way of resisting capitalism?
- Some critics (see section 6.13) would say that the high rate of black street crime in the 1970s was not a myth.
- Neo-Marxism appears to say little about how crime and deviance are gendered.

For consideration

1. Do criminals try to justify their crimes, and if so, how?

2. Can criminals' justifications of crime be seen as explanations of crime?

↬ Classic Study

Policing the Crisis (1978) is regarded as a key text in Marxist explanations of crime and race. It is a highly theoretical account of the development of the moral panic over 'mugging' by young black men in the 1970s. The study draws on Cohen's theory of moral panics (see section 6.17) as well as Gramsci (see section 3.8) and uses secondary media sources and statistics to place the events of the 1970s into the social and historical context of race relations in Britain. Despite its sophistication, critics might point to its relative lack of empirical detail.

● Synoptic Link

Paul Willis's study, *Learning to Labour*, is a good example of sub-cultural Marxism, and is an excellent study to use as a synoptic link between crime and education. Willis's study shows how a group of working-class boys actively create an 'anti-school sub-culture'. This is an act of deviance. Willis explains this deviance in terms of a sub-cultural resistance to the dominating authority of school and work.

◆ What, when and why?

The development of the New Criminology was a response to the criticisms made of the more standard versions of Marxism in the 1960s and 1970s but also to the overwhelmingly positivist study of crime in the UK in the late 1960s. The authors of *The New Criminology* were also involved in the creation of the National Deviancy Conference, formed in 1968, which aimed to provide a sociological alternative to the functionalist-inspired views of crime dominant amongst policy makers and researchers at that time.

✓ Top Exam Hint

Where it is relevant to the set questions, it is a very good idea to show that you have a high level of knowledge and understanding by indicating that there are several types of Marxism. You can say that this shows that theoretical ideas are always changing. Willis provides a good example of a Marxist trying to resolve the structure/action debate. Remember, no single theory can provide all the answers.

What do interactionists say about crime and deviance?

MERTON

66 99 Key Definition

Labelling is the idea that groups or individuals with an authoritative role in society can affect how people see themselves by placing labels on them, i.e. 'underachiever' or 'naughty'. After constant reinforcement, the individual comes to believe their label, and takes on this role. The label then becomes a self-fulfilling prophecy.

✳ Key Idea

'Social groups create deviance by making the rules whose infraction constitutes deviance, and by applying these rules to particular people and labelling them as outsiders. From this point of view, deviance is not a quality of the act the person commits, but rather a consequence of the application of others of the rules and sanctions to an offender. The deviant is one to whom the label has successfully been applied; deviant behaviour is behaviour that people so label.'

(Becker 1963, page 9)

Howard Becker is one of the key sociologists in the field of labelling theory, and has conducted research on medical students, teachers, drug users and jazz musicians.

What does this mean?

Interactionist theory focuses on how people's actions are motivated and the meaning that social action has for those participating in it. As such it offers a very different view of crime and deviance to that offered by functionalism and Marxism, since they are structural theories and see crime as the result of structural forces that people have no control over. Interactionists, by contrast, argue that social order is constantly being negotiated and constructed. This means that what counts as crime, and what counts as deviance, are much more open to negotiation than either functionalist or Marxist theory suggests.

How do interactionists define crime and deviance?

Howard Becker has made one of the most important contributions to understanding crime and deviance through the development of **labelling** theory. Becker's theory starts with the assertion that no act is criminal or deviant until it has been labelled as being such by others. This means that whether an action is criminal or deviant has nothing to do with the act itself, but in fact has much more to do with the social reaction to the act. Becker therefore agrees with the idea that crime and deviance are socially constructed, but he interprets this in a much more radical way than structural theorists. For labelling theorists, crime and deviance is much more about the social reaction to certain types of behaviour, rather than about the meaning that the activity has for the person who commits the act.

What does this tell us about crime and deviance?

Labelling theory provides sociologists with a number of fresh insights into crime and deviance.

Becker's studies show that being labelled as a deviant can have important consequences for a person's identity. If the label of criminal or deviant is successfully applied, the negative label becomes a master status, which cancels out the other statuses that an individual has. This can effectively exclude the individual from many social activities, such as work. Excluded from mainstream society, deviants find support with other similar individuals. This is likely to reinforce a deviant lifestyle, and the development of further deviant activities may lead to a deviant career. All of these processes can culminate in the creation of deviant sub-cultures.

How can we evaluate labelling theory?

Many criticisms have been made of labelling theory. The following are just a few of the most important ones.

- It does not explain why people commit deviant acts in the first instance.
- It is deterministic (denies that people have free will and the power to act).
- It neglects power and social structure and therefore cannot explain why certain types of people are regularly and repeatedly identified as criminal.

British sociologist Ken Plummer has defended labelling theory against these criticisms (1979). As he reasons, labelling theory is not a perfect theory, but it can provide convincing responses to all of the above points. Firstly, labelling theorists identify individual deviant acts as ways of gaining status and self-esteem. The theory is not deterministic, as it puts great stress on the way that labels are always the outcome of negotiation. Certainly, concepts such as self-fulfilling prophecy can be interpreted as being deterministic, but they can be used more cautiously, without involving that implication. The most serious criticism is that labelling theorists neglect questions of power and structure. Undoubtedly, as action theorists, interactionists are bound to place less emphasis on action than structure. However, as Plummer has pointed out, the whole point of labelling theory, as it is developed and used by sociologists such as Becker, is to show the inequalities in the operation of the law, and it was labelling theory that helped sociologists begin to raise questions about this.

Conclusion

- Crime and deviance can only be understood by examining how people define actions as criminal or deviant.
- What counts as crime is continually being negotiated and constructed as a result of many individual interactions between different groups of people.
- Criminality or deviance is not a characteristic of any activity. Actions become criminal or deviant if society reacts to them in a particular way.

↝ Classic Study

Becker's study *The Outsiders* (1963) introduced a range of important concepts and approaches to sociologists in the 1960s. The book consists of a selection of essays explaining the interactionist view that deviance is best thought of in terms of social reaction to actions. The book includes a famous study of 'dance musicians' and how people 'learn' to become marijuana users. The book gives some indications on how Becker conducted his research but, like much interactionist work, positivists may criticise it for its apparent lack of rigour and openness to subjective interpretation.

⌾ Methods Link

Sociologists interested in labelling theory and interactionism take an interpretivist approach to social behaviour and favour studying on the micro level. This means that they will use qualitative methods such as observation and informal interviews. Of course, this also leads their work to be criticised as being unrepresentative, subjective, and liable to distortion through the interviewer/Hawthorne effect.

✓ Top Exam Hint

If you are evaluating labelling theory it is a good idea to link it to the structure/action debate. A good point to make is that the weaknesses of labelling theory in relation to power and structure simply reflect its position in that debate. This does not mean that sociologists such as Becker ignore power and structure, just that they explain it more at a micro level.

For consideration

1. Can labelling theory tell us why some people are more likely to be labelled than others?

2. Would it be useful to synthesise labelling with a structural theory? If so, why and which one?

Are there criminal sub-cultures?

What does this mean?

Functionalist explanations of crime are based on the idea that crime and deviance will increase when shared culture and social controls are weakened. However, some functionalists have argued that there is not simply one set of shared values. They argue that all societies will contain groups who develop their own distinctive **sub-cultures**. Such groups will share some of the values of the mainstream culture, but they will develop some of their own values. These groups are called sub-cultures.

What do functionalist sub-cultural theorists say about crime and deviance?

The work of American sociologists Walter Miller (1962), Cloward and Ohlin (1961), and Albert Cohen (1955), provide good illustrations of the functionalist sub-cultural approach. All of these sociologists were influenced by Robert Merton's approach to crime and deviance (see section 6.6), but unlike Merton, they did not agree that there was one set of cultural values that all deviants adapted to.

- Walter Miller argued that what he called the 'lower class', in contrast to Merton's view, did have a distinctive set of norms and values which set them apart from the rest of society (1962). Miller argued that lower working-class culture focused on the values of 'toughness', being 'smart' in appearance, and put a great emphasis on the need for 'excitement'. Miller argues that these sub-cultural values inevitably mean that young lower-class males form gangs and get into trouble with the police.
- Cloward and Ohlin contended that there were in fact three types of sub-culture; criminal, conflict and retreatist. A criminal sub-culture develops where there are already many adult criminals, and this provides 'an illegitimate opportunity structure' which enables young people to be drawn into criminal activities. Conflict sub-cultures, though, involving vandalism, hooliganism and gang violence, develop where there is little adult criminal activity, and so there are few opportunities for young people to get involved in more serious crime. Retreatist sub-cultures, characterised by high levels of drug use but relatively little other crime, develop where young people have failed to succeed in mainstream society, but they have also failed to become criminals in any of the other two sub-cultures mentioned. Cloward and Ohlin see this last sub-culture developing in certain lower-class areas.
- Albert Cohen argues that Robert Merton's approach seems to assume that all crime is committed for some material gain. He also argues that Merton's analysis only explains why particular individuals get involved in crime and deviance. Cohen argues that deviant action has to be seen as a collective phenomenon, something which social groups rather than just individuals

commit. Cohen uses the concept of status frustration to explain why young working-class males are often involved in crime. Cohen argues that the ability of young working-class men to achieve the goals which bring high status in modern society is blocked by their social position (they are culturally deprived). Such young men therefore reverse or replace the dominant cultural goals by getting involved in delinquent activities. Activities such as fighting, vandalism, and 'joyriding' do not make criminals rich, but they do bring prestige and status within a sub-culture.

Does this mean that criminals do have different values to everyone else?

Functionalist sub-cultural theories do suggest that criminals have different values to other members of society. However, sociologist David Matza argues that criminals actually have the same cultural values as others (Matza 1964). Matza claims that we can deduce this because delinquents, criminals, and deviants frequently use what he calls **techniques of neutralisation** to justify their actions. They may, for example, deny that what they have done is wrong, justify themselves by arguing that they only steal from shops, do not use violence, do not steal from old people, or they may appeal to higher loyalties, for example, 'I had to steal to get clothes for my children'.

Matza concludes that criminals are not that different from other people, and reasons that criminals just drift into crime due to circumstances. He claims that all societies have what he calls 'subterranean values'. This means that there are many activities that many people will indulge in when they think they can get away with it. These values coexist with mainstream values. Delinquents and criminals simply express these values in the wrong places and times, whereas those in other social groups manage to conceal their 'subterranean values' more effectively.

Conclusion

Use the following points to help evaluate functionalist sub-cultural theories.

* Sub-cultural theorists still believe that there is a dominant set of shared values.
* The theories are still structural and see action as determined.
* The theories still appear to neglect differences of race and gender.

For consideration

1. Do criminals have the same values as other people?

2. Are there such things as 'subterranean values'? Discuss some examples.

∞ Methods Link

Radical sociologists would argue that sociologists' own cultural values can distort their views of crime, and that it is significant that sub-cultural functionalists focus on working-class crime and appear unaware of crimes committed by the powerful. Our views about crime are inevitably shaped by our culture, and this criticism highlights the difficulty of studying crime in terms of cultural values. It also raises the issue of whether sociologists can avoid making value judgements.

❝❞ Key Definition

Techniques of neutralisation: Matza uses the term 'techniques of neutralisation' to refer to the excuses people use to justify what the wider society sees as deviant or criminal acts.

✓ Top Exam Hint

In evaluating these approaches, remember that functionalist theories are still open to the criticism that they do not adequately explain power relations since they neglect the economic bases of power differences. They also only focus on particular types of crime, such as delinquency, and neglect crimes of the powerful. Make the point, therefore, that sub-cultural functionalist explanations can be seen as being based on a narrow view of crime and deviance.

Are joyriders trying to resolve status frustration?

How is crime and deviance related to locality?

Is inner city crime a result of social disorganisation?

☐ Key Fact

Evidence from the 1998 British Crime Survey found huge differences in the risk of being a victim of violent crime for adults from different social groups.

- 4.8 per cent of men from high-income, rural households were victims of violent crime in 1997, compared with 9 per cent of men from low-income, inner city households and 18.9 per cent of men from private rented accommodation in inner city areas

- the corresponding figures for women were 2.9 per cent, 7 per cent and 8.9 per cent respectively.

(Mirrlees-Black et al 1998)

What does this mean?

A number of research studies have found a strong relationship between crime and locality. In the UK, the most recent research has found that those living in inner city locations are more at risk of being victims of crime than people living in rural areas (Mirrlees-Black et al 1998). Sociologists have therefore been concerned to investigate this relationship and find out how it can be explained.

How have sociologists explained the relationship between crime and locality?

Some of the most well known research on the relationship between crime and locality was conducted in the 1930s and 1940s by American researchers Shaw and McKay. Shaw and McKay were based at the University of Chicago, and their work helped develop the ecological approach to crime, which argued that the best way to study crime was by examining the environment in which it occurred. Shaw and McKay (1942) conducted a detailed statistical examination of crime rates in the various boroughs of Chicago. They found a strong statistical pattern. The highest crime rates occurred in the centre of the city (called the central business district or CBD), and as one moved further away from the CBD, crime rates fell.

Shaw and McKay explained that the CBD was a 'zone of transition', or an area characterised by a constantly changing population. The central area would also have a high proportion of immigrants, of families living on low incomes, and a high level of people moving in and out of the area. Shaw and McKay argued that this led to 'social disorganisation'. By this, they meant that there were few community relationships and organisations, little social control, and therefore more opportunities for crime. It was this, they argued, that could explain the patterns of criminal activity revealed by crime rates.

What criticisms can be made of these studies?

Several studies in the UK have led to criticisms of Shaw and McKay's explanation of the relationship between crime and locality.

- Morris's study of crime levels in Croydon (1957) argued that the highest rates of crime were actually found in particular council estates, not the CBD. Importantly though, his study raises the issue of how the concept of social disorganisation should be operationalised. Morris points out that the estates he studied were tightly-knit communities where everybody knew everyone else, in contrast to the middle-class areas where neighbours kept themselves to themselves. More critical, Morris argued, in creating high crime rates in particular areas was the policy of the council to house 'problem families' in the same area.

- Baldwin and Bottoms' (1976) study of crime in Sheffield argued that it was not social disorganisation which caused high crime rates, but the council's segregating of 'problem families'. However, Baldwin and Bottoms say that other tenants also contributed to this pattern, since they would refuse to accept housing on a 'problem' estate. The result was that particular estates filled up with those who had been in trouble with the law, tipping an estate into lawlessness and creating 'sink estates' that law-abiding residents did not want to live in.
- Even more critically, Owen Gill's observational study of a poor area in Liverpool suggested that some areas are labelled (1977). This leads to increased levels of police monitoring, and even a self-fulfilling prophecy, as residents adopt a tough self-image and identity.

Social disorganisation then, is a difficult concept to operationalise accurately, and studies and findings such as those from Shaw and McKay may lack validity.

Is location still an important factor?

Despite these criticisms, the relationship between locality and crime remains a key focus for contemporary sociologists and policymakers. Recent attention has focused on 'wild spaces' where normal social rules are suspended (Lash and Urry, 1994). Some sociologists, such as Muncie and McLaughlin (1996), have argued that the geographical distribution of crime reflects the way some areas are criminalised, marginalised, and socially excluded. Others, such as Amitai Etzioni (see section 6.12), have argued that high rates of crime in decaying urban areas reflect the decline of community bonds, and that policies need to foster the regeneration of community ties. In some quarters this has led to calls for a tougher response to crime, which can include the so-called zero-tolerance approach whereby all breaches of the law are treated seriously (see also sections 6.12 and 6.14).

Conclusion

In order to evaluate the relationship between crime and location, focus on the following points.

- The research here focuses on a narrow definition of crime (see section 6.18).
- Social disorganisation is difficult to operationalise accurately and reliably.
- The validity of official crime statistics can be questioned (section 6.19).

⚭ Methods Link

Shaw and McKay operationalise social disorganisation using indicators such as the proportion of immigrants and numbers of owner-occupiers. Baldwin and Bottoms' study also identified factors such as the number of rooms, number of inhabitants per dwelling, and whether the property was owner-occupied or rented, as being significant indicators. Use of these indicators can be questioned. Morris, for example, claims that 'social disorganisation' was most common in middle-class areas where people did not even know the names of their neighbours.

● Synoptic Link

This point can be linked to the theme of socialisation, culture and identity. As Gill's study indicates, it is not simply a matter of the inhabitants of an area deciding that they want to be seen in a certain way. The identity an area acquires will be strongly influenced by the way it is seen by others. This may be based on key social factors such as the class or race of the people living there.

✓ Top Exam Hint

The concept of social disorganisation is very similar to Durkheim's concept of anomie. You can criticise this from a Marxist viewpoint and point out that perhaps crime levels and perceptions of crime and locality are best explained in terms of power and the ability of some groups to criminalise others. Does more crime really occur in inner city areas, or is this just labelling?

For consideration

1. How would you operationalise 'social disorganisation'?
2. Do Shaw and McKay give a valid picture of crime? Explain your answer.

6.12 | Why do we not all commit crime?

☀ Key Idea

The key idea of control theory is nicely summed up in this comment from Hirschi.

'The question "Why do they do it?" is simply not the question the theory is designed to answer. The question is, "Why don't we do it?"'

(Travis Hirschi 1969, page 34)

◆ What, when and why?

Control theory developed in the late 20th century in the USA (see Key idea above), as crime rates in the USA rose. Arguably, it was particularly popular from the 1980s onwards. Some of the ideas of control theory came to be reflected in 'zero tolerance' policies in the 1980s. These policies were devised in response to the growing rates of disorder and crime in American cities, particularly New York in the 1980s.

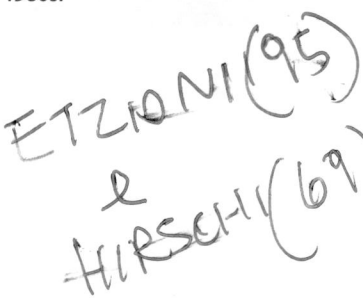

What does this mean?

Most sociological theories on crime and deviance start from the point of trying to explain what makes people act in criminal or deviant ways. Control theory cleverly works from the belief that we should instead invert this question, and ask what prevents most people, most of the time, from breaking the rules.

What is control theory?

Control theory has its origins in Durkheim's ideas about the relationship between crime and social control. Durkheim argued that rapid social change led to a lack of integration, anomie, and thus weak social controls and higher rates of crime and deviance. Control theorists take this idea and develop it further.

Travis Hirschi, for example, has argued that crime levels are related to the degree to which social bonds exist (1969). Hirschi identifies four types of bond: attachment, commitment, involvement and belief.

- If people are attached they will care about others.
- If people have some stake in society and the social order they will be committed.
- If people are involved in their society, through membership of social and community groups and indeed through employment, they will feel involved.
- If strong social bonds on these bases exist, a fourth bond, that of belief in social values and rules, will also be evident.

The four elements of social bonding are needed to control behaviour and prevent crime.

How has control theory influenced social policy on crime?

Amitai Etzioni is an American sociologist who has applied some of these ideas to social policies aimed to reduce crime. Etzioni (1995) maintained that policies need to develop community organisations, such as Neighbourhood Watch schemes, or youth development projects. Etzioni argues that schemes need to bind people into a range of community networks. This helps to create social integration and that will create the controls that prevent crime. This sort of approach closely reflects Hirschi's views about social bonds. Etzioni is referred to as a 'communitarian', and he believes that modern societies need to rebuild a sense of community. His ideas have some similarity with Giddens' notion of the 'third way' (see sections 2.16 and 6.18). The influence of all of these ideas can be seen in the policies of recent New Labour governments with their catchphrase 'Tough on crime, tough on the causes of crime' (see section 6.13). Some theorists have developed control theory and applied it to gender and crime, and to age, and these are discussed in sections 6.20 and 6.21.

Jock Young has noted that control theory is closely related to the demands of 'administrative criminology' (1988), a term used to refer to studies of criminality sponsored by and conducted on behalf of the state. Critics argue that this approach often avoids asking more difficult and interesting questions about crime, for example about the nature of and definition of crime, and contents itself with narrowly empirical studies. However, a mix of control theory and administrative criminology has led to the development of current policies such as installing CCTV in shops, malls, car parks and town centres, with the idea that this will make it harder to commit crime in these crime 'hot spots'. This is sometimes known as 'target hardening'.

Another policy closely related to control theory is 'zero tolerance'. Zero tolerance was devised in New York in the 1980s. The idea is that if even the most minor breaches of the law are punished, then gradually crime will be reduced. Zero tolerance therefore shares the Right realist assumption (see section 6.13) that minor criminal acts lead to a downward spiral of lawlessness, but it also reflects the views of control theorists and communitarians such as Etzioni, who believe that stronger controls and community organisations make it harder for crime to take hold in an area.

Conclusion

Control theory provides some interesting insights into crime and deviance, but numerous criticisms have been made of it. Use the three criticisms below to help you evaluate control theory. The points for consideration give clues to two further issues.

- Control theory has a selective view of crime, mainly focusing on violent offences, theft, delinquency and street crime.
- Control theory cannot adequately explain fraud and white-collar crime since, arguably, white-collar criminals are embedded in exactly the sort of social networks which should exert control on such activities (section 6.16).
- Marxists, radical criminologists, interactionists and feminists, would argue that this view neglects the role of the state and the criminal justice system in actively constructing crime and criminals.

+ UP 2 Date = MRE THN OTHER THEORIES

☀ Key Idea

Communitarianism is the idea developed by American sociologist Amitai Etzioni, which argues that, in the late 20th century, many of the problems of modern society could be solved by policies that focus on rebuilding a sense of community in mass society. Communitarians believe that modern society is fragmented and therefore aim to recreate social integration by strengthening institutions such as the family, and emphasising the importance not just of rights, but also of responsibilities.

☞ Who is this person?

Amitai Etzioni was born in Cologne in 1929. He survived the upheavals of the Second World War and was educated at the Hebrew University in Jerusalem, and gained his PhD from the University of California, Berkeley, in 1958. Etzioni has acted as a consultant and adviser on a multitude of government and think-tank committees in the USA, and believes passionately that sociology can contribute to social policy.

For consideration

1. Does control theory assume that consensus is attainable? Does it neglect the fact that there may be conflict over values and rules?

2. Are all people naturally selfish?

What are realist theories of crime and deviance?

◆ **What, when and why?**

An unusual mixture of New Left realist and Right realist thinking is reflected in Labour's slogan 'Tough on crime, tough on the causes of crime'. This was developed by Tony Blair in the early 1990s (Blair 1993) at a time when crime rates were rising despite the policies (considered harsh by some) of a Conservative government which aimed to reduce crime. Labour's slogan enabled them to sound simultaneously tough and progressive.

☞ **Who is this person?**

Jock Young (born 1942) has been a key figure in British criminology. In the 1970s he was one of the co-authors of *The New Criminology*, and in the 1980s he was a co-author of other publications which led to the development of New Left realism. Apparently, Young's views on crime were affected when he witnessed a particularly unpleasant assault on the underground railway in London. There is some tension between the two approaches, and Young's shift shows that sociologists can change their views in the light of experience.

What does this mean?

Realist approaches to crime were developed in the 1980s when crime appeared to be rapidly increasing. There are two versions of realism: left realism and right realism. These reflect different political and sociological approaches to crime. Left wing views in politics are those which are associated with a broadly socialist outlook on life, and put a particular emphasis on equality. Right wing views are usually associated with a broadly conventional or 'conservative' outlook. They emphasise the need for authority, order and hierarchy, and generally view social change as disruptive and negative.

What was New Left realism?

New Left realism developed as a critical response to the New Criminologists (see section 6.8). The New Left realists (NLRs) argued that the New Criminologists had romanticised crime, portraying crime as the justifiable response of oppressed working-class people desperately trying to survive in an unequal society. The NLRs argued that this was a highly prejudiced view of crime, which neglected the harsh realities of crime.

One of the key NLR authors was Jock Young, who had also co-authored *The New Criminology*. In the 1980s Young became disenchanted with what he saw as 'Left idealist' views of crime. Young argued that such views were based on the assumption that crime would simply not occur in a more equal society. This led the 'Left idealist' criminologists to argue that the only solution to crime was the creation of a socialist society. Young and his fellow NLRs argued that, as the creation of a socialist society was highly unlikely in 1980s Britain, the task for sociologists was to develop a more realistic understanding of crime. Young argued that sociologists should provide practical policy recommendations to reduce and prevent crime.

The New Left realists believed that crime was the result of relative deprivation, marginalisation and the development of sub-cultures, but they made the following key claims about the nature of crime.

- Street crime was a real social problem, and official statistics were broadly correct in showing that most crime was committed by young, black, working-class men.
- It is young working-class men who are predominantly the perpetrators of crime, and, at the same time, their victims are usually other working-class people.
- Crime should not be 'romanticised' and seen as some sort of political protest. Criminals in modern Britain are not Robin Hood characters, robbing the rich to give to the poor.

The policy recommendations of the New Left realists moved far away from the idea of reducing inequalities, and suggested developing community organisations in the administration of criminal justice through citizens' juries and neighbourhood watch type schemes.

What is Right realism?

At around the same time that the New Left realist view was being developed, other sociologists with a more right-wing approach to politics, were developing Right realism. These sociologists believed that crime rates were rising as society was fragmenting due to the decline of community and a consequent lack of respect for authority.

Wilson and Kelling (1982) argue that when control is absent, crime can spiral and areas fall into decline. This is likened to the situation where a window is broken in a disused building (hence this is sometimes known as the 'broken windows thesis'). If no repairs are made and there is no attempt to stop the damage recurring, gradually more vandalism will occur. Local people will feel vulnerable because of the decay and feel less commitment to the area (i.e. will not attempt to address deterioration/deter vandals). As this happens, so further minor crimes occur, and gradually an area will gain a reputation. Crime will become an increasingly bigger problem as possible offenders will be attracted to the area because it has become more vulnerable and less protected.

Wilson and Kelling draw the conclusion that the control of disorderly behaviour in public places, even for minor offences, is vital in order to prevent the escalation to more serious crime. This view was one of the most important influences that led to the policy of a zero-tolerance approach to crime, which was developed and applied in New York City in the 1980s (see section 6.11).

Conclusion

Both Left and Right realism have had a strong influence on law and order policies introduced by Labour governments elected in 1999 and 2001. However, both views are open to similar criticisms.

- Do official statistics provide a generally accurate picture of the scale and nature of crime?
- Both views neglect the crimes of the powerful.
- Both views (arguably) neglect the role of inequality in creating crime.

∞ Methods Link

New Left and Right realists both assume that official statistics provide a broadly accurate picture of crime. This is contested by sociologists who remain influenced by a more radical approach. Here we can see once again how sociologists' values shape their methods and how these in turn both reflect and shape their view of crime.

✓ Top Exam Hint

It can be argued that both types of realist theory neglect the crimes of the powerful and white-collar crime, due to their overriding focus on 'street crime'. Crime committed by working-class offenders is real enough, but the point made by those such as Steven Box, that law enforcement is selective, still remains the case.

For consideration

1. Is the NLR view closer to Merton's view of crime than Marx's?

2. Is it acceptable for sociologists to change their views?

What do postmodernists say about crime?

✳ Key Idea

Social fragmentation refers to the idea that social groups, such as class, race and gender, are now much less important than they were in modern societies. Postmodernists argue that people are now free to create their social identity free of the constraints imposed in modern society by structures such as class, race and gender. Much more important now is the role of the media, which provides people with most of their knowledge of the world, and which is a key influence on identity.

What does this mean?

Postmodernism is a relatively new theory in sociology which claims that society is fragmenting. Postmodernists claim that key social structures such as class, and ethnic and gender differences are fragmenting, leaving people much freer to create their own identity in contemporary society. Although postmodernists have not often written directly about crime and deviance, many other sociologists have used some insights and ideas from the theory to explain crime and deviance.

How can postmodernism help us understand crime?

Sociologists influenced by postmodernism have argued that society is undergoing changes which may be contributing to shifts in the type and extent of crime. Postmodernists argue that contemporary society is fragmenting. This means that social groups are less important, and postmodernists claim that now the most important influence on individual identity is consumption. They argue that it is through our spending patterns that we try to create an identity and distinguish ourselves from others. Several key points can therefore be made by sociologists who are influenced by postmodernist ideas.

- Lash and Urry (1994) argue that contemporary societies are fragmenting, and this has led to the creation of 'wild spaces' where the normal rules no longer apply. They are thinking here of the many urban areas of severe deprivation in Britain and the USA, where ethnic minorities and other socially-excluded groups develop a criminal lifestyle and identity.
- A postmodernist-influenced view of contemporary cities can point to the way that the very rich and the very poor now often live in very close proximity. This can lead to an increased fear of crime on the part of the rich, who isolate themselves in gated communities. As American academic Mike Davis notes (1994), city authorities may employ security features ranging from private security guards and closed-circuit television to architectural security features such as water sprinklers in parks which prevent 'down and outs' sleeping rough in public places.
- Other sociologists have developed the postmodernist idea that we now live in a consumer culture, where people are free from constraints and there is, therefore, less social control. However, not all individuals have an equal chance to create their identity. There is a **polarisation of identities**, as increasingly individuals distrust those who appear to be different to themselves. This leads to a 'culture of resentment' as inequalities increase. People come increasingly to think of themselves as individuals rather than members of social groups. This means that they have fewer obligations to other people. This process is called individualisation. This can mean that there are fewer constraints preventing people from committing crime, and can lead people to the view that crimes committed against others are acceptable, therefore enabling a tolerance of crime to develop.

This last concept is one which is closely associated with French thinker Michel Foucault (not best described as a postmodernist). Foucault explains the term in more detail arguing that individualisation means crime is seen as an individual problem and an individual responsibility. Foucault believed that since it is very difficult for modern states to monitor and control all citizens, they have to try and develop other forms of discipline or social control. Modern societies see the creation of a culture whereby individuals monitor or control themselves. Professional experts (police, psychiatrists, legal experts and criminologists) make what Foucault calls 'normalising judgements' about what sorts of people are criminals. These definitions become influential, but they also create the illusion that crime and deviance are purely individual matters, and do not acknowledge that the 'normalising judgements' by which some come to be seen as insane or criminal, for example, are socially constructed.

Conclusion

Postmodernist-influenced views of crime and deviance may seem very persuasive. However, use the following points to critically evaluate postmodernist views.

- A 'culture of resentment' and 'polarisation of identities' may not be an entirely new phenomena. Postmodernism, therefore, exaggerates the extent of social change.
- The social changes identified by postmodernist theory may be better explained by other theories, such as functionalism, Marxism or control theory.
- It is hard to see how postmodernist theories can be operationalised and tested.

✓ Top Exam Hint

You can use postmodernism to evaluate other theories such as Marxism and functionalism. To simplify, postmodernists claim that all of the older or classical theories in sociology are flawed. However, a counter-argument is that postmodernism neglects the importance and existence of structures. It therefore leans heavily towards the action side in the structure/action debate.

For consideration

1. Is there a culture of resentment?

2. Are all social groups fragmenting?

| # Do official statistics give a true picture of crime?

Key Fact

The British Crime Survey (BCS) has been carried out on an annual basis since 2001. It currently uses a sample of around 40,000 respondents. A recent finding was that 44 per cent of crimes reported in the survey were reported to the police. This provides some basis on which to estimate the total amount of crime in a given year, however, the rates vary a lot depending on the type of crime.

✳ Key Idea

The idea that there is a dark figure of crime, suggests that statistics only show crimes known to the police. The so-called dark figure refers to all those crimes which have been committed but not reported or identified. The term 'iceberg principle' refers to the fact that the largest proportion of an iceberg remains submerged under the surface; crime statistics, in this sense, are only the 'tip of the iceberg'.

What does this mean?

Official statistics on crime are collected by the government through the recording of crimes by the police and courts and through the British Crime Survey (BCS), a large-scale victim survey. The problem with both of these sources is that they lack validity and obscure the true extent of crime – the so-called 'dark figure' (unknown) or the 'tip of the iceberg' (only one-seventh of an iceberg is visible on the surface, the rest is hidden beneath the water). Sociologists therefore need to understand how crime statistics are constructed in order to evaluate how useful they are as sources of data.

What problems are there with using official statistics?

The problem with police recording of crime is that it only shows 'crimes known to the police'. This depends both on police activity and the public's willingness to report crime. Clearly the police are unable to identify all criminal offences, but research by Holdaway shows that the police work selectively (1983). In doing this they reflect public views of crime as well as shaping and reinforcing public attitudes. Holdaway conducted participant observation on the occupational culture and working practices of the police. He found that the occupational culture led to police officers creating their own view of the priority and seriousness of offences and a strong belief that police officers had the right to exercise 'discretion' over how they dealt with offences. In practice, Holdaway argues that this also means that officers would apply the law in ways which were to their own benefit. This might mean for example that minor offences were neglected, possibly to avoid extra paperwork, or arrests were made in order to be able to return to the police station instead of remaining outside in unpleasant conditions. Senior officers may try to exercise control over these processes, but they too will have 'discretion'. The whole process of policing therefore contributes towards the social construction of crime.

...e public too will not have a simple response to crime. People may have
...ny reasons for not reporting crime to the police, ranging from a lack of trust
...tion 6.11) to a belief that a crime is too minor or can best be dealt with
...ately, or they may not realise that they have been a victim of a crime (see
...ion 6.16).

...crime is socially constructed and this is why official statistics lack validity
...only show us a part of the picture about crime. Official statistics possibly
...s more about this process of construction than about crime itself.

...y do sociologists use official statistics?

...te these problems, official statistics on crime are still a useful resource as
...as they are used critically. Official statistics provide a cheap and easily

available resource, they provide some ability to analyse change over time, and they consist of a large number of cases. Sociologists can therefore gain some insights into crime using this resource. They can combine official statistics with the results from victim surveys and self-report studies to estimate the 'real' rate of crime.

What other methods can sociologists use to measure crime?

There are several other methods that researchers can use in addition to the official crime statistics. The two most important methods are victim surveys and self-report studies. Victim surveys aim to encourage members of the public to reveal whether they have been the victim of a crime and other relevant details, such as why they did not report the crime. Self-report studies attempt to persuade respondents to confess to offences they have committed but which may not be known to the police. There are, however, disadvantages with both of these methods.

- Not all respondents take part in victim surveys, and those who do not may be aware of crimes that would change the overall picture of crime.
- Respondents may not report all crimes for various reasons.
- Views about crime change so people's willingness to report or confess may change over time.

Conclusion

- The picture of crime provided from official statistics lacks validity.
- However, crime statistics can be useful if combined with self-report and victim surveys.
- If official statistics lack validity, then sociological theories of crime and deviance based on such theories may be flawed.

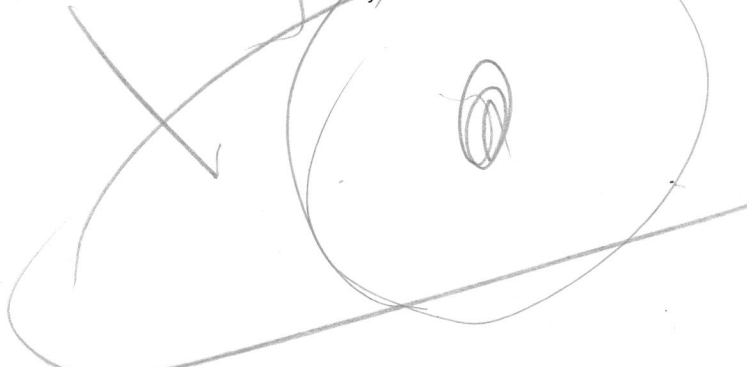

⤳ **Classic Study**

Hobbs, '*Doing the Business*', 1988: Hobbs argues that there was a reciprocal relationship between the police and people in the East End of London. Hobbs argues that both police and criminals needed each other, and they developed complex relationships involving the trading and bartering of information and favours. This study therefore helps to reinforce the criticisms made of official statistics by showing the context in which they are constructed.

✓ **Top Exam Hint**

According to official statistics, the typical criminal is young, male, working class, black, poorly educated, and likely to have had a disturbed childhood. However, the implication of this section is that before trying to provide sociological explanations of this, we should consider carefully whether official statistics in fact provide us with a valid picture of crime and criminals.

For consideration

1. If official statistics lack validity, should sociologists avoid using them?
2. What sort of crimes are people likely to report? Why?

| # What is white-collar crime?

How many crimes can you see being committed here? Sociologists argue that white-collar crime is an important, but frequently hidden, form of crime.

✳ Key Idea

The idea of white-collar crime was first explained by Edwin Sutherland in the following terms. Sutherland claimed that

'persons of the upper socio-economic class engage in much criminal behaviour … this criminal behaviour differs from the criminal behaviour of the lower socio-economic class principally in the administrative procedures which are used in dealing with offenders'.

(E Sutherland 1949).

∞ Methods Link

White-collar crime is hard to research, due to the difficulties in identifying it, and the unwillingness of individuals and organisations to discuss it. However, white-collar crime is also important because its _____ ce and relative neglect, sugge_____ gical theories of _____ 'street crime', _____ e powerful and _____ d image of

What does this mean?

The idea of white-collar crime refers to crimes committed by professionals or members of the middle classes. The term is interesting because it seems to imply that white-collar crime is somehow unusual and that criminals are usually from a different class, such as blue-collar or manual workers. Investigating white-collar crime may lead us to revise our views about what sort of social groups criminals come from and which theoretical explanations of crime we find most convincing.

What is white-collar crime?

The concept of white-collar crime was invented by American sociologist Edwin Sutherland in the 1940s. Sutherland defined white-collar crime as *'crimes committed by persons of respectability and high social status in the course of their occupations'* (1949). Sutherland had in mind crimes such as fraud and embezzlement. However, white-collar crime can also include a range of other activities, some of which may be considered by some people to be normal business practice. Examples of this might be the fairly common practice of not paying bills until well after the agreed credit terms, or salvaging waste from a job and re-selling it, or dumping toxic waste into the environment. Critics of Sutherland have taken different views of this definition. Some have argued that it is simply an anti-capitalist and business bias. Others have argued that Sutherland's definition is too vague, and does not, for example, distinguish between those who commit crime in the course of their occupations for their own benefit, and those who commit it for the benefit of their employer. This has led several sociologists, including Hazel Croall (1992), to distinguish between two types of white-collar crime.

- Occupational crime: this refers to crimes committed by professionals, senior or junior executives or others, in the course of their occupation. This could include fraud, for example, various types of electronic or computer crimes are increasingly common.
- Corporate crime: this refers to crimes committed by corporations or businesses. It can include a wide range of activities from pollution, fraud, breaking health and safety regulations to negligence or corporate manslaughter.

Croall would argue that we can broaden this further. She claims that what is at issue is in fact 'crimes of the powerful', and suggests that we can also use the term 'organisational crime' to refer to crimes committed by governments or public organisations. Muncie and McLaughlin in a similar way refer to 'crimes of the state'.

Is there much white-collar crime?

Michael Clarke (1990) points out that white-collar crime is difficult to research because it is easily concealed and disguised. Many firms are embarrassed to acknowledge that their employees can act criminally and therefore do not report incidents. Clarke also points out that as white-collar crime such as fraud or accounting scams can be complex and hard to investigate, requiring highly specialist knowledge and skills, the police are not likely to prioritise it. Clarke notes that in 1987 only 5 per cent of British detective manpower was allocated to fraud squads.

It is hard to estimate the extent of white-collar crime, but recent research by Professor Susanne Karstedt and Stephen Farrell (University of Keele) suggests that white-collar crime is increasingly common and could be costing around £14 billion per year, which is five times more than the cost of burglary (Radford, 2003). This is a finding which bears out the views of Steven Box, who argues that white-collar crime is important because it shows us how relations of power are vital in shaping our perceptions of crime. The ability of the powerful to avoid criminalisation and the low number of convictions for white-collar crime help increase the focus on the crimes of the less powerful. This process is therefore an ideological device which distracts our attention from the reality of crime. It is another example of selective law enforcement.

Conclusion

- The difficulties in measuring white-collar crime remind us once again of the methodological difficulties in studying crime.
- White-collar crime can lead us to reflect on the validity of theoretical explanations of crime. Perhaps theoretical explanations should focus more on what makes people obey the law than what makes them break it.
- White-collar crime may also lead us to reflect that the differences between so-called 'criminals' and those from higher social groups are exaggerated and distorted.

For consideration

1. What methodological criticisms might be made of the findings of Karstedt and Farrell?

2. Give examples of crimes of the state.

☐ Key Facts

In a cross-cultural study with a sample of 4000 people aged 25–65 in England and Wales and West Germany, Karstedt and Farrell (2003) found that many respondents admitted to exaggerating insurance claims (7 per cent in England and Wales, 22 per cent in Germany), or paying cash to avoid taxation (34 per cent and 54 per cent). Karstedt and Farrell argue that contemporary society is aptly described as 'predatory' (people prey on others, like animals), and that market societies are not necessarily moral societies.

✓ Top Exam Hint

White-collar crime raises important questions about the nature of crime and challenges the view implicit in many sociological theories, that crime is mainly a working-class activity. Use this insight to evaluate the sociological theories which have been discussed so far.

How does the mass media portray crime and deviance?

Does the mass media portray a realistic picture of crime? Or do sensational headlines such as this contribute to moral panics and a social construction of crime?

Classic Study

Stan Cohen, *Folk Devils and Moral Panics*: the research on which this study is based was conducted between 1964 and 1966. Cohen used primary and secondary sources and a wide range of methods. He used newspapers and many documents, questionnaires, interviews, participant observation, non-participant observation, and a survey on attitudes to delinquency amongst councillors, lawyers, magistrates and similar official figures. This is interesting because it shows that although strongly influenced by interactionism, like most other sociologists, Cohen has used a complex mix of methods.

What does this mean?

Sociologists argue that our knowledge of crime and deviance is socially constructed. This means that our views of what crime is, what causes it, and what should be done about it, are ideas which we learn from institutions and other people in society. One of the key institutions through which dominant ideas about crime and deviance are transmitted is the mass media. Sociologists argue that the mass media can have a powerful influence on our views about crime and deviance.

How does the mass media contribute to the social construction of crime?

A range of research into the content of the mass media suggests that a highly selective view of crime is transmitted by the media. Research by Williams and Dickinson (1993) indicated that 12 per cent of the content of current affairs coverage was devoted to crime, and that over 60 per cent of this focused on crimes involving violence. In the early 1990s, however, violent crime represented only some 5 per cent of all crime recorded by the police. This indicates a highly selective view of crime. Sociologists have made various explanations for this phenomenon. Chibnall's study (1977) put crime reporting firmly into the context of news production. As Chibnall found, news production follows the principal of 'newsworthiness' according to which news is defined in terms of five factors.

- It must be highly visible and spectacular.
- Sexual and political implications are highly desirable.
- Graphic presentation is essential (dramatic pictures).
- It must involve individual pathology (sickness, abnormality).
- It must involve deterrence and repression.

Certain types of crime 'stories' provide these elements, and these are the type journalists will be most likely to publicise. It is for this reason that violent crimes involving innocent young victims; spectacular crimes involving risk, excitement and violence; or crimes which are particularly shocking or sickening will gain a high media profile. The more mundane cases of crime, which are the vast majority, will attract little interest.

How do audiences react to the mass media's portrayal of crime and deviance?

Stan Cohen has argued that the media plays a crucial role in constructing the social reaction to crime and deviance. In a key study, *Folk Devils and Moral*

Panics, (1973) Cohen argued that exaggerated and distorted reporting by the media was able to create a public reaction to crime and deviance which could lead to the public labelling of a group as deviant. Cohen argued that this process involved several stages, but it concerned a problem being identified and seen as being caused by one group, who were then stigmatised and labelled. The media focus on this deviant group leads to further reporting, but Cohen's study showed that this only led to further public outcry, and the attention of what he calls 'moral entrepreneurs' – public officials such as editors, senior police officers, members of the legal profession and politicians. This interest, in turn, leads to both further reporting by the media, who see a developing story that must be reported, and a determination to tackle the perceived problem by the forces of law and order. The media interest and exaggerated reporting therefore leads to a social reaction and amplification (or a deviancy amplification spiral), as more interest in fact leads to the identification of more of the offending behaviour.

Cohen uses the example of the moral panic over the 'mod and rocker' riots of the late 1960s to illustrate this. Other sociologists, such as Fishman (1978) and Chibnall (1977) argue that in fact 'crime waves' are nothing but moral panics. Other examples of moral panics would include the response to dance music and ecstasy use in the last twenty years. However, Sara Thornton (1995) has used this example to criticise aspects of Cohen's concept. Thornton argues that the idea of one social reaction to deviance is oversimplified, and that in contemporary society there may be many reactions to such exaggerated reporting. She also uses the idea of reflexivity, arguing that, in fact, many deviant and sub-cultural groups, such as the ravers of the 1980s and 1990s, actively sought to gain media and public notoriety. It is through such means that some groups and sub-cultures can shock and create a distinctive identity in what Thornton sees as a fragmented and postmodern world.

Conclusion

In evaluating the role of the mass media it is useful to remember the following points.

- Giddens argues that people are reflexive. This means they interpret media output rather than just accept it.
- As Thornton contends, it is more accurate to talk about social reactions in the plural, not just social reaction.
- Study of the mass media indicates that crime is a social construction.

For consideration

1. What are the dominant images of crime in the media?
2. Does the media present a biased image of crime?

✳ Key Ideas

- The idea of reflexivity suggests that sociologists need to see people as actively creating society, not as passive dupes or puppets. This is important to bear in mind when evaluating media effects research or Cohen's study discussed here. It may lead us to challenge the conclusions reached by the sociologist.

- The concept of deviance amplification enables us to understand the processes involved in the social construction of crime. It should also remind us to think back to labelling theory, discussed in section 6.9, because there we learned that according to interactionists one of the key ways in which crime and deviance are constructed is through the social reaction to deviant acts. Deviance amplification can be seen as an important element of social reaction.

● Synoptic Link

Cohen's study shows us that we have to make links to other topics in order to understand how crime is socially constructed. Here the main link is to the media and media representations, but there are also important links to theory and the structure/action debate.

What does the study of drugs tell us about crime and deviance?

Sociologists argue that whether an action is seen as deviant or not depends on the social reaction.

What does this mean?

The way that drugs are used in society, and the way that society responds to drug use, provides a good case study of what sociologists mean when they say that crime and deviance are socially constructed.

How do drugs affect people?

Howard Becker (1963) interviewed marijuana users and claimed that drug use cannot be explained simply in biological terms. Becker found that users have to learn how to feel the effects of smoking marijuana, for example, by learning how to respond to the drug, how to recognise the symptoms of a 'high', and the correct ways to signify enjoyment.

Those who use the drug may not necessarily become regular users, but using marijuana is likely to lead them to commit themselves to the outlook of those they share the activity with. Becker argues that regular users may develop a deviant career as marijuana use becomes a more important part of their identity and becomes a 'master status'.

How does society react to drug taking?

Jock Young (1971) argues that it is the way in which society responds to drug taking that is of chief importance. Young's research into drug users in London led him to conclude that what mainstream society disliked about drug users was not so much their drug use, but rather their cultural values. The drug users Young studied in the late 1960s were critical of the work ethic and placed higher value on leisure. Young also argued that the stigmatisation and marginalisation of drug users was counter productive. Young argued that excessive police attention in fact led to deviance amplification, as drug users found it difficult to shed their master status. This was therefore a process of criminalisation, and fears about drugs often lead to the creation of moral panics (section 6.17). Young claims that the media created a fictional account of drug takers and their world, but these processes led to the fiction becoming a reality, as a powerful self-fulfilling prophecy was set in motion.

Becker's and Young's studies are therefore good illustrations of the way that crime and deviance are socially constructed. Other drugs, such as alcohol and tobacco, do not meet with such strong social disapproval, even though they cause more deaths than other drugs (South 2002).

How are society and crime changing?

Drug use has changed since Becker's and Young's studies in the 1960s and 1970s, with the use of different drugs and increased levels of use (see margin items). As Jock Young has shown, sociologists have also begun to look at society in different ways, with new theoretical frameworks and new concepts. Jock Young draws on a number of these in his recent work, and argues that crime, in general, is increasingly seen in terms of social exclusion (2002). Young suggests that many policy makers, government officials and politicians, now explain crime in the following terms.

- In a fragmented and diverse society, crime is caused by social exclusion (section 6.14).
- Crime is predominantly caused by a small number of people, living in close proximity (see sections 6.11 and 6.13).
- Crime is largely the result of the development of a socially-excluded underclass in a dependency culture (see section 6.13).
- Crime is the outcome of these factors, which lead to social disorganisation and a chaotic lifestyle centred around drug use (see section 6.11).

However, Young counters this picture by arguing that it is, in fact, neo-liberal policies which have caused fragmentation, inequality and social exclusion, by promoting the idea that government should not interfere in the process of wealth creation by initiating social policies. Young argues that this inevitably means that the gap between rich and poor increases, and an 'underclass' develops. Neo-liberal policies also promote globalisation, which is essential to understanding the rapid increase in drugs use from the 1970s onwards (South 2002). Young argues that so-called 'third way' policies on crime, as advocated by Giddens, by communitarians such as Etzioni, and politicians such as Tony Blair, neglect the power of neo-liberal policies to create huge inequalities. Inequality is an inevitable consequence of such policies, and leads to a situation where crime and the drugs trade become alternative career paths for those without the resources to compete in more socially acceptable ways.

Conclusion

- Globalisation has led to an increase in drug use in the late 20th century.
- Drug use and other crime and deviance, can be seen as the outcome of social exclusion.
- Sociologists have to consider critically what factors cause social exclusion.

For consideration

1. Has drug use become normal?
2. Why are alcohol and tobacco acceptable drugs in the UK?

☀ Key Idea

This extract from the classic study 'Outsiders' illustrates Becker's view that becoming a drug user and experiencing the effects of drugs is a social process.

'See, like I didn't know the first thing about it – how to smoke it, or what was going to happen, or what. I just watched him like a hawk – I didn't take my eyes off him for a second, because I wanted to do everything just as he did it. I watched how he held it, how he smoked it, and everything. Then when he gave it to me I just came on cool, as though I knew exactly what the score was. I held it like he did and took a poke just the way he did.'

(Becker, *Outsiders*, 1963, page 48)

↪ Classic Study

Jock Young's '*The Drugtakers*' is one of the first key studies of drug use and how it comes to be socially constructed as a deviant activity in British sociology. Most textbooks describe it as a study, and while the book is based on participant observation of a group of drug users in Notting Hill between 1967 and 1969, the reader is hard pressed to find much detail of how the study was carried out. This makes the study a rather easy target for the common criticisms levelled at qualitative research.

◆ What, when and why?

Neo-liberal policies argue in favour of letting countries and businesses trade wherever they like, without government restrictions. Many sociologists see these policies as being one of the causes of globalisation (see Chapter 3). Nigel South points out that the production, sale and consumption of drugs now has to be seen in its global context. Events in a distant place can affect our own lives, but, because this is a global phenomenon, it is hard for governments to control these events. Third way policies have been devised in the late 1990s by sociologists such as Giddens and taken up by politicians such as Tony Blair. These argue that crime is a serious and real problem, which can only be solved by a mixture of firm punishments and improved welfare provisions to help young people in deprived areas.

6.19 | The social distribution of crime: are ethnic minorities more criminal than whites?

Why are young black people eight times more likely to be stopped and searched than whites?

🗋 Key Facts

- **19 per cent of male prisoners are from ethnic minorities**

- **25 per cent of female prisoners are from ethnic minorities.**

As ethnic minorities form around 6–7 per cent of the UK population, ethnic minorities are disproportionately represented in the prison population.

Source: Morgan 2002

- In 2001–02, The Home Office found that black people were eight times more likely to be stopped and searched than white people.

Source: Home Office, *Race and the Criminal Justice System*, 2002

What does this mean?

A major concern for sociologists and others has been whether there is any evidence that crime is more prevalent amongst certain ethnic minority groups. This issue arises from the data produced by official statistics showing British prisons having a disproportional number of ethnic minority inmates. This finding raises the question of whether ethnic minorities really are more criminal, or whether there is bias and selective law enforcement.

How do sociologists explain the relationship between crime and ethnicity?

Official statistics show that a high proportion of offenders come from ethnic minority groups. Sociologists can explain this pattern by applying any of the theories discussed in this chapter. In the 1980s, however, sociological explanations came to focus on one key debate which still concerns sociologists and criminologists today.

- On the one hand, neo-Marxist-influenced researchers such as Stuart Hall (see section 6.8), argue that black criminality is a myth. Black people are no more criminal than any other group in society, but are seen as such because of distorted media reporting and inadequate statistics.
- On the other hand, researchers generally associated with the New Left realists (see section 6.13) such as Lea and Young (1993), argue that official statistics are generally accurate, and young black men really are committing more offences than other groups.

In trying to choose between different theoretical explanations, sociologists have to combine theory with empirical evidence, so let us now examine the research evidence on crime and race.

What evidence is there of racial discrimination in the criminal justice system?

Since recorded crime only provides a partial view of crime, trying to investigate whether the criminal justice system is racist is very difficult. The criminologist Robert Reiner (1994) has argued that it would require much more self-report data and other comparable data to make a judgement, and given that this is not available it is probably impossible. However, this has not prevented some sociologists from trying, and several pieces of recent research can provide evidence from which tentative conclusions can be drawn.

- In 1983 the PSI published a report entitled *Police and People in London*. Researchers used a range of qualitative methods, including non-participant overt observation ('shadowing' police officers) and interviews to investigate the attitudes of Metropolitan Police officers. The researchers found that the use of racist language and jokes was common and had become part of the institutional culture.
- Simon Holdaway has conducted qualitative research into the occupational culture of the police, and he has also found evidence of the widespread use of racist language and attitudes.
- A large multi-method research project carried out in 2001 by Marion Fitzgerald and Michael Hough, *The Policing For London Survey* (PFLS), found that although many people stopped by the police were satisfied with their treatment, there had been a decline in confidence in police effectiveness. Dissatisfaction with the police was highest amongst young people, black suspects, and those living in poor areas. The study found that the best predictors of being stopped by the police were 'being young, being male, being black, being working class and being single' (2002).

The evidence of these research findings seems to give considerable support for the view that policing practices are often institutionally racist. However, as indicated above, there are methodological problems with all research in this area. Other researchers, while acknowledging the existence of racism in British society, express a note of caution. Phillips and Bowling (2002), for example, point out that the structural context of ethnic minorities in British society cannot be neglected, while Smith (a co-author of the 1983 PSI report) argues that the over-representation of black people is so great that it cannot all be explained as the result of **institutional racism**. Others might well argue that while structural factors (inequality) may lead some ethnic minorities towards crime, the evidence of institutional racism simply underlines the selective nature of law enforcement and suggests there is a high probability that black people are no more likely to be criminal than other sections of the population (see sections 6.15 and 6.16). This in no way justifies any law breaking, but it does put it into a different context.

Conclusion

Remember the following points when evaluating debates on crime and ethnicity.

- Official statistics lack validity and researchers need to use a range of evidence in examining race and crime.
- Ethnicity may just be one element in a complex web of causes.
- Sociologists should never neglect power relations. Consider which social groups have most power in making and applying the law.

For consideration

1. Do only some ethnic groups have criminalised identities? If so, why?
2. What is the best way to research race and crime?

◆ **What, when and why?**

A concern over the issues of policing, crime and race relations has been a long-running theme in British society. This concern was heightened following the racist murder of Stephen Lawrence in 1993 while he was waiting at a London bus stop. The Macpherson Enquiry in 1999 argued that the Metropolitan Police was institutionally racist in its actions concerning the investigation of his murder. As a result his killers have not been held accountable. The murder of 10-year-old Damilola Taylor in 2001 was seen as the Metropolitan Police's first big test on the murder of a black youth since the Stephen Lawrence case. However, the trial collapsed in 2002 due to police and Crown Prosecution failings, according to official investigations.

✳ **Key Idea**

In *Policing the Crisis: Mugging, the State and Law and Order* (1978), Stuart Hall et al criticise what they argue is the distorted and often racist reporting of black crime in the British media. They argue that in times of economic crisis, crime statistics can be politically manipulated to provide reason for the failure of the economy. Using the example of the mugging crisis in the 1970s, Hall et al argue that this results in the scapegoating of a particular group of people – in this case, black youths (see section 6.8).

❝❞ **Key Definition**

Institutional racism refers to the way in which the rules and procedures of an institution can work. Where institutional racism occurs, there are systematic biases in the way that they are applied to people. These biases do not have to be intentional or involve a deliberate attempt to discriminate on the part of individuals or an institution.

∞ **Methods Link**

The PFLS research provides a good demonstration of the complexity of professional research. The researchers used a multi-strategy approach that involved qualitative and quantitative methods and a sample of 5700 Londoners. The study involved a survey (which had a response rate of 49 per cent) and also used focus groups with members of the public and with police officers, depth interviews, and observation. See the activity on the CD-Rom for furt

The social distribution of crime: are women less criminal than men?

Are women naturally less criminal than men?

⚮ Methods Link

Feminists have been critical of the malestream bias of sociology and have argued that feminists can use different approaches to produce more valid research. Perhaps one of the key biases is that, until fairly recently, sociologists have failed to question and investigated the highly gendered nature of crime.

What does this mean?

Official statistics show that far fewer women are convicted of criminal offences than men. This raises the question of whether women are really less criminal than men, and if so, why. It also raises the question of whether women are fairly treated by the criminal justice system, or whether biases exist in the way it operates.

What evidence is there that women are less criminal than men?

In a review of research into this issue, Heidensohn (2002) argues that the overwhelming conclusion to be reached is that women do indeed commit less crime than men. However, the situation is more complex than this fact suggests.

- Self-report studies indicate that, while women are less involved in criminal activity than men, the difference is not quite as large as official statistics suggest. Heidensohn reports that the ratio of male compared with female offending was around 6:1 in 1999, but that self-report studies revealed a figure nearer to 3:1.
- Moreover, Heidensohn notes that the share of crime committed by women is slowly increasing, and that women do commit all types of crime. However, the proportion of offences committed by women varies considerably between different offences.

How do sociologists explain women's role in crime?

In trying to explain women's role in crime, all of the theories examined in this chapter can be applied to the data above. Here though we are going to focus on three main explanations.

Biological explanations

Developing Lombroso's original research (see section 6.5), Lombroso and Ferrero (1895) argued that women's biology prevented them from becoming criminal, as they were more passive and naturally more inclined to childrearing than aggressive physical activity such as crime. Other researchers have seen biological differences leading in a different direction. Otto Pollak (1950) argued that women were by nature devious and manipulative. Pollak concluded that women committed more crime than was apparent from official records, were more skilled at concealing their crimes, and that they focused their efforts on particular types of crime, such as shoplifting.

The chivalry thesis

In the 1980s, some researchers argued that women offenders gained more lenient treatment from the police and courts; Campbell (1981), Allen (1987). Carol Smart, however, has argued that women can be treated more harshly or unsympathetically by courts in some cases (1989). Women who are seen to be particularly deviant may therefore be stigmatised with a negative identity, for example, 'monster'. Recent research by Gelsthorpe and Louck (1997), based on 197 interviews with lay (part time, unpaid) and stipendiary (paid) magistrates from five courts in England and Wales, found no evidence of deliberate discrimination by magistrates. However, the researchers did find that magistrates were more inclined to take account of family circumstances in cases involving women, and women were more likely than men to be treated with leniency when they had dependants. Also, in finely-balanced cases where the magistrates were unsure whether the sentence should be custodial or non-custodial, personal circumstances were more important for female offenders than for male offenders.

Control and the gendering of crime

Frances Heidensohn (1996, 2002) argues that women have a gendered identity in British society, and that crime is a gendered activity. She argues that women's identity in British society is constructed in such a way that criminal activity is not seen as a desirable feminine activity. Socialisation into gender roles and patriarchal social control in the family and household limits the opportunity that women have to become involved in crime. Heidensohn therefore uses control theory (see section 6.12), as well as feminism to explain gender and crime. This supports Gelsthorpe and Louck's findings, suggesting that women's treatment in the criminal justice system is gendered, and that this reflects the gendering processes in the wider society. However, Heidensohn makes the important point that women have the ability to choose how to act, and that they actively construct their gender activities. Sociologist Bob Connell (1985) makes the same point about male gender identities. For Heidensohn the implication of this is that sociologists, rather than posing the question of why female crime rates are so low, should instead be asking what it is about masculinity that leads so many young men into crime.

Conclusion

In evaluating competing explanations of the evidence showing that women are less criminal than men, bear in mind the following key points.

- Crime is a gendered activity.
- Explaining the relationship between gender and crime has to involve examining both masculinity and femininity.
- People actively create their identities, but in doing this they are constrained by structural forces.

For consideration

1. What structural conditions might encourage women to commit crime?

2. Why and how could criminality be seen as a positive feature of male identity?

| # The social distribution of crime: age and crime

Are young people just more likely to be seen breaking the law or are they really more criminal?

☐ Key Facts

- 25 per cent of all recorded crime is committed by children aged between 10 and 17

- 40 per cent of all crime is committed by persons under the age of 21.

Source: Criminal Statistics (2000)

According to the National Prison Survey (Walmsley et al 1992):

- 40 per cent of male prisoners left school before the age of 16, compared with 11 per cent of the male population

- over a quarter of prisoners had been in local authority care at some time, compared with 2 per cent of the general population.

66 99 Key Definition

- **Folk devils:** the largely exaggerated or even fictitious group that moral panics are linked to.

- **Social** ___ l refers to the social a___ ___ resources which a ___ to. The concept was ___ oleman and it ___ lationships and ___ vantages on ___ y providing ___ f support.

What does this mean?

According to official statistics, crime is strongly associated with youth, and sociologists are interested in investigating why this is the case and whether it is a valid portrayal of crime.

Is youth crime a modern phenomenon?

Sociologist Geoffrey Pearson has pointed out that while crime by young people is nothing new, the way it is seen and the type and extent of crime and deviance by young people, is a modern phenomenon (1983). The concept of 'youth' is socially constructed and varies over time and place. Industrial capitalism has constructed a child-centred society, where the role of children is such that they are sheltered from the labour market until reaching adult status and often until well into their twenties. From the 1950s onwards, sociologists have been particularly interested in the creation of youth cultures, and have noted that such cultures are often seen as being a social problem for the wider, adult society. Youth cultures have, therefore, often been associated with crime and deviance and constructed as **'folk devils'** (see section 6.17), and sociologists have applied all the theories discussed in this chapter to explain this relationship. The rest of this section therefore focuses on some of the more influential and recent explanations of youth crime.

What are the more current explanations of youth crime?

As has already been indicated (see sections 6.18 and 6.14), many contemporary views of crime have been strongly influenced by the idea that modern society is increasingly consumerist and individualistic. Also related to this view is the idea that most crime is committed by a dysfunctional underclass. Some of these views are reflected in American sociologist James Coleman's concept of **social capital** (Coleman 1987), which has come to be increasingly influential in recent years amongst some researchers and policy makers. Although published in 1987, these ideas currently provide a strong focus for policy makers.

Coleman uses the term social capital to refer to the relationships within a family, the networks of support, and the structures of relationships between individuals and groups within a community. The presence of social capital can therefore be indicated by:

- strong family relationships and low levels of single-parent families
- high levels of interaction between parents and children
- clear and firmly-held sets of norms and values.

Coleman argues that these factors are associated with very low rates of juvenile crime, and the lack of social capital is correspondingly associated with high rates of juvenile crime. Coleman therefore concludes that youth crime is the result of low levels of social capital.

As Newburn has pointed out (2002), views based on this theory have been taken up by policy makers and politicians in power in the UK since 1997. A social capital approach to youth crime has helped to promote the idea that juvenile crime and delinquency is the result of disruptive families or dysfunctional families and poor parenting.

What criticisms can be made of social capital theory?

Social capital may seem to provide an analysis which fits well with the images of crime which we all see through the media and perhaps even in our own lives. However, sociologists have to be careful of generalising from their own experience, and from the media whose information-gathering processes are based on the principle of 'newsworthiness' (see section 6.17). Accordingly, we can draw on a range of theories and concepts to critically evaluate Coleman's theory.

- The idea of social capital appears vague and hard to operationalise. It also seems likely to involve value-judgements on the part of the researcher. Single-parent families, for example, can provide very secure environments for childrearing.
- This leads to an alternative suggestion that the key association is the link between social class and juvenile crime. Poor parenting may also occur as much, perhaps in different ways, in middle-class families, and it may be that it is their social class position which helps rule out the need or inclination for crime.
- It is also important to recall Steven Box's claim that criminal activity is not restricted to the lower social classes (see section 6.16).

Conclusion
- There is a strong relationship between youth and crime in official statistics.
- Official statistics lack validity.
- Many youth identities are constructed as 'delinquent' by adults.

[Handwritten margin notes:]
① Subculture
② underclass
③ social capital
④ W/C = MARXIST
⑤ functionalist poor socialisation
⑥ NEW Right = family diversity

must consider other factors such as social class ethnicity

What has suicide got to do with crime and deviance?

What does this mean?

Many students are perplexed to find suicide as a topic in crime and deviance, especially if they have already studied it in theory and method. However, you need to remember that deviance is a broad category, and can include the study of mental health and drug taking, for example, as well as crime. Also, suicide provides some important insights into crime and deviance. Suicide used to be illegal in the UK (and many other countries) and its status as a crime continued until the 1960s. This will remind you that crime and deviance are relative to time and place. Suicide is relevant to the study of deviance because it has for a long time been considered to be a deviant act. The study of suicide can therefore tell us a great deal about deviance, crime and social order, as well as being a useful topic because of its methodological significance.

What did Durkheim say about suicide?

In his classic study, *Le Suicide* (1897), Durkheim argued that suicide was best explained as being the result of social factors. It could not, Durkheim argued, be understood purely as the result of an individual's psychology or biology, or seen as some form of mental illness. Durkheim hypothesised that suicide was related to the level of social integration in a society. He tested this hypothesis by using official statistics derived from coroners' reports from a wide range of European societies. Durkheim argued that social integration could be indicated by the religion practised in an area or country. His reasoning was that Catholic societies would have higher levels of integration than Protestant societies, and that therefore suicide rates would be higher in Protestant societies. Durkheim believed that the Catholic religion, with its stricter rules, integrated its members much more tightly into the community. Protestantism on the other hand, encouraged its followers to question and interpret religious belief, and ultimately this led to communities that were less tightly integrated around a set of rigid beliefs and values.

What criticisms can be made of Durkheim's study of suicide?

Durkheim's findings appear to provide strong support for his hypothesis, but it can be seen in a very different light. Interpretivist critics of Durkheim, such as Atkinson (1971) and Douglas (1967), make several key points.

- Durkheim is not sensitive enough to the view that suicide is socially defined and constructed. Coroners have to interpret evidence and they may do this in very different (and inconsistent) ways.
- Suicide, therefore, has to be seen as a socially-constructed category. The interpretivist approach draws on the idea that in Catholic communities the act of suicide would lead to the individual involved (and probably their

✳ Key Idea

Social integration is a functionalist concept and in using it, functionalists are claiming that shared values are needed to hold society together. You will see that other theorists, such as control theorists, Right realists, and some of the ecological theorists (see section 6.11) also share this view. Remember, though, that social integration is hard to measure, and not all sociologists agree that it is the best way to look at society.

∞ Methods Link

Durkheim's study on suicide is important in sociology precisely because it tells us so much about methods. Durkheim took a positivist approach to sociology and tried to apply scientific methods to the study of society. Interpretivist critics have argued that since people are reflective and have reasons for acting as they do, other methods offer a better way to study social behaviour. One of the criticisms of Durkheim's approach is the idea that we all agree on what 'suicide' or family) being stigmatised. Suicide, in other words, is deviant, and to commit suicide would lead a person to have a **stigmatised identity**. This could well mean that coroners in Catholic societies would be more likely to avoid categorising deaths as suicides, since they would be aware of the shame it would bring on families.

Conclusion

Durkheim's study shows us that crime and deviance cannot be seen just in terms of individual characteristics. However, taken together with the criticisms of it, the study has a wider significance for our understanding of crime and deviance.

- Crime and deviance do need to be seen as socially-constructed categories. How people think about crime and deviance has important social effects.
- It shows us how deviant (and stigmatised identities) are constructed.
- Positivist approaches to crime and deviance, involving quantitative and statistical data, can present us with a distorted or partial view of reality, and will thus lack validity.

66 99 Key Definition

A deviant or a **stigmatised identity** is one which society reacts to negatively. Interactionists would not say that this implies a consensus (as functionalists would) but rather that it shows the importance of differences in power.

✓ Top Exam Hint

Durkheim's study is a really good example to use in questions involving a discussion or evaluation of the use of official statistics. Using it in a careful and relevant way will enable you to demonstrate your methodological and theoretical awareness and sophistication.

For consideration

1. What other indicators of social integration could Durkheim have used?

2. Is deviance always stigmatised? Is it ever celebrated?

READ

6.23 How can we make crime and deviance synoptic?

✓ Top Exam Hint

In addition to learning some key studies from your AS topics to use in synoptic questions (see section 6.2), make sure that you also learn some key points or examples to illustrate the links with the course themes of socialisation, culture and identity, and stratification and inequality. Do the same for theory and method.

● Synoptic Link

You must be able to link crime and deviance to all the themes here as well as to the other topics you studied at AS level. You key goal is to show that you understand that crime is socially constructed. You can do this convincingly by using your knowledge of other topics and of theory and method appropriately.

Why is synopticity important for crime and deviance?

Synopticity is all about making links between the different component parts of sociology. By learning about the way that crime and deviance is linked to other topics in sociology, you will improve your understanding of all topic areas and of sociology in general. In a way then, you cannot really understand crime and deviance without also understanding about key areas in sociology, such as culture, identity, inequality, deviance, and stratification and differentiation. This section therefore helps you to identify the way that crime and deviance are linked to these key course themes.

How does crime and deviance link to families and households and education?

This has been discussed in section 6.2, but it is worth raising a few points here. Crime and deviance links very easily to the studies of families and households, because family background can play a big role in the likelihood of a person getting involved in crime. This can be a result of factors linked to stratification, for example, household income and standard of living, but it is also important to remember that gendering processes start in the family. Education is also easily linked to crime when one bears in mind that 40 per cent of the male prison population leave school at the minimum leaving age (section 6.21), and that this population is characterised by a low level of attainment.

How does crime and deviance link to methods?

This is a vital link to make as we have seen, throughout this chapter, the way sociologists define and measure crime has a strong influence on their findings. As we have discussed, there are many debates about the validity of official statistics, but it is important to remember that the more positivist inclined researchers also question the validity of qualitative research methods such as participant observation (see the case studies on the CD-Rom for more useful examples on this topic).

How does crime and deviance link to issues of culture?

Sociologists have always been interested in culture, but in recent years there has been renewed interest in it. Sociologists have been keen to demonstrate that our ideas about crime and deviance are cultural constructions. This means that different societies define crime and deviance in different ways and also that these definitions change over time. Linking culture to power helps us to realise that cultural norms and values are often the values of particular social groups. Cultural values are upheld through social control, so powerful groups can ensure that the dominant culture is their culture. They can use this power to criminalise other cultures or aspects of other cultures.

How does crime and deviance link to issues of identity?

Crime and deviance is central to the way that our identities are constructed. Even if we are not criminal or deviant, we are marked out as a certain sort of person, for example, 'law abiding citizen', 'normal' or 'honest'. This will help define our identity, our status and the roles which we are able to adopt in society. These sorts of identity will be positively sanctioned. On the other hand, if our activities lead us to be labelled as criminal or deviant, we will find our identity is more likely to be what Goffman has called a stigmatised identity. This too will mark out a particular status and role for us in society, a predominantly negative identity, which will be most likely to lead to negative sanctions being applied.

How does crime and deviance link to issues of deviance?

It is important to remember that not all criminal acts are deviant, and equally that not all deviance is criminal. Deviant behaviour can be concerned, for example, with alternative cultural values and practices. Ethnic minority groups, for example, may often find themselves labelled as deviant and be portrayed as having a stigmatised identity. Homosexuality is widely regarded as being deviant by many people in British society, and gay identities are frequently stigmatised by the wider society, though there is perhaps growing tolerance.

How does crime and deviance link to issues of inequality?

Inequality features as a key focus in many sociological explanations of crime and deviance. Marxists and those influenced by them, argue that law and order is selectively enforced. Sociologists also point to the relative neglect of white-collar crime and the more lenient approach which the law appears to take towards white-collar criminals, corporate crime, and even crimes of the state. A slightly different focus on inequality suggests that the effect of large inequalities in capitalist societies is a direct cause of crime. This comes about because inequality leads to despair, envy and crime.

How does crime and deviance link to issues of stratification and differentiation?

Stratification refers to the structured inequalities of class, ethnicity, gender, and societies can be stratified by other criteria, such as age. A key issue running throughout this theme is power, and many sociologists would argue that power varies according to an individual's or group's position in society. In the middle of the 20th century, sociologists devoted most attention to the relationship between class and crime and deviance. More recently, though, interest has shifted to consider how all of these forms of stratification are interrelated.

Key points to remember

- To fully understand crime and deviance it has to be linked to other topics in sociology.
- It is particularly important to link crime and deviance to stratification and differentiation. This key topic and course theme shows us how crime and deviance is linked to issues of power, and to class, race and gender differences.
- We also have to link crime and deviance to culture and identity, as we can only understand how some actions are defined as criminal or deviant if we understand how a particular culture constructs these definitions.

✳ Key Idea

Power is an absolutely vital concept to grasp if you are to demonstrate a real understanding of sociology. It is important in this topic as it will shape your answer to questions such as 'Who has most power to make the laws and rules?' and 'Who benefits most from law and order?'. It will also influence which questions you think worth asking about crime and deviance. See Chapter 2 for more discussion of power.

∞ Methods Link

Synopticity is not just about linking crime to other topic areas such as families and households, and education. One question in your exam will require you to demonstrate the links between methods and crime and deviance. As we have shown throughout this chapter, there are many links between the methods researchers use and the resulting picture of crime and deviance which they produce.

6.24 | Pushing your grades up higher

1. Practice writing introductions and conclusions for long answers and get friends or your teacher to look at what you have written. This exercise forces you to summarise your thoughts on debates and theories in a very compressed way.

2. Get copies of past question papers and work through the questions. Also consult the chief examiner's report on the most recent sitting of the examination. This will contain useful advice and tips on what to do and what not to do in the exam.

3. Make a spider diagram or a list of the links between crime and deviance and other topics, sociological theories, and methods and methodology. Use your diagram/list to write down the names of key studies, concepts or sociologists that you can use in the exam.

4. Make a list of key 'link' or 'signpost' words, phrases or constructions. These will help you show readers how paragraphs in your essays are linked together. They will help you to make your argument flow logically by explaining your points and reasoning in careful detail. Examples of signpost words or phrases are: 'however', 'it can be argued that', 'this view is supported by evidence from'.

5. Make your own glossary of key terms and concepts in crime and deviance. Review, revise and test yourself by using it regularly.

6. Avoid 'restricted evaluation'. This means that you have tried to evaluate, but have not explained your points in sufficient detail and elaborated (spelt out) why your argument is a good one and why it is preferable to alternative views. A brief, one sentence justification for your views in a long essay answer will not be sufficient. If it is not supported by reasoned argument and some evidence, it is just an assertion.

7. Remember to show an awareness of current debates and social change, where they are relevant, in your work. This does not mean waffling on about some obscure report you have read in the local newspaper or TV news. It means that you might argue, for example, that the changing climate of opinion regarding drug use is a good example of the way in which crime and deviance are relative to time and place. It also means that you should try to use an understanding of current theories, such as postmodernism or globalisation, where you can see the relevance of such theories to your answer. These theories, debates, and aspects of social change may be helpful in critically evaluating older theories or studies.

8. This is a synoptic paper, so remember to integrate your general sociological knowledge. You can do this throughout the exam, but pay particular attention to the links which each question requests you to make. Use a direct style to draw the reader's (examiner's) attention to these links. You can use constructions such as, 'in studying this area, sociologists have to be

aware of a number of theoretical issues…', or 'the idea of deviance is also relevant in other topics such as the family…'

9. Do not quote large or even short excerpts from the data items in the exam. This nearly always makes you look either lazy or gives the impression that you do not know anything else. The best strategy is to 'refer' to the item. You can do this by using sentence constructions such as 'as the information in Item A suggests, functionalists see crime as…' This is a more skilful and appropriate way of writing in the context of your sociology exam. It is more appropriate because instead of re-writing the item, you are drawing attention to the particular part that is of interest. Rather than just copying it out, you are directing the reader's attention to what is important in the item. In short you are making a point.

10. Remember to write as clearly as you can and to set your answers out neatly in the exam. It is really helpful if you leave a couple of lines between each separate answer and label each question carefully. It is also helpful if you leave lines where questions ask you to, for example, identify and explain two points. If you write your answers in a simple style, for example, 'one point is…' and then leave a line and write 'another point is …', it will be much clearer to the examiner. It does not matter if you forget something and want to add it later. You can write your extra comments and put an asterisk or maybe a letter or number by the material. Then just repeat the symbol where you want the extra material to be joined and add a brief margin note, and it should be clear, even to an examiner, that you want the material to be read.

Key points to remember

- Use your knowledge and understanding carefully and appropriately – the exam is not simply a test of how much you have remembered.
- Evaluate and present well-reasoned arguments in response to the longer questions.
- Think synoptically and relate your knowledge to other relevant parts of the specification.

☀ Key Idea

Evaluation is one of the key AO2 skills and it is vital to understand it in order to maximise your marks in the exam. In order to evaluate, you must show that you can use sociological theories, concepts and research findings critically. You must identify strengths and weaknesses, and weigh up the strengths and weaknesses of different studies, theories and findings, and then show how you can reach a conclusion.

Frequently asked questions

Q. Why are sociologists more interested in male criminals than in female ones?

A. Some sociologists would say that this is because most crimes are still perpetrated by male offenders. However, feminist sociologists would take a more critical view of this. They would argue that there is a bias within mainstream sociological studies on crime, and in criminology, towards viewing crime as a predominantly male activity. So, feminists argue, not only is crime gendered, but so is our understanding of crime. Feminist sociology has forced researchers to look at this issue more critically, and investigate those women who are involved in crime, as well as studying the way the criminal justice system deals with female victims and offenders.

Q. Can sociologists ever really know about crime?

A. Positivist sociologists would argue that scientific methods will indeed present the truth about crime, but interpretivists would be more sceptical. However, many sociologists would be cautious in answering this question and would agree that sociological knowledge about any topic is always partial and provisional. This does not mean that it is pointless to attempt sociological research, but rather that knowledge is always partial and therefore it can only help make a contribution to understanding. This is not the same as the postmodernist view that no such thing as the 'truth' exists; it just means we cannot be absolutely certain that we always know what the truth is.

Q. Will we ever live in a society without crime?

A. Marxist-inspired sociologists can argue that crime will decline in a more equal society. However, arguably the most convincing answer comes from Durkheim, who argued that crime was inevitable and would never be eradicated. Durkheim points out that no matter how tolerant societies are, will have rules and there will always be occasions when the rules are . In an imaginary society of saints, Durkheim says, what seem to us misdemeanours will come to be regarded as more serious breaches. laws will always change, but they will never be abolished, and ime, or law breaking, will always take place.

Chapter 7

Stratification and differentiation

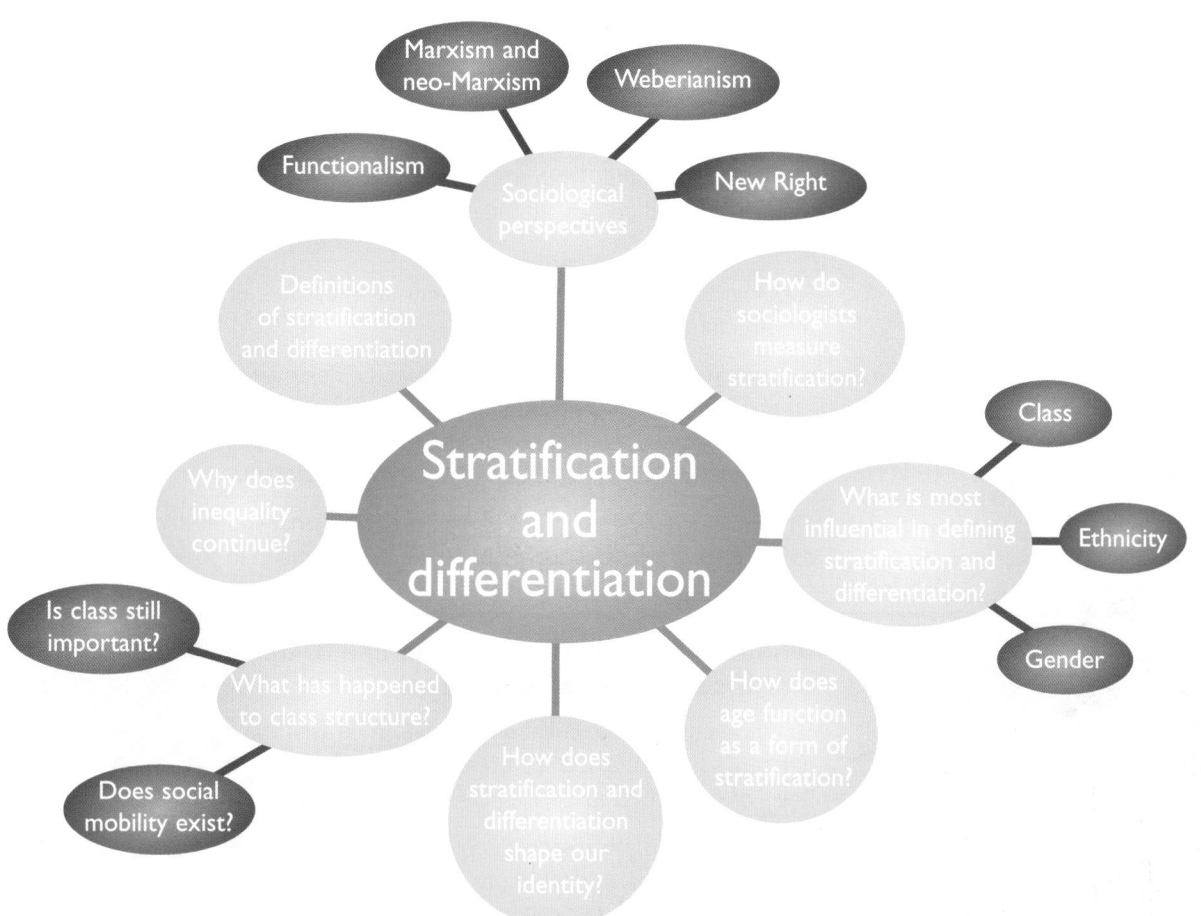

Key issues in stratification and differentiation

❝❞ Key Definitions

- Sociologists use the term **stratification** to refer to structured social inequalities and hierarchies. Systematic social inequalities (regular and repeated patterns of inequality) can develop and be justified on the basis of any perceived or real characteristic of a group, for example, class, ethnicity, gender or age.
- **Differentiation** refers to the way that social groups and categories of individuals are distinguished from one another. Sociologists are increasingly using this term as a general name for social differences such as class, ethnicity and gender. Differentiation is not the same as stratification because it focuses on differences not inequalities. This emphasis reflects the use of the word in postmodernist theory.

What are the important issues in stratification and differentiation?

All societies have ways of organising and classifying people into different categories or groups. **Differentiation** refers to the processes whereby people are categorised as being different to others. **Stratification** is the process whereby the different social groups that emerge from differentiation are organised into a hierarchy. The sociological study of stratification has changed a great deal in recent years and some of the important issues now facing sociologists in this topic area include the following.

- How many classes are there in British society?
- Which element of stratification (class, ethnicity, gender or age) is most important?
- How should sociologists define, operationalise and measure stratification?
- Is stratification natural and inevitable or socially constructed?
- How is stratification related to the structure/action debate?

Why are sociologists interested in stratification and differentiation?

Sociologists want to know about stratification and differentiation because class, ethnicity, gender and age can have considerable effects on many aspects of our lives. These range from the sorts of jobs we get and how long we will live, to our social and political attitudes, to our leisure interests, and even our personal identity.

Sociologists are also interested in stratification because of what it tells us about the structure of society.

- Sociologists agree that stratification and differentiation tell us something about the nature and distribution of power in our society.
- Sociologists agree that stratification and differentiation tell us something about how society is held together (or is integrated).

Of course, sociologists do not agree *exactly* on what stratification and differentiation tell us about either power or integration in society, as you will see in this chapter.

What are the key ideas we can use to think about stratification and differentiation?

Stratification and differentiation are concerned with the divisions between different social groups. Until recently, sociologists have focused on two main types of social division.

- Class: sociologists disagree about how class should be defined but class can be summed up as referring to a group with a shared economic and social position.

- Status: status refers to the social prestige a group of people have. This could be social groups such as community organisations, professions, leisure clubs, or categories of people, such as members of ethnic minority groups, or age groups or those belonging to a particular gender.

Groups of both types can use a range of economic or cultural resources to maintain or improve their position in the social hierarchy, for example wealth, income, power, or symbols, image, and so on.

What does the exam board say about stratification and differentiation?

Not all students will take an exam (in Unit 6) in stratification and differentiation, but all students need to understand the basic concepts and theories in this topic because it is a synoptic topic. It is vital for a full understanding of all the other areas you will have studied. The exam board emphasises the importance of this topic by making social differentiation, power and stratification a core theme. If you have a good understanding of this topic, you will find that it gives you a great advantage in evaluating debates and findings in all the other topics that you have studied.

What are the key problems in stratification and differentiation?

As with all other sociological topics, you will find that the key concepts you learn about are contested concepts. This means that there is dispute about what the concepts mean, how they should be defined and how important they are. There are several key issues which are contested in stratification.

- How do we define and measure class? There are big differences, notably between Marxist- and Weberian-influenced sociologists.
- How many classes are there? Again, a key difference exists between Marxists and Weberians.
- Are some types of stratification more important than others? In the mid-20th century, many sociologists would have said that class differences were the crucial aspect of stratification in society. Now opinions are more divided.

Key points to remember

- Stratification and differentiation is a vital topic in sociology whether you are covering it in the examination or not, because of its focus on power and for what it has to say about the way society is integrated or held together.
- Traditionally, sociologists' interest in stratification has been focused on class, and there have been different views about how it should be defined and measured. These have led to competing sociological views of the class structure in Britain.
- Contemporary sociologists are very interested in other aspects of stratification, especially gender and ethnicity. Many contemporary sociologists recognise the need to examine how class, gender and ethnicity are linked, but there is no clear agreement about how the three are related, or whether any one type of stratification is the most important of the three.

✳ Key Idea

One important concept to remember is the difference between objective and subjective views of class. Objective views of class are the ways that sociologists define a person's class in terms of their employment conditions and income. Subjective class refers to people's own views about social class. The two may vary considerably and are both important. How people think about themselves shapes their behaviour, but so does the reality of their position in the stratification system.

◆ What, when and why?

Postmodernist and feminist thought has led to a shift away from the focus on inequality to an interest in social differences and the way different identities were created. Postmodernists have argued that people are free to create identities and are largely free from social constraints in doing this. This view has been heavily criticised by sociologists, but many sociologists acknowledge the importance of studying all aspects of stratification and the way that they are interrelated.

7.2 How does stratification and differentiation link to the AS course?

● **Synoptic Links**

- Stratification and differentiation have many links with topics you will have studied at AS, such as families and households, education, health or mass media. Make sure that you check through your notes and identify studies which found evidence of systematic social inequalities and differences by class, gender, ethnic group or age.
- If you take the Unit 6 exam, there will be three questions in the topic of stratification and differentiation, offering 8, 12 and 40 marks. One question will require you to link stratification and differentiation to sociological methods, another will require you to link stratification to other topics you have studied, and the third will require you to link stratification to sociological theory.

🔲 **Key Fact**

'There has been a widening gulf between households in which there are two earners and households in which there are none (and the latter group of households has increased owing to both rising unemployment and an increase in early retirement). Indeed, the gap between households in which at least one person has a full-time job, and those without an earner, has widened dramatically. Average incomes have risen in earner households, whereas households without a full-time earner have lower average incomes, in real terms, than in 1979.'

(Crompton 1998, page 220)

Why are links to AS important for sociology?

Stratification and differentiation are the backbone of the discipline of sociology.

- All sociologists will discuss stratification (i.e. class, ethnicity, gender, or another aspect of stratification) at some stage in their work. The views that a sociologist has on stratification and differentiation will shape the way they see society.
- This, in turn, will shape the sorts of questions which sociologists ask about society.

You therefore need to have a good understanding of stratification and differentiation, even if you are not answering a specific exam question on it in Unit 6. Remember, you cannot understand sociology properly unless all the parts are linked together carefully, and the concepts of stratification enable you to link the different topics you have studied together.

Why is stratification and differentiation so important in sociology?

Research shows that factors such as class, ethnicity and gender have a huge impact on people's life chances.

Sociological research on stratification demonstrates that social inequalities are patterned. This means that differences between various social groups in, for example, health, income or educational level, are systematic, and repeated over time with great regularity. However, there are different sociological explanations of these patterns and, indeed, different views about what the patterns look like. Some sociologists see such differences as natural and inevitable, while others feel that differences and inequalities are mainly socially, not naturally, constructed and reflect differences in power between different social groups.

Stratification and differentiation is therefore a vital topic in sociology, because it forms a key part of a sociologist's overall picture of society. The core of any sociological view is its view on power and stratification and social differences. Different schools of sociological thought tend to produce very different views of the nature of society based upon the way they conceptualise stratification and the stratification system. This means that if we want to evaluate a sociological perspective (such as Marxism, functionalism, feminism, the New Right, or postmodernism) really effectively, we need to have a very good understanding of the way that perspective views stratification.

What links can be made to other topics?

There are many links between stratification and differentiation and AS topics such as education and families and households.

- There are (still) large class differences in educational attainment, and class is a key explanatory variable in the work of many researchers, such as Bernstein (1971), Bourdieu (1986), JWB Douglas (1964), and Halsey, Heath and Ridge (1980) and Willis (1977).
- There are many studies on education and gender which demonstrate that students are treated differently on the basis of gender, a process which still leads to inequalities in educational attainment.
- Ethnicity is also a key dimension of differentiation within schools. David Gillborn (2002) argues that schools perpetuate a process of **institutional racism**. Again, these are processes which lead to inequalities of educational attainment.
- In families and households, the importance of gender is evident in studies of conjugal roles, divorce, and domestic violence.

All of these processes help reproduce inequalities and reproduce social divisions and a hierarchy of class, ethnic and gender differences.

Key points to remember

- Stratification and differentiation is taught as a synoptic topic and you will have to make links between it and the substantive topics you have studied, as well as between methods, and between theories.
- Stratification and differentiation is also a core theme so it is relevant and useful even if you are not answering a question on it in Unit 6.
- Inequalities are prevalent in all areas of society, whether we talk about the family, education, health, media or crime. Sociologists argue that an understanding of stratification contributes a vital element to our understanding of how society functions.

✳ Key Idea

Institutional racism: this was discussed in *Heinemann Sociology AS for AQA*, but it is worth reminding yourself of it now. Institutional racism refers to the way that the rules and practices of institutions in society may systematically discriminate against groups on the basis of ethnicity. It may well be unintentional. It is a very subtle form of discrimination which is widely misunderstood. Institutional racism can be important in understanding education, crime, work, and wealth, poverty and welfare.

✓ Top Exam Hint

Use your knowledge of stratification and differentiation, and the way it links to key concepts such as power, to evaluate studies and findings in other topics you study. Do not compartmentalise your knowledge and understanding of key concepts in sociology.

How can we find out about stratification and differentiation?

How have sociologists tried to measure stratification and differentiation?

Until quite recently, the main focus in sociological attempts to measure stratification has been on class. Because class is an abstract concept, it has proved difficult to operationalise and measure. Most researchers have operationalised class by using occupation as an indicator. It has usually been the occupational title of the head of a household that has been used as a **unit of analysis** to give the class position of a whole family or household. Once occupational data has been collected, researchers then place the occupation in a class category using an occupational classification scheme or scale, of which there are several. Occupational scales are supposed to rank different jobs hierarchically, so that the jobs providing the best life chances are the highest, and those with the least are at the bottom of the hierarchy, although there are numerous criticisms of these scales (see section 7.5).

Sociologists have also tried to measure gender and ethnic stratification. These are generally not so difficult to classify, though there have been many disagreements over the terminology used to define ethnic groups.

What methods do sociologists tend to use to study stratification and differentiation?

There are two broad traditions in studies of stratification. Rosemary Crompton has described these approaches as the employment aggregate approach, and the class formation approach (1998).

The first of these is the dominant type, and advocates the use of the large-scale survey. This is because the aims of stratification research, to map and measure the class structure, neatly fall into a positivistic framework. Measuring the class structure and movement and change within it, is only really viable if the research is quantified. Data from occupational classification readily lends itself to quantitative analysis, and quantitative techniques are the best way to display this sort of data. Because of this, the study of the class structure is an area of sociology where rigorous and sophisticated techniques of statistical analysis are used.

However, the alternative approach aims to focus on the way classes form as active social groups and can involve using methods more influenced by qualitative approaches, such as case studies or interviewing. These are necessary in order to shed light on the processes by which classes as active social groups can be studied, since it is qualitative methods which best reflect people's motivations and the meanings which social structures have for them.

What problems with definition are encountered in stratification and differentiation?

The problem of definition is a key issue in the study of stratification and differentiation. As you will remember from your study of theory and methods (see Chapter 4), how sociologists define key concepts can have a big influence on their findings. There are several important problems in defining class.

1. There are differences in how class is defined in different sociological theories.
2. There is the problem of whether sociologists should use an objective or a subjective definition of class. Objective definitions are the definitions devised by sociologists and which should apply to everyone, regardless of their own opinion. Subjective definitions are the way individuals see themselves. These can be very important, since they can affect people's actions, but sociologists would argue that they may not be sociologically accurate.
3. Sociologists disagree as to what should be the unit of analysis of class. Should class be examined on the level of the individual or the family? Whose occupation should be used as an indicator? Some feminist sociologists have argued that in dual-career families, the occupations of both adults need to be included as data, and have devised a new scale.
4. In terms of other aspects of stratification, a key issue has been about the construction of ethnic categories and indeed debate over the use of the terms 'ethnicity' and 'race' (see section 7.14). Terms such as 'Asian' have been criticised because they can put discrete groups with very different life chances, for example Bangladeshis and East African Asians, into the same category, thus distorting our understanding of how these groups are stratified.

Key points to remember

- The main focus of sociological interest has been on class, but this is a difficult concept to define and operationalise.
- Two main approaches to the study of class are the employment aggregate model and the class formation model.
- Sociologists do not agree on which model provides the best picture of the class structure. Class is a contested concept.

☀ Key Ideas

- The employment aggregate model of class analysis studies the class structure by using occupation as an indicator of class position. The idea of the class formation approach to studying class involves examining the way people think about their class position.

- Questionnaires often suffer from an 'imposition problem'. This is because as the sociologist chooses the questions in the first place, they are imposing their own views on the answers people can give. They are limiting some responses, ignoring others by simply not asking questions about certain things, and therefore they are finding the answers they want because they are asking the questions they want to in the first place.

⚭ Methods Link

The employment aggregate model of class analysis involves the use of large-scale surveys. A class formation approach involves using more qualitative methods and case studies. Either approach clearly entails problems, with the quantitative approaches running the risk of the 'imposition problem' and qualitative approaches being susceptible to the Hawthorne effect (see section 4.2).

What is stratification and differentiation?

What does this mean?

Sociologists say that people in society are differentiated. This simply means that society does not classify and identify all people in the same way. For example, society classifies people on the basis of age, and identifies the very young and the very old as being less capable of acting independently. People are also differentiated in other ways that become socially significant, such as in terms of their class, ethnicity or gender. Sociologists claim that the idea that differentiation does occur, is supported by strong evidence of differences in life chances. This leads to the creation of different roles and identities (see sections 7.11–7.21).

Sociologists argue that the process of differentiation does not just affect individuals, but also leads to the creation of different social groups based on these processes. These social groups are stratified, which means that they are organised on a hierarchical basis.

What are the main types of stratification?

Social characteristics such as class, gender, ethnicity, or age, can all be used as factors to differentiate between people, and as a result privilege or discriminate against certain groups. All of these types of social differentiation are forms of stratification, but sociologists have, until recently, argued that they create two main types of stratification system: **status** systems and class systems.

- In status-based systems, social position tends to be **ascribed**, that is, it is achieved on the basis of fixed characteristics which are difficult to change. Status positions which are shared by a group of people become status groups, such as women or members of ethnic minorities, for example.
- In class-based systems of stratification, social position can be seen as being something which is **achieved**, usually through the attainment of educational qualifications or success in a particular job. Class is, therefore, a form of division which is focused on economic factors.

The position of a class or status group in society is maintained by social exclusion. This refers to the ways that class and status groups have of restricting membership to the group. Exclusionary practices control or limit entry to the group and are usually achieved through the management of economic or cultural resources that lead to membership of the group, such as marriage, educational and professional qualifications, or income or wealth (see also section 7.7).

Sociologists disagree as to which of these elements of stratification is most important, but most would agree that we need to try and understand how both class and status systems are interrelated. This matters since status characteristics such as gender or ethnicity may also influence a person's chances of success in the class system. However, see case studies for recent findings on this. Also many contemporary sociologists would now argue that theories of stratification have to include gender and ethnicity, and not focus so narrowly on class.

66 99 Key Definition

Status refers to social prestige or reputation. One can have high or low status, based on one's job, gender, ethnicity, or age. People may have various statuses depending in different social situations, for example, at work or in a friendship group.

✳ Key Ideas

- Sociologists make an important distinction between societies where status is seen to be mainly ascribed, and those where status is achieved. **Ascribed status** refers to a status which you are born with, and **achieved status** refers to status which a person gains through their own efforts, for example through gaining a high status occupation. However, sociologists also note that while status in modern society is often achieved, many status distinctions are still ascribed, for example gender, ethnicity and age.

- Social exclusion is a concept which is increasingly being used by sociologists and others. Some sociologists are critical of this tendency, since it can focus more on cultural differences and neglect the economic aspects of structured social inequality.

Can people change their position in the stratification system?

Sociological research shows that people can change their position in the stratification system. In terms of class, sociologists have identified several types of social mobility, (movement) up or down the class scale.

- Intergenerational social mobility: this measures the changes between different generations, usually by comparing a person's occupational class with that of their father. (Many sociologists measure class using the father's occupation on the grounds that this will be the main/largest income. See section 7.10.) So if your father was a bus driver and you are a Managing Director then you have undergone upward intergenerational mobility.
- Intragenerational social mobility: this measures the changes within an individual's lifetime. So if a person starts working life as an unskilled factory worker but ends up as a barrister they have undergone upward intragenerational mobility.

Sociologists refer to the degree of social mobility in a society by the terms **open** or **closed system**. A system which is completely closed is one where there is no social mobility at all, but this is extremely rare. Usually sociologists would refer to a degree of **closure**, and they would be able to quantify the mobility chances for people in that society. An open system or society is one where there is much social mobility. However, it is important to note that for a society to have a truly open stratification system, there must be both upwards and downwards mobility.

Gender and ethnicity may appear to be categories which we cannot change because they are based on natural differences. However, sociologists would point out that both of these are socially-constructed differences and therefore change over time. While only a few people do actually change their sex, sociologists have noted that gender inequalities may be altered by a person's ethnicity and class, and people can use these factors to create different types of gender identity. In the case of ethnicity, sociologists have observed that increasingly people do create a range of identities, or what Hall calls hybrid identities (1992).

Conclusion

- Social differentiation refers to the way that society classifies and identifies people. People and social groups may be differentiated on many different characteristics, but class, ethnicity, gender and age are some of the most important social differences.
- Social differentiation provides a basis upon which stratification can occur.
- Sociologists argue that there are two main forms of stratification, status systems and class-based systems.

For consideration

1. Is stratification inevitable?
2. Are sociologists guilty of over-generalising when they argue that society differentiates and stratifies on the basis of key social characteristics such as gender, ethnicity, class and age?

Prince William is the second in line to the throne, after his father, Prince Charles. This is a good example of ascribed status (a status fixed at birth), since Prince William has no choice in the matter.

❝❞ Key Definition

Open society: an open society is one where there is a high degree of social mobility, involving movement up and down the class system. **Closure** refers to a lack of social mobility, and in a completely **closed society** there would be no social mobility. In reality, sociologists argue that all societies are characterised by degrees of openness or closure.

How can we measure stratification?

Does the wealth achieved by winning the lottery make the winner upper class?

66 99 Key Definition

Indicators are criteria which sociologists use to identify abstract social phenomena. An indicator will tell us when some object or phenomenon is occurring or about to occur. The most widely-used indicator of class position is occupational title, but this may not always give a completely valid measure or picture of the class structure.

∞ Methods Link

The problems of measuring and operationalising class shows how sociologists' findings are always dependent on their theoretical views and definitions. Marxists and Weberians, for example, define stratification and class in particular ways. Feminists are highly critical of both approaches, arguing that they reflect malestream approaches to stratification and neglect the employment of women.

✓ Top Exam Hint

Remember, classes and occupations are not the same thing. Sociologists use occupation to *indicate* class position only.

What does this mean?

The idea of class inequality means that there are systematic differences and inequalities in the life chances of different social groups. Sociologists have devised a number of different ways of trying to measure these inequalities.

How can we measure stratification?

The main type of stratification which sociologists have tried to measure is class. To achieve this, sociologists have had to pick an **indicator** of class and then measure inequalities in terms of these indicators.

The most commonly-chosen indicator has been occupation. Sociologists have created several occupational class scales (see margin box). Most sociologists using these occupational scales have been influenced by Weber's idea of life chances and market situation, and they have tried to rank the different social classes in order of life chances. All of these scales have therefore ended up with the top social class groups consisting of professional occupations such as lawyers and accountants; intermediate groups consisting of administrative and clerical workers; and lying below these, skilled and unskilled manual workers.

Sociologists using the various occupational class schemes would argue that the scales are valid measures of the class structure because they have revealed systematic differences between each group. For example the registrar-general's scale has consistently revealed health inequalities in terms of infant mortality and mortality rates. However, other sociologists have been critical of occupational scales.

Are there any problems with these ways of measuring stratification?

It has been argued that occupational scales do not produce a valid measurement of social class. To understand these criticisms you need to remind yourself about the concepts of operationalisation and validity.

Since class is an abstract concept, sociologists can only study it by operationalising the concept in terms of an indicator. In the case of the occupational class schemes discussed here, the chosen indicator is occupational title. Occupational titles can then be graded in terms of their market situation and working conditions. This means that sociologists are interested not just in how much a person earns, but in all their rewards, privileges and conditions, for example hours worked, holiday entitlement, and whether they have authority over others in their job.

Those using occupational scales claim that they can produce a valid picture of the class structure. However, critics argue that the picture that emerges may not be valid for the following reasons.

- Not everybody has a job. The unemployed, royalty, the very rich, the retired, and housewives, will all be excluded from occupational scales. So how can their class be measured?
- Occupational scales confuse class with subjective views of status. For example, vicars are in Class 1 in the Registrar-General's scale, but their earnings are the same as those in many manual jobs.
- Marxist's such as John Westergaard (1976, 1995) argue that occupational scales either leave out capitalist owners or put them into the same group as professionals such as managers or accountants. Marxists argue that this completely distorts and misunderstands the nature of the class structure, which is defined as the relationship to the means of production, not as differences in market and work situation.
- Feminist sociologists, such as Arber and Ginn (1991), have argued that basing the class of households on the occupation of the male neglects the growing importance of women's paid employment. They contend that women's incomes can make a significant difference to household income and life chances, and sociologists therefore need to examine joint incomes. They also argue that most occupational scales represent a 'malestream' view of class, and present a sexist bias by using only the occupation of men or 'breadwinners'.
- Occupational class scales do not show us how factors such as gender, ethnicity and age, affect (or 'cross-cut') class differences. For example, having a professional job may benefit your life chances generally, but this advantage will vary depending on your ethnicity, your gender or your age.
- Occupational class scales produce a static picture of the class structure. They do not show how a person's class may change through their life.

Rosemary Crompton argues that research based on occupational scales shows us data about 'employment aggregates', and is useful because it tells us about patterns of inequality. However, we must not confuse occupation with class relationships, nor with status groups, and we need other research methods (such as qualitative data) to find out about the social groups and relationships which they create.

Conclusion

You will have to apply your knowledge of theory and method to evaluate attempts to measure stratification in sufficient detail.

- Theoretical differences in defining class will lead to differences in how class is operationalised and measured.
- Occupational scales lack validity, focus on structure rather than action, and are static.
- Occupational scales only attempt to measure one aspect of stratification.

For consideration

1. What factors apart from occupation could be used as indicators of class?
2. Which provides a better unit of analysis for class, the individual or the household?

Class scales

The Registrar-General's Scale (devised by the government)

I	Higher professional/managerial (e.g. doctors; company directors)
II	Lower professional/managerial (e.g. police; managers)
III N	Supervisory and lower/routine non-manual
IIIM	Skilled manual
IV	Semi-skilled manual
V	Unskilled manual

The National Statistics Socio-Economic Classification (a new scale which the government devised to replace the RG Scale and used in the 2001 census)

1. Higher managerial and professional
2. Lower managerial and professional
3. Intermediate
4. Small employers and self-employed workers
5. Lower supervisory, craft and related
6. Semi routine
7. Routine
8. Long-term unemployed or never worked

Goldthorpe's Class Scheme (although revised during the 1980s, this scheme identifies the three key classes.

Service class
1. Higher professionals, higher administrators, managers of large industrial concerns, large proprietors
2. Lower professionals, higher-grade technicians, lower-grade administrators, managers in small businesses and supervisors of non-manual employees

Intermediate class
3. Routine non-manual, e.g. clerical and sales personnel
4. Small proprietors and self-employed artisans
5. Lower-grade technicians and supervisors of manual workers

Working class
6. Skilled manual workers
7. Semi-skilled and unskilled manual workers

The Surrey Occupational Class Scale (developed by Sara Arber, Angela Dale and Nigel Gilbert of the University of Surrey. This aims to avoid the sexist biases of other scales. It classifies women on the basis of their occupations and takes account of the gendering of occupations, as is clear by the splitting of class 6 into two categories.)

1. Higher professional/administrators/ managers and large proprietors
2. Employers and managers
3. Lower professional
4. Secretarial and clerical
5. Foremen and self-employed
6a. Sales and personal services
6b. Skilled manual
7. Semi-skilled
8. Unskilled

7.6 | What is the functionalist view of stratification?

What does this mean?

All sociological perspectives provide views about stratification and differentiation which reflect their general assumptions about the nature of society. Functionalists assume that modern society requires a complex division of labour, but argue that this social system has to be characterised by harmony and value-consensus. They therefore provide a theory of stratification and differentiation which acknowledges differences and inequalities, but which also claims that these are legitimate (fair) and beneficial to society.

How do functionalists define stratification and differentiation?

Functionalists think of stratification in terms of a continuous hierarchy of occupational ranking. They are aware that the many different occupations in a complex modern society can be ranked in terms of both their prestige and their different privileges and rewards. Functionalists see these different ranks as being like strata, or layers of rock in the Earth, arranged in a hierarchy. The layers are all different, but they are closely packed together and all are needed to be in place if the Earth's crust is to be stable.

There are problems with defining stratification in this way.

- Firstly, it means that functionalists tend to neglect differentiation on the basis of ethnicity and gender. While functionalists such as Parsons (1964), for example, discuss sex role socialisation, they also tend to see gender differences as inevitable and natural. Individual functionalist researchers might be aware of racial discrimination, but functionalist theory can offer no systematic explanation of it, since functionalists believe that stratification in modern societies is usually considered to be legitimate. Weberian views of stratification, in contrast, would be able to recognise that ethnicity is a form of status grouping which can be used as either a means of privileging or discriminating against other groups.
- Secondly, Marxist-influenced sociologists would argue that functionalism ignores the real economic relationships which class is based on and is simply descriptive rather than analytical or relational (see section 7.7).

What are the key features of stratification and differentiation in modern society?

For functionalist sociologists such as Durkheim and Parsons, stratification and differentiation in modern societies is important because it marks a decisive break with earlier types of society. In pre-industrial society, people's position in the stratification system was generally ascribed or fixed at birth. In modern societies though, social position is something which individuals achieve through their own efforts. For Parsons and other functionalists, this means that modern society is a meritocracy, where what you achieve reflects your own efforts, and does not depend on who your parents were or on other characteristics such as your ethnicity or gender. Parsons argues that the process of structural differentiation, by which modern societies become increasingly complex and organised, creates many opportunities for us. It means that our roles and identities are increasingly differentiated (different) and this frees us from the narrow constraints that were common in traditional society.

What is the purpose of stratification and differentiation in modern society?

Functionalists argue that stratification and differentiation is a functional prerequisite. A prerequisite is something which is essential, or 'pre-required', in order for something else to happen. Functionalists argue that stratification is essential for various reasons.

- Firstly, stratification enables society to maintain a set of common values. The rewards given to only some members of society help to reinforce social values and create an incentive for others to aspire to the same goals and values.
- Secondly, stratification in modern society becomes a key mechanism for what functionalists call **role allocation**. Role allocation refers to the part that people play in society, particularly the work they do.

Davis and Moore argue that stratification is essential for efficient role allocation (1967). They say that all jobs can be ranked in terms of their functional importance. The most important jobs have to be more highly rewarded than the lesser jobs. They claim that if this did not happen then there would be no incentive for people to compete or go to any effort to gain the top jobs. Stratification, or structured inequality, is therefore functionally necessary to motivate and reward people to aspire to the most important jobs. This is why top surgeons earn more than factory workers. Davis and Moore argue that this leads to a meritocratic system, which is essential if stratification is to be seen as legitimate. If it is believed that people are recruited to the top positions or roles in society through fair and free competition, inequality will be accepted by the rest of the population.

Conclusion

Use the following points to help you evaluate the functionalist approach to stratification.

- Critics of functionalism argue that there is no consensus on which jobs are functionally the most important in our society.
- There is much evidence (see section 7.11) that ascribed characteristics rather than merit are still important in determining occupational roles.
- Functionalist accounts of stratification and differentiation focus mainly on occupational ranking. Other forms of stratification (gender, ethnicity) appear to be neglected.

For consideration

1. How could the functionalist approach to stratification explain why top sports stars and musicians are so highly paid?

2. Functionalists argue that structured inequalities are beneficial to society. Could they have any less positive effects?

✳ Key Idea

Meritocracy is the idea that people's position in society is achieved on the basis of merit. This means that someone has achieved a certain position through hard work, effort and ability, rather than by inheriting a position or paying to be appointed. In 18th century Britain, for example, people who could afford it were able to buy themselves a position as an MP, or a job in the civil service, the army or the navy.

66 99 Key Definition

Functionalists use the term **role allocation** to refer to the way that jobs are distributed in modern industrial society. Functionalists say that the most efficient way for jobs to be distributed in modern society is by having a meritocratic education system, as this makes the best use of the talents and abilities that exist in any population. In this respect, and in terms of the belief in meritocracy, the views of the New Right are very similar to functionalism. The New Right believe that inequalities are both inevitable, due to varying skills and abilities, and necessary for a competitive economy.

☐ Key Fact

- The Office of National Statistics (ONS) figures from 1997/8 showed that professionals had a participation rate of 80 per cent in higher education, compared with 19 per cent for those from a skilled manual background. The participation rate for all social classes was 34 per cent. Participation rates measure the proportion of people from different social classes currently enrolled on full-time higher education courses

- *'Of the top 200 schools in Britain in 1996 (in terms of A level performance), all but 22 were in the private sector. The private sector accounts for only 7 per cent of the school population, but for over half of the entrants to Oxford and Cambridge universities.'*

(Rosemary Crompton 1998, page 221)

What is the Marxist view of stratification?

What does this mean?

While different social groups in capitalist society do indeed come to depend on each other, as functionalists such as Durkheim argued, for Marx the relationship between different social groups was not an equal one and was characterised by structured inequalities. This led Marx to present a radically different view of stratification in modern society.

How do Marxists define stratification and differentiation?

Marxists define stratification and differentiation in terms of class differences. Two main classes are identified.

- The bourgeoisie: these are the owners of the **means of production**. The means of production is anything that is used to make wealth, such as land, a factory and the equipment in it, or an office. Because the bourgeoisie are the owners, Marxists say that they do not need to work in order to earn a living; rather other people work for them.
- The proletariat: members of this group do not own the means of production and therefore have to work for the bourgeoisie to earn a living.

Marxists, therefore, define classes as groups of people with a shared economic position. People are either owners or workers, and Marxists say that an individual's class position is determined by their **relationship to the means of production** – whether they are owners of means of production or are workers. Marx was aware of other classes, such as the petty bourgeoisie, who are owners of small businesses, but saw these groups as being less important than the two main classes.

What are the consequences of class inequality in capitalist society?

Marxists see stratification as playing a key role in leading to social change, and argue that class conflict creates social change through the process of **polarisation**.

- This will occur because of the economic dynamic (or nature) of capitalism. Competition between the bourgeoisie to make the most profit would drive down wages, but some owners would fail, and would therefore join the ranks of the working class.
- Over a period of time, the numbers in the bourgeoisie will decline, but those who remain will become richer, since they will be more able to pay wages at the rate they prefer as there is less competition from other employers.
- At the same time, the working class will increase in size. This will create an increasing supply of labour, and will therefore drive wages down.
- Polarisation therefore means that the two main social classes become further and further apart, economically, as the bourgeoisie get richer, and the working class get poorer. Marx said that the working classes would become pauperised (this is sometimes called emiseration).

Marxists such as Braverman argue that office workers have been 'deskilled' and are really proletarians

66 99 Key Definitions

- The **means of production** refers to the machinery and equipment that is used at work. This usually means factories and factory equipment, but it can also include buildings, offices and land. Some people own these resources (capitalists, the employers) and they can employ other people (workers, the proletariat) to work for them.

- The **relationships of production** refers to the relationships that people are thrown into because of these economic arrangements. For example, workers live under the authority of capitalists, and this is characterised as being a relationship of conflicting interests.

- **Polarisation** is the process by which the two main social classes become economically further and further apart.

What does Marxism tell us about stratification in contemporary capitalist society?

Some sociologists argue that Marxist theory on class is not relevant to our understanding of contemporary society, because the process of polarisation has not occurred. Instead, societies in countries such as Britain have actually seen the growth of a large 'middle class' of white-collar workers and professionals. Some of the responses Marxists can give to these criticisms are:

- Marx's work on class provides a useful alternative to functionalism. Marx argued that the form of stratification in capitalist society did not lead to meritocracy at all, but to class domination. Sociologists influenced by Marx therefore point to the mass of empirical evidence showing systematic (regular and patterned) inequalities between different classes. Marx's theory is still useful because his account of class shows us how our social position and life chances are crucially linked to our access to economic resources. This access also means that some groups have more power than others.
- Marx's theory suggests that functionalists are wrong to argue that our identity and social position are created on the basis of what we achieve in life. Marxist analysis indicates that these too vary according to our position in the system of economic relationships. Marxism also points out how the reduction of all social relationships to economic relationships is part and parcel of capitalism, and claims that this alienates and dehumanises people.
- Harry Braverman (1974) argued that many clerical jobs in the USA were being deskilled in the late 20th century. This meant clerical jobs were being made simpler and American employers were therefore able to employ workers on lower wages. Braverman showed that wage levels for routine clerical workers declined over the 20th century. This process is called 'proletarianisation'. Braverman's study provides evidence to support the Marxist idea that classes would polarise in capitalist society.

Conclusion

Use the following points to evaluate the Marxist approach to stratification.

- Marxists define class predominantly in terms of relationship to the means of production. However, there are other sources of status and many forms of benefit which can set workers apart, such as income levels, qualifications required to do a job, hours worked, conditions of work, and perks such as working flexi-time.
- Marxists tend to consider people's feelings about their class identity as being irrelevant. However, people's feelings about their class position can affect their actions. For example, a working-class person may think of him/herself as better off than others, and this could influence his/her voting behaviour. This is relevant to evaluating the proletarianisation theory.
- Marxist theories such as proletarianisation give a static view of the class structure. This means that Marxists regard it as static, not as a process. Not all people in routine clerical jobs will spend their whole life in such jobs. They may undergo upward intragenerational mobility.

For consideration

1. Has class polarisation occurred?
2. Have routine clerical workers been proletarianised, or are they members of an intermediate class group between the bourgeoisie and the working class?

⁝ Key Idea

Proletarianisation refers to the process whereby those groups of workers existing between the two main classes of the bourgeoisie and the proletariat, are pushed down into the same position as the proletariat. Their wages and conditions of work are continually eroded.

◆ What, when and why?

In the 20th century, many Marxist-influenced sociologists agreed with this view. However, the increased focus of sociologists on other forms of stratification in the 1960s and 1970s led many Marxist sociologists to argue that ethnicity and gender were indeed important forms of stratification, but that they were ultimately the result of class inequalities.

● Synoptic Link

The 'reserve army of labour' is a Marxist concept which can be usefully applied to aspects of stratification as well as other topics. Marxists argue that ethnic minority and gender inequalities can be explained in terms of the way these groups form reserves of potential employees. Their existence (even if unemployed) helps to keep wage levels low. It also controls the proletariat by leading them to focus their attention on protecting their jobs from the competition posed by these 'rival' groups.

What is the Weberian view of stratification and differentiation?

☞ Who is this person?

Max Weber (1860–1924) was one of the chief founders of modern sociology, along with Emile Durkheim and Karl Marx. Weber had a wide range of academic interests, and held academic posts in law, economics, and political economy before ending his career as Professor of Sociology at the University of Munich in 1918. One important contribution he made was the 'verstehen approach', which is the idea that sociology has to be aimed at understanding the motives and views of individual actors.

✳ Key Idea

Weber defines the difference between class and status in the following terms.

'With some over-simplification, one might thus say that "classes" are stratified according to their relations of production and acquisition of goods; whereas "status groups" that are stratified according to the principles of their consumption of goods are represented by special "styles of life".'

(Max Weber in Gerth and Mills 1948)

In other words, two groups of people may have similar incomes (for example, junior police officers and university lecturers) but lead very different lifestyles, mix with different groups of people, and have a different status in society.

What does this mean?

Max Weber was a German sociologist famous for arguing that sociology had to focus on the experiences and motivations of individuals. This made him critical of approaches such as Marxism, which put too much emphasis (in his opinion) on structural factors.

How did Weber define stratification and differentiation?

Weber (1948) recognised the importance of the difference between owners and workers (bourgeoisie and proletariat) but argued that differences within the working class were also significant. Weber defined class in terms of a person's situation in market terms. Clearly, different types of workers can gain very different levels of pay and working conditions, and Weber thought these were more important than Marx did. Defining class in this way allowed Weber to identify important differences in the class structure and he identified four main classes: the propertied upper class (owners), the property-less white-collar workers (managerial, administrative and clerical workers), the petty bourgeoisie (self-employed workers and small business owners), and manual workers.

Classes, therefore, are simply groups which share a similar market situation and **life chances**. They may not necessarily have shared values.

However, Weber, in contrast with Marx, argued that three types of stratification were important in modern capitalist societies: class, status and party. He was keen to point out that stratification in modern society could occur on the basis of non-economic factors.

Weber defined status as an 'effective claim to social esteem' (1948), which can refer either to positive or to negative levels of social respect. Status may be related to ethnicity, gender, caste group, religion, attendance at a particular school or university, the values or lifestyle of a group, or membership of a particular occupational group, for example, medicine or law. Status groups are competitive, and aim to achieve 'social closure', which means that they try to exclude other groups from their position of privilege. Weber also observed that status could cut across class differences or even divide a class group.

The final aspect of stratification identified by Weber – party – can be defined as a group that forms in order to gain power, and in so doing reflects and promotes the interests of any social group. Organisations such as trade unions or professional societies, or groups such as Greenpeace or Outrage! are all examples of party. They reflect the idea that status groups, as well as economically-based class groups, can form a basis for political action.

What does the Weberian approach tell us about stratification in modern capitalist societies?

There are several reasons why Weber's theories of stratification are still relevant.

- Weber's theory of stratification shows that stratification can be achieved in terms of social as well as economic divisions.
- Weber's focus on intermediate groups in the class structure indicates the importance of differences in market situation and a variety of forms of payment or reward. It therefore focuses on position rather than the relationship between different classes.
- Weber's analysis reminds us that we should understand that the boundaries between class groups will inevitably be 'fuzzy' because they involve the attempt to distinguish different positions in the labour market on the basis of levels of income.
- People may define themselves in terms of any aspect of stratification or none at all, so we should not be surprised if people do not think of themselves as members of a certain class.
- Class and stratification still have a vital influence on people's life chances, but in an affluent society we can use Weber's ideas about status groups to remind ourselves that people may create their identities more around consumption patterns than class groups.
- Class differences in the 20th century developed in a different way to that suggested by Marx. Some sociologists influenced by Weber argued that rather than polarisation occurring, more and more people were becoming middle class and moving to the centre of the spectrum rather than opposite ends. This process is called 'embourgeoisement'.
- Sociologist David Lockwood (1958) has synthesised elements of Weber's analysis with Marxism and has defined class in terms of 'market situation', 'work situation' and 'status situation'. This analysis has been used by Lockwood, and other neo-Weberian sociologists, to analyse class structure in contemporary Britain.

Conclusion

Weber's theory of stratification and differentiation shows us that theories of class are also always theories about power.

- Weber's theory suggests that there are other sources of power besides economic power.
- Weber's theory therefore provides some useful insights into the nature of gender and ethnic differences in modern societies.
- However, critics might argue that Weber's theory does not provide any way to distinguish between the relative importance of the different types of stratification.

For consideration

1. How would a sociologist influenced by Weberian theory describe and explain the social position of sports and pop stars?

2. How can class be 'cross cut 'by status?

66 99 Key Definition

Life chances are the opportunities, advantages and disadvantages that a person will have in life depending upon their social position. Weber does not ignore the idea of natural differences between people, but he maintains that our chances in life will vary, regardless of individual talents, according to our social position. A good example of the way life chances influence the course of our life is given by mortality statistics which show that life expectancy in Britain varies systematically according to class.

✳ Key Idea

The idea of 'embourgeoisement' claimed that middle-class values and standards of living were being adopted by more and more people in the middle of the 20th century. This was not an idea developed by Weber, but rather by sociologists influenced by functionalism, although it does reflect Weber's focus on the importance of the intermediate classes. Neo-Weberian sociologist, John Goldthorpe, tested the theory in a famous study, 'The Affluent Worker' and found little evidence for the view that the working classes and middle classes were becoming identical.

What is the neo-Marxist view of stratification?

Neo-Marxist Erik Wright is Professor of Sociology at the University of Wisconsin-Madison.

☞ Who is this person?

Erik O Wright (born 1947) is one of the few contemporary sociologists who claims to actively work on class analysis in the Marxist tradition. He studied at the Universities of Harvard and Oxford, before studying for a PhD at the University of California, Berkeley.

✳ Key Idea

Wright uses the term 'contradictory class locations' to refer to the large number of workers in intermediate positions between the bourgeoisie and the proletariat. These workers do not own the means of production, but they are in a position of authority over other workers. This means that they help to exploit workers, while at the same time they are themselves exploited by capitalists.

What does this mean?

Neo-Marxism is the name given to more recent versions of Marxist theory which have attempted to improve the basic theory in the light of social changes in the 20th century. In particular, neo-Marxist sociologist Erik Wright has tried to develop new ways of understanding groups in the middle of the stratification system.

How do neo-Marxists define class?

Erik Wright (1997) argues that class is the most important type of stratification in modern capitalist societies. However, he maintains that this has to be defined in Marxist terms. For Wright this means that class is about the social relationships created in the capitalist process of production. He argues that capitalist production leads to exploitative relations between different groups in the production process (in the work place) based on the type of control that different groups have over production. Wright identifies three types of resources to control: investment, the means of production and labour power. There are, though, four levels of control: full, partial, minimal and no control. The capitalist class have full control over all of these dimensions while the working class have control over none of them. This means that other groups are in an intermediate position, having one or two types of control.

What do neo-Marxists say about the class structure in modern society?

Wright's analysis claims that class in capitalist society is more complex than Marxist theory originally acknowledged. He agrees that there are important intermediate groups in the class structure, but argues that these groups can be understood as occupying contradictory class locations. By this Wright means that those in intermediate positions exploit others, while at the same time they are themselves exploited by the capitalist class. For Wright this is an important point to make, because it is this which helps to preserve the Marxist orientation of his approach.

Marxists claim that classes are formed as a result of the relationship to the means of production, with the key difference being that between owners and workers. Marxists also maintain that owners exploit workers, because most of the value produced by the workers is retained by capitalist owners. Wright aims to develop a theoretical view of class in contemporary society which maintains this element of Marxist theory, but also allows it to be applied to those classes existing between the owners and the workers.

Wright considers that managers and white-collar workers are in contradictory class positions. His views about control lead him to point out some of the differences between workers and explain why they exist in contradictory class locations. Wright argues that managers, for example, make decisions about investments and 'hiring and firing', but they are also employees themselves and do not have complete control over the means of production (factories, offices, machinery). More-junior white-collar workers will exercise authority over 'labour power' by, for example, supervising manual workers.

What criticisms can be made of this view of stratification?

Wright's theory can help to explain the complexity of contemporary class structure, showing how non-owners are divided, and why the class structure has not developed as Marxists thought it would. However, it also raises a number of important theoretical issues.

- Wright's unit of analysis is the individual and he focuses on using what Rosemary Crompton calls **employment aggregates** to operationalise class (1998).
- Crompton means that Wright is simply assuming that the groups of people occupying similar employment situations do have some shared, collective identity, and do act as a social group. This needs to be demonstrated using empirical evidence, since people do not always adopt a class identity.
- This means that Wright's analysis is overly structural, and does not account for the fact that some people may see their identity in very different ways to those in which Wright characterises them.
- Crompton argues that Goldthorpe's neo-Weberian analysis also shares the same problem.
- It can be argued that Wright's scheme ends up measuring an occupational hierarchy (not relations as he claims), and is therefore closer to Weber than to Marx.

Conclusion

Wright's theory raises key questions about the way class is defined and operationalised.

- An 'employment aggregates' analysis of class neglects people's own views about their social identity (structure/action debate).
- This definition produces a static picture of class at one point in time and does not show us how people's class situation may change over their lifetime.
- Employment aggregates only show part of the picture of stratification. Sociologists need to use different types of research (qualitative as well as quantitative) and link structure and action.

For consideration

1. What unit of analysis other than the individual could Wright use?
2. Do people's subjective views of their class matter? If so, why?

✳ Key Idea

Marxists argue that workers are always exploited by capitalists. Marxists use the idea of surplus value to explain this view. Surplus value refers to the value which workers help to produce through their work. Marxists claim that it only takes a small proportion of a worker's labour to pay his/her wages. The rest of this value, the surplus value, is kept by the capitalist as profit. Marxists who agree with this 'theory of surplus value' therefore argue that workers do not receive a fair share of the rewards from their work.

66 99 Key Definition

The idea of **employment aggregates** simply refers to a way of defining class by grouping together jobs which have similar levels of reward. This may not match up very well to the way people in society define class groups, nor, as some sociologists believe, does it explain the 'lived relationships of class' in society.

✓ Top Exam Hint

Wright's theory is intended to be a relational theory of class. This means that it attempts to explain stratification in terms of relationships between different social groups (formed on the basis of relations in the production process), not simply to rank groups in terms of the amount of income or status they possess. Critics such as Mike Savage (1992) claim this is what Wright does, making his theory more like Weber than Marx.

What is the New Right's view of stratification?

Prime Minister John Major stated that Britain in the 1990s was a 'classless society'.

☞ Who is this person?

Peter Saunders is a Professor (Emeritus) of Sociology at the University of Sussex. He began his academic career in the field of urban studies, and his interests in housing policy in the 1980s led him into issues of stratification and differentiation.

66 99 Key Definition

The term **consumption cleavages** refers to gaps or differences in spending patterns. It implies that the differences between groups are not very significant and may even be the result of simply having made different choices.

What does this mean?

New Right thinkers argue that stratification and differentiation are not only inevitable, but also beneficial to the efficient functioning and growth of a capitalist economy. New Right sociologists have not formed the sort of rigorous definitions of stratification produced by Marxists or Weberians, but they make important claims about stratification in modern society. The 'New Right' is a political ideology rather than a sociological theory, but it is important because it has been so influential in British society. Prime Minister John Major clearly expressed one key belief of the New Right, when in 1990 he said that we live in a 'classless society'.

What do New Right sociologists say about stratification in modern society?

Sociologists influenced by the New Right have presented a number of claims about the nature of stratification in modern society.

- Saunders (1990) argues that the key source of differentiation in contemporary society is in consumption patterns not relations of production or differences of market situation. By consumption patterns, Saunders means the difference between those who rely on state services for housing, health and education, and those who purchase these services privately. It is these **consumption cleavages** which are increasingly the most important form of stratification in contemporary society.
- Saunders (1996) claims that while there is an economic elite, its power is limited. Most managers and directors are company employees not owners, and have worked hard to gain their positions. Differences in society are the result of equal opportunity, so those in higher classes deserve greater rewards. New Right sociologists therefore agree with the functionalist idea of meritocracy. Saunders argues that there is considerable mobility in Britain. He argues that ability and motivation are the key factors determining class position (see section 7.11).
- New Right sociologists contend that a combination of these economic trends and a decline in cultural and moral values standards leads to the creation of an **underclass**; a large group of people at the very bottom of the stratification system, below the working class (see also section 7.19).
- Charles Murray argues that the underclass develop a distinctive set of cultural values. The most important of these he argues, is a fatalistic outlook on life which he terms 'welfare dependency' (1989). This means that members of the underclass come to depend on the welfare state to support them and believe that they are powerless and incapable of solving their own problems.

How can we evaluate the New Right view of stratification and differentiation?

A number of criticisms have been made of these views.

- Saunders' view, that consumption cleavages are better indicators of differentiation, neglects gender and ethnic inequalities and evidence on life chances, and it does not explain why there are consumption differences in the first place. Arguably, it is indeed market situation and relationships of production which determine a person's ability to consume (spend) in the first place.
- The term underclass includes people who survive on benefits for very different reasons.
- Lydia Morris argues that there is a long tradition of those at the bottom of the stratification system being stigmatised as worthless and representative of a dangerous social problem (1994). It can therefore be argued that the idea of an underclass is more of a cultural bias on the part of some sociologists than an empirical reality or useful analytical concept. Morris's argument illustrates how the links between identity and stratification are socially constructed to the advantage of the powerful.

Conclusion

You can evaluate New Right approaches to stratification and differentiation by using your theoretical and methodological knowledge. Use the following points.

- New Right ideas are important as theories of society in their own right, but they have also been very important politically. They developed at a time when some politicians wanted to stress the importance of individual responsibility, and when there was strong support for the belief that free market principles were the best way of organising society.
- New Right theories seem to make the assumption that while power is not spread equally, it is not as unequal as Marxists, for example, would argue. Like functionalists, New Right thinkers believe in the existence of meritocracy.
- These views of power are reflected in the ideas about structure and action evident in New Right thinking about stratification. New Right theories see society consisting of individuals (not groups) who are free to make choices. This is in sharp contrast to most structural approaches in sociology.

For consideration

1. Are the powerful advantaged by the ability to portray those in the underclass as a dangerous social problem?

2. What evidence could be given to reject the view that social position is mainly determined by ability and effort?

⋇ Key Idea

- The term **underclass** is an important idea in contemporary sociology. While this term is not only employed by New Right sociologists, its use is often heavily criticised. Two reasons for this can be seen in this section. Firstly, the idea of an underclass is vague and encompasses a wide range of different types of people, who are impoverished for very different reasons. Secondly, the term often involves thinly-hidden value-judgements. This is reflected in Murray's characterisation of the underclass as 'fatalistic' on the basis of very weak empirical evidence.

- The New Right argued that society was best organised on the basis of free market principles, or 'the free market'. These are concepts from economics. Market principles are simply the rules which permit buying and selling with few restrictions or controls imposed by the state. From a more Marxist position, the disadvantage of this is that it means that workers have no safeguard of minimum conditions (or wages), and it assumes that capitalists will always give workers a fair deal.

Does social mobility exist?

Pupils at Harrow. Do state school pupils have an equal chance of making it to the top?

66 99 Key Definition

Social mobility refers to movement within the class structure. Mobility may be upwards or downwards.

✳ Key Idea

It is important that sociologists consider movement both up and down the class scale in order to measure the extent of mobility in a society. There may be a lot of upward movement for groups lower down, for example, but if this is not matched by downward mobility for those in higher groups, it means that more room has been created at the top, but it also means that those in the higher groups still had a better chance to maintain their position of relative privilege.

What does this mean?

Social mobility is the term sociologists use to refer to the process whereby people change their class position. There has always been debate about how much social mobility there is in British society and this section will examine the different viewpoints on this issue.

Why is social mobility important?

Studying social mobility enables sociologists to measure one aspect of stratification, class, by quantifying the amount of movement up and down the class structure. Estimating the degree of social mobility therefore enables sociologists to comment upon the degree of openness or closure exhibited by the class structure. It is important to have this information in order to be able to judge whether a society is meritocratic or not.

Social mobility is also important because when mobility is restricted, it means that a class boundary becomes a firmer social barrier. When mobility rates are less restricted the opposite occurs. This means that social mobility has a key role in constructing the boundaries between different social classes. It is also important because people's subjective perceptions of social mobility influence the extent to which class membership becomes seen as an important part of their identity.

How is social mobility measured?

There are two main forms of social mobility, relative and absolute mobility.

- Relative social mobility means measuring the relative chances of those from different social classes of moving to a higher-class group. 'Relative chances' means the chances of one class compared with those of another class.
- Absolute social mobility refers to the amount of movement in a class structure. This means the total number of people who have moved up or down the class scale.

Sociologists also distinguish between intergenerational social mobility and intragenerational mobility. Intergenerational mobility is social mobility between different generations, for example, whether a son or daughter has moved up or down compared with their parents. Intragenerational mobility measures the degree of upward or downward movement an individual experiences within their own lifetime.

How much social mobility is there in Britain?

There have been several large-scale studies of social mobility in Britain and numerous analyses of secondary data. The main findings of these studies can be summarised as follows.

- The 1972 Oxford Mobility study conducted by a team led by John Goldthorpe (1980), found high rates of absolute mobility, but importantly, it also found big differences in relative mobility rates between different social classes.
- The Oxford study identified three classes – service, intermediate and working class – and found that the relative chances of a person reaching the service class depended upon the class of their father. Of those with fathers in the service class, 55 per cent gained service class positions themselves, while for those from an intermediate class origin the figure was 25 per cent, and for those with a working class father the figure was 14 per cent. This meant that a boy from the service class had about three and a half times more chance of ending up in the service class than a boy from a working-class background.
- More recent research by Gordon Marshall (1988) also found big differences, and calculated that those from a service class origin were around seven times more successful in gaining a service class position than someone from the working class.
- These results have been criticised by Peter Saunders. Using data from the National Child Development Study (NCDS) (1996) he argues that absolute mobility is a more important measure, and that there has been a considerable increase in this; 52 per cent of those in a sample of around 11,000 had experienced some upward intragenerational mobility. On the basis of the NCDS data, including tests of ability, Saunders concludes that British society is a meritocracy and that effort and ability, not class of origin, are the key determinants of success.
- In response to Saunders, it may be agreed that effort and ability are important, but so too is the class of origin in determining class destination. Marshall and Swift found that 43 per cent of men from the service class as opposed to 15 per cent of men from the working class, all qualified up to A Level, reached service class destinations (1993, 1997).

Conclusion

Sociologists need to remember that society and social change are linked in a two-way relationship, and they need to be aware of both.

- The occupational structure has changed, and there are fewer manual jobs.
- Absolute mobility has increased, but this is because of the changes in the occupational structure.
- Crompton (1998) argues that people are probably more aware of changes in absolute mobility, hence the common belief in meritocracy.

● Synoptic Link
You might draw links here between stratification, class and education. Basil Bernstein (1990) for example, argues that middle-class children use the same language as that of teachers and so perform better than working-class children's use of restricted codes. Boudon (1974) argues that middle-class children tend to perform better and aim higher because their social structure (family, friends) encourages this.

↷ Classic Study
The 1972 Oxford Mobility Study was conducted by a team of sociologists led by John Goldthorpe at Oxford University. The study used a sample of 10,000 men between the ages of 20 and 64. The class background of these men was analysed and compared with the class background of each man's father.

☐ Key Fact
The proportion of service sector jobs in the UK increased by 36 per cent between 1978 and 2000. Between 1978 and 2000, manufacturing sector jobs decreased by 39 per cent (Bilton 2002, page 304). This is important because it suggests that one reason why mobility has increased is simply because the occupational structure has changed. It is therefore not necessarily best seen as an increase in the openness of the class structure.

For consideration

1. What other types or aspects of stratification should sociologists consider in discussing meritocracy and social mobility?

2. What is reflexivity and how is it demonstrated in the conclusion above?

What has happened to class: are we all middle class now?

What does this mean?

In the 1960s some sociologists argued that the differences between the middle classes and the working classes were disappearing. One of the key reasons why this claim was put forward was that some sociologists thought that poverty and inequalities in wealth were being eradicated as incomes and the average standards of living rose. It was suggested that the population was becoming increasingly middle class in its attitudes, and in terms of its income and wealth. This process was called 'embourgeoisement'. This claim is still important as some sociologists argue that increasing affluence means that class differences are disappearing or becoming less important.

What evidence would be needed to support this theory?

Most contemporary sociologists have used definitions of class which are based on Weber's ideas (see section 7.8). They would therefore argue that to test the embourgeoisement thesis (or theory) we need to look at several key areas.

- Economic relationships and factors: these would include not just how much people earn, but how hard they have to work to get their reward, as well as any perks or benefits, and the amount of authority they have at work. The embourgeoisement thesis also suggested that the working class would share middle-class attitudes to work. It was assumed that the middle classes were more involved in their work and gained more satisfaction from it, whereas the working class had a more instrumental attitude to work (they aimed to make as much money as possible from it and were less concerned about 'satisfaction').
- Norms, values and social relationships: the idea of embourgeoisement assumed that the working class would increasingly have friends from outside their own class as both middle and working classes started to share similar incomes and lifestyles. There would be more social mixing. The research also aimed to find out whether different social classes have distinctive sets of norms and values.
- Image of society: the embourgeoisement thesis suggested that both working and middle classes would have a similar outlook on society. Unlike the 'us and them' (conflicting) views of the past, a fairer and more affluent society would lead to a more harmonious view of society on the part of both the working and the middle class.
- Political attitudes: the embourgeoisement thesis suggested that the political attitudes of the working class would become similar to those of the middle class.

⊂⊙ **Classic Study**

The Affluent Worker

This study was based on questionnaire and interview research conducted with a sample of 229 manual workers and 54 white-collar workers. The workers were drawn from three large factories in Luton: The Skefco Ball Bearing Company, Laporte Chemicals, and the Vauxhall Car Plant. The findings of the research were published in the book, *The Affluent Worker in the Class Structure*, by Goldthorpe et al (1969).

What evidence has sociological research identified?

In the 1960s a team of sociologists led by John Goldthorpe and David Lockwood decided to test the theory by conducting a large-scale research project (see Classic Study). The researchers picked Luton as a good place to do the research, reasoning that its growing working class population and full employment in skilled manufacturing work would make it a place where, if any embourgeoisement was occurring, they would find evidence of it. In fact, though, the research team found very little evidence to support the thesis.

Economically, workers still had very instrumental attitudes towards their work. In terms of their social relationships, very few members of the sample mixed with people from other social classes. In terms of 'image of society', the affluent workers viewed society in terms of what the researchers termed a 'pecuniary model', in other words, in terms of money; 56 per cent of the workers saw society in this way. They felt the only difference between those higher in the class scale and others was that they had more money than other people; they did not take the view that such people were superiors in any way. The middle class, in contrast, was acutely aware of positions in a hierarchy, and sometimes put more emphasis on this than on the level of financial reward people received. Politically, the affluent workers mainly expressed a different set of interests and values from the middle class, with the majority voting for the Labour Party (the traditional party of the working class). The researchers noted, though, that support for Labour owed less to a sense of 'class loyalty' and more to a perception of self-interest – they thought they would personally benefit more from Labour policies.

In fact, the research found that there were only two limited ways in which the working class and the middle class were becoming similar.

- Both classes had a home-centred and 'privatised' (individual, private) lifestyle.
- Both classes were becoming increasingly instrumental in their attitudes to work, as white-collar workers were joining trade unions to help improve their pay and working conditions.

Conclusion

The Affluent Worker study is a classic study in sociology and it tells us at least three things about stratification and differentiation in contemporary society.

- How researchers define and measure class will have a big impact on their view of the class structure.
- The so-called 'affluent workers' may have been much better off than their parents' generation, but this did not make them middle class.
- In the late 1960s, Britain was not becoming an increasingly middle-class society. This suggests that levels of income and wealth may improve over time, but important differences and inequalities can remain.

For consideration

1. How important are economic factors in defining class?

2. The Affluent Worker study focuses in detail on people's attitudes about class. Is class just a matter of attitude?

✳ Key Idea

The idea that there is an inevitable link between position in the class structure and certain types of behaviour, values, or action (including political action), has to be treated very carefully. As Crompton has argued, this is an area where sociological theories are in need of development. Sociologists need to be cautious, as Goldthorpe and Lockwood were, and most recognise that class action is always a potential, not an inevitable, outcome of class membership. This reflects the structure/action debate which runs throughout the study of stratification and differentiation.

∞ Methods Link

How concepts are operationalised is very important in sociology. The embourgeoisement thesis provides a good example of why sociologists need to think carefully about how class should be defined. Advocates of the embourgeoisement theory were suggesting that the most important aspect of class was income or wealth, but as we have seen, many sociologists argue that class is more complex than this, and Goldthorpe and Lockwood define class here in terms of market and work situation (see sections 7.1, 7.6, 7.7 and 7.13).

☐ Key Facts

- Over the course of the 20th century, the proportion of the UK population working in manual occupations has declined.

- Routh (1980) estimates that in 1911, 79 per cent of the workforce consisted of manual workers. By 1975, however, manual workers composed only 55 per cent and, by 1994, 46 per cent of the work force.

- Sociologists argue that this means that the class structure is inevitably affected by changes in the occupational structure.

What has happened to class: are we all working class now?

- **The bourgeoisie**: a French term used by Marx to refer to the owners or the capitalists.

- **The proletariat**: at term used by Marx to refer to the working class.

- **White-collar workers** is a term which refers to non-manual office workers. The sort of routine clerical (office) work performed by white-collar workers is judged to be of a lower level of skill than professional work, but higher than that of manual work. It is important because it represents a boundary between the working and middle classes, although generally considered to belong to the lower end of the middle class hierarchy.

☀ Key Idea

Deskilling is an idea devised by Marxist Harry Braverman (1974). He argued that manual working-class jobs were being deskilled, that is, they were continually being simplified by the introduction of modern technology. This would have the effect of lowering wages and, Braverman claimed, of 'proletarianising' the bulk of the work force in capitalist societies. This has not happened because while technology simplifies some jobs, it also creates new ones, of varying levels of skill.

What does this mean?

A theory that the population in the UK was becoming more working class (although it was also considered to be occurring in other societies, such as the USA) was developed in response to the embourgeoisement thesis in the early 1970s (see section 7.12). This alternative theory was called 'proletarianisation', and its supporters claimed that rather than the population becoming increasingly wealthy, in fact, the inequalities between workers and the **bourgeoisie** were widening.

As we have already seen in section 7.7, this theory of stratification is associated with Marxist sociologists such as Braverman. This theory focuses on the position of **white-collar** or clerical workers, and argues that they are being 'pushed' down into the working class. The theory suggests that this process will go on, leading to the sort of class polarisation envisaged by Marx (see section 7.7).

What evidence would be needed to support this theory?

The theory of proletarianisation suggests that the pay and skill levels associated with occupations in the middle of the class structure are gradually being eroded. If a process of proletarianisation is occurring, then it should be possible for researchers to observe the following features.

- A decline in the pay differentials between manual workers and white-collar workers and professionals.
- A decline in the benefits and perks available to white-collar and professional workers.
- A decline in the amount of skill required to do white-collar jobs, making them easier to do and requiring less training.

What evidence have researchers identified?

One important study arguing against proletarianisation is David Lockwood's study, *The Blackcoated Worker* (1958). Lockwood argued that while the differences in pay between manual workers and white-collar workers did indeed decline in the early 20th century, there were still important differences between them. These included differences in promotion prospects, job security, and other benefits such as holidays and time off, and differing health risks in their workplaces. This is now a very dated study, but it is very important because it maintained that class is composed of two key elements; market situation and work situation (see Key Idea), and this is something which many sociologists still believe has to be taken into consideration.

More recent studies, such as those of Stewart et al (1980) and Marshall et al (1988) echo Lockwood's findings. Stewart's study makes the point that many of those working in white-collar jobs later move up the class hierarchy, and so in some ways the issue of whether white-collar jobs are being proletarianised is irrelevant, since they still form an important gateway for those hoping to progress to higher and better-paid professional positions.

Marshall's research in the 1980s claims that clerical workers are not deskilled. However, Marshall's research used the approach of asking clerical workers themselves whether they thought that their work needed more or less skill than it had when they began working. It is of course possible that the respondents are wrong, or are making a judgement on the basis of a short range of experience. Marshall, however, does note that the 1980s saw the beginning of a big change with the development of relatively low-skilled jobs in the service sector, such as shop assistants and call centre operators. Marshall argues that in terms of pay and conditions, these jobs cannot be seen as being similar to the bulk of middle-class occupations. This does not support the idea of proletarianisation as it applies only to a small section of service workers, but it does indicate that class is changing (see section 7.14).

Conclusion

These studies provide useful material with which to evaluate the proletarianisation thesis. The following points can be made in conclusion.

- These studies are now slightly dated. However, more recent evidence suggests that important differences between white-collar jobs (including other middle-class professions) and working-class occupations persist and are significant.
- There was a decline in the pay of white-collar workers in comparison with the wages of skilled manual workers in the 20th century. Even today, wage differentials between white-collar workers (and many lower professionals such as social workers, teachers and nurses) and skilled manual workers are narrow; indeed, some skilled workers can earn more than these occupations.
- Nevertheless, Lockwood's classic study illustrates that determining class position involves examining more than just pay. Status is also important. On this basis, the case for proletarianisation is unconvincing.

☀ Key Idea

The distinction between market and work situation as elements of class is a vital one in sociology. Lockwood is drawing on Weberian theory and suggesting that sociologists can identify classes by using these two indicators. Market situation refers to the ability of an individual to gain high rewards for their work. It does not just refer to wages, though, and can include a range of perks and benefits. Work situation refers to the amount of authority a person has in their occupation, or their ability to avoid being closely supervised by others. Lockwood says that class is the sum of both of these things.

⬜ Key Fact

In the late 1980s, Marshall et al (1988) pointed out that the routine non-manual category consisted of 39 per cent of women workers and only 6 per cent of male workers. This suggests that this type of work is heavily gendered.

For consideration

1. Is computer technology deskilling white-collar jobs?

2. Having read this section, which theory of class do you find more useful – Marx or Weber?

What is the class structure like today?

What does this mean?

In sections 7.12 and 7.13 we have looked at two of the most important theories on class structure to be developed in the late 20th century. It has been found that there is insufficient evidence to support either theory. This section suggests that in fact what has happened in the late 20th century is that the class structure has fragmented.

What is the class structure like today?

In the 1970s and 1980s, studies of social mobility by sociologists such as John Goldthorpe and others (1980) suggested that in reality what had happened to the class structure was best described by using a visual image; class structure had developed into a diamond shape. This meant that it had a large, extended middle, and two shorter and narrower ends. The upper and working classes had shrunk and the middle classes had expanded. This does not mean that the embourgeoisement thesis was correct though, because the differences between those in the middle class and other classes were still significant. However, it did mean that class differences were becoming more blurred, as class was cross-cut by status divisions.

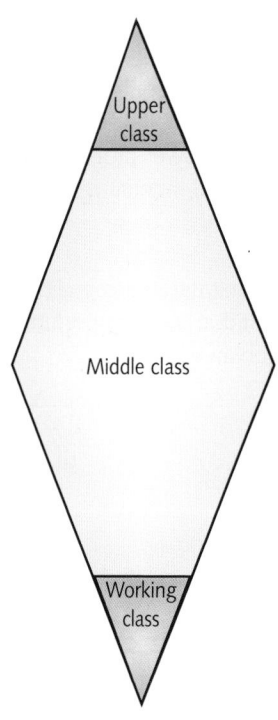

Goldthorpe has argued that the cross structure is best represented as a diamond shape.

More recently, other sociologists have added to and qualified this picture of the changing class structure. Some, influenced by postmodernism, have suggested that class is no longer important as a determinant of life chances (see sections 7.21 and 7.22). Others have argued that class remains an important structure in contemporary society. For example, Rosemary Crompton (1998) argues that class remains an important structural force shaping life chances, but that it has changed over the second half of the 20th century, with class divisions becoming much more blurred than they used to be. Crompton suggests that to fully understand what has happened to the class structure, we have to look at class both as an objective structure as well as looking at how people view class subjectively. Crompton says that both of these two senses of class are linked.

Sociologists argue that the decline of manufacturing industry in the UK has led to a big change in the class structure.

✷ Key Ideas

- Weberian-influenced theories of class tend to see the boundaries between different classes as being blurred, due to the 'cross-cutting' effects of status divisions. This means that status differences such as gender or ethnic divisions can sub-divide or fragment classes. This would probably mean that not all members of a class group (for example, middle class professionals) would be seen as having a common social position because they would be differentiated by their gender or ethnicity. Theorists more influenced by Marxism will still see the boundaries as being sharp, because they tend not to recognise status divisions as being of crucial importance.

- The idea that both objective and subjective views of class have to be examined is a key strategy. Marxist theories have tended to focus on the objective elements of class, leading to a highly structural view which some have criticised as being rigid and neglecting actors' own views about class. Those influenced by Weberian theory (such as Goldthorpe, Marshall) have, in contrast, tried to combine objective and subjective elements of class in order to produce a picture of class which reflects both structure and action.

What has happened to the class structure?

In terms of objective class, Crompton argues that the UK class structure has undergone a number of important changes since the late 1970s. In the workplace, manual jobs have declined and technological changes have created new types of work and new jobs. This has led to an increasingly large 'middle' section of the population, although it has many sub-divisions within it in terms of income and lifestyle. At the same time, the old-fashioned manual working class of the early and mid-20th century, employing men in heavy industries such as steel manufacturing, coal mining and shipbuilding, has died out. This process can be described by the term **class fragmentation**.

This aspect of change draws mainly on the objective sense of class, referring to changes in the way that people work and what they do to earn a living. However, Crompton argues that changes in objective class have had a big impact on people's subjective views about class. Whereas in the early and mid-20th century it was more common to find people describing themselves as members of a class, now class fragmentation has led to another process, **individualisation**.

However, these changes do not mean that class has disappeared. Objective class, or 'employment aggregates' still remain, but they do not necessarily create social groups which give people an identity. Crompton's strategy of considering both the subjective and objective aspects of class structure enables us to understand that the objective structures of class can change and, by doing so, can effect changes in the way people see their class position.

Conclusion

Crompton's summary of changes in the class structure sheds considerable light on the way the class structure has changed, and allows us to draw several key points in conclusion.

* Both embourgeoisement and proletarianisation theories were wrong and in recent years the class structure has fragmented.
* This has been caused by changes in the occupational structure and changes in technology.
* In order to fully understand these changes, we have to be aware of both subjective and objective aspects of class and the way that these different views of class are interrelated.

For consideration

1. Who can best describe your class position – you or a sociologist?
2. Which theory of class do you think is best able to explain the changes described here?

---

66 99 Key Definition

* **Class fragmentation**: the process by which traditional working-class communities of the early and middle 20th century, exemplified by mining villages or working class areas in big cities, have largely disappeared, as these social groups and identities have been fragmented by social change.

* **Individualisation** is the process by which people now see themselves as individuals rather than as members of a class. A sense of class is therefore now less likely to exist and less likely to have an influence on a person's identity.

◆ What, when and why?

Crompton argues that class structure and stratification changed in the late 20th century as a result of several factors. Occupational change has occurred, with the development of a large service sector creating many jobs requiring little training. Technological change has meant the decline of many manual jobs and the creation of new jobs and professions. Changes in gender relations, with more women working, have led to important differences between households. Political decisions and policies on issues such as taxation and welfare benefits also had an important influence on shaping inequalities.

☐ Key Facts

* Since 1977, the proportion of the UK population with less than half the average income has trebled (Rowntree, 1995). This demonstrates that class differences are widening.

* The effect of class origin on class destination does seem to have weakened over the last twenty years according to Marshall et al.

'the odds [chances] *of a man reaching the middle classes from a Class 1 or Class 2 background* [Nuffield/Goldthorpe categories] *have been approximately halved, relative to those for a man from an unskilled background'*.

Marshall (1997)

How does ethnicity shape our life chances?

66 99 Key Definition

Harriet Bradley defines ethnicity in the following terms.

'Ethnicity refers to belonging to a particular collectivity or community, sharing a culture, possibly with a distinct language.'

(Bradley 1996, page 17)

☐ Key Facts

- In 1950, ethnic minorities accounted for 1 per cent of the UK population, while the figure in 2002 was 7.6 per cent.

- Only 1 per cent of senior managers employed by the top 100 UK companies are from an ethnic minority.

- 67 per cent of Pakistanis and Bangladeshis in the UK live in poverty.

Sources: The Commission for Racial Equality (1998) and *Sociology Update 2003*

What does this mean?

You may have noticed that the theories of stratification considered earlier in this chapter generally seem to have little to say about stratification and differences in life chances which are based on ethnicity or race. This neglect has been the source of many debates in sociology. In this section we will look at the nature of ethnic inequalities and consider how they are best explained.

What is the evidence about ethnic differences and inequality?

There is a wide range of evidence about the relationship between ethnicity and inequality in contemporary UK society. Sociological researchers have identified a number of key inequalities which vary according to ethnic origin.

- Scott and Fulcher (1999) note that two-thirds of Pakistani and Bangladeshi families are in the bottom fifth of income distribution in Britain.
- Ethnic minorities are disproportionately likely to be unemployed, although recorded unemployment levels vary amongst different ethnic minority groups. In 2000, the government Labour Force Survey found unemployment levels of 5 per cent for whites, 8 per cent for Asian Indians and 17 per cent for Pakistanis and Bangladeshis.
- The Commission for Racial Equality (1998) reported that a 1998 survey in Greater London found that ethnic minorities were three times more likely to be homeless than whites.
- A recent Department for Education and Skills study (2003) showed that in 2002–3, black Caribbean pupils were three times more likely to be permanently excluded from school than white pupils, and that black, Bangladeshi and Pakistani pupils consistently performed less well than white pupils at all levels. However, Chinese and Indian pupils were shown to outperform all groups.

How do sociologists explain these inequalities and differences?

Modernist sociological theories have offered a number of ways of trying to explain these inequalities.

- Marxists argue that inequalities between different ethnic groups are best understood as being primarily caused by relations of production. In other words, Marxists have acknowledged that these inequalities exist, but they argue that they are not really caused by the cultural and ethnic differences themselves, but simply by the fact that ethnic minority groups occupy the less skilled positions in the working class. This sort of approach was reflected in work by sociologists such as Robert Miles (1989) and Castles and Kosack (1973).

- Functionalists have argued that ethnic inequalities have been the result of low skill levels amongst migrant ethnic minority labourers. Functionalists have taken the optimistic view that such inequalities are therefore not the result of discrimination and in time would decline as ethnic minorities worked their way up the career ladder.
- Weberian-influenced sociologists, such as Rex and Moore (1967) and Rex and Tomlinson (1979), argued that ethnic minorities formed a secondary labour market (they have the worst jobs, less pay, worse conditions, least security), due to the lower levels of their skills, but also due to the influence of their lower cultural status. Weberian theory therefore acknowledges that cultural discrimination exists and that stratification is not purely economic; the existence of status groups, such as those based on ethnicity, show that stratification can also occur on the basis of cultural factors.
- Some sociologists have also argued that there is a black 'underclass', which is even more exploited and deprived as a result of both economic and cultural (status) discrimination. This concept will be discussed in section 7.19.

Critics have argued that Marxist explanations do not treat ethnicity as an important factor in its own right (because they are mainly interested in economic differences) and that Marxist theory has been 'race blind'. Functionalism has been considered unduly optimistic in the light of continued and, in some cases, worsening inequalities on the basis of ethnicity, and in so doing appears to neglect the reality of racial discrimination. Weberian-based explanations seem more promising due to their acknowledgement that status differences on the basis of culture can complicate class differences.

Conclusion

As a result of these criticisms of modernist theory, some sociologists (including those influenced by postmodernism) have argued that ethnicity is indeed an important aspect of stratification and differentiation in its own right, and not just a side effect of economic inequality.

- Tariq Modood (1988, 1990) has argued that stratification and differentiation involves economic and cultural elements. In particular, he emphasises the need to examine how inequalities between ethnic groups are shaped by class, colour and creed (religion).
- This means that sociologists need to acknowledge that there are important differences between ethnic minority groups – they are not all the same. Certainly in general they suffer discrimination, but this can vary according to other factors such as class position.
- Sociologists have therefore more recently been concerned to examine the way in which ethnicity is cross-cut by other aspects of stratification, such as gender, class, and even age (see section 7.17).

● **Synoptic Link**

Remember to use ethnicity to see the links between different topics. Inequalities between ethnic groups are also clearly demonstrated in the study of crime and deviance, and in figures on differences in educational attainment.

✓ **Top Exam Hint**

If you get questions on stratification and ethnicity in the exam, use the material here but also remember to apply material from sections 7.5–7.9, 7.17 and 7.19, in order to create a full and detailed evaluation.

For consideration

1. Are ethnic identities changing in contemporary Britain?

2. What is racism?

Why are gender differences and inequalities in life chances important in stratification?

What does this mean?

Just as is the case with ethnicity, most of the sociological theories considered earlier in this chapter neglected to consider the role of gender in stratification. For a long time in sociology, gender differences and inequalities were not questioned or studied very seriously. Since the 1970s, some sociologists have argued that gender inequalities are less important than class inequalities. In this section we will examine the extent and causes of gendered inequalities and differences in life chances based on gender.

Crompton suggests that while women have increasingly entered paid employment in the late 20th century, the increase has not been equally distributed and has generally amplified already existing patterns of gender segregation. For example, the biggest increases between 1981–1991 were in public service jobs, financial management, and sales and marketing (20 per cent, 11.4 per cent and 16.5 per cent respectively).

What evidence is there about gender differences and inequalities?

Despite years of political campaigning by feminists, and often to the surprise of many women today, considerable gender inequalities persist in British society.

- Women are more likely to be in part-time or low-paid employment than men. According to the Equal Opportunities Commission (2003), 43 per cent of women and 9 per cent of men work in part-time employment, and 79 per cent of those employed in administrative or secretarial jobs are women.
- Research by Crompton and Jones (1984) indicated that clerical work is a mainly female occupation. In Crompton and Jones' study 70 per cent of workers were female, and the researchers found that these subjects were less likely to gain promotion than men.
- Despite recent improvements in women's employment opportunities, researchers have noted the existence of a **glass ceiling** restricting females from being promoted to the highest levels in business (Crompton 1998).
- More women head single parent families than men. This means that single parent families tend to have lower incomes than families with two adults.
- Women are more at risk of falling into poverty than men (Arber and Ginn 1991 and 1995).

☐ Key Facts

'Skilled minority ethnic women are twice as likely to be unemployed as white women.'

(Bradley 1996, page 108)

'Research in the late 1980s showed that 39 per cent of women, but only 6 per cent of men, were in Goldthorpe's class III (routine non-manual).'

(Crompton 1998, page 95)

66 99 Key Definition

- The term **glass ceiling** refers to the idea that there is an invisible barrier in institutions and firms, beyond which women cannot pass.
- **Equal Pay Act, 1970**: this act gave all individuals the right to the same pay and benefits as a person of the opposite sex working in the same job.
- **Sex Discrimination Act, 1975**: this act made it unlawful for any individual to be discriminated against in the workplace because of their gender (i.e. promotion, selection for a job, sexual harassment).

How do sociologists explain these inequalities and differences?

Modernist sociological theories have tended to explain gender inequalities and differences in terms of other factors, such as class, or else have argued that they are not as important as other forms of stratification.

- Marxist theories, for example, tended not to question women's role in society too closely until the development of Marxist-feminism in the 1970s. Marxist-feminists, however, argued that gender stratification was actually caused by capitalism, and believed that gender inequalities were functional for capitalism. Gender inequalities help capitalism by providing a female reserve army of labour and by maintaining and reproducing labour power (caring for men, bringing up children).
- Functionalist theories of stratification also tended to see gender inequalities as either an inevitable outcome of role allocation, or else took a more progressive stance believing that gender inequalities would gradually decline as social change created new norms and values regarding women's role in society. In the 1970s, legislation such as the **Equal Pay Act** and the **Sex Discrimination Act** helped give this explanation some credibility.
- Weber's concept of status, and his distinction between class, status and party, suggests that cultural differences (including gender) can be recognised as a distinct basis for stratification. In the 1980s, Weberian sociologist John Goldthorpe (1984) argued that gender was a distinct aspect of stratification. However, Goldthorpe used this point to argue against feminist claims that his methods for defining and measuring class were sexist. Goldthorpe suggested that the class of a household was best indicated by the occupation of the head of household, who should be the main wage earner. Feminists saw this method as sexist, since it meant that the earnings which women brought into families, and the class position which their occupations gave them, were being neglected. In response, Goldthorpe reasoned that a woman could be the head of household, but the key point was that class inequalities were more important than gender inequalities.

Conclusion

Contemporary sociologists are, in general, more likely to be critical of all of these previous positions, and would want to recognise that gender and class inequalities are linked and can interact with each other.

- Feminists are right to see gender as an important element of stratification.
- The concept of patriarchy helps to explain why gender divisions and processes of gendering arise.
- However, it is also increasingly recognised that women's experience of gender interacts with other elements of stratification, such as class, ethnicity and age (see sections 7.17 and 7.20).

How far have we come since the equal rights legislations of the 1970s?

∞ Methods Link

The debates about gender and stratification are a good example of how sociologists' theoretical assumptions shape their findings. Goldthorpe and others following his approach refused to operationalise class in terms of gender. Feminists have been keen to challenge this and have developed alternative ways of measuring stratification.

● Synoptic Link

Stratification and differentiation on the basis of gender also relates to other topics. Crime and education are both aspects of social life which are heavily gendered. Crime is a predominantly male activity, and women's crime is generally restricted to particular types of non-violent crime. The education system can be seen to be gendered, and helps to push women into certain subjects, which reinforces later work roles and choices.

For consideration

1. Is the family (a key area for gender relations) becoming more democratic?

2. How are women's experiences of gender inequalities influenced by class, ethnicity and age?

What are the links between class, gender and ethnic inequalities?

◆ What, when and why?

Modernist sociology developed in the 19th century. Modernist sociologists were optimistic that sociology could help bring about social change and improvement, and would identify the truth about the social structures governing our lives. Postmodernism developed from around the 1970s and 1980s when social progress seemed much harder to believe in given the troubled history of the 20th century. This led to a general scepticism about the possibility of progress and universal truth, and at the same time, changes in the division of labour and in the class structure made belief in the relatively simple categories of modernist theories less credible.

What does this mean?

In recent years sociologists have become interested in examining how the different aspects of stratification are related and in discovering whether any particular type of stratification is most important. Modernist sociologists (for example Marxists, Weberians, and functionalists) have argued that class is the most important type of stratification, and that other types, such as ethnic or gender divisions, are less important. Sociologists influenced by postmodernism, though, have argued that all the different aspects of stratification are linked together in complex ways. This section examines these viewpoints.

How do sociologists explain the links between class, gender and ethnicity?

Modernists

Traditional or modernist sociological theories have tended to argue that the most important aspect of stratification is class. For these views, the central divisions in modern society are class divisions. These are seen to have a determining influence on an individual's life chances. This has meant that some theories could relegate the importance of gender and ethnic inequalities. Indeed, some sociologists taking this approach argued that other inequalities were the result of class inequalities, as, for example, Marxist sociologists Castles and Kosack claimed in their study of the position of ethnic minority migrant workers (1973).

Feminists

More recent sociological perspectives have seen these claims as over-generalising. In the 1980s, some feminists criticised the idea that women's life chances could be predicted simply from the class position of their husband, pointing out that women's own employment could make a significant difference. Third wave feminists argued that women's experiences also varied according to their ethnicity. In the 1990s, Sylvia Walby argued that there were in fact three systems stratifying women's experience; class, gender and race (1990). Walby argues that all three of these elements of stratification are important, but that they form an overlapping network of structures which shape life chances.

Postmodernists

Sociologists influenced by postmodernist ideas have also been highly critical of modernist sociological theories of stratification. Postmodernist-influenced approaches vary, but there are several key points they all make.

- Postmodernists have been highly critical of general, overarching theories and claims, for example the claim that class is the key determinant of life chances.
- Postmodernists have argued that it is more important to examine diversity and the differences within the groups identified by sociologists, such as differences within classes, ethnic groups and gender groups. This helps us to understanding the complexity and plurality of contemporary life.
- This has led sociologists to look at the complex ways in which class, ethnicity, gender and age are linked. This can mean that more complex patterns are identified, for example, gender is less of a disadvantage to white, middle-class women than it is to working-class women, or can be yet another basis of discrimination for women from ethnic minority groups.
- Postmodernists have argued that society should be looked at in terms of the categories and ideas which people themselves use to explain things. This means examining how people themselves define gender, ethnicity or class, and how they perceive it affecting them.

Which is more important, inequality or difference?

The differences between modernist and postmodernist approaches to stratification are considerable. Two very different views of and approaches to stratification are being offered.

1. Modernist theories suggest that stratification is the result of social structures, and that these powerful forces shape our lives. These structures are largely, though not exclusively, the result of economic power resulting from a position in the division of labour. Modernist theories argue that inequality is the key feature of modern societies, and the most important concept to grasp in order to understand them.
2. Postmodernist theories claim that what is most important in stratification are cultural differences. Postmodernists argue that these are socially constructed and vary tremendously in different cultures. Therefore, they have to be studied on a more individual basis. Postmodernists place much less emphasis on structural economic differences; indeed, in the most extreme examples, they neglect them. Contemporary societies can be best understood by examining the way culture leads to the construction of social differences and life chances.

Conclusion

Sociologist Harriet Bradley offers some useful points to consider in evaluating these differing views.

- There is no way to determine whether it is inequality or difference which is the most important form of stratification.
- Both cultural and economic aspects of inequality are important.
- Bradley suggests that sociologists need to look at class, ethnicity and gender as interacting dynamics.

For consideration

1. Can individuals choose their own identity?
2. Does social change mean that we can now ignore older theories of stratification, such as those of Marx and Weber?

66 99 Key Definition

Third wave feminism developed around the 1980s when black feminists argued that previous generations of feminism had neglected to consider other dimensions of inequality, such as race. Third wave feminism has therefore contributed to the focus on diversity and difference, and to the idea that different forms of stratification are linked together in more complex ways.

✳ Key Idea

Power is important in terms of both cultural and economic approaches to stratification. In both cases, the ability of individuals or groups to gather and use cultural and/or economic resources to differentiate themselves from others is vital. Arguably, postmodernist approaches to stratification and differentiation neglect power, while modernist approaches have sometimes exaggerated the constraining influence of power differences.

✓ Top Exam Hint

Use postmodernist approaches to evaluate older debates about stratification such as those on embourgeoisement and proletarianisation. Postmodernist theories suggest that the class structure is best seen as fragmented, something which the modernist theories neglect in their over-emphasis on stability and structures. However, you must not forget the criticisms of postmodernism, and here Bradley's synthesis may be a very useful way to conclude.

How does age affect our life chances?

Is 'old age' a natural condition or is it a social construction?

📋 Key Fact

In 1901, boys had a life expectancy of 45 years and girls, 49 years. In 2000, the corresponding figures are 75 years and 80 years respectively.

Of those aged 65 in 2000, professional men can expect to live another 17.5 years, and women another 20.8 years. There is still a sharp class difference though: men from the unskilled working class can only expect to live another 13.4 years, and women another 16.3 years (on average).

Source: Denscombe M, *Sociology Update* 2003

What does this mean?

Age might seem to be a purely natural category, and therefore something which sociologists have little to say about. However, sociologists have pointed out that while ageing is a natural process, how age is regarded, how it affects life chances and the way it is used as a basis for differentiating between people, is a social process. Sociologists have therefore been interested to investigate age-based inequalities and to find out how differentiation and stratification on the basis of age occurs.

What inequalities and differences arise from age?

There is a range of research findings showing that age is a significant aspect of stratification and differentiation.

- In 1999/2000, government statistics indicated that about 19 per cent of those in poverty were pensioners. Government statistics also revealed that around 1.3 million pensioners received only the basic state pension (DSS 2001).
- Recent figures indicate that around five million children in the UK live in poverty. Two million of these children live in households where no adult has a job, and the other three million live in households where the income is less than half of the national average (Howarth C et al 1999).
- Inequalities are also evident in the field of employment. In 1971, 31 per cent of men aged 65–69 were in employment. In 1981 the figure was 16 per cent, and in 1991 it was only 6 per cent (Bradley 1996).

How do sociologists explain age stratification?

There are several main ways in which age stratification can be explained.

- Functionalist explanations: in the mid-20th century, a basic theory of age stratification was constructed by sociologists such as Parsons and Eisenstadt. They both argued that age groups were culturally defined and had a key role in shaping identity, roles and social expectations of individuals on the basis of age. Both also saw social differentiation on the basis of age as serving important functions in society. For example, both Parsons (1954) and Eisenstadt (1956) saw the role of the youth stage in American society as helping to ease the change to adulthood. Eisenstadt saw age groups as helping individuals to learn new roles. Within this view, though, some age groups can become dysfunctional, as is the case with the role of the elderly, which Parsons recognises as becoming problematic as members of this group in modern societies become 'functionless'.
- The explanation from political economy: another main explanation of age stratification takes some of its ideas from Marxism. The political economy

approach to age stratification argues that social divisions based on age are caused by capitalism. It is argued that capitalism creates **structural dependency**, whereby the young and the old are forced out of the labour market and depend upon others to support them. This happens because the most powerful social groups wish to restrict access to jobs and rewards. This view criticises the functionalist approach for making the assumption that age differences are experienced in the same way by all members of an age group. Functionalist accounts, therefore, ignore the fact that a person's experience of age varies according to their class.

- Postmodernist explanations: postmodernist theories suggest that we are now living in a new period of time where the older and familiar social structures and rules are being eroded. Thus Featherstone and Hepworth (1991), for example, argue that age boundaries in contemporary postmodern culture are becoming blurred. It is now possible for older people to escape the limitations previously imposed upon them in traditional society. Featherstone and Hepworth refer to this as a process of **de-differentiation**, whereby the differences which used to be perceived between age groups are eroded and blurred. While this approach is helpful in highlighting the fact that age groups are social constructions and vary over time, it is arguably less convincing in its claim that age differentiation is becoming blurred. Evidence such as that provided by Bradley and the idea of structural dependency, can be seen as indicating that prejudice and negative stereotypes persist, and old age is arguably still predominantly a stigmatised identity.

Conclusion

In examining the role of age in stratification and differentiation, sociologists need to bear these points in mind.

- Age is a natural phenomenon but it is also a socially-constructed category. To understand this we need to question our assumptions about age.
- There are strong relationships between age and poverty. Sociologists need to examine how age is linked to other elements of stratification.
- Age is frequently used as a basis for stigmatising certain identities, and this can apply to the young (and very young) as well as the old.

⁎ Key Idea

Some sociologists have argued that age differences become key structures shaping our lives. Social institutions, such as retirement and the minimum school leaving age, force people into structural dependency (Townsend 1979). Therefore, as these findings indicate, age is an important dimension of social inequality. Socially-constructed age group categories create social differences. These in turn lead individuals belonging to different age groups to have varied access to wealth, power and status.

❝❞ Key Definitions

- **Structural dependency**: dependency is a state of depending on others to look after you. By structural dependency, Townsend simply means that this state is built into the rules of society. This is because we have laws which state when a person can begin to work and when they must retire. These rules therefore force individuals, whatever their own wishes, to be dependent on other people at certain times in their life. This dependency, though, will vary depending upon the class, gender and ethnicity of the individual.

- **De-differentiation**: this is the opposite of differentiation. In other words, social differences become blurred. This term is associated with postmodernists, and some 'reflexive modernisers' such as Lash and Urry (1994).

For consideration

1. Is British society child-centred? How is childhood socially constructed in contemporary society?

2. How does the experience of old age vary in British society?

Changes in the class structure: is there an underclass today?

Charles Murray

☞ Who is this person?

Charles Murray is an American academic. He is usually associated with a New Right perspective. He became well-known in the 1980s in Britain and the USA following the publication of his controversial pamphlet on the underclass. He has worked as an advisor to various think tanks and to the US Government.

What does this mean?

In recent years some sociologists have argued that a new class is developing at the bottom of the stratification system. This class has been called the **underclass**. The underclass is defined in different ways by different sociologists, but it is often seen as consisting of the long-term unemployed, those living continuously on welfare benefits, the homeless, and broadly, the 'poorest of the poor'.

Who invented the theory of an underclass?

The idea of an underclass in recent sociological work was developed and used by several sociologists in the 1980s. One of the most important of these sociologists was Charles Murray. Murray published an article in the *Sunday Times* in 1988, arguing that there was an urban underclass in the USA and that a similar group was developing in the UK. Murray claimed that this group had several key distinguishing features.

- It included a variety of types of people: the unemployed, young single parents, drug addicts, and those involved in petty crime. The group also tended to include many young black males.
- All of these types belonged to what Murray termed 'a dependency culture'. This meant that they were unwilling to accept personal responsibility for their own well-being, and were dependent upon state benefits to survive.
- Murray argued that the underclass had been created by the welfare state. He claimed that by the time of the late 1980s, governments in the USA and the UK were providing a welfare system that was too generous, and this meant that for many of those at the bottom of the stratification system, there was no incentive to work.

An alternative view of the underclass was devised by another American sociologist, William Julius Wilson (1987). In his book *The Truly Disadvantaged* he argued that there was indeed a group of extremely poor people who formed a distinct class at the bottom of the stratification system. However, he disagreed that these people had a distinctive dependency culture, or did not want to work. Their position was the result of a lack of power in the face of economic and social structures of disadvantage.

How can we evaluate this concept?

These views have met a great deal of criticism from other sociologists. Many criticisms point us back to the definitions of class (see sections 7.1 and 7.4) and argue that using the category of underclass involves putting people into a common class for very many different reasons. The underclass has thus come to include single parents, the unemployed, the sick, the elderly, the disabled, criminals, drug addicts, the homeless and others. All of these different categories of people may be in impoverished circumstances for different reasons. Equally, it is possible to be a criminal or a drug addict, and to be fairly well off financially. Critics therefore conclude that the underclass is not bound together by a shared market and work situation, one of the key means contemporary sociologists use to define a class.

In her book, *The Dangerous Classes* (1994), Lydia Morris argues that the idea of the undeserving poor is a very old one. Morris reasons that the identification of such a group, and its labelling as a scapegoat for society's ills, is a form of social exclusion which reflects the fears and concerns of the dominant classes in capitalist society. Morris argues that the increased popularity of the concept came about at exactly the time (the late 1980s) that globalisation led to important changes in the UK labour market, in particular a decline in manual work and the growth of a large service sector. These changes have helped to fragment the class structure. In doing this, inequalities in wealth have become increasingly polarised. Morris argues that the concept of an 'underclass' is useful, as long as it is seen as a cultural category rather than an economic category. Morris suggests that the concept is more helpful for showing how dominant and mainstream groups use cultural values as a basis for excluding and stigmatising those who are considered to depart from the norm.

Conclusion

Sociologist Rosemary Crompton (1998) suggests that it is best to resolve this debate by referring back to, and using, basic concepts.

- Those arguing for the existence of an underclass are, in fact, referring to differences in status, not class.
- However, economic class differences are often the basis on which status differences are created.
- Contemporary sociologists therefore need to focus more on the ways that class and status divisions are linked and interact together.

For consideration

1. Do any value judgements enter the underclass debate?
2. Can new classes be created?

How do stratification, differentiation and inequality affect our identity?

⊂⊙ Classic Study

- 'The Emerging British Underclass'(1989): Charles Murray's pamphlet on the British underclass is a classic study in stratification which has much to say about identity and stratification. One interpretation is that Murray was claiming that a position in the underclass led to the development of a dependency culture. However, it could also be considered that Murray was claiming that people fell into the underclass because they were predisposed to idleness and dependency. Either way, this study had very little empirical evidence to support its claims.

- Pakulski and Waters' book, *The Death of Class* (1996) challenged the dominant view that class and stratification were the key determinants of life chances and social identity. They argued that class is unfashionable in today's society, and that people no longer feel they are part of class groups. Pakulski and Waters believe that ethnicity, gender and age are now more important forms of stratification. However, the book was a largely theoretical study, using secondary evidence. As ever in sociology, theories cannot simply be proved by accumulating data. Data has to be interpreted and this can only be done by using theoretical ideas.

What does this mean?

Stratification, differentiation and inequality are all things which can have a big impact upon our identity. The classical sociologists such as Marx, Weber and Durkheim were interested in this question, and they suggested that in modern society people could be alienated, experience feelings of isolation and individualism (anomie), or become very strict and self-denying (Weber's Protestant ethic). Sociologists are now especially interested in the ways that stratification affects our identity, but they have developed these ideas in new directions.

What do sociological theories say about stratification and identity?

Marxism

In Marxism, identity was seen to follow on very simply from class position. Other types of identity, such as gender or ethnic identity, were relatively neglected; since Marxist theory assumed that the most important aspect of stratification was class, other factors could only have at best a secondary influence. According to Marxist theory, the prospects for identity in capitalist society were not good. People would lead lives and develop identities stunted by the inequalities created by capitalism, and would be alienated.

Functionalism

Identity in functionalist theory is seen as something which, in modern society, is achieved not ascribed. Functionalists therefore have a very optimistic view of the way that individuals can shape identity in modern society. They do recognise some differences, such as gender roles, but tend to emphasise how roles are now much more flexible and are the outcome of consensus rather than being imposed through social control.

Weberianism

Weber's work on stratification is important partly for raising the importance of status differences and so reminding sociologists of the complexity of stratification. However, Weber is also important because the concept of status brings the idea of culture into stratification. By including status differences in his account of stratification, Weber shows us that it is not just economic differences which are important. This is because status differences, such as those between different ethnic groups or those arising from gender differences, reflect cultural beliefs. Weber's analysis shows us that identity depends on cultural as well as economic factors and that, while in many ways we can create our identity, there are also important structural constraints.

What do contemporary sociologists say about stratification and identity?

Contemporary sociologists have noted that the late 20th century was a time of considerable social change. Ideas drawn from two new theories, postmodernism and post-structuralism, have had a particularly strong influence in sociology. This has led sociologists to turn away from economic differences, and to focus more on the way that culture can be used to actively create identity and differences. A well-known example of such a view is apparent in Pakulski and Waters' book, *The Death of Class* (1996) (see Classic Study and section 7.21).

While many sociologists have been highly critical of these new approaches, they have nevertheless borrowed insights from them. As Bradley has argued (1998), sociologists are now recognising the need for better ways of theorising stratification. Several key changes do seem to have occurred in relation to stratification and the way it relates to identity.

- The class structure has fragmented, in the sense that class no longer seems to form a key aspect of people's self-identity.
- Gender identities are now considered to be much more flexible and varied. Sociologist Bob Connell (1987) has argued that genders have to be seen as constructed and as involving a range of masculine and feminine identities. These may vary, for example, on the basis of class, age or ethnic origin.
- Ethnic identity is changing in the UK, as those from immigrant backgrounds form hybrid identities. Hybridity refers to the creation of a new identity which is the product of a mixture of two different cultures, for example a person whose parents are from Bangladesh, but who was born in the UK might describe themselves as a 'British Asian'. (See Hall 1992, and M. Song, in Abbott 1998.)
- Sociologists are also keen to explore new aspects of stratification and identity, such as the way that age groups can shape identity and inequality.
- Giddens (1990) argues that social change has led to a society where we can now be said to be living in a post-traditional social order. People's identity is no longer constrained by traditional rules, and they are able to create and mould a 'plastic identity'.

Conclusion

As a result of changes in society and in sociology, many sociologists would argue that sociologists need to do at least three things to study stratification properly:

- develop new theories of stratification and identity
- examine the way that groups and their cultures can create social exclusion and stigmatised identities
- examine the way that stratification and identity are shaped by globalisation.

For consideration

1. Are people free to choose their identity in contemporary society?

2. How does a person attain a high status identity in contemporary society?

✳ Key Idea

Postmodernism and identity: postmodernists have suggested that identities are no longer constrained by social structures such as class, race and gender. They have argued that people are now free to construct their identity as they wish. As social structures have fragmented, people are strongly influenced in doing this by the mass media. Post-structuralism is a theoretical approach which has turned attention to culture, identity and differentiation, pointing out that people are able to use culture and cultural symbols as a way of actively creating identity.

✓ Top Exam Hint

Remember that the structure/action debate is directly relevant to these debates about identity and stratification. Point out this link and use it to make criticisms of both perspectives. For example, postmodernism puts too much emphasis on action and neglects the importance of structures, and modernist theories can neglect the importance of reflexivity.

| # How has globalisation changed inequality and stratification?

❋ Key Idea

Globalisation is a process which can have many different effects, shaping political, economic, social and cultural life.

- Governments may have less control over their own country.

- The economic success of a country depends on events in other countries.

- Socially, people may lose a strong sense of national identity.

- Different societies may become increasingly the same in terms of their culture.

What does this mean?

In the previous section we have seen that sociologists have noted how stratification has changed considerably. One of the factors leading to change is the process of globalisation. The concept of globalisation claims that we are living in an increasingly interconnected world. This means that it is no longer possible to understand stratification and inequality in the UK without considering the impact of global relationships. Globalisation is a highly controversial concept, but in this section we will examine how it has been claimed to shape stratification.

How does globalisation affect stratification and inequality?

There are two particularly important explanations of how globalisation affects stratification and differentiation in contemporary society.

- Pakulski and Waters (1996) have argued that globalisation reflects a new period of time which is characterised by the development of a postmodern culture. This view suggests that class is no longer so important in a postmodern culture because the economic aspects of globalisation have created a world where class identities are increasingly less important. Pakulski and Waters argue instead that identity is mainly centred round what they call 'status-conventionalism'. This means that status differences are much more important than class differences.

  Pakulski and Waters reason that manual work and the class structures that went with it in advanced industrial societies have declined. Economic globalisation has led to the creation of affluent service economies and, in these societies, status is more important than class, and is achieved through consumption patterns.

- Anthony Giddens (1990, 1999) and Ulrich Beck (1992) are two social theorists associated with the approach termed 'reflexive modernisation'. Like postmodernists, they agree that there has been considerable social change, but they have a different view of it. These theorists argue that we live not in a postmodern society, but in a de-traditionalised society. This means that position and status are much more the result of individual achievement and choice, rather than being determined at birth by structural forces such as class origin. People reflexively construct their individual identity and are much less constrained by factors such as class. This means, according to Giddens and Beck, that collective identities, such as class identities, have a much lesser role to play in contemporary society. While they do acknowledge that inequalities persist, they take the view that inequalities between different societies are now the most important aspects of stratification (see Key Fact).

What criticisms have been made of these views?

Views such as those described above have helped to create a situation where some sociologists have questioned whether class remains a useful concept in sociology (see section 7.14). However, many sociologists, while wanting to acknowledge social change, would argue that the extent of such change has been exaggerated by some contemporary sociologists. Rosemary Crompton is a good example of those who take this view.

Crompton argues that the cases put forward by both postmodernists and reflexive modernisers are exaggerated. Crompton makes the following points.

- The case for de-traditionalisation has not been made in a completely convincing fashion. Empirical evidence demonstrates that there is still considerable difference in social mobility for members of different social groups and classes (see section 7.10). In addition, contemporary societies are still characterised by the persistence of customs and irrational prejudices against certain social groups; consider, for example, the underclass, ethnic minorities, homosexual groups and so on.
- Both theories also tend to neglect the role of coercion, force and power. They present a picture of a world where these features do not appear to play a very important role in social affairs. For example, it may be true that we can construct our identities through consumption, and that we may lead very individualised and reflexive lives. However, the ability of an individual to create any particular identity will vary systematically depending upon their social position.
- Both theories also neglect the role that governments play in creating and reinforcing stratification and differentiation (see section 7.22). Governments have the power to shape patterns of stratification through the policies they make. Postmodernists are right to suggest that the power of governments is limited in a global economy, but governments are not as powerless as they suggest.

Conclusion

All of these views have something useful to tell us about stratification, differentiation and inequality in contemporary society:

- Stratification in Britain has been changed by global social change (globalisation) and it is not possible to fully understand inequalities without knowledge of this.
- Inequalities between different nations and different parts of the world are therefore a very important aspect of inequality which sociologists need to examine in order to understand stratification in any one society.
- Status and consumption differences have been neglected, but economic differences still exist and are still important.

For consideration

1. Who will benefit from globalisation?
2. Is globalisation a new phenomenon?

☀ Key Idea

The concept of de-traditionalisation is one which is used extensively by reflexive modernisers such as Giddens and Beck. They argue that modern societies have seen the sweeping away of the traditions and rules that bound pre-industrial eras. However, this is a highly controversial view, which makes sweeping claims about the lack of dynamism in pre-industrial society, and indeed neglects the role of tradition and the re-invention of tradition in modern societies, for example, the creation of national and ethnic identities.

✓ Top Exam Hint

It is important to keep up to date with social change. Another aspect of globalised inequality nowadays is access to information technology. Sociologists such as Manuel Castells (1997) talk of the 'information rich' and the 'information poor'. Lack of access to a computer can affect your educational and career opportunities.

Why do stratification and inequality persist?

Key Fact

Despite popular belief that inequalities in the UK are narrowing, the government's own statistics show that the reverse is true. In 1979, the richest fifth of the population earned 35 per cent of all income. In 1999/2000, the richest fifth earned 44 per cent of all income. The poorest fifth, by comparison, earned 9.6 per cent of all income in 1979, and only 5.9 per cent in 1999/2000.

Source: Department of Social Security 1997, 2001

What does this mean?

In the 1960s, some sociologists thought that class was becoming less important and that inequalities were being eroded, with most people adopting a middle-class lifestyle and income. From the late 1980s onwards, sociologists influenced by postmodernism have claimed that class is no longer a significant aspect of identity, and that growing affluence has enabled people to choose whichever lifestyle most appeals to them. However, as we have seen, inequalities have increased, although they have also become more complex. This section examines how sociologists explain these persisting inequalities and patterns of stratification.

How do sociologists explain the persistence of stratification and inequality?

As we have seen, sociologists influenced by postmodernism have tended to underplay the existence and importance of inequalities. Their focus instead has been on differentiation, and they have been keen to point out the varieties of differentiation which are generated by human cultures. However, sociologists drawing their inspiration from other sociological approaches, see and explain stratification and inequality in other ways.

Functionalist views of stratification and inequality are worth carefully distinguishing from postmodernist views and the views of those such as Beck and Giddens. Functionalists argue that inequalities do exist, but they argue that some of these are inevitable and necessary. Closely related to functionalist thought here, is the liberal view (a political approach) that unjustified inequalities, such as differences between men's and women's pay, are gradually being eroded by legislation. Liberals and functionalists believe that the state can be trusted to act fairly in the best interests of all.

Marxist-influenced sociologists would argue that class conflict continues, though capitalist societies have changed considerably since Marx's day. Despite this, the central insight of Marxism remains; we live in a capitalist society, and this means that conflicts and inequalities on the basis of ownership are inevitable.

Weberian-influenced sociologists can reasonably argue that in a period of mass consumerism and high levels of affluence (for some), the study of status differences has indeed become more, rather than less, important. However, they would argue that postmodernists distort the importance of this insight, and that this is mainly a result of their inability to appreciate that stratification is the result of inequalities of wealth and power. Arguably, the Weberian approach is much more aware of these and provides concepts which allow us to understand them.

Danish sociologist, Gosta Esping-Anderson, has become well known for his analysis of the ways in which welfare systems preserve inequalities, and help create new ones (1990). Esping-Anderson argues that this can happen in two ways.

- Firstly, those who receive benefits can become stigmatised. This can happen, for example, where those who receive free school dinners are easily identified. This means that status differences are in fact likely to be accentuated. Arguably, another example of this can be seen arising from the stricter benefit rules in the UK over the last 20 years. These have helped to create a highly visible group of homeless people living on the streets. These people gain a generally stigmatised identity.
- Secondly, universal benefits can, in fact, highlight inequalities. This occurs because, in societies where there is not already a high level of equality (i.e. there is much stratification and inequality), the affluent gain further benefits and find their privilege boosted, since they gain universal benefits as well as earned income. An example of this is the way that all families in the UK, regardless of income, can claim Child Benefit allowance.

How are stratification and inequality changing or disappearing?

One way of summarising the debates here is to note that what many of the current discussions boil down to is whether or not stratification and inequality continue to be a key feature of our society. Postmodernists and other sociologists influenced by postmodernism have argued that both of these features are of declining importance. They suggest that a process of de-differentiation (blurring) is occurring, providing individuals with the opportunity to shape new identities. Other sociologists, however, may insist that while stratification is becoming more complex, it does not necessarily follow that we are living in a period when inequalities are no longer important constraints on our actions.

Conclusion

In evaluating these viewpoints, these key issues need to be addressed.

- Sociologists must not generalise from their own or limited experience.
- Social change has complicated stratification and made it harder to identify the effects of stratified inequality.
- Sociologists' views of power and the structure/action debate will shape the way they answer this debate.

Gosta Esping-Anderson

☞ Who is this person?

Gosta Esping-Anderson is a Danish sociologist. His book, *The Three Worlds of Welfare Capitalism*, has become a classic in contemporary sociology. In this book, Esping-Anderson argues that different types of welfare system always create new forms of stratification or else preserve existing inequalities.

∞ Methods Link

Postmodernist accounts of class and differentiation tend to be theoretically rather than empirically based. This should be regarded as a weakness because theoretical ideas in sociology need empirical support. If postmodernist approaches were to be more methodologically sound, they would tend to focus more on people's perceptions of class and stratification.

✓ Top Exam Hint

Remember to use the idea of social exclusion when discussing the persistence of stratification and differentiation. The idea of stigmatising groups because of various non-economic characteristics, for example, gender, ethnicity, age or other factors, is another reason why stratification persists and indeed can be continually reinvented in different ways, varying between different cultures and different times.

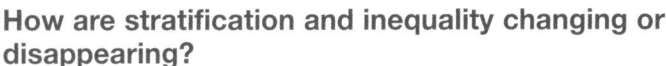

For consideration

1. Are social inequalities inevitable and necessary?

2. Are there more opportunities for the development of individual identity in contemporary society than in the past?

7.23 How can we make stratification and differentiation synoptic?

❝❞ Key Definitions

- **Synoptic**: a synopsis is a summary or an overview. A synopsis of a book or a film will provide you with an overall picture of how the book or film progresses and what happens in the end. The synoptic unit therefore requires you to provide an overview, showing how the different topics you have studied fit into a whole picture. To make your work synoptic, therefore, you have to show how the different elements fit together to produce a coherent picture.

- **Core themes**: there are two core themes in the AQA specification: socialisation, culture and identity; and social differentiation, power and stratification. These themes should be linked to all the other topics you study. As you can see, this means that stratification is a vital topic – even if you are not aiming to answer a question on stratification in the exam, it is still a vital topic to understand.

Why is synopticity important for stratification and differentiation?

Synopticity refers to the way that different topics are linked together. Examining how stratification and differentiation (which are also **core themes**) runs through the different topics you have studied will help improve your understanding of each one. Synopticity is also important in this topic because, if you choose this topic in the exam, you will have to make synoptic links to other topics you have studied in AS Sociology and to theory and method.

How does stratification and differentiation link to families and households?

The family is a highly gendered institution as contemporary studies of conjugal roles have demonstrated. This differentiation is also reinforced and reflected in social policies which privilege men and have tended to assume that women's place is in the home, looking after children and dependants. In this chapter (see sections 7.16 and 7.17), the influence of women's work on household incomes is seen by Crompton as reflecting the changing role and importance of women's position in the stratification system. As many sociologists now argue, class and gender are both important aspects of stratification, and both of these structures have a big impact on the family, and the family is a key site where gendered identities are created.

How does stratification and differentiation link to education?

One of sociologists' key interests in the sociology of education is to explain the varied patterns of educational attainment which have been observed. Systematic differences in attainment occur on the basis of class, ethnicity and gender. Stratification is also an important issue in the meritocracy debate, where the opposing claims reflect different views of the stratification system. Educational policies since the 19th century have reflected the idea that different social classes exist and require different types of education. Differentiation in terms of ethnicity and gender is also relevant to the issues of institutional racism and to the gendering of the curriculum. The education system is a key site where class identities, and ethnic and gendered identities, are created and reinforced.

How does stratification and differentiation link to power and politics?

Stratification has often been seen as a key factor in explaining voting behaviour. Many sociologists, though, have been critical of the idea that there is any 'automatic' link between stratification and voting, and political scientists such as Ivor Crewe have argued that a process of class dealignment occurred in the UK in the 1980s. However, there are still important links between class, ethnicity and gender and voting behaviour, but as stratification has become more complex, so has the way it is linked to voting behaviour.

How does stratification and differentiation link to theory and methods?

Theory and methods are linked to stratification and differentiation because different theories provide competing descriptions and explanations of stratification and differentiation.

In terms of methodology, there are important issues about how class is operationalised and measured, as well as issues about how class relates to structure and action (see section 7.1 for more on the latter). For example, feminists (see sections 7.16 and 7.10) have argued that many sociological views of stratification have neglected women's role in stratification. This claim has led to debates about whether women are a class and how women's class position is best identified and operationalised. In the case of race and ethnicity, some sociologists have argued that theoretical perspectives such as Marxism were 'race blind' since racial and ethnic differences were seen to be based primarily on class position, not on race or ethnicity itself.

How does stratification and differentiation link to culture and identity?

Sociologists often argue that cultures enable social groups to become integrated around unifying beliefs or values. However, cultures can also promote stratification and differentiation. In British culture, for example, there are important rules based on social differences such as gender, age, class and ethnicity. Those who do not maintain cultural rules may find that they are socially excluded. Stratification and differentiation, therefore, is very much concerned with cultural differences and the cultural bases of stratification, and is not simply about economic differences. The way that cultures stratify and differentiate people also has an important impact on identity. In order to attain a favourable identity in British society, a person must follow certain cultural rules; failure to do this can lead to social exclusion.

Key points to remember

- Theories of stratification and differentiation are one of the key ways that sociologists try to explain how societies are integrated or held together. This topic is therefore relevant to all other topic areas.
- Different sociological theories describe and explain stratification and differentiation in very different ways. However, this provides you with lots of ideas and material for debating and to use for evaluation.
- Do not forget to link stratification and differentiation to issues of culture and identity (a core theme). Stratification shapes our identity and the identities that are available to us, and it also reflects cultural rules.

✓ Top Exam Hints

- Use the concept of power to evaluate different explanations of stratification. Marxist and feminist views of power tend to see it as something which is unequally shared out. This helps to explain the continuity of inequality. Functionalists, though, claim that power is equally shared and do not believe that there are any major conflicts of interest in capitalist society. These views lead the theories to reach very different conclusions about the nature of stratification.

- Identify key studies for each of these topic areas which demonstrate the importance of stratification and differentiation.

7.24 Pushing your grades up higher

⁎ Key Idea

The idea of the 'sociological imagination' was developed by American sociologist, C Wright Mills, in the 1950s (Mills 1980). Mills argued that the key aim of sociology should always be to show how what appear to be purely private details of our individual lives are always linked to social processes. In this way, Mills argued that sociology is able to help us understand our lives more completely and to see that all behaviour is social behaviour, or is influenced by social processes.

✓ Top Exam Hint

Postmodernism is a good theory to use in this respect. You can use postmodernist ideas as a way of evaluating the more traditional theories, such as Marxism, neo-Marxism and functionalism.

● Synoptic Link

Remember to make the synoptic links required by the question you are answering. A handful of good references throughout the question will show that you are making links with another topic. Make it clear what you are doing by using phrases which make the nature of the link explicit.

1. Identify and learn five key facts about the extent of inequalities in contemporary Britain. The A2 exam does, of course, give you more marks for interpreting, evaluating, applying and analysing your knowledge, but it is easier to do all these things when you have a sound base of knowledge.

2. Remember to use your sociological imagination. Show the links between our individual lives and social processes.

3. Remember to point out that stratification and differentiation in contemporary society have changed considerably in recent years. Use this point to evaluate older studies.

4. Make a habit of reading from a range of textbooks to gather different points of view and fresh insights and data. Also read a few articles on this topic. Your teacher will be able to point you towards relevant articles in books of readings or magazines such as *Sociology Review*.

5. Make your own glossary of terms for this topic, taking care to explain the terms in your own words. This will be better than just using glossaries from textbooks because you will have to think carefully about the terms to do this. You should understand something better if you have written about it yourself. Keep adding terms to your glossary for as long as possible – the more you stretch yourself the better.

6. Make your own summary chart about stratification and the other topics you have studied. Use a piece of A4 paper in landscape format. You should make a column on the left to note down summaries of each of the major theories of stratification. Add other columns such as, 'view of the class structure', 'key strengths', 'criticisms', 'links to other topics', and any others you think are important. The rows cutting across the columns will be for the main theories; you should have at least five rows so that you can include the following theories: Marxist, Weberian, functionalist, feminist, postmodernist.

7. Make a list of all the things which you do not think you fully understand about this topic. Compare your list with other students and, with the help of your teacher, have a lesson when you try to iron out these problem areas.

8. Obtain a copy of the previous year's exam paper, the mark scheme for the exam, and the subsequent chief examiner's report. Study these carefully to see exactly what was required in order to do well.

9. Organise a time when you can make your own presentation or talk about one aspect of this topic to another student studying sociology. This is a good way of finding out if you really do understand the topic well. You could try this in class and give the talk to a group of students.

10. Make a second glossary. This one should be for non-technical (i.e. non-sociological) words which you have had to look up in the dictionary. Make sure that every time you find a word that you do not know the meaning of in the course of your reading for sociology, you look it up in the dictionary and record and define it. This will expand your general vocabulary and improve your communication skills, which are vital in a subject like sociology.

11. Make it a priority to work on your language skills, especially essay writing. Use any specialist books you can find in your school or college library. Ask friends and teachers for advice on essay writing and try to look at other people's essays. Find good examples of essay writing and analyse them, identify their strengths and try to use similar techniques and styles in your own work.

12. Do not use personal pronouns in your essays, for example 'I' as in 'I think that…' Use impersonal pronouns such as 'It' as in 'It can be argued that…' This is the conventional style for academic essays because it makes your essay sound more reflective and objective.

13. Always make sure that you evaluate ideas, theories, concepts and studies explicitly. This means that you need to make it clear how and why you are criticising something and tell the reader of your work/essay why your point is relevant. For example, 'This is relevant since…' or 'This helps answer the question because…'. Do not assume that your point will be obvious or clear to the reader unless you have made an effort to make sure that it is. Also remember that in long essay answers you are trying to construct an argument in response to a question. This means that you need to present a number of points which support your conclusion.

14. Be sure to label and set out your answers clearly.

Key points to remember

- Demonstrate your understanding by using sociological terms.
- Work hard to develop a good essay style and explain why your points are relevant.
- Try to show that you are aware of social change and the impact it may be having on stratification and differentiation.

✓ **Top Exam Hint**

With short answers that require you to do several things, for example identify and explain, it is often a good idea to leave a line between each part of your answer.

Frequently asked questions

Q. Why are sociologists always worried about stratification?

A. Sociologists are certainly interested in stratification because they see it as an important aspect of society, although they have very different views about how and why it is important. Sociologists are not necessarily 'worried' about stratification – some of them (functionalists) see it as a beneficial feature that is essential if modern industrial societies are to continue to function effectively.

Q. Why do sociologists spend more time talking about class than anything else?

A. Even if this was true in the past, it is almost certainly no longer the case. Sociologists are now increasingly aware that class is only one element, although a very important one, of stratification in contemporary societies. They are therefore keen to explore the links between class and other forms of stratification such as gender, ethnicity and age. Moreover, as we discussed in this chapter, there are many sociologists who dispute the importance of class in contemporary society. So despite the popular image of sociology which sees it as dominated by 'radical' and 'left wing' ideas, it is actually a very diverse discipline. Sociologists nowadays are just as likely to 'spend more time talking' about culture, gender, identity or globalisation. Which one of these they will be talking about will vary from individual to individual. Of course, they might also be talking about all of these, as sociologists are very aware of the way that social life is influenced by all of these factors!

Q. Why is stratification synoptic?

A. What sociologists want to understand is how society is organised and functions, and this involves considering how different elements of society influence each other. In AS and A2 sociology you learn about individual topic areas, but it is important to see how they link together. For example, we can better understand the differences between and within families and households once we have an understanding of stratification. Ideas about stratification and differentiation help us to understand gender differences in the family. Stratification can explain class differences between families, or the way that family structures and the sharing of resources varies according to the ethnic group involved. A person's role in the family will also depend upon their age.

So stratification is a very important topic which can link together all of the different topic areas which you have studied in sociology and it will provide you with various ways of explaining the different patterns of social inequality that are revealed by sociological research such as inequalities in health, official statistics on crime, or patterns of educational attainment.

Part 3 SKILLS FOR SUCCESS IN SOCIOLOGY

Chapter 8

Coursework skills

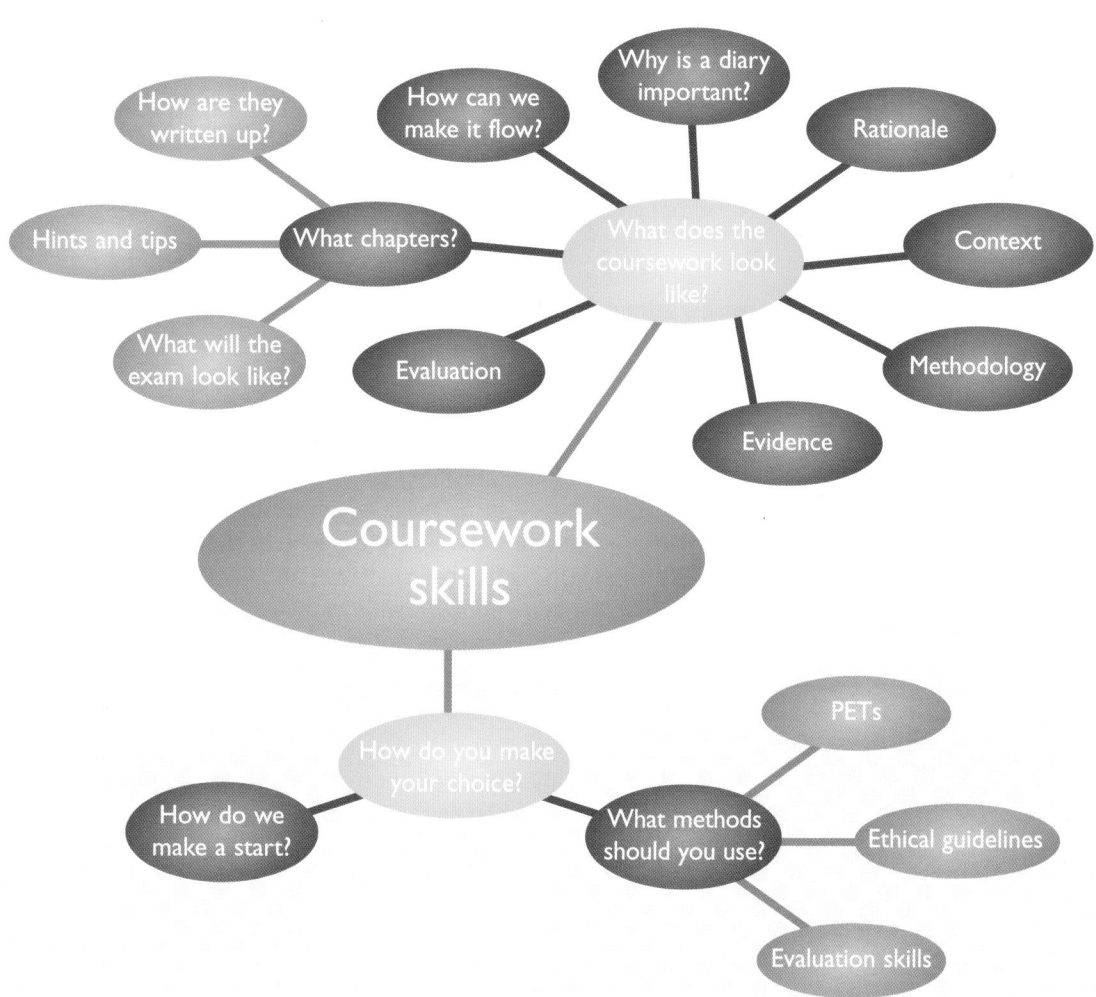

Key issues in coursework

What is the coursework?

The A2 coursework is for Unit 5 of the second year course. Many schools and colleges start preparations for the coursework towards the end of the AS year. The final deadline will be set by the school or college that you attend, but the coursework is sent to the examination body for marking and moderation by Easter of each year.

The coursework itself is an individual piece of research, written up in a format prescribed by the examination board. The coursework counts for up to 15 per cent of the final A2 mark, and is optional. You will either do the coursework or sit an examination on theory and methods which lasts one hour and 30 minutes, following the same format as the examination papers for Units 4 and 6.

What should the coursework look like?

The coursework should ideally be word-processed, since it will save time later on. You will probably be drafting each part or chapter of the coursework so often that not to word-process it and save each draft as a separate file would be a waste of your time in the long run. Your coursework must follow these criteria.

- It is recommended that the coursework is roughly 3500 words long.
- The choice of topic to research is up to you, although you must follow the guidance of your teachers.
- Although the choice of topic is yours, you must make sure that you are safe at all times while carrying out your research and that those you study are also safe.
- For ethical reasons, the exam board will not want you to research a 'vulnerable group' without really thinking and explaining how you can do your research in an ethical fashion.
- You must follow, and show that you are following, the British Sociology Association's (BSA) ethical guidelines for research practice.
- The coursework is divided up into five sections or chapters: rationale, context, methodology, evidence and evaluation.
- The coursework must have a bibliography of all sources used.
- You are required by the examination board to keep a research diary, and to include some pages from this with your final project.

Why is a diary important?

A research diary is important for two reasons.

1. It is an examination requirement that you submit some pages from your diary with your finished piece of work.
2. It will be useful for you to keep a diary, especially when it comes to writing up the final sections of your project.

Use the diary for the following, and make sure that you keep it safe and use it right from the start.

✓ Top Exam Hint

The ethical guidelines provided by the BSA are available on their website which you can access through www.heinemann.co.uk/hotlinks.

Make sure that you do not only follow the guidelines, but you show that you are following them, in order to gain important evaluation marks. You might like to quote from the guidelines as long as you fully reference what you use.

- The most important use of the diary will be as a place to log or record problems and issues with your research as you carry out the collection of your data. Make a list of all the problems that occurred and mistakes that you made; you can use these in the evaluation chapter. If you do not record them, you might be in danger of forgetting them once the end of the project is in sight. Keep a record of what you are doing and how you think it is going.
- Record in your diary any books you use or refer to. Make sure you note the author; title; date it was published; and what pages you used.
- Record in your diary any other sources you used, such as newspapers or websites. This way you will have a running record of everything you looked at ready for the bibliography at the end of the project.
- Record feedback you get from teachers. If you have an individual appointment with your teacher for advice or support, make a note of the issues raised.
- From time to time, maybe at the end of each week, make a quick note of what you have done during that period of time.

Key points to remember

- You will be asked to keep a diary.
- You can choose what to do, with the guidance of your teacher.
- The exam board decides what the sections of your project should be.

The coursework is an opportunity for you to find out what it feels like to conduct real research.

How is the coursework written up?

Part of getting the best grade you can in coursework, as in any examination, is to give the examiner what they want. There are some very simple tips and tricks to follow when writing up your coursework to make it as clear and well presented as possible. This is discussed below.

What does the coursework need to look like?

Make sure your coursework is word-processed, the pages are numbered and that the chapters are in order. The following advice will help you with your presentation.

1. Do not use an arty font or spend ages making a front page. Make it look simple and professional.
2. Look at how this book and others like it reference the names of sociologists. Look at how our bibliography is presented, and copy the same format.
3. You might like to include footnotes. You do not have to do this but it is a good idea. Most word-processing programmes will allow you to insert a footnote which is different from a footer. A footnote is when you insert a number in the main body of the text, which then relates to a numbered entry at the very bottom of the page (hence the name). In this entry you simply provide the details of where you got the information from. Again, make everything really clear to the reader.
4. You might choose to put all quotes in bold or italic – this way they stand out.
5. If you are producing quantitative data, make sure that all graphs etc are clearly labelled and each graph has a discussion along with it.
6. If you are producing qualitative data, you might put all quotes from your respondents in bold or italic. Change their name for ethical reasons, and say that you are doing this. Make sure you present what they say exactly how they said it in order to make it valid.
7. Always refer back to your aim at every opportunity. Show that everything is relevant to the main focus of what you are trying to do.
8. You might put PETS in bold every time you use the words practical, ethical, theoretical and sensitivity. This way it will look like these are themes that are building up over time and it is an easy way to signpost evaluation.
9. Make sure you read through your coursework when it is finished, and check your grammar and spelling.

How should it be presented?

- Your name and candidate number should appear on every page. Insert this as a footer or a header.
- Make sure that you do not mention the name of your school or college in the coursework. This is for ethical reasons and also because the examiner should not need to know exactly what educational institution you attend.

- Print it off and treasury tag it all together in the top corner and put the whole project in a single plastic wallet.
- Make sure you photocopy two or three pages of your diary to go at the very back of the project.
- You might want to add an appendix, but do not overdo it.
- Include a contents page.
- Keep a copy printed off and a copy saved to disk just in case.
- Your teachers will ask you to sign a sheet from the exam board to say it is all your own work. This should go right at the front of the project.

What should the appendix be used for?

An appendix is a section at the end that allows you to include extra background information. It is not included in your word count.

- Do not overdo it with an appendix. Only put things in if you need them.
- The appendix is not marked, but will be read by the examiner.
- Do not include something in the appendix instead of putting it in the main project. This is a waste since it can only get marked if it is in the main part of the project itself.
- You may like to include letters asking permission from organisations you might have needed to contact during the course of your research.
- You might show an example of a questionnaire completed by a respondent but there is no need for you to put every single one in.
- You might like to type up (**transcribe**) a section of an interview and present it here to show that you took the research experience seriously.
- You might like to include notes from doing the actual research, although this should all really be included in the diary in the first place.
- Do not include all your data as this will make the project too bulky.
- Do not include copies of articles and newspaper sources. If you need to use them, perhaps in your rationale as a secondary source, then quote from them and fully reference them instead.

Key points to remember

- Make your coursework look professional.
- Make sure you present your findings clearly, follow the advice above.
- Make sure everything is fully referenced and footnoted.

❝❞ Key Definition

When we say '**transcribing** an interview' we mean the process of typing up a record of the conversation that took place. If you do this, it is important that interviews are tape-recorded and that you ask permission of the respondent beforehand. This is something else you might write about in the methodology chapter. Also, be aware that the presence of a recorder might actually affect the outcome of the interview in some way. Make sure you transcribe it exactly as it was said, including all the words and noises and half-finished sentences. People do not speak in a perfect way so do not try to fake an interview – it will be easy to spot.

What does each of the chapters do?

What does this mean?

The AQA examination body have pre-set the sections or chapters of your project and you must follow these. Each section does a different thing, and it is important that you find ways to link the sections together so that the project as a whole flows.

The sections are:

1. rationale
2. context
3. methodology
4. evidence
5. evaluation.

What is the rationale?

The rationale is like the introduction. As the name suggests, it is where you tell the reader what you are going to be doing and how you will be doing it. In this first section you are required to state your aims clearly, and to explain what the point of the research is going to be. If you are producing quantitative data you will need to clearly state your **hypothesis** in this section.

What is the context?

The context is similar to a 'literature review'. In this chapter or section you have to show what other sociologists have done on the topic that you have chosen. You might present some ideas that you are going to up-date, or ideas that you will disagree with during the course of your research. This must all be relevant to the point of your particular research. This chapter 'sets the scene'.

What is the methodology?

Arguably this could be seen as the most important chapter of all. After all, the point of doing the coursework is that you need to show how much you understand about the process of carrying out research. In this chapter you present your method. You will be asked to discuss strengths and weaknesses and to explore the problems and solutions you had when conducting your research. Write this in the future tense – you have not done the method yet.

What is the evidence chapter?

The evidence chapter is where you show and comment upon your findings – the data you have produced. It is vital that you analyse and interpret what you have found, and that you evaluate it. Do not just present it as a fact and not provide any commentary. Go back to your aim and go back to your context. What have you found? What do you think it all means?

66 99 Key Definition

A **hypothesis** is a statement that can be tested and shown to be right or wrong. It should not be a question and it should be as clear as possible. You will need to define carefully any problem words that you use in this statement so the reader understands what you mean.

✓ Top Exam Hint

Make sure you get the rationale to a reasonable standard before you do anything else with your coursework. Until your aim is clear, there is no point trying to go any further.

What is the evaluation chapter?

The purpose of the evaluation chapter, the last section of your project, is to take the findings of the previous chapter and to think about the success of the research as a whole. What did you find? What does it mean? Are there any problems with what you found? Could it have been done any differently? Are there recommendations for any future research?

How are the marks divided up between the chapters?

The whole project, like each of your examinations, is marked out of a possible 60 marks. You will be asked to choose only one method and to decide whether to do a **primary** or a **secondary** piece of research.

The coursework is marked according to the two different skill areas or 'assessment objectives'.

1. Knowledge and understanding is worth up to 24 marks.
2. Identification, analysis, interpretation and evaluation is worth up to 36 marks.

Each section of the project does a different thing in terms of how it is marked, and this therefore should affect what you write in each section and how you write it.

- The first set of skills (knowledge and understanding) is marked in the context and methodology chapters, with a maximum of 12 marks for each of these two sections of the project.
- The second set of skills is marked as follows: a maximum of 18 marks for how you apply your method and how you present and interpret your findings; and a further maximum of 18 marks for your rationale, evaluation and the conclusions that you draw.

Key points to remember

- There are five sections to the project.
- Each section is marked in a specific way.
- You can only choose one method, and can do either a primary or a secondary method.

✍ Coursework Suggestion

Evaluation is very important when you write up your coursework. You must show the difficulties and problems you face, and what possible solutions you should investigate. You must make sure that the project becomes like an ongoing discussion of what you are thinking and what you are trying. Research is like problem-solving, so show the process that you are going through for as many evaluation marks as possible.

66 99 Key Definitions

Primary research means you gather the data yourself. The data would not exist if you did not undertake the project.

Secondary data means you use data gathered by others. The data existed before you carried out the project.

✍ Coursework Suggestion

If you do a primary project, you can still use a small amount of secondary research in order to back up what you find, or to compare and contrast with your findings. You might even do a piece of research to explore whether a piece of secondary data might be valid or not.

8.4 | How do you decide what to do?

Producing successful coursework is often a result of finding a clear route through the process of planning your research, carrying it out and writing it up. Do not make the point of your research too complicated or confused, or you will not know what direction to turn in.

✎ Coursework Suggestions

* **Most ideas for coursework that work well are very simple. Do not take on too much. Decide on a clear aim, a method that is suitable and a theory that you can see through the eyes of. If you cannot explain your idea in very simple terms, then you might not really understand what you are doing. Do not fall into this trap early on. Spend some time, but make sure you understand what you are doing and what the point of it is. Otherwise, you simply will not be able to write a sensible and meaningful rationale.**

* **Many students take an old sociology study and play around with it. You could see if it is still true today. You could use a different variable by taking an existing piece of sociological research that did not look at ethnicity or gender and do the research again with the new variable. You could change the location. Take a piece of research done in one location, and try it in another.**

What does this mean?

Getting started is the hardest thing about coursework. Because the decision of what to do is so open, it is very difficult to narrow down the options and to make a decision. Do not worry about this, and most importantly, do not make a quick, rushed decision and then regret it later.

It is also important that your idea is not too big. A real problem every year for many students is that they simply try to do too much, or to take on too many ideas. Aim for a straightforward idea, but try to find something you will be interested in doing. After all, you will be working on this piece of work for a considerable period of time. Make sure you are not going to get bored.

What will you need to decide?

In order to progress, you are going to have to make a few decisions.

* What topic area in sociology will you study? Do you choose a topic you have studied at AS, at A2, or something different?
* What method will you use to test your hypothesis?
* What type of data will you try to produce – quantitative or qualitative?
* What will your hypothesis be if you are producing quantitative data?
* Who exactly will you study? Where will you find these people? Will they actually allow you to do your research?
* What theoretical ideas will be most closely associated with your project?
* Will you do a primary or a secondary project?

The question is, where do you start? What decision comes first?

Where do you start?

Here are some ideas to consider in helping you to get started.

* What have you enjoyed most in sociology so far? What debates or topics or even theories have interested you most? Can you link a project to one of these?
* You could up-date an old study that you have been taught and which has interested you. You might wish to see if it is still true, or to try and prove it wrong.
* You could work backwards. Do not think about the topic, but think about the method you might use. Are there any methods you might prefer? You simply might be more interested in them. Are there any methods you just would not want to use? Why?
* Is there a theory that you have enjoyed over the past year? You could try to conduct a piece of research into an idea or concept that the theory is associated with.

- What sorts of people would you enjoy studying the most? Who can you easily get access to?
- Think about what issues are current in the media. Might they form the basis of a project?

What sources can help?

In order to make a decision on what kinds of sources to use, you might try to get hold of the following.

1. A sociology textbook is the simplest source to use. Are there any ideas you are interested in? Use the contents page and the index to find an interesting topic.
2. What about the web? Are there any interesting news stories that you might like to investigate?
3. Can your teacher show you some old projects? Clearly, this project must be your own work, but if you look at what others have done you might see what sorts of things people do each year.
4. Do you get a free local newspaper sent to your home? Do you ever read it? Maybe there are some items of local interest that you could investigate?

Once you have your idea, you will find the rest of the project much easier, but take your time. It is important to get this first stage right.

Key points to remember

- Think about what issues you have enjoyed the most.
- Think about what method and theory you might like to use.
- Make sure you have an ethical idea.

∞ Methods Link

Make sure that whatever you choose to do, it is ethical. Make sure your idea is not going to put you or others in danger and think very hard about the ethical nature of covert methods. Consider the BSA guidelines carefully (see section 8.1).

✍ Coursework Suggestion

Do not forget that running throughout this book are these margin boxes with coursework hints and ideas for you to try. You can print them off from the CD ROM that accompanies the book so you can find them all easily. Also remember that the AS book in this series also has many other ideas for you to think about.

How do you decide what method to use?

You must decide on what method to adopt for your research and there must be clear reasons for your choice. What sort of data do you want to produce and why?

What does this mean?

Once you have decided on your aim (what you want to find out) you need to give some serious consideration to the method you want to use. You will need to think about the topic, the data you want and the potential success of anything you try to do.

Your reasons why you have chosen a particular method should appear in some detail in your methodology chapter, but a brief discussion should also appear in the rationale chapter.

What choices do you have available?

The coursework only requires you to choose one method, and to make the decision between a primary or a secondary piece of research. You must think of the following issues when choosing a method.

- How much time do you have available?
- What other resources might you need – dictaphone, photocopier, computer, video camera?
- Where would the method need to be carried out? For example, if you are doing interviews, would you need a quiet room somewhere?
- What data do you need? Do you need to produce a statistical summary of different variables or do you need detailed information about people's thoughts and feelings?
- Do not forget that some methods have sensitivity and ethical issues. Can you guarantee to limit or at least to reduce these as much as possible?
- All methods have strengths and weaknesses, but can you make sure that the strengths outweigh the weaknesses?
- You could try and work backwards. Do not think about what method to choose, but rather, what methods you can rule out. Do not forget to have a brief discussion in your methodology chapter not only about those methods you have chosen, but also an analysis of why you rejected others. This is good for evaluation marks.

You will need to answer all these questions so as to be able to decide what to use and why to use it. These questions will also help you in your methodology chapter since you will be required to provide an extended discussion of your choice of method and the reasoning and thinking behind it.

You will also, at all times, need to show your thinking. The coursework should be written as if it is a discussion of the problems involved in doing and planning research, as well as actually showing what you did do.

∞ Methods Link

Do not forget that many feminist thinkers have rejected quantitative data, feeling that qualitative data is better for 'empowering' those that you study. If you are going to take a feminist approach in your project, you will need to consider this and discuss it in some depth in your methodology and rationale chapters.

✍ Coursework Suggestion

Do not forget that every method has problems – you will need to think about these in advance of your actual choice to make sure it is still the most suitable option. Think about PETS – practical issues, ethical issues, theoretical issues and sensitivity issues. How do these relate to your choice of method?

What methods are available?

There are many methods available to the researcher, and each has its own strengths and weaknesses. You have the following to choose from.

- Questionnaires/surveys: you need to think about whether the questions should be open or closed or both.
- Interviews: they could be structured or semi-structured.
- You might wish to do joint interviews (interviews with more than one person).
- Rather than joint interviews you could choose a focus group.
- Covert methods might be unethical, but are there ways in which you might use them?
- Observation: could be participant or non-participant.
- You could study media products using content analysis or semiology.

What will you need to write about?

Whatever method you choose, you will need to be able to justify its use and choice. You will always need to consider and write about the key methodological issues of reliability, representativeness and validity.

You will need to write about the following in your methodology chapter.

- Why is your choice the most appropriate for your study?
- How will you carry it out?
- What potential problems can you predict? What PETS do you have?
- How will you solve PETS issues?
- How will you gain access to those in your sample?
- Why did you reject other methods?
- Why are you producing the type of data you are creating?
- Make sure you discuss issues of reliability and validity.

Key points to remember

- All methods have both strengths and weaknesses.
- Try to link PETS to your choice of method.
- Show your thinking and problem-solving when you write up your method choice in your methodology chapter.

◯─◯ Methods Link

The Surrey University website has some really useful articles that you might find helpful about doing research and using methods. The website can be found at www.heinemann.co.uk/hotlinks and you will need to look at the sociology homepage to find *Social Research Updates*. This is a series of printable articles by researchers about the process of research. Do not forget to write published material in your own words and reference clearly the names of the authors in your methodology chapter. Use your diary to take notes and put the full reference in the bibliography.

What goes in the rationale?

What does this mean?

The rationale is like the introduction. As the name suggests, it is where you tell the reader what you are going to be doing and how you will be doing it. In this first section you are required to state your aims or hypothesis clearly, and to explain what the point of the research is going to be.

What do you need to do?

Be very clear about your aims and objectives. State them as clearly as you can and as early as you can in this opening chapter. Try to really find the easiest description of what you are doing and then explain it in more depth. Say what you think the point of the research would be; in other words, why is it sociological? Why is it interesting?

To illustrate your reasons for choosing your topic you might be able to find a statistic as a secondary source to show that the project has some significance or relevance to modern-day society. Perhaps this could be a government, official statistic?

Equally, you might be able to find a newspaper source that links your project to 'real-life'. This could be from a national newspaper or a local one. You could find both in order to try to locate the research into both regional and social contexts.

What must you include?

* Make sure you define all key terms as clearly as possible. This process is known as **operationalisation.**
* State the theory you will adopt and the method you will use.
* Briefly state the type of sampling you will be doing.
* Briefly state why you will be producing this type of data.
* Are there names of key sociologists who are important to this research? People you are following, testing, trying to prove right or wrong? Briefly mention them here, but leave the detail for the next context chapter.

How should it be written up?

Avoid making lists. Treat the rationale as an extended discussion but try to keep it to one side of typed writing (500 words). It should be a short and clear introduction to what will be coming next. The rationale will have to be written in the future tense as it is written before you have carried out the actual data gathering.

✓ Top Exam Hints

* Try the website of the National Statistics. It is full of official statistics, organised under topics.

* Try *The Guardian* website. There will be lots of searchable detailed articles and the site organises news stories from *The Guardian* around topics and ongoing debates.

   These websites can be accessed at www.heinemann.co.uk/hotlinks.

* Do not forget those sociological variables – class, gender, ethnicity, age, location, globalisation etc.

66 99 Key Definition

To **operationalise** is to define clearly what is meant by a term and how you intend to use it. This must be made clear in your rationale right from the start.

Key points to remember

- Make it clear and to the point.
- Make sure it is obvious what you will be doing and how.
- Do not make lists but discuss.

How do I build a context?

✓ Top Exam Hint
Do not forget the four ingredients of all good sociology writing – theory, key words, named studies and evaluation. These are the backbone of the context.

✍ Coursework Suggestion
You will need to keep coming back to your context once it is written. It will shape the questions you ask and it will also be used to interpret your findings.

What does this mean?

The context is similar to a literature review. In this chapter or section you have to show what other sociologists have done on the topic you have chosen. You might present some ideas that you are going to up-date, or ideas that you will disagree with during the course of your research. This must all be relevant to the point of your particular research and should place your study in context.

What do you need to do?

- You should start by reminding the reader of your aims. This is important, so that you make sure that you link your context back to your aims. Remember, this is a 'context'. This means it provides the background to the study that follows. You must make sure that you use this context in the methodology, evidence and evaluation chapters.
- Once you have discussed your aims, try to link them in with your theory. Go into some depth on your chosen theoretical perspective in general, and then apply it to the issue of your coursework topic in particular.
- Do not forget to link your project to important sociological and theoretical key words and concepts.
- Make sure that every named example you provide is fully referenced in the bibliography at the back, and footnoted at the bottom of the page if you do this.
- Try to identify three or four named examples that most link to your project. They could be historical or contemporary, but it would be better if you can get a mixture of the two. It might be that you are doing something different from the named studies you have chosen, but that they still link. Explain how they link in to what you are going to do, as well as providing an extended discussion of what they have to say.
- As with the rationale, you could put key words in bold or italic type so that they stand out.
- Try to find some secondary sources that you can briefly use to back-up your project. These might be statistical or otherwise. But, if you use them here, they must link to the ideas in your context in an obvious way. Make sure you spell out these links.
- Try to find a named study or example of something your project disagrees with – an idea test. Spell it out here and show how your project is trying to be different.
- It is important that you do more than simply list all these ideas. Discuss them and show how they compare and contrast.
- The final thing to do is to show how your context is relevant to your aim, and, most importantly, how what you are doing is similar to and different from the ideas you have presented here.

How should it be written up?

Think of this chapter as basically an essay. Write it with an introduction, main body and a conclusion. Make sure that it really is, however, a genuine 'context'. It provides the background for what comes next in an obvious way. It sets the scene.

Key points to remember

- Make sure it is a genuine context – it is really the background for your study.
- Try and present ideas that both complement and contrast with what you think you will find.
- Make sure that you use this context in the methodology and evidence chapters.

What goes in the methodology?

What does this mean?

Arguably this could be seen as the most important chapter of all. After all, the point of doing the coursework is that for Unit 5 you need to show how much you understand about the process of carrying out research. In this chapter you present your method. You will be asked to discuss strengths and weaknesses and to explore the problems and solutions you will have when conducting your research.

What do you need to do?

For this chapter you will need to explain in very precise terms why you are going to use the method that you have chosen. Think of this as an exercise in problem solving. You will need to explain in detail every aspect of your method, why you have chosen it and how you will try to carry it out. Discuss what problems might be involved and how you might solve them.

* Start with your aim again; remind the reader of it.
* Provide a short discussion of **positivism** and **phenomenology**. Try to locate your project within one of these two traditions. What does your methodology imply you are trying to do, and what sort of knowledge are you trying to explore? Why have you chosen one over the other?
* Explain very briefly, as part of this discussion, why you have not chosen the alternative methodology? Why have you rejected it? Remember, every decision to do one thing, is a decision to reject something else!
* Link the methodological tradition you are locating yourself in with the type of data you will produce. Say why this is the right sort of data for what you want to find.
* Now begin explaining what the strengths and weaknesses of the method are in general. Then go on to explain how these strengths and weaknesses apply in the case of the particular research you will be carrying out.
* Give a sense of why you are not choosing some methods that still might be relevant. Be careful here. Do not just list all methods and reject them in a simplistic way. Clearly some would not be appropriate depending on what you are trying to do, but there are always choices. So, why have you made the decisions you have?
* Link the potential problems you might have to PETS. This is vital. Remember to offer solutions as to how you will try and overcome these problems. You might put the words practical, ethical, theoretical and sensitivity in bold type and use them as much as possible. Actually quote from the BSA guidelines (see section 8.1).
* Think about your sample. What method will you choose? Why is it the right choice? Explain exactly how you will carry it out.
* How will you gain access to your sample? Explain how and try to predict potential problems with this.

⁑ Key Idea

Positivism is referred to as scientific sociology that uses quantitative data and seeks generalisation. **Phenomenology** or 'interpretive' sociology looks to produce qualitative data and is small-scale.

∞ Methods Link

You will need a number of 'tools' to become a sociologist and to carry out research: a theory, a method, data, and a research tradition such as positivism or phenomenology.

- Actually show your method. Show your questions and explain why you are asking them; show how they link to your context. Explain why you have chosen the questions you have.
- Try to give a sense of exactly how you will carry out the research, in as much depth as possible.

Things to think about

To explain exactly what you will be doing, think about these issues.

- How will you introduce the aims of the project to your respondents?
- How will you settle and put your respondents at ease?
- If you are recording an interview, how will you explain this to the respondent so they are comfortable?
- Where (what location) will you carry out your research? What are the advantages and disadvantages of this?
- How will you prompt the respondent if you need to? Will you have back-up questions?
- How will you ensure confidentiality?
- How will you treat your respondents with sensitivity?
- How will you try to act and speak when you are with your respondents?

What goes at the end?

At the end of this chapter should be the consideration of a pilot study. Show what you have done, carry it out and then evaluate it. After this, show how you have changed your method accordingly. You can even use the pilot results in the next chapter as additional data. Now you are ready to actually carry out the research.

How should it be written up?

Like the two preceding chapters, think of this chapter as written in the future tense, until it gets to the last part, where you present your pilot. Since we are suggesting that you evaluate the pilot here, this will be the point at which the project changes from future to past tense. This is then continued into the next chapter, the evidence, since you will have already gathered it by the time you come to write the chapter up.

Key points to remember

- Spell out the reasons for every decision.
- Every decision to do something is also a decision not to do something else. Make this clear.
- Do a pilot study at the end and evaluate it.

⁂ Key Ideas

- We tend to refer to those who agree to take part in research as 'respondents' and not as 'subjects' since this suggestions an unequal power relationship.

- Do not forget that feminists reject the use of quantitative research since they feel there are power inequalities between the researcher and the researched. How will you overcome these problems?

⌗ Methods Link

A pilot study is a much shorter version of the study that you try out before the main research in order to test your method. You can make last minute changes and evaluate what you have done.

How do I show my results?

What does this mean?

Once you have carried out your method, you will be left with lots of data. The question is, what do you now do with it? How do you present your results, and what do you do with them? The evidence chapter is where you present and analyse your results.

How you present your results differs according to whether you have produced quantitative or qualitative data, but there are some general pointers to follow first.

- Make sure you label everything, even quotes and graphs. It should be obvious what everything means.
- Do not let the 'facts speak for themselves'. They do not. You will need to work quite hard now to explain to the reader what you think you have found out.
- Make sure you start this evidence chapter by reminding the reader of your aim. This is laborious, but it allows everything to be clear right from the start.
- Also at the start of this chapter, make sure that you make a comment on the nature of your sample. Discuss in some detail what sorts of people responded – what the 'make-up' of the sample was. Did you have any **non-responses**? Was there any **sample attrition**?
- Make sure that you spell out that you have kept to the BSA guidelines in relation to confidentiality and anonymity. Say this at the start. Change people's names, the name of places you went to etc.

What do I do with quantitative data?

If you have produced quantitative data you will need to present this as tables, graphs and charts. Make sure each has a title, and make sure they mean something by always offering an interpretation. Try to relate variables to each other, rather than simply presenting each separate question as a separate graph. Make sure you comment on each graph. What does it mean? Why do you think you got the answers you did? Try to compare the graphs. Make sure you conclude, and use your context as a resource through which to interpret what you have produced. Evaluate your results. Are there reasons why you might have produced the data that you did?

What do I do with qualitative data?

Make sure you quote directly from those you studied, in *exactly* their own words. This will really affect your word count, but you have no choice! Put these in bold or italic to make them stand out. If you need to shorten what people say then put in omission marks (…) to represent a cut.

66 99 Key Definitions

- **Non-response** means, quite literally, potential respondents who do not take part – they 'do not respond'. If too many respondents drop out, then this might affect your data.

- **Sample attrition** refers to the situation of people dropping out during the course of the research. They have taken part in some aspects, but have left before the end. It is a bit annoying when this happens, but remember those BSA guidelines. People have the right to refuse! Make sure you discuss this in the results.

✓ Top Exam Hint

Reflect upon who was in your sample by thinking about the key sociological variables – class, gender, ethnicity, age, location etc. Did you get the people you wanted? How might these variables affect their answers?

Most importantly, comment on the data. Compare what different respondents say to each question; try to look for patterns, confusions, contrasts. Link what they say to what sociologists in your context say. You might like to provide a sample transcript in the appendix, but if you do, do not rely on it as a source of data. If you want it marked, put it in here.

Make sure that you reflect upon why you think people said what they did. Finally, make it obvious who is saying what.

Key points to remember

- Do not just let the facts speak for themselves. They do not.
- Make sure you use your context as a tool to analyse the results with.
- 'Bounce' results off each other: make comparisons and contrasts, look for patterns and contradictions. Do more than simply show them!

⁜ Key Idea

When you decide to choose some comments over others, you are actually being selective and therefore biased. You have no choice since you cannot show everything, but what about the things you leave out? If someone has decided they are relevant to say to you, do you have the right to cut them? You are setting the questions and then choosing what bits of the answers you like the best. This is called the 'imposition problem'. Try and evaluate your research within this concept.

Where and how do I make conclusions?

What does this mean?

In *both* the evidence and in the evaluation chapters you are required to come to some sort of conclusion about the nature of your research. There are, in fact, a number of different issues you will need to conclude now that you have carried out your research, interpreted your data and reflected upon the experience.

What different conclusions are there?

With hindsight, now it is all over, you need to decide

- whether your method was the most appropriate choice
- whether your data was the most appropriate choice
- whether your theory was the most appropriate choice
- what you think your results mean
- how your results compare with each other
- how your results compare with your context
- what your results mean for your aim
- how successful the research carried out was
- whether the problems outweighed the solutions or vice-versa
- what you would do differently and why
- where you would go next with this
- how you think this research might be of benefit to sociology.

You are going to need to develop an answer for each of these questions although, as you can see, they overlap quite considerably. Some of these should be discussed in the evidence chapter, and some in the evaluation chapter. Some might be appropriate for both, as follows.

◥◣ Methods Link

Try to write in such a way that you are able to show the big difference between what the textbooks say about methods, and what it is like in real life when you try to do research. Show that research is an unpredictable business, full of unexpected problems and difficulties.

How do you conclude in the evidence chapter?

You will need to answer the following in a clear way.

- Was your method the most appropriate choice?
- Was your data the most appropriate choice?
- Was your theory the most appropriate choice?
- What do you think your results mean?
- How do your results compare with each other?
- How do your results compare with your context?
- What do your results mean for your aim?

In a sense, it does not matter what data you find; it is what you think about your method and how well or badly it went that is more important since the point of the project is for you to demonstrate how much you know about methods.

You will need to approach your conclusions with sensitivity and maturity.

- Do not make massive generalisations that you cannot support given the size of your sample.
- Do not gloss over any problems; be honest and reflect upon them.
- Do think about PETS all the way through the process of drawing conclusions.
- Do try to think about how the data you produced is selective. You have asked certain things and got what you were looking for. This is called the imposition problem and you might like to reflect upon this.
- Do think about the validity, reliability and representativeness of your research.
- Do not ignore your context. Use it to make sense of what you have found. Compare your results with your context.

How do you conclude in the evaluation chapter?

You will need to answer the following in a clear way.

- How successful was the research carried out?
- Did the problems outweigh the solutions or vice-versa?
- What would you do differently and why?
- Where would you go next with this?
- How do you think this research might be of benefit to sociology?
- Do you have recommendations for further research?

The point of this chapter is to pull it all together and then to push it all forward, into the future. Try to think about what happens next. What would you do differently? How might your results be used now that you have them? Reflect upon the experience of trying to be a sociologist. How did it make you feel? How did others respond to you? Did they take you seriously? Do not forget to record these feelings in your research diary at the time.

Key points to remember

- Think about the different sorts of issues you will need to draw a conclusion about.
- Do not forget that concluding comments appear both in the evidence and evaluation chapters.
- Try to be reflective and self-critical at all times for those important evaluation marks.

What goes in the evaluation chapter?

What does this mean?

The purpose of the evaluation chapter, the last section of your project, is to take the findings of the previous chapter and to think about the success of the research as a whole. What are your conclusions? What did you find? What does it mean? Are there any problems with what you found? Could it have been done any differently?

What do you need to include?

You should start this final chapter by once more reminding the reader of your original aims and also, now that you have written the evidence chapter, of what you think you have found and what you think it means. Do this very briefly, but make sure that you do it so that everything is obvious and the chapter clearly flows from the previous one.

Since this is the last chapter of the project, it is time to take stock, to assess how you felt the research went and what problems really got in the way. The worst evaluation you could write would simply gloss over problems and just say that it went well. This is totally unrealistic. Just think of it like this. The examiners know you will have problems and will have made mistakes; they understand that research is an unpredictable and complicated business, so show them how this was true for you. They are actually giving you marks for admitting mistakes, as long as these are not too trivial, and as long as you offer solutions.

Coursework Suggestion

You could write this chapter under the headings of the previous chapters. Use these as sub-headings through which to organise your thoughts.

Evaluation of the rationale

• Was your aim reasonable?
• Was your method the right choice?
• Have you found what you wanted to?

Evaluation of the context

• Was your theory the right choice?
• Does your data agree with your theory, or might you need to reject what you previously thought?
• Did you find something similar to the ideas in your context or different? Why do you think this is?

Evaluation of the methodology

• Did the strengths outweigh the weaknesses or was it the other way around?
• Was it the right choice of method?
• Did the sampling work as it was intended to?
• Were the problems you predicted actually present, or were there unforeseen problems that occurred?
• Were you able to keep to the solutions you predicted in the first place?
• What went well?

Evaluation of the evidence

- Is your data valid? How can you tell?
- Is your data reliable? How can you tell?
- Is your data representative? How can you tell?
- Are there problems interpreting what the data might mean?
- Are your results the product of problems with the method? How?

Please note that you still need to include evaluation throughout the project, as well as in this chapter. Do not leave the evaluation until the end. You can also use this chapter to remind the reader of problems you predicted might come up and how successful or otherwise your solutions were once you actually tried them for real.

Do not forget PETS

For all the problems and difficulties that arise, make sure that you use the PETS distinction that we have talked about before – **practical, ethical, theoretical and sensitivity issues**. Use these words and put them in bold so that they stand out.

You should think about whether or not you were successful in avoiding ethical problems. Make sure you fully discuss this. Do some of the BSA guidelines contradict and conflict with other more practical problems? In fact, many of the PETS problems themselves contradict each other, causing some quite complex issues all of which would need to be evaluated here.

- Might informed consent lead to a Hawthorne effect where respondents do what they think you want them to?
- Respecting confidentiality might mean there are some things you cannot write up in your project.
- Some people might ask you to turn off your tape recorder. What will this do for your data?
- Some questions might be uncomfortable and might lead to sensitivity problems.
- People might not respect you since you are young; they might not take the research seriously.
- You might have an imposition problem since you are going to be setting the questions and therefore getting what you want from people. Consider what you do not ask. Are you just collecting data in a biased way to prove you are right?
- Did you lead people towards certain answers? Did you have interviewer bias?

Drawing a conclusion

Do not forget to finish the project. Say what it felt like to be a researcher (your personal thoughts and reflections); what you would do differently next time; what you will do with the results; and how you think sociology will benefit from what you have found.

Key points to remember

- Evaluate under the headings of the previous chapters.
- Include PETS at every opportunity.
- Draw a clear conclusion by showing that you understand the connections between your study, sociological thought and research methods.

✐ Coursework Suggestion

As we have said before, research is a messy and unpredictable business and the general rule is that what can go wrong probably will go wrong. If you are reading this before carrying out your research do not start to get worried. This is just how it is, so you must reflect this reality in what you comment on in this chapter.

❝❞ Key Definitions

Practical issues: problems with the actual carrying out of the method itself.

Ethical issues: problems with the morality of your research.

Theoretical issues: problems with trying to detach yourself from your views while doing research.

Sensitivity issues: problems with people's emotions and feelings caused by your research.

✳ Key Idea

The British Sociological Association (BSA) says that research must allow respondents:

- to choose freely to be involved
- to not be harmed or upset in any way
- to have their privacy respected
- to understand what they are volunteering for
- to understand they can say 'no' at any time
- to understand what the point of the research is.

How do I make my chapters link together?

Try to find the simplest, shortest and clearest way to explain what you are doing, in as ordinary a language as possible. You will need the sociological depth, but try also to be as clear as possible.

⊙⊙ Methods Link

Make sure that you always evaluate your choice of method. Think about PETS, and about validity, reliability and representativeness. Discuss these issues throughout the project as a whole.

What does this mean?

Since you might be writing each chapter at a different time, coursework sometimes has a habit of becoming quite disjointed. It feels as if you have produced separate broken-up chapters which are not part of a unified whole. There are some simple tricks you can follow to make sure that it all links and flows together.

What tricks are there?

- State your aim clearly at the start of the rationale.
- Go back to your aim at both the start and the end of the context; make sure that this means your rationale and context chapters link together.
- Refer to your aim at the start of each chapter. This enables the reader to see how the aim of your project links to each of the sections you are producing.
- Put the PETS words in bold or italic throughout – practical, ethical, theoretical and sensitivity. Over the chapters, this will build up as a theme that will stand out to the reader. PETS will need to go in every chapter expect possibly the context. Even the rationale can refer to the major PETS problems that the project will face and need to overcome.
- Put all quotes in bold or italic to make a common way of presenting information.
- Think about what key ideas or concepts your project is trying to test. Are there particular sociological words that really link to your project or ideas that are central to your aims or the context? Make sure that this stands out in some way.
- Refer back to your context in both the methodology and the evidence chapters. In the methodology chapter, try to show how what you ask is related to the context. Use your methodology to test the ideas that appear in your context. Use the context as a background for your methods. Go back to your context in the evidence chapter – what have you found and how does it link to your context? What have you found and what did they find? Do you agree or disagree and why might this be the case?
- Choose a theory through which to approach the project and then use it now and again as a theme. Mention it briefly in the rationale. Go into depth in the context and explain why it is the most appropriate choice. Refer back to your theory in the methodology and explain why your choice of data is appropriate for the theory you are following. Finally, actually use your theory to interpret your results in the evidence chapter. What would your theory make or think about the results that you have produced? Use it to tell you what it might all mean.
- Make sure that your conclusion to your research (once you have interpreted and evaluated your data) is both at the end of the evidence

chapter and again at the start of the evaluation chapter. This is important for how the project is marked.

- Write your evaluation chapter under the side-headings of the previous chapters of the project in order to make it all link together.
- Go back to PETS in the evaluation chapter; show what did and did not work, what you solved and what you did not end up being able to solve. Be honest but also reflective and self-critical.
- Evaluate your project in every chapter. Think of your project as an exercise in problem-solving. What are you trying to do, and how? What are the problems and difficulties that might get in the way? What are you going to do about them? If you write like this, then it will tie the project together since it will be full of self-reflection and criticism.

Key points to remember

- Use PETS all the way through.
- Try to see your project as an exercise in problem-solving.
- Use your aim all the way through the project as a way of being relevant and clear, and bringing it all together.

8.13 Pushing your grades up higher

In this section we will simply summarise the key points from this chapter. Follow the advice this book gives you and make sure you use this as a checklist. This information is also available on the CD-ROM to be printed off. Use it as a checklist and keep it in your folder. Tick off each piece of advice once you feel you have successfully completed it.

- Follow, and show that you are following, the British Sociology Association's (BSA) ethical guidelines for research practice.

- Make sure you get the rationale to a reasonable standard before you do anything else with your coursework. Until your aim is clear, there is no point trying to go any further.

- Do not forget that every method has problems – you will need to think about these in advance of your actual choice to make sure it is still the most suitable choice. Think about PETS – practical issues, ethical issues, theoretical issues and sensitivity issues. How do these relate to your choice of method?

- The Surrey University website has some really useful articles about doing research and using methods that you might find helpful. The website can be found at www.heinemann.co.uk/hotlinks and you will need to look at the sociology homepage to find *Social Research Updates*.

- You will always need to think and write about the key methodological issues of reliability, representativeness and validity.

- Show your thinking and problem-solving when you write up your method choice in your methodology chapter.

- Always refer back to your aim at every opportunity; show that everything is relevant to the main focus of what you are trying to do.

- Make it look professional and check your punctuation, spelling and grammar.

- Make sure you present your findings clearly, follow the advice given.

- Make sure everything is fully referenced and footnoted.

- Be very clear about your aim. State it as clearly as you can and as early as you can in the opening chapter. Try to really find the easiest description of what you are doing and then make it harder and more complex.

- Try the National Statistics website at www.heinemann.co.uk/hotlinks. It is full of official statistics, organised under topics. You are sure to find something interesting here.

- Try the *Guardian* website www.heinemann.co.uk/hotlinks. There will be many searchable detailed articles, and the site organises news stories from *The Guardian* around topics and ongoing debates.

- Do not forget those sociological variables – class, gender, ethnicity, age, location, globalisation etc.

- Make sure you define all key terms as clearly as possible. This process is known as 'operationalisation'.

- Make sure it is obvious what you will be doing and how.

- Did the strengths outweigh the weaknesses or the other way around?

- Research is a messy and unpredictable business and the general rule it that what can go wrong, will go wrong. But, don't worry. You should reflect this reality in what you comment on in the evaluation chapter.

Frequently asked questions

Q. How do I decide on what to do?

A. This is the most difficult part of the project. Once you have the idea, then you can really make a start but until you do it is very difficult to know where the inspiration might come from. Think about what you would find the most interesting. Do not do something because it is the first thing you have thought of. You will be working on your coursework on and off for quite a few months so it must be able to keep you interested and motivated. Look at textbooks and think about the sorts of things that sociologists do. Make sure your aim is simple and clear – do not take on too much.

Q. How should my coursework be presented?

A. Word-process everything since you will probably re-draft your work a number of times, it is a false economy to do anything else. Read through your work when it is finished to make sure it reads as one document. Make sure that all sources are fully referenced in a bibliography and you might also use footnotes. Do not use bulky folders, just put it in a simple plastic wallet and treasury tag it all together. Put your name on each piece of paper as a header or footer and follow the five sections provided by the exam board. Include a contents page, a bibliography and your research diary. Do not overdo it on the appendix if you have one.

Q. What should go in the appendix?

A. Concentrate on samples of things, but do not overdo it as you won't be marked on your appendix. You might like to include a sample questionnaire or an interview schedule. Perhaps you could transcribe part of an interview, but do not include every single one. You may like to include a video or a tape if it is relevant.

Chapter 9

A2 examination skills

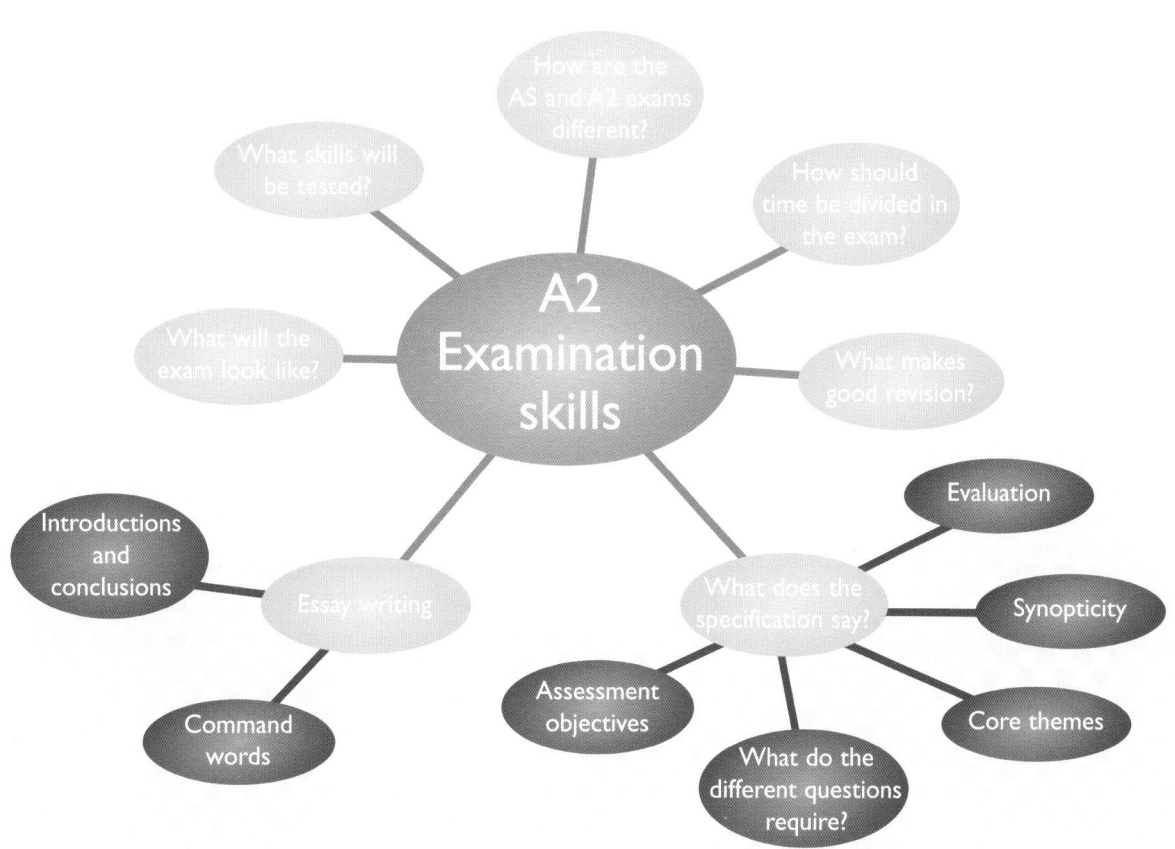

 CD-ROM

9.1 Key issues in developing good exam skills. What will the exam look like?

What does this mean?

It is important to know the sort of examination you are working towards. You already have an idea of what sociology exams look like, since you have already taken AS exam papers. Let us remind ourselves what the AS exam consists of.

- One 2-mark question: define a key term
- One 4-mark question: identify two things
- One 6-mark question: make a list of three things
- One 8-mark question: identify and explain two things
- Two 20-mark extended questions: (e) primarily testing knowledge, and (f) primarily testing evaluation skills.

The A2 examination is different. It is one hour and 30 minutes long. It has one source item and only three questions.

- One 8-mark question: identify two things
- One 12-mark question: discuss some aspects of an issue
- One 40-mark question: an essay question.

While the marks for the total paper also add up to 60, as you can see, what is required of you is very different this time around.

How different is the A2 examination?

Clearly, the questions are asking you to produce more-detailed pieces of writing, that is more-extended discussions of ideas and concepts, but you are still basically manipulating the same elements or ingredients as before. You still have:

- theory
- key words
- named examples
- evaluation.

The ingredients of sociology remain the same, but you are now required to do different, or at least more-detailed, things with them. You have, after all, had an extra year by the end of the course with which to become accustomed to using them. You are now being asked to:

- write more
- produce more depth
- show more evaluation
- show more connections between ideas and issues.

✓ Top Exam Hints

- Use these four ingredients as a simple way to plan essay answers under timed conditions: theory, key words, named examples, evaluation.

- Use these ingredients (theory, key words, named examples, evaluation) as a checklist through which to evaluate your own answers. Re-read your work and try to see how much of each ingredient you use and how evenly spaced throughout your answers they are.

- You can also use these ingredients as a way to plan your essay answers. Divide up a piece of A4 paper into four boxes – one for each of the ingredients. Make a list of the ideas that you will need to use to answer the question and then number them. This is a very simple yet effective way to plan an essay.

What tricks are there to writing a good answer?

You are expected to produce a more-detailed response. This is not actually the same thing, though, as simply writing more words, although in the case of the 40-mark essay question you will need to do this as well. You are actually being asked to consider things more fully; to show a deeper insight, a more-rounded understanding. You should not just compare theories with each other, but go further and try to see how and why theories say what they do.

Some of the following ideas might help you to make a more detailed answer.

1. Try to think about the underpinning debates that most theories battle over:
   - macro/micro
   - freewill/determinism
   - feminism/malestream
   - consensus/conflict.
2. Try to show that you can link theories to the political ideologies and values that underpin them. Show the biases at work in the views they have of society.
3. There is usually a hidden methods issue behind most sociological questions. For example, this might be an issue of how we might measure or define something. Try to spell this out in your writing.
4. Try to locate the theoretical ideas in the time period that they come from. What theories propose are a reflection of when they were written and what society was like at that time. It may very well be different now. If you think this, then say it. Be confident enough to say that you think something is out-of-date, as long as you say why.
5. Make a distinction between social problems and sociological problems.

As you can see, A2 answers are about depth. They are about looking at things in more detail and showing more understanding and sensitivity.

Key points to remember

- The A2 exam asks you to use the same basic ingredients of sociology as the AS exam.
- The A2 course requires you to look at issues in more depth.
- The A2 course asks you to be more sensitive to the underpinning reasons behind why theories say what they do, rather than simply learn them off by heart at a surface level.

✓ Top Exam Hint

A really important way to make sure you produce a good exam answer is to make sure that you plan your time in the exam, and that you also plan your answers. On section 9.3 of this book, you will find some advice on how to do this.

Writing a good exam answer is like being a juggler, you need to keep lots of ideas and concepts going all at the same time.

What skills are needed for the A2 course?

What does this mean?

When you learn sociology, as with all other subjects, you are not just learning a body of knowledge, but you are practising what to do with it. The exam asks you not only to remember things, but also to be able to do things with the knowledge you remember in different ways. To truly show and prove that you understand something you need to be able to manipulate it – to do something with it.

Therefore the AS exam is different from the A2 exam in terms of *skills*. A skill is a practised ability; you are able to show the degree of ease with which you can do the required task. In A2 sociology, you are not just required to know about sociological ideas, you are also being asked to show the ease with which you can do things with the ideas you know.

What skills are important?

The AQA sociology specification divides up skills into two main areas:

- Assessment Objective 1 (AO1) – the skills of knowledge and understanding
- Assessment Objective 2 (AO2) – the skills of identification, analysis, interpretation and evaluation.

In AS, the emphasis was more upon AO1, but in A2, you will need to have a much more developed sense of AO2. As a quick example, in the examinations, the 40-mark essay question will be marked equally for these skills. This shows you that evaluation is much more important this year than last.

What is knowledge and understanding?

The AQA specification says that the skill of knowledge and understanding can be seen as three related elements.

- **The nature of sociological thought**: how we use ideas to think about society; theories, macro- and micro-perspectives; how values might affect sociological thinking; looking at order and control and power; looking at how sociological ideas might affect and influence social policy.
- **Knowledge and understanding of methods**: how sociologists create data; the strengths and weaknesses of their methods of data collection; problems in carrying out research etc.
- There are important themes that run throughout all sociological thinking which students need to both know and understand – power, control, socialisation, identity, culture, inequality etc. These are important since they are the 'tools' that sociologists use to think about the world they are studying.

Like every other skill, you have to train to do well in sociology. You need to practise the action you are trying to perfect so that it can then actually become a skill. A skill is simply something that you can demonstrate with some ease. You are trying to pass exams by showing what you know, so get used to manipulating the ingredients of sociology as much as possible.

✓ Top Exam Hint

It is really important that you familiarise yourself with what the exam paper will actually look like. Sometimes just the look of an exam paper can put people off, so know exactly what you can expect before you go into that exam hall. Ask your teacher for a copy of an exam from last year. Make sure it makes sense.

What are identification, analysis, interpretation and evaluation?

These skills, arguably, are harder than those of knowledge and understanding, and in some senses they are much more 'creative' and 'imaginative'; they also probably take longer to get to grips with and to feel comfortable in demonstrating.

Students need to be able to show they can:

- take ideas, theories and pieces of data/sources and show what they mean, and relate other sociological ideas to them
- discuss the strengths and weaknesses of ideas, theories, and research
- organise evidence in such a way as to make an argument
- understand the role of values and bias in the arguments of others
- use theories and concepts to understand different topics and different issues.

As you can see, these skills are very *active*; they are about you being able to use sociological ideas in various ways.

What other important elements make up A2 sociology?

You will need to get used to being much more free thinking this year. You should be able to see the connections and interrelationships between the ideas from one topic and another, and see the connections between aspects of society. Sociology has always been like this – there have always been lots of connections between the ideas and the topics, but at A2 sociology you will actually be tested on this. This is called **synopticity**.

There are also some very important 'integral elements' in the whole of your sociology course, which must be a foundation for everything that you do. These are theories, methods, key concepts and the connections between topic areas using these. As you know, sociology has a number of ingredients and you are being assessed on the ease with which you can show your understanding of them, their connections and how you can manipulate them into an exam question answer.

Finally, the AQA specification identifies 'core themes'. These will underpin all that you do. They are the things that make sociologists see society how they do. The core themes are the ideas of *socialisation, culture and identity*, and the ideas of *differentiation, power and stratification*. These exist everywhere in all sociology – in every theory, every case study and every topic.

Key points to remember

- There is more to 'doing sociology' than just remembering and repeating things.
- Evaluation is a really important skill at A2.
- You must make sure you understand what the A2 exam requires of you to be able to demonstrate that you can manipulate sociological ideas.

● **Synoptic Link**

Use the terms that the exam board say are 'themes' in order to be synoptic. These themes or 'synoptic tools' include socialisation, culture, identity and power, inequality, stratification, differentiation. Try to see how they underpin every topic, both at AS and at A2.

How should I divide up my time in the exam?

✓ Top Exam Hints

- Try getting past exam papers from your teacher and practise this advice over and over again.

- Answering the question directly is really important. It does not matter how good you are at the other skills listed. If you cannot give the examiners what they want, you will not do yourself justice. A key factor in providing good examination answers is to think about the time on offer, and what you should and should not be doing during it.

- Use the four ingredients of sociology in order to plan your essay questions. Make a list of the theories, the studies and their key words. List them in the order they will appear in your answer. Try to decide which ideas and approaches would agree and disagree.

What does this mean?

It is important to remember that examinations are not really about how much you know, or how much you can remember, but rather, they are more about what you can demonstrate. They are about what you can get out of your head and onto that exam paper, as long as it is relevant. You must always actually directly address and answer the question set.

You will be required to demonstrate a number of things:

- how much you know
- how much you understand
- how you can interpret exam questions
- how you can apply your knowledge
- how you can evaluate
- how you can directly answer the questions set.

What should you do at the start of the exam?

During the first ten minutes of the examination, spend the time thinking. Read the paper. You must not simply rush into the exam, turn over the paper and start writing without fully considering the questions in front of you. Spend time now, to save time later on.

1. *Do not start writing straight away!* This is hard, especially when you see lots of others people around you in the hall doing just this. Be brave – you have a plan! When you do start putting pen to paper it will be to plan first.
2. *Do have a watch in front of you.* Again, this is an obvious piece of advice, but an absolutely essential one! Make sure you know how long you have and how long to spend on each question. Look at your time. Do not assume that your watch and the exam hall clock will say exactly the same time.
3. *Do read the questions.* Read all of them, and more than once. Highlight the key words of the question. Think about the command words of the title; what is it actually asking you to do? Look at the key words in the titles; which words will need defining in your answer? What theories would be associated with the words? What other issues link in?
4. *Now check the items on the paper.* Read them two or three times. Get a pen and highlight key words. Look at the author and the date, if it is provided. What does this tell you? While you are reading the items, make some notes on the item at the side. What does it mean? What key words come to mind? Do you know of any studies that might agree or disagree with the item? What would theories say?
5. *Make a choice of essay question.* You cannot do this on the Unit 6 exam because there is no choice, but you can for Unit 4. Consider both the questions. Do not assume you know what they mean and fall into the trap of writing what you *think* you are being asked, rather than what you are *actually* being asked.

6. *Now start brainstorming*. Start by remembering the key sociological variables: class, gender, age, culture, identity, location, ethnicity, and globalisation. How might these help in your answers? What about the synoptic tools (see section 5.4). How can they be applied? Think about the studies you have learned.
7. *Finally think about the introduction and the conclusion*. Think about the formula for writing good introductions and conclusions (see section 9.6). Start to think about what the question is asking you, and what your approach will be to tackle it.

Yes, all this can be achieved in ten minutes but, like anything else when it comes to exams, you must make sure that you practice doing it a few times before you actually have to do it for real.

What about the rest of the time?

The exam is one hour and 30 minutes long, so you now have one hour and 20 minutes left. The exam is worth 60 marks as usual, and you have three questions: one 8-mark, one 12-mark and one 40-mark question.

Let's work backwards:

- you will need five minutes at the end to read through what you have produced
- you will need to spend about 55 minutes on the actual essay question — so five minutes planning the answer in a little bit more depth than you did at the beginning of the exam and 50 minutes to write it
- that leaves 20 minutes
- since the 8- and 12-mark questions add up to 20 marks, that is roughly a minute per mark – just like the shorter questions on the AS exam last year.

As you can see, you do have time but make sure you use it wisely.

How can I best plan my answers?

- Use the four ingredients of sociology (section 9.1) as a way to plan your essay answers. Divide up a piece of A4 paper into four boxes, one for each of the ingredients. Make a list of the ideas that you will need to use to answer the question and then number them. This is a very simple yet effective way to plan.
- Another thing you can try while writing homework or class essays is to use your revision cards as a plan. Put all the theories and case studies onto cards and then sort them into those that are relevant for the essay title you are writing. Simply arrange them on the table in the order you think flows best, and then you can start writing. Simple!

Key points to remember

- Do not start writing straight away.
- Make sure you plan.
- Make sure you think about what the questions are asking you to do.

✓ Top Exam Hint

Do not forget that the sociology 40-mark essay questions are always a debate; there are always at least two sides to the question, sometimes even more than that. As part of your planning time, try to brainstorm the different possible interpretations the question might have for a truly detailed and wide-ranging answer.

9.4 | How do I write good essays?

✓ Top Exam Hint

Your job when writing an essay is to answer the question and to address the question all the way through. Everything you write must lead eventually to the answer you provide and it must be clear that it is coming. Make sure you directly show the relevance of all that you write by using the command and key words from the title in your answer.

What does this mean?

The purpose of an essay-style question is to allow you to enter into an extended discussion of what you have learned in your two years of sociology. There are some important elements to writing good essays:

- being able to understand sociological ideas
- being able to describe sociological ideas in an accessible fashion
- being able to manipulate sociological ideas together in order to form an answer to a specific question
- being able to structure your answer in a clear and logical way
- being able to communicate effectively in writing.

A good essay must provide an answer to the question set. The answer should take all the relevant sociological elements and put them together in such a way that a logical and sensible answer emerges. You are showing the reader that you have understood the point of the question and what sociologists would think about the issue in as clear a fashion as possible.

What are command words?

All essay questions and, in fact, all exam questions of any sort, are made up of two important elements.

- **Key sociological words**: these are important sociological ideas that will need to be defined in the introduction and then used throughout the answer to demonstrate your relevance in answering and addressing the question set.
- **Essay command words**: these are the words in the title that tell you what sort of essay is required from you; they tell you what the point of the essay is.

Command words do different things, and the point of writing an essay is that you give the reader what the question asks you to give them.

Consider, define, describe, examine, outline, state: these terms indicate that you are required to enter into descriptions of ideas and concepts. You are to show good knowledge and understanding. These terms are often used in short-answer questions that require a quick, short, to-the-point answer.

Analyse, evaluate, describe, assess, to what extent: some terms indicate that you are being asked to do more than simply show knowledge; rather, you are being asked to do things with the knowledge you have, to manipulate it in some way. These terms show that essays are asking you to sum-up and weigh-up evidence for different view points.

Discuss, compare/contrast, critically consider: some terms are associated with both being asked to describe ideas and, at the same time, being asked to evaluate the ideas you are using.

It is important that you do what is being asked of you. You should think about what the essay question (or whatever exam question it might be) is actually asking from you.

What makes a good answer?

Good answers to essay questions should follow this checklist.

- Does the introduction answer the question set and use the key words from the title?
- Does the main body start in a logical place?
- Does the main body address and answer the question set?
- Does the main body use the command words and the key words from the title?
- Is the order logical?
- Does the answer flow?
- Are key terms used for depth throughout the answer?
- Are key terms defined within the flow of the writing?
- Is the content up-to-date and relevant to the question set? Is it clear that your writing answers the question?
- Does evaluation run all the way throughout the answer?
- Are enough studies and theories used for depth?
- Does the conclusion sum-up the argument and debate and does it answer the question set?
- Are spelling, punctuation and grammar satisfactory?
- Does the essay draw out synoptic links (for Unit 6)?

Key points to remember

- Essays must actually answer the question set.
- Exam questions show you what they want from you by the command words they use.
- Essays must follow the checklist above in order to produce a good answer.

✓ **Top Exam Hints**

a Look at an essay of yours (or you could try this with a friend) and go through this checklist. How much of this advice have you included in your essay?

• Get three coloured pens: one for all the key words you use in your essay, one for the evaluation in your answer and one for the times you use the words from the title in your answer. Go through your essay and underline or highlight each time you do these things. What does this tell you about the quality of your answer?

How can I show good evaluation skills?

What does this mean?

By evaluation we often mean criticism. In sociology, we mean something more specific:

- making criticisms
- pointing out that there might be problems in evidence
- showing that there are comparisons between ideas
- showing that there are contrasts between ideas
- saying what is good about an idea
- saying what is useful about an idea
- having an opinion, which we can back up with evidence.

Evaluation is a really important skill, and it is actually very hard. In fact, along with learning about strange new theories, it is having to be evaluative that students often find quite challenging if they are new to sociology. But, do not worry. In time, students actually end up liking evaluation – it is a really important thing to be able to do, and something that few other subjects really focus on. What more could you want than to have the opportunity to actually criticise what you are learning?

Why is evaluation important?

Sociology is marked and assessed according to certain skills, as set out by the examination boards. We collect these skills together, and call them 'Assessment Objectives' (AO). There are two sets of skills, evaluation being very important for the second set:

- Assessment Objective 1: the skills of knowledge and understanding
- Assessment Objective 2: the skills of identification, analysis, interpretation and evaluation.

The first set of skills are the main focus for the AS course, and the second set become more important as you move from AS to A2.

Even if you end up doing the exam and never thinking about sociology again, and even if you forget in time the ideas you were taught, evaluation skills will be really important for the rest of your life.

How can you be evaluative?

It might be useful to identify different types of evaluation that you might like to try. These could act as a checklist that you might use to think about the quality of the answers you are producing.

✓ Top Exam Hints

- In the exam, some questions require you to be more evaluative than others. Questions that ask you to 'assess' are asking you to be evaluative.

- Evaluation will also give you depth and detail in any question that is not simply a short-answer question. If you can show an awareness of why two theories or why two studies disagree, then this is understanding as well as evaluation.

☼ Key Idea

This emphasis upon evaluation is central to what C Wright Mills calls the 'sociological imagination' – the distinctive worldview that sociology gives us.

1. Use theories to criticise other theories.
2. 'Think through the eyes of theories'. Imagine what it would be like to think in a particular way.
3. Make methodological criticisms; attack a study for how it carried out its research.
4. Use 'real life' examples. Argue that an idea or theory might not be true or might be true because an event in the contemporary world provides us with evidence that we can use to access what sociologists are saying.
5. Use historical examples to support or criticise a theory for saying something, where history might agree or show something else has happened.
6. Some named sociologists did research in order to 'prove' or 'disprove' other research; make sure you spell out these links.
7. Use synoptic tools to think about a theory or study: link an idea to class, gender, culture, identity, power etc, and in doing so you can discuss it in more depth, and in interesting ways.
8. Make a note of when the idea, study or theory was invented. If it was a long time ago, this will help you to think about its use today.
9. You could not only say what is bad about an idea, but also what is good about it.
10. You could try to point out political biases and value-judgements behind the theory. Some ideas might be left or right wing, and this might affect how the proponents see society.
11. Another really impressive thing to do is to try and 'assess the contribution' made to sociology by a theory. Try to say what we would miss or lack if the idea had not been invented in the first place.

Key points to remember

- Make sure evaluation runs all the way throughout essay answers. Do not just leave it until the end.
- Make sure that you try to use different types of evaluation – vary it a bit.
- Try to spell out evaluation, do not assume the reader can recognise it. Make it obvious by using signposted phrases (see section 9.7).

✓ **Top Exam Hint**

Use the ways of evaluating. Try them out and see if they work for you. They will take time to master, but will improve your exam answers once you have.

✳ **Key Idea**

As you can see, evaluation is really important for your exam, and also really important if you want to think like a sociologist.

9.6 | How can I write good introductions and conclusions?

What does this mean?

Something that many students find difficult is the beginning and end of their essay answers. This is actually quite a hard skill to master, but it is an important one.

- The introduction is the first thing to write. Where do you start? How can you get over having a blank sheet of paper staring back at you? The introduction is the first thing to be read by the examiner, so it has got to be interesting; you need to make an impact right from the start.
- Since the introduction is first, you will need to explain what your answer is all about – this means that you need to know what you are going to write, before you actually write it. In other words, you will have to plan before you write the introduction (see section 9.3 for information on how to make a plan).
- You will need to address the question all the way through your answer, but you must actually answer the question finally at the end.
- The conclusion has to pull together all the interwoven threads of your essay in a concise, reasoned judgement of the initial question.

What do essays do?

Think about what the purpose of an essay is. Its purpose is to answer a question, but also to take the reader along a journey to the answer at the end. Your job is to be the guide, but to a certain extent you are also the referee between different sides. You must get the reader to the end, but then weigh up the battle and decide on the winner if you can.

In essence you need to do four things when writing an essay:
- say what you are going to write
- write it
- remind the reader what you wrote
- decide on what the answer to the question is.

Are there any tricks to introductions?

In order to get the introductions and conclusions right, there are a number of things you can do. The following structures or formulae will help you write good introductions and conclusions.

For introductions, you must make sure that you do the following:
- Begin with an opening 'seductive sentence or phrase' that awakens the interest of your reader; a sentence that takes the essay title and explains how and why it is an 'important' title for sociology or even for society. You might try to link the title to a current world event or show why the title is sociologically significant. 'Seduce' your reader; show them it is worth reading your answer by giving them a taste of what is to come.

- Re-write the aims of the essay in your own words. You might start this by saying 'the aim of this essay is to …'. Show that you understand the point of the question. You can demonstrate here what you think the different interpretations of the question are.
- Define the key words from the question. Not the command words, but the key sociological words. Show that you understand what the words mean and how they link to the debate in the title. You might also want to think about other key words that link to the title and define these as well. Show your reader what you think the question is about in as clear a way as possible.
- Give a sense of essay order and structure. Say what you will be looking at first, second, third etc. Show what the main disagreement is and say which side you will look at first. You might like to link these 'sides' of the answer to different theories or to different sociologists.
- Raise potential problems or issues that underpin the essay title. Most have these; for example, a problem defining a word or a problem measuring something. Spell these out for evaluation marks at the start of your answers.

Make sure that the introduction sets the scene of the essay. Its purpose is to explain to the reader what you understand to be the point of the question. What do you think you are being asked to do? What are the key sociological issues that are part of the question?

Are there any tricks to conclusions?

For conclusions, you must make sure that you do the following:

1. In order to make it obvious to the reader, you could start the conclusion by saying 'In conclusion …'.
2. Briefly summarise what the general argument is. Remind the reader what they have read, but only as a short sentence or two. Do not repeat too much, and certainly do not make lists.
3. Explain why there might be different sides to the debate you have described. Why are the sociologists disagreeing? What are they disagreeing over exactly?
4. Actually answer the question set. Is the title asking you 'to what extent?', or to 'compare and contrast?' etc.
5. Suggest ways forward. What have sociologists not looked at? Can we combine ideas together?

The point of the conclusion is to do more than just summarise; it should directly comment on the extent to which the question is answerable. Avoid ambiguous statements such as 'the answer will depend on the type of sociologist or theory'. Avoid this; your examiner will have heard it all many times before. Show exactly what the disagreement is, rather than simply say that there is one. Of course the examiner will know that there is a debate, otherwise how could you write the essay in the first place?

Key points to remember

- Plan the essay before you start writing, so you can make sure that the introduction and the conclusion link together.
- Follow the formulae given in this section.
- Practise writing introductions and conclusions as part of your revision.

✓ Top Exam Hints

- Once more the four key ingredients of sociology come in here. Use them in your introductions as a way of getting depth, especially the idea of having to define key words right from the start. The four ingredients are discussed in more detail in section 9.1.

- Try practising only writing the introductions and conclusions to essay answers. Time yourself. You could try to write six introductions and conclusions in a one hour period.

- Many students ignore introductions and conclusions. They go straight into the main body of the essay, and actually disregard answering the question at the end. Another common mistake is that students spend too long on the introduction; they actually introduce the introduction. Go straight into explaining what you think the point of the title means. Be direct, but also be thorough.

∞ Methods Link

Most essay questions have a hidden methods issue or a definitional problem behind the title. For example, a question on power requires us to define and measure what power actually is, but in fact this is not clear, and many sociologists disagree on how to do this. Often sociologists disagree because of their definitions or measurements and this is why there are different sides to a debate. Try to spell this out. This point might be useful in a conclusion as well.

How can I get my essays to flow?

What does this mean?

A good essay is a discussion rather than a list of points. It is important that you can move from point to point in a smooth way. Your essay should have a structure and an order that is not just a random list of unconnected points.

What tricks are there?

Try the following ideas.

- Make sure you always plan your answer (see section 9.3). An effective way to do this is to use the four ingredients of sociology (see section 9.1) and to brainstorm what ideas link to your title. Number the ideas in the order you wish to present them before you start.
- You could always start with the 'for' argument and then do the 'against' and show that this is what you are doing. This is a simple but effective structure for some essays to show an argument.
- You could say 'referring back to the question' as a way to show the reader when you are addressing the question.
- You could start the main body with a paragraph on the theory that agrees the most, and then link this to a relevant study.
- You need to make sure that evaluation runs throughout the answer, not just at the end.
- Use the command words from the title over and over again to link what you do back to the title (see section 9.4).
- Use the key sociological words from the title that you defined at the start of your introduction throughout the answer, in order to link what you do back to the title (see section 9.6).
- You might like to try to spell out comparisons and contrasts between ideas or thinkers in order to connect the different ideas you are using.

What are 'signpost phrases'?

In order to develop and to show the reader that you have good evaluation skills, you might wish to use certain sorts of phrases that allow your answers to show evaluation, sound sophisticated and clearly allow your answers to flow from one point to another. Such signpost phrases might be:

- the relevance of this is …
- this is similar to/different from xxx because …
- the implication of this is ….
- this can be applied to …
- the usefulness of this is …
- this is confirmed by …
- a strength of xxx is …

- the main problem with this is ….
- this can be seen by …
- I disagree because ….
- this assumes that xxx is true, however …
- this makes little sense because …
- this lacks evidence because …
- this does not take into account …
- this is questioned by …

For conclusions (see section 9.6) you might like to use these phrases:

- to sum up …
- having weighed up …
- the balance of the argument suggests that …
- the weight of the evidence suggests that …
- to conclude, …

These phrases will give your answers an important 'gloss'; they will allow you to link your points together rather than simply jumping from point to point. Remember, it must be an ordered discussion rather than simply a list of points.

These phrases will also help your evaluation skills. It is much better to spell out evaluation than to simply **juxtapose**. In other words, it is better to evaluate ideas, rather than simply placing opposite ideas together and leaving it up to the reader to figure out that they are opposite to each other. Spell everything out as much as you can. This is how you get good marks in essays.

Key points to remember

- Do not make lists, but try to make points connect with each other.
- Use the signpost phrases.
- Make sure you plan so you do not forget something and then end up just adding it in when you do think of it later during the writing of the answer.

✓ Top Exam Hint
Think of other phrases that allow your essays to flow from point to point.

● Synoptic Links
- 'Signpost phrases' can also be used to demonstrate good synoptic skills in your writing. You can actually start sentences by saying 'synoptically-speaking …' to really highlight to the reader what you are doing.

- Remember, you do not have to wait until the Unit 6 exam in order to demonstrate your ability to write and think in a synoptic fashion; to make relevant and interesting links between ideas and topics. This is an important sociological skill even if it is not actually being tested in the exam. By doing this you can create a wider answer and can also provide a more original answer to gain your reader's interest.

❝❞ Key Definition
To **juxtapose** means to place two opposites together without commenting on why they are opposites.

How will my essays be assessed?

What does this mean?

In order to produce a good essay answer you need to understand what you are being required to do. You need to understand how you will be assessed and what your examiners are looking for. Then you can give it to them.

What skills are important in essay writing?

As we have discussed elsewhere, the A2 examination is based upon two sets of skills:

- **Assessment Objective 1**: knowledge and understanding
- **Assessment Objective 2**: identification, analysis, interpretation and evaluation.

Each of these skills ask different things of you.

- **Knowledge**: What do you know? What ideas have you learned?
- **Understanding**: How much do you understand the ideas you have learned?
- **Evaluation**: Can you **assess** the ideas you have learned?
- **Analysis**: Can you pull the ideas you have learned apart? Can you question them?
- **Interpretation**: Can you take what you have learned and apply it in different ways to other ideas and to questions set?
- **Identification**: Can you think about what questions mean, and respond accordingly?

How will I be assessed?

Your essay answers will be marked twice – once for the skills of knowledge and understanding, and once for the skills of evaluation, analysis, interpretation and identification. You will have two different marks out of 20 each for these, giving you a total mark out of 40. Unlike the AS year, as you can see, evaluation is as important as knowledge at A2 level.

The AQA examination board marks your essays in a series of 'bands' or 'grade descriptors' that describe, in a qualitative fashion, what the marks might actually mean about the quality of the answers you are producing. These are as follows:

For the AO1 skills: (knowledge and understanding):

- 0 = no evidence of the particular skill in question
- 1–5 = limited skills; too much commonsense and not enough sociology; too much description
- 6–10 = limited skills; some basic relevance; lack of depth and of examples; too few points explored

Do not try to guess what the exam questions might be or what the examiners want. Concentrate on reading the questions and really understanding what they are actually asking you to do. Take your time.

✓ Top Exam Hint

While answering exam questions, it is important to think what the skills you are being asked to display might be. Think about the command words (see section 9.4) being used. What does the question want from you?

66 99 Key Definition

To **assess** means to weigh up; to consider all the views on and interpretations of something.

- 11–15 = reasonably good levels of depth, detail and knowledge shown; largely relevant; some good use of key terms and most aspects of the question explored
- 16–20 = a wide answer; clear and detailed; lots of ideas, discussed in a relevant fashion; few if any mistakes.

For the AO2 skills (evaluation, analysis, interpretation, identification):

- 0 = no evidence of the particular skill in question
- 1–5 = limited skills; too much commonsense and not enough sociology
- 6–10 = limited skills; some basic evaluation, but largely simple juxtaposition; does not flow through the whole answer
- 11–15 = broad skills; balanced and quite sensitive; good conclusion
- 16–20 = detailed answer; the title is addressed throughout; strong conclusion; sophisticated evaluation.

Key points to remember

- Make sure you understand what the marks are given for so you can give the examiners what they want from you.
- Make sure you understand what the different skills mean, since you will be asked to demonstrate them.
- Make sure you understand what makes a good exam answer, so you can provide it.

✳ Key Idea

Philosopher Nietzsche referred to philosophy as the 'art of mistrust' and the same can be said for sociology. Evaluation is important to how sociologists think about society, and what they make of the ideas of other sociologists. Evaluation is an important skill for you to show in your exam. You will be assessed on it.

✓ Top Exam Hint

How do you demonstrate, as it says here for 16–20 marks, 'sophisticated evaluation'? One simple way to do this is to use the key signpost phrases as described in this book in section 9.7. Another way is to use evidence to support the points you make in your answer.

What makes good revision?

What does this mean?

Many students take revision for granted. It is assumed that students know what to do when they are 'revising' and that they know how to do it. Perhaps this is not the case. We should think hard about revision; what is the purpose of it and what are the best ways of going about it?

What makes good revision?

Learning is not the same for everyone. We might learn in different ways, and we may need to revise in different ways too. Each of us will find some ways of working and studying easier than others, but we should experiment and try them all out to see what works best.

Think about how you learn best.

- Do you find it easier to remember when you write things down?
- Do you need to colour-code revision notes to help you think about them?
- Do you need to shorten your notes? Are there just too many to learn without doing so?
- Do you need to write things out from your head, not just read them?

We are all different learners, and it is important to remember this. You must find out what works for you; this might be different from what works for other people. But you must also make sure you experiment with different types and techniques of revision. Otherwise how will you really know which method actually suits you the best? Despite the fact that we are all different, there are some basics that we can use as a starting point in order to think about good revision.

Some things that you should do:

- make sure that you engage in what is called 'active' revision, which is about writing and doing (not passive reading, which really is not the most effective way to revise)
- make sure that you have all the notes from your folder shortened, perhaps onto index cards ready to revise from
- think about evaluation skills while you revise; practise making lists of how theories and thinkers would criticise each other
- practise past exam papers obtained from your teachers
- try to revise by manipulating the four key ingredients of sociology (see section 9.1); try to link theories to words to studies etc.

Some things you should not do:

- do not simply rely upon reading as revision; it is not effective since it is too passive

- do not leave sorting out and shortening down your notes until the end of the course; making notes is not really revision; do not fool yourself into thinking that it is
- do not see revision as a process of putting things into your head; see it as a process of taking things out of your head and putting them onto paper. This is after all what you are doing in the exam, so it is what you should be doing in the revision also!

Conclusion

Think about learning to drive a car. You do not sit in your kitchen and look out of the window at the car. You get in the car, and you actually drive; you practise the thing you are actually being tested on. It should be the same in exams. Practise past papers; practise writing things from memory.

Experiment with all these ideas and try to find what works best. Make sure you do this early on in your course, especially for mock or trial exams. Do not leave revision until the final examination; it might be too late then for you to experiment with different revision methods. You do not want to be experimenting with revision before the real exam and you should already know what works best for you.

Key points to remember

- Make sure your revision is 'active'.
- Make sure you practise past essay questions.
- Make sure you find what works for you!

✓ **Top Exam Hint**

Try writing descriptions of theories using the key words for depth. Then try adding studies and linking them to other studies. This will help you to practise the detailed writing skills needed in some parts of the exam.

Frequently asked questions

Q. Why is evaluation so important this year?

A. Evaluation is important for four reasons: it is a higher-weighted skill in the exams you will be sitting than at AS level; it is an important ingredient in the writing of a quality essay answer; it is vital for a detailed piece of coursework; and finally, it is an essential part of being synoptic.

Q. What does a good essay look like?

A. A good essay is really about how you manipulate the four key ingredients of sociology that we have spent so much of this book demonstrating to you. A good essay should start by clearly showing the reader that you understand the point of the question and that you can clearly define the key terms in the question itself. You should then start with the theory most associated with the 'for' side of the answer, and write about the theory in depth using the key words. This enables you to show knowledge and understanding, but it is vital that you spend some time relating this back to the topic or issue of the question itself in order that it is relevant. You must provide studies or named examples as evidence of this theoretical point of view, and then proceed to show comparisons and contrasts with other theories on the same issue. Insure that you use the key words at all times for depth. Finally, summarise and try to solve the issue – actually answer the question, whatever it was. In the exam, you will have about 55 minutes to do all this, and you will need to produce about three to four sides of A4 writing to get a top grade.

Q. How can I revise essay technique?

A. There are a number of different things you can do. You can brainstorm essay questions, five to ten minutes per title, as if you were in the actual exam. Use the four ingredients of sociology in order to think about what content should go in each answer. You can also practise simply writing introductions and conclusions for each essay title, following the formula presented in this chapter. Finally, make sure you practise timed essay questions. Nothing can substitute for practice according to the timed conditions of the real thing.

Bibliography

Abbott, D. (1998) *Culture and Identity*, London: Hodder and Stoughton.

Abbott, P. and Wallace, C. (1990) *An Introduction to Sociology, Feminist Perspectives*, London: Routledge.

Abercrombie, N., Hill, S. and Turner, B. (1980) *The Dominant Ideology Thesis*, London: Allen and Unwin.

Alberto, M (1989) *Nomads of the Present: Social Movements and Individual Needs in Contemporary Society*, London: Hutchinson Radius .

Allen, H. (1987) *Justice Unbalanced: Gender, Psychiatry and Judicial Decisions*, Milton Keynes: Open University Press.

Althusser, L. (1971) *Lenin and Philosophy and Other Essays*, London: New Left Books.

Althusser, L. (1971) 'Ideology and Ideological State Apparatuses' in *Lenin and Philosophy and Other Essays*, London: New Left Books.

Anderson, P (1976) 'The Antimonies of Antonio Gramsci', *New Left Review*, 100.

Annual Report of the Registrar-General (1911) London: HMSO.

Arber, S. and Ginn, J. (1991) *Gender and Later Life*, London: Sage.

Atkinson, J. M. (1978) *Discovering Suicide – Studies in the Social Organization of Sudden Death*, London: Macmillan.

Bagguley, P. (1995) 'Protest, Poverty and Power: a Case Study of the Anti-poll Tax Movement in Leeds' in *Sociological Review*, 43. 4.

Baldwin, J. and Bottoms, A.E., (1976) *The Urban Criminal*, London: Tavistock.

Barker,E.(1984) *The Making of a Moonie: Choice or Brainwashing*, Oxford: Blackwell.

Barker, E. (1995) *New Religious Movements: A Practical Introduction*, London: HMSO.

Baudrillard, J. (1993) *Simulations*, New York, Semiotexte.

Bauman, Z. (1989) *Modernity and the Holocaust*, Cambridge: Polity Press.

Bauman, Z. (1991) *Modernity and Ambivalence*, Cambridge: Polity Press.

Bauman, Z. (1992) *Intimations of Postmodernity*, London: Routledge.

Bauman, Z. (1992) *Mortality, Immortality and Other Life Strategies*, Cambridge: Polity Press.

Bauman, Z. (1993) *Postmodem Ethics*, Oxford: Blackwell

Bauman, Z. (1995) *Life in Fragments*, Oxford: Blackwell

Bauman, Z. (1997) *Postmodemity and Its Discontents*, Cambridge: Polity Press.

Bauman, Z. (1998) *Globalisation*, Cambridge: Polity Press.

Bauman, Z. (1998) *Work, Consumerism and the New Poor*, Buckingham: Open University Press.

Bauman, Z. (1989) *Legislators and Interpreters*, Cambridge: Polity Press.

Beck, U. (1992) *Risk Society*, London: Sage.

Becker, H. (1963) *Outsiders*, New York: Free Press.

Bell, D. (1973) *The Coming of Post-Industrial Society*, New York: Basic Books.

Bellah, R. (1966) *Civil Religion in America*, NewYork: Daedalus.

Bellah, R. (1970) *Beyond Belief*, New York: Harper Row.

Bellah, R. (1965) 'Religious Evolution' in Lessa, W. and Voight, E. *Reader in Comparitive Religion: An Anthropological Approach*. New York: Harper Row

Bellah, R. (1970) *Beyond Belief*, New York: Harper and Row.

Berger, P. and Luckmann, T. (1967) *The Social Construction of Reality*, New York: Doubleday.

Berger, P.L. (1969) *The Social Reality of Religion*, London: Faber and Faber.

Berger, P.L. (1990) *The Sacred Canopy: Elements of a Sociological Theory of Religion*, New York: Anchor Books.

Berger, P.L. and Kellner, H. (1974) *The Homeless Mind: Modernisation and Consciousness*, Harmondsworth: Penguin.

Bernstein, B. (1975) *Class, Codes and Control*, London: Routledge and Kegan Paul.

Best, S. (1997) 'Agency and Structure in the Writings of Anthony Giddens' in *The Social Science Teacher* 26.

Best, S. (1998) 'Zygmunt Bauman: Personal Reflections from the Mainstream' in *Journal of Sociology*.

Bhattacharyya, G., Ison, L., Blair, M., (2003) 'Minority Ethnic Attainment and Participation' in *Education and Training: Department for Education and Skills*, July 2003.

Bilton, T. et al, (2002) *Introduction to Sociology*, London: Palgrave.

Blair, T. (1993) 'Why Crime is a Socialist Issue', *New Statesman*.

Bocock R., (1985) 'Religion in Modern Britain' in Bocock R and Thompson K., [eds] *Religion and Ideology*, Manchester: Manchester University Press.

Bottomore, T. (2002) *The Frankfurt School and its Critics*, London: Routledge & Kegan Paul.

Bourdieu, P. (1986) *Distinction: A Social Critique of the Judgement of Taste*, London: Routledge.

Bowlby, J. (1946) *Forty Four Juvenile Thieves*, London: Tindall and Cox.

Box, S. (1983) *Crime, Power and Mystification*, London: Tavistock.

Bradley, H. (1996) *Fractured Identities: Changing Patterns of Inequality*, Cambridge: Polity Press.

Braverman, H. (1974) *Labor and Monopoly Capital*, New York: Monthly Review Press.

Bruce, S (1999) *Choice and Religion: A Critique of Rational Choice Theory*, Oxford: Oxford University Press.

Bruce, S. (1992) 'The Twilight of the Gods: Religion in Modern Britain' in *Social Studies Review*, November 1992.

Bruce, S. (1995) *Religion in Modern Britain*, Oxford: Oxford University Press

Bruce, S. (1996) *Religion in the Modern World: From Cathedrals to Cults*, Oxford: Oxford University Press.

Butler, C. (1995) 'Religion and Gender: Young Muslim Women in Britain' in p18–22 *Sociology Review* Vol 4, No 3, February 1995.

Campbell, A. (1981) *Girl Delinquents*, Oxford: Blackwell.

Campbell, B. (1996) 'The Dangers of New Labour's Communitarian Ideals' in *Sociological Review*.

Castells, M. (1996) 'The Rise of the Network Society' in *The Information Age: Economy, Society and Culture*, Vol I, Oxford: Blackwell.

Castells, M. (1997) 'The End of Millenium' in *The Information Age: Economy, Society and Culture*, Vol II, Oxford: Blackwell.

Castells, M. (1997) *The Information Age: Economy, Society and Culture*, Oxford: Blackwell.

Castles, S. and Kosack, G. (1973) *Immigrant Workers and Class Structure in Western Europe*, Oxford: Oxford University Press.

Bibliography

Chambliss, W. (1973) 'Vice, Corruption, Bureaucracy and Power' in Chambliss, W. (ed) *Sociology Readings in the Conflict Perspective*, pp353–378, Reading, Massachusetts: Addison-Wesley.

Chambliss, W. (1988) *On the Take: From Petty Crooks to Presidents*, Indianapolis: Indiana University Press.

Chibnall, S. (1977) *Law and Order News*, London: Tavistock.

Ciulla, E. and Nye J.S. (1999) *Democracy.com? Governance in a Networked World*, Hollis New Hampshire: Hollis.

Clarke, J. (1975) 'The Skinheads and the Magical Recovery of Community' in Hall and Jefferson (eds) *Resistance through Rituals: Youth Sub-cultures in Post War Britain*, London: Hutchinson.

Clarke, M. (1990) *Business Crime*, Oxford: Polity Press.

Cloward and Ohlin (1961) *Delinquency and Opportunity*, New York: Free Press.

Cohen, A. K. (1955) *Delinquent Boys*, New York: Free Press.

Cohen, S. (1973) *Folk Devils and Moral Panics*, London: Paladin.

Cohn, N. (1957) *The Pursuit of the Millennium*, London: Secker and Walburg

Coleman, J. and Hoffer, T. (1987) *Public and Private High Schools: the Impact of Communities*, New York: Basic Books.

Comelia, N. (2000) *Internationalism and the State in the Twentieth Century*, New York: Routledge.

Commission for Racial Equality (1998) *Education and Training Factsheet*.

Commission for Racial Equality (1999) *Housing and Homelessness Factsheet*.

Connell, R. (1987) *Gender and Power*, Cambridge: Polity Press.

Crewe, I. (1992) 'Why Did Labour Lose Yet Again?' *Politics Review*, September 1992.

Croall, H. (1992) *White Collar Crime*, Milton Keynes: Open University Press.

Crompton, R. and Jones, G. (1984) *White-collar Proletariat: Deskilling and Gender in the Clerical Labour Process*, London: Macmillan.

Crompton, R. (1998) *Class and Stratification*, Cambridge: Polity Press.

Dahl, R. (1971) *Polyarchy*, Yale, Yale University Press.

Dahl, R. (1998) *On Democracy*, New Haven: Yale University Press.

Davie, G. (1989) 'Religion' in M. Haralambos (ed.) *Developments in Sociology* vol 5, Ormskirk: Causeway Press.

Davis, K. and Moore, W.E. (1967) 'Some Principles of Stratification' in Bendix and Lipset (1967) *Class, Status and Power*, London: Routledge and Kegan Paul.

Davis, M. (1990) *City of Quartz*, London: Verso.

Day, G. and Robbins, D. (1987) 'Activists for Peace: the Social Basis of a Local Peace Movement' in C. Creighton and M. Shaw (eds.) *The Sociology of War and Peace*, London: Macmillan.

Dean, H. and Taylor-Gooby, P. (1992) *Dependency Culture*, Hemel Hempstead: Harvester-Wheatsheaf.

Denscombe, M. (2003) *Sociology Update*, Leicester: Olympus Books UK.

Denver, D. (1994) *Elections and Voting Behaviour in Britain*, 2nd edn, Hemel Hempstead: Harvester Wheatsheaf.

Department of Social Security (DSS) (1997, 2001) 'Households Below Average Incomes: A Statistical Analysis 1978–1994/5', London: The Stationary Office.

Derrida, J. (1991) *A Derrida Reader: Between the Blinds*. Hemel Hempstead: Wheatsheaf.

Diani, M. (1992) 'The Concept of Social Movements'. *Sociological Review*, 40, 1.

Domhoff, G. W. (1967), *Who Rules America?*, Englewood Cliffs, NJ: Prentice Hall.

Douglas, J. (1967) *The Social Meanings of Suicide*, Princeton New Jersey: Princeton University Press.

Douglas, J.W.B. (1964) *The Home and the School*, London: MacGibbon and Kee.

Downes, A. (1957) *An Economic Theory of Democracy*, New York: Harper and Row.

Dunleavy, P. and O'Leary, B. (1987) *Theories of the State: the Politics of Liberal Democracy*, Basingstoke: Macmillan Education

Durkheim (1964) *The Division of Labour*, New York: Free Press. Originally published 1893.

Durkheim (1979) *Suicide: A Study in Sociology*, London: Routledge. Originally published 1897.

Durkheim, E. (1912) (trans1961) *The Elementary Forms of Religious Life*, London: Colliers Books.

Durkheim, E. and Pickering, W. (1994) *Durkheim on Religion*, Atlanta, Georgia: Scholars Press.

Eisenstadt, S. (1956) *From Generation to Generation*, Free Press: Chicago.

Esping-Anderson, G. (1990) *The Three Worlds of Welfare Capitalism*, Cambridge: Polity Press.

Etzioni, A. (1995) *The Spirit of Community*, London: Fontana.

Featherstone, J. and Hepworth, M. (1991) 'The Mask of Aging and the Postmodern Life Course' in M. Featherstone et al. (eds) *The Body: Social Process and Cultural Theory*, London: Sage.

Feyerabend. P. (1993) *Against Method* (Third Edition), London: Verso. Originally published 1975.

Finer, S. (1987) 'State and Nation-building in Europe: the Role of the Military' in S. Finer (1979) *Five Constitutions*, Harmondsworth: Penguin.

Fitzgerald, M. and Hough, M. (2002) 'Policing For London Survey', http://www.policingforlondon.org/

Foucault, M. (1977) *Discipline and Punish: The Birth of the Prison*, New York: Pantheon.

Foucault, M. (1978) *History of Sexuality*, Vol 1, London: Penguin.

Foucault, M. (1982) *This is not a Pipe*, California: University of California Press.

Foucault, M. (1990) *The Order of Things: An Archeology of the Human Sciences*, New York: Routledge.

Gelsthorpe, L. and Louck, N. (1997) *Understanding the Sentencing of Women*, Home Office Research Study 170.

Giddens, A. (1984) *The Constitution of Society*, Cambridge: Polity Press.

Giddens, A. (1974) *New Rules of Sociological Method*, London: Hutchinson.

Giddens, A. (1981) *Social Theory and Modern Sociology*, Cambridge: Polity Press.

Giddens, A. (1985) *The Nation State and Violence*, Cambridge: Polity Press.

Giddens, A. (1990) *The Consequences of Modernity*, Cambridge: Polity Press.

Giddens, A. (1994) *Beyond Right and Left*, Cambridge: Polity Press.

Giddens, A. (1999) 'Runaway World', *The BBC Reith Lectures*, London: BBC Education.

Gill, O. (1977) *Luke Street*, London: Macmillan.

Gillborn, D. (2002) *Education and Institutional Racism*, London: Institute of Education, University of London.

Goffman, E. (1974) *Frame Analysis: An Essay on the Organisation of Experience*, Harmondsworth: Penguin.

Goldthorpe, J. (1980) *Social Mobility and Class Structure in Modern Britain*, Oxford: Clarendon Press.

Goldthorpe, J. (1984) 'Women and class analysis: a reply to the replies', *Sociology*, Vol18, No 4.

Goldthorpe, J. et al (1969) *The Affluent Worker in the Class Structure*, Cambridge: Cambridge University Press.

Gordon, D. (1976) 'Class and the economics of crime' in Chambliss and Mankoff (1976) , *Whose Law? What Order?*, New York: John Wiley.

Gramsci, A. (1977) *The Modern Prince*, New York: International Publishers.

Greeley, A. (1994) 'A Religious Revival in Russia' in *Journal for the Scientific Study of Religion*, vol 33, no 3, p253–72.

Habermas, J. (1973) *Legitimations Crisis*, London: Heinemann.

Hall, S. (1992) 'New Ethnicities' in Donald, J. and Rattansi, A. (eds.) *Race, Culture and Difference*, London: Sage.

Hall, S. and J. (eds.) (1983) *The Politics of Thatcherism*, London: Lawrence and Wishart.

Hall, S. et al, (1978) *Policing the Crisis, Mugging, the State and Law and Order*, London: Macmillan.

Hall, S. et al. (1992) *Modernity and its Futures*. Milton Keynes: Open University Press.

Halsey, A. H., Heath, A. and Ridge, J.M. (1980) *Origins and Destinations*, Clarendon Press: Oxford.

Hammond, P. E. (1985) *The Sacred in a Secular Age*, Berkeley: University of California Press

Haseler, S. (1989) cited in Horsman, M. and Marshall, A. (1994) *After the Nation State*, London: Harper Collins.

Heath, A., Curtice, J., Evans, G., Jowell, R. and Witherspoon, S. (1991) *Understanding Political Change*, Oxford: Pergamon.

Heath, A., Jowell, R. and Curtice, J. *How Britain Votes*, Oxford, Pergamon.

Heath. A. (1992) 'The Attitudes of the Underclass' in D.J. Smith (ed.) *Understanding the Underclass*, London: PSI.

Heidensohn, F. (1996) *Women and Crime*, Basingstoke: Macmillan.

Heidensohn, F. (2002) 'Gender and Crime' in Maguire, M., Morgan, R., and Reiner, R. (eds.), *Oxford Handbook of Criminology*, 3rd edition, Oxford: Oxford University Press.

Held, D. (1992) in Hall, S. (ed.) *Modernity and Its Futures*, Cambridge: Polity Press.

Heller, A. and Feher, F (1988) *The Postmodern Political Condition*, Cambridge: Polity Press.

Herberg, W. (1956) Protestant, *Catholic, Jew*. Garden City, New York: Doubleday.

Hirschi, T. (1969) *Causes of Delinquency*, Berkeley, California: University of California Press.

Hirst, P. (1988) *Politics After Thatcherism*, London: Macmillan.

Hirst, P. (1993) *Plurist Theory of the State*, London: Routledge.

Hobbs, D. (1986) *Doing the Business*, Oxford: Oxford University Press.

Holdaway, S. (1983) *Inside the British Police*, Oxford: Blackwell.

Home Office, (2002) *Race and the Criminal Justice System*, London: HMSO.

Howarth, C. et al (1999) *Monitoring Poverty and Social Exclusion*, York: Joseph Rowntree Foundation.

Inglehart, R. (1971) 'The Silent Revolution in Europe: International Change in Post-industrial Societies', *American Political Science Review*.

Inglehart, R. (1990) 'Values, Ideology and Cognitive Mobilisation in New Social Movements' in R.J. Dalton, *Challenging the Political Order*, Cambridge: Polity Press.

Johnston, R.J., Pattie, C.J. and Allsopp, J.G (1988) *A Nation Dividing?*, Harlow: Longman.

Jones, S. (1994) *The Language of the Genes*, Harmondsworth: Penguin.

Jordan, B. (1987) *Rethinking Welfare*, Oxford: Blackwell.

Joseph Rowntree Foundation (1995) 'Inquiry into Income and Wealth', York.

Karstedt, S. and Farrell, S. (2003) Paper presented to the British Academy Annual Conference, Sociology and Social Policy Section.

Kellner, P. (1997) 'The 1997 General Election', http://bbbc.co.uk/news.

Kirby, M. (1995) *Investigating Political Sociology*, London: Collins Educational.

Kuhn, T. (1970) *The Structure of Scientific Revolutions*, Chicago: University of Chicago Press.

Lacan, J. (1977) *Ecrits: A Selection*, London: Tavistock.

Lane, D. (1996), *The Rise and Fall of State Socialism*, Cambridge: Polity Press.

Lasch, C. (1980) *The Culture of Narcissism: American Life in an Age of Diminishing Expectations*, London: Abacus.

Lash, S. and Urry, J. (1994) *Economies of Signs and Space*, London: Sage.

Layder, D. (1994) *Understanding Social Theory*, London: Sage.

Lindblom, C. (1977) *Politics and Markets*, New York: Basic Books.

Lloyd, J. (1997) 'New Deal', *New Statesman and Society*, February 1997.

Lockwood, D. (1958) *The Blackcoated Worker*, London: Allen and Unwin.

Lombroso and Ferrero (1895) 'The criminal type in women and its atavistic origin' in *The Female Offender*, London: Fisher Unwin, reprinted in McLaughlin, Muncie, Hughes (eds.) (2003, 2nd edn), *Criminological Perspectives*, London: Sage.

Luckmann, T. (1967) *The Invisible Religion: The transformation of symbols in industrial society*, New York: Macmillan

Luckmann, T. (1978) *Phenomenology and Sociology*: Selected Readings, Harmondsworth: Penguin.

Lukes, S. (1974) *Power: A Radical View*, London: Macmillan.

Lyotard. J-F. (1984) *The Postmodern Condition*, Manchester: Manchester University Press. Originally published 1979.

Macmurry, J. (1962) *Self as Agent*, London: Faber and Faber.

Malinowski, B (1954) *Magic, Science and Religion*, New York: The Free Press.

Mann, M. (1993) *The Sources of Social Power*, Cambridge: Cambridge University Press.

Manning, T. (1995) [untitled] Gay Times.

Marcuse, H. (1964) *One Dimensional Man*, London: Routledge and Kegan Paul.

Marshall et al. (1988) *Social Class in Modern Britain*, London: Hutchinson.

Marshall, G., Swift, A., and Roberts, S. (1997) *Against the Odds?*, Oxford: Clarendon Press.

Marshall, G. and Swift, A. (1993) 'Social class and Social Justice', *British Journal of Sociology*, June 1993.

Marshall, G., Newby, H., Rose, D. and Vogler, C. (1988) *Social Class in Modern Britain*, London: Hutchinson.

Marshall, G. (1997) *Repositioning Class: Social Inequality in Industrial Societies*, London: Sage.

Marx, K. (1857) *On Religion*, Moscow: Progress Publishers.

Marx, K. (1985) *The Communist Manifesto*, London: Penguin. Originally published 1848.

Mason, A. (1995) [untitled] Gay Times.

Matza, D. (1964) *Delinquency and Drift*, New York: John Wiley and Sons.

Mayo, E. (1975) *The Human Problems of an Industrial Civilisation*, London: Routledge.

McAllister -Groves, J. 'Learning to Feel: the Neglected Sociology of Social Movements'. *Sociological Review*, 43,3.

Mednick, S., et al, (1987) *The Causes of Crime: New Biological Approaches* (eds. S. Mednick, T. Moffit, and S. Stack), Cambridge: Cambridge University Press.

Melucei, A. (1972) *Anti- Nuclear Protest*, Cambridge: Cambridge University Press.

Merton, R. (1947) *Mass Persuasion*, New York: NYFP

Merton, R. (1968) *Social Theory and Social Structure*, New York: Free Press. Originally published 1949.

Mestrovic, S. (1994) *Balkanization of the West: The confluence of Postmodernism with Postcommunism*, London: Routledge.

Michels, R. (1949) *Political Parties*, Glencoe: The Free Press.

Miles, R. (1989) Racism, London: Routledge.

Miliband, R. (1969), *The State in Capitalist Society*, London: Weindenfeld & Nicolson.

Miliband, R. (1973) *State in Capitalist Society*, London: Quartet.

Miller, W. (1958) *Lower Class Culture as a Generating Milieu of Gang Delinquency*, The Journal of Social Issues, 14, 3, 10.

Mills, C. Wright, (1980) *The Sociological Imagination*, Harmondsworth: Penguin.

Mirrlees-Black, C, et al., (1998) *The 1998 British Crime Survey*, London: Home Office.

Modood, T. (1988) 'Black Racial Equality and Asian Identity', *New Community*, 14 (3), pp397–404.

Modood, T. (1990) 'British Asian Muslims and the Salman Rushdie Affair', *Political Quarterly*, 61 (20), pp143–160.

Morgan, R. (2002) 'Imprisonment – A Brief History, The Contemporary Scene, and Likely Prospects' in *The Oxford Handbook of Criminology* (3rd ed), Oxford: Oxford University Press.

Morris, L. (1994) *Dangerous Classes: The Underclass and Social Citizenship*, London: Routledge.

Morris, T. (1957) *The Criminal Area*, London: Routledge Kegan Paul.

Muncie, J. and McLaughlin, E. (1996) *The Problem of Crime*, London: Sage.

Murray, C. (1989) *The Emerging British Underclass*, London: IEA.

Newburn, T. (2002) 'Young People, Crime, and Youth Justice' in *The Oxford Handbook of Criminology*, Oxford: Oxford University Press.

Nordlinger, E. (1981) *The Autonomy of the Democratic State*, Cambridge, Massachusetts: Harvard University Press.

Pakulski, J. and Waters, M. (1996) *The Death of Class*, London: Sage.

Parsons, T. (1954) *Essays in Sociological Theory*, New York: Free Press.

Parsons, T. (1970) *Societies: Evolutionary and Comparative Perspectives*, Englewood Cliffs, New Jersey: Prentice-Hall.

Parsons, T. (1951) *The Social System*, New York: Free Press.

Parsons, T. (1977) *The Evolution of Societies* (ed. J. Toby), Englewood Cliffs, New Jersey: Prentice Hall

Bibliography

Patrick, J. (1973) *A Glasgow Gang Observed*, London: Methuen.

Pearce, F. (1976) *Crimes of the Powerful: Marxism, Crime and Deviance*, London: Pluto.

Pearson, G. (1983) *Hooligan: A History of Respectable Fears*, London: Macmillan.

Phillips, Z. and Bowling, B. (2002) 'Racism, Ethnicity, Crime, and Criminal Justice' in *The Oxford Handbook of Criminology*, Oxford: Oxford University Press.

Plummer, K. (1979) 'Misunderstanding Labelling Perspectives' in Downes, D. and Rock, P. (eds.) *Deviant Interpretations*, London: Martin Robertson.

Pollak, O. (1950) *The Criminality of Women*, Philadelphia: University of Philadelphia Press.

Poulantzas, N. (1973) *Political Power and Social Classes*, London: Verso.

Raskovic, (I990) *Diminishing Expectations*, London: Abacus.

Radford, T. (2003) 'Meet criminals who cost the UK £14bn : the middle class', The *Guardian*, 12/9/03.

Reiner, R. (1994) Policing and the Police, in Maguire, M. et al (eds.) *The Oxford Handbook of Criminology*, Oxford: Oxford University Press.

Rex, J. and Moore, R. (1967) *Race, Community and Conflict*, Oxford: Oxford University Press.

Rex, J. and Tomlinson, S. (1979) *Colonial Immigrants in a British City*, London Routledge Kegan Paul.

Rorty, R. (1989) *Irony, Contingency and Solidarity*, Cambridge: Cambridge University Press.

Rorty, R. (I991) ' Objectivity, Relativism and Truth': *Philosophical Papers*.

Rose, S., Lewontin, R. and Kamin, L. (1984) *Not in Our Genes*, Harmondsworth: Penguin.

Rosenail, S. (1995), *Disarming Patriarchy: Feminism and Political Action at Greenham*, Buckingham: Open University Press.

Roth, A. Parliamentary Profiles: London Parliamentary Profiles.

Routh, G. (1980) *Occupation and Pay in Great Britain, 1906–79*, London: Macmillan.

Sarlvik, B. and Crewe, I. (1983) *Decade of Dealignment*, Cambridge: Cambridge University Press.

Saunders, P. (1990) *Social Class and Stratification*, London: Routledge.

Saunders, P. (1996) *Unequal but Fair? A Study of Class Barriers in Britain*, London: IEA.

Savage, M. et al. (1992) *Property, Bureaucracy and Culture: Middle Class Formation in Contemporary Britain*, London: Routledge.

Sayer, A. (1984) *Method in Social Science*, London: Hutchinson.

Scott, A. (1990) *Ideology and the New Social Movements*, London: Unwin Hyman.

Scott, J. (1991) *Who Rules Britain?*. Cambridge: Polity Press.

Scott, J. and Fulcher, J. (1999) *Sociology*, Oxford: Oxford University Press.

Shaw and McKay (1942) *Juvenile Delinquency and Urban Areas*, Chicago: University of Chicago Press.

Skopol, T. (1979) *States and Social Revolutions*, Cambridge: Cambridge University Press.

Smart, C. (1989) *Feminism and the Power of the Law*, London: Routledge.

Smith, D.J. and Gray, J. (1983) *Police and People in London*, London: PSI.

South, N. (2002) 'Drugs, Alcohol and Crime' in *The Oxford Handbook of Criminology*, Oxford: Oxford University Press.

Stark, R. and Bainbridge, W.S. (1985) *The Failure of Religion: Secularisation, Revival and Cult Formation*, Berkeley: University of California Press.

Stark, R. and Glock, C. (1968) *American Piety: The Nature of Religious Commitment*, Berkley: California Press.

Stephens, P., Leach, A., Taggard L. and Jones, H. (1998) *Think Sociology*, London: Stanley Thomas.

Stewart, A. et al. (1980) *Social Stratification and Occupations*, London: Macmillan.

Sutherland, E.H. (1949) *White-collar Crime*, New York: Holt, Rinehart and Winston.

Taylor, I., Walton, J. and Young, J. (1973) *The New Criminology*, London: Routledge and Kegan Paul.

Thompson, K. (ed. and trans.) (1985) *Readings from Emile Durkheim*, London: Routledge.

Thornton, S. (1995) *Club Cultures: Music, Media and Subcultural Capital*, Oxford: Polity Press.

Tilly, C. (ed.) *The Formation of Nation States in Europe*. Princeton, New Jersey: Princeton University Press.

Townsend, P. (1979) *Poverty in the United Kingdom*, Harmondsworth: Penguin.

Turner and Killian (1986) *Sovereign Individuals of Capitalisms*, London: Allen and Union.

Turner, B.S (1991) *Religion and Social Theory*, Atlantic Highlands, New Jersey: Humanities Press.

Tyler E.B. (1970) *Religion in Primitive Culture*, Gloucester: Peter Smith

Veblen, T. (1912) *The Theory of the Leisure Class*, New York: Macmillan.

Walby, S. (1990) *Theorising Patriarchy*, Oxford: Blackwell.

Wallis, R. (1984) *Elementary Forms of the New Religious Life*, London: Routledge.

Walmsley, R., Howard, L. and White, S. (1992), The National Prison Survey 1991: Main Findings, *Home Office Research Study* No 128, London: HMSO.

Walter J., Kickert, M. and Stillman, R. (eds.) (2000) *The Modem State and its Study: New Administrative Sciences in a Changing Europe and United States*, Northampton, Massachusetts: Edward Elgar.

Weber, M. (1905) *The Protestant Ethic and the Spirit of Capitalism*, London: Allen and Unwin.

Weber, M. (1948) 'Class, Status and Party', in H. Gerth and C. W. Mills (eds.) (1948) *From Max Weber*, London: Routledge.

Webster, F. (1995) *Theories of the Information Society*, London: Routledge.

Westergaard, J. (1995) *Who Gets What?* The Hardening of Class Inequality in the Late Twentieth Century, Cambridge: Polity Press.

Westergaard. J. and Resler (1976) *Class in a Capitalist Society: A Study of Contemporary Britain*, Harmondsworth: Penguin.

Williams, P. and Dickinson, J. (1993) 'Fear of Crime: Read all about it? The Relationship between Newspaper Crime Reporting and Fear of Crime', *British Journal of Criminology*, No 33, pp33–56.

Willis, P. (1977) *Learning to Labour: How Working Class Kids Get Working Class Jobs*, London: Saxon House.

Wilson, B. (1966) *Religion in a Secular Society*, London: CA Watts.

Wilson, J.Q. and Kelling,G.L. (1982) 'Broken Windows: The police and neighbourhood safety' in *The Atlantic Monthly*, March 1982, pp29–38.

Wilson, W. J. (1987) *The Truly Disadvantaged: Inner City Woes and Public Policy*, Chicago: University of Chicago Press.

World Health Organisation, (1988) 'Application of the International Classification of Diseases', Geneva: World Health Organisation.

Worsley, P. (1970) *The Trumpet Shall Sound*, London: Palladin.

Wright, E. (1997) *Class Counts*, Cambridge: Cambridge University Press.

Yinger, J. (1970) *The Scientific Study of Religion*, London: Macmillan.

Young, J. (1971) *The Drugtakers*, London: Paladin.

Young, J. (1988) 'Radical Criminology in Britain: the Emergence of a Competing Paradigm', *British Journal of Criminology*, 28, 2, 289–313.

Young, J. (2002) 'Crime and Social Exclusion' in *The Oxford Handbook of Criminology*, Oxford: Oxford University Press.

Index

Index

Index

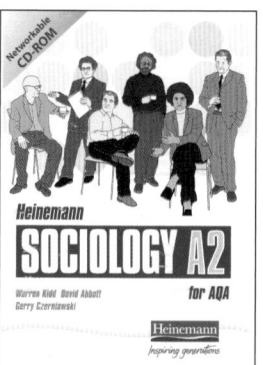